State and Society in Contemporary China

State and Society in Contemporary China

EDITED BY

Victor Nee and
David Mozingo

Cornell University Press

ITHACA AND LONDON

First published 1983 by Cornell University Press.
Published in the United Kingdom by Cornell University Press Ltd.,
Ely House, 37 Dover Street, London W1X 4HQ.

International Standard Book Number (cloth) 0-8014-1570-5
International Standard Book Number (paper) 0-8014-9253-X
Library of Congress Catalog Card Number 82-46010
Printed in the United States of America

The paper in this book is acid-free and meets the guidelines for permanence and durability of the Committee on Production Guidelines for Book Longevity of the Council on Library Resources.

*To George Homans and
Thomas Berry*

Contents

9

Contents

Acknowledgments

The idea for this volume came from the State and Society workshop held at Cornell University in April 1978, sponsored by the China-Japan Program and the Center for International Studies. The participants believed that an interdisciplinary study of state and society in contemporary China was long overdue. The editors wish to express appreciation for the insights of the participants in the workshop: Steven Andors, Martin Bernal, Sherman Cochran, Debra Friedman, Edward Friedman, Richard Kraus, Paul T. K. Lin, Richard Madsen, Mei Tsu-lin, Maurice Meisner, Carl Riskin, Vivienne Shue, Theda Skocpol, Benedict Stavis, and Kam-ming Wang. Preparations for this volume began in 1979.

We thank others who have helped us along the way: Mark Selden and an anonymous reviewer for providing useful criticism and suggestions; Bobbie Pearson for her typing; and Trudie Calvert for her careful copyediting.

The Pinyin romanization is employed except in reference to works published in English which used the Wade Giles system.

VICTOR NEE
DAVID MOZINGO

Ithaca, New York

Contributors

Edward Friedman is Professor of Political Science at the University of Wisconsin—Madison. He is the author of *Backward toward Revolution: The Chinese Revolutionary Party* (1974), co-author of *Ascent and Decline in a Socialist State* (1981), and author of numerous articles on contemporary Chinese politics. He is presently completing a book, *A Chinese Village in a Socialist State*, with three colleagues.

Richard Kraus has taught in the Department of Sociology at the University of Illinois and is presently teaching at Dickinson College. He is the author of *Class Conflict in Chinese Socialism* (1981) and has published articles on contemporary Chinese society in such journals as *American Journal of Sociology* and *China Quarterly.*

Richard P. Madsen is currently Assistant Professor of Sociology and coordinator of the program in Chinese studies at the University of California, San Diego. He is the author of *Morality and Power in a Chinese Village* (forthcoming) and, with Anita Chan and Jonathan Unger, co-author of *Chen Village: The Recent History of a Peasant Community in Mao's China* (1983).

Maurice Meisner is Professor of History at the University of Wisconsin—Madison. His books on modern Chinese history include *Li Ta-chao and the Origins of Chinese Marxism* (1967), *Mao's China: A History of the People's Republic* (1977), and *Marxism, Maoism and Utopianism* (1982). He currently is working on studies entitled "An Inquiry into the Fate of Socialist Revolutions" and "Post-Maoist Chinese Marxism: A Study in Ideological Deradicalization."

David Mozingo is currently President of Califas Ltd., an investment banking firm. He was formerly Professor of Government at Cornell University and a staff member at the Rand Corporation. He is the author of *Chinese Policy toward Indonesia, 1949–1967* (1976) and *United States in Asia* (1976).

Victor Nee is Associate Professor of Sociology at the University of California, Santa Barbara, and has taught at Cornell University. He is the author of *The Cultural Revolution at Peking University* (1969), co-author of *Longtime Californ': A Documentary Study of an American Chinatown* (1973), and co-author and co-editor of *China's Uninterrupted Revolution* (1975). He is currently completing a book on village life in China (forthcoming, Pantheon Books).

Dorothy J. Solinger is Associate Director of the Asian Studies Program and Adjunct Associate Professor in the Department of Political Science at the University of Pittsburgh. Her publications include *Regional Government and Political Integration in Southwest China, 1949–1954* (1977) and *Chinese Business under Socialism* (1983). She has written on central-local relations, economic policy, commercial affairs, and minorities in the People's Republic.

Benedict Stavis, a political scientist, is currently Associate in Research at the John Fairbank Center for East Asian Research at Harvard University. He has taught at Michigan State University and was a Research Associate at Cornell University. His publications include *China's Green Revolution* (1974), *People's Communes and Rural Development in China* (1974), *Politics of Agricultural Mechanization in China* (1978), and *Turning Point in China's Agricultural Policy* (1979). He has published numerous articles on the politics of China's rural development.

Tang Tsou is Professor of Political Science at the University of Chicago. He is author of *America's Failure in China* (1963), and *Quemoy Imbroglio: Mao, Chang, and Dulles* (1958), co-author and co-editor of *China in Crisis* (1967), and editor and co-author of *Select Papers from the Center for Far Eastern Studies* (1981).

Gordon White is a Fellow at the Institute of Development Studies at the University of Sussex. He is the author of *The Politics of Class and Class Origin* (1976), co-author of *Micropolitics in Contemporary China* (1979), and co-editor of *China's New Development Strategy* (1982).

State and Society in Contemporary China

Introduction

DAVID MOZINGO AND
VICTOR NEE

In a fundamental sense, all social revolutions result in new states. The elites and social forces that subsequently arise in the transformed society require special institutions and structural arrangements to bring about the changes they desire. Whether these changes can be made seems, however, to depend not only on the particular transformation introduced but also on the capacity of the old society's traditions to survive and, to a certain extent, co-opt the revolution. The French Revolution thus appears as a particularly shattering historical example because it represented a complete destruction of, and break with, the past. On the other hand, most students of Russian history have been impressed with the basic continuities between some of the social outcomes produced by the Bolshevik Revolution and some facets of imperial Russian society.

The modern Chinese state has been shaped by the confluence of traditional as well as radical influences, which to some extent accounts for the difficulty scholars face in interpreting its outcome. It is not therefore surprising to find that no clear perception of the present Chinese state has emerged from the writings of Western historians or social scientists — certainly not a perception that could be described as consensual. By contrast, certain basic notions about state and society in the old Confucian order have been widely accepted for decades. Before any new consensus about the People's Republic can develop, there needs to be greater agreement than presently exists on the utility of concepts such as bureaucracy, totalitarianism, democracy, class, mobilization, popular consent, legitimacy, and participation. The contributors to this volume claim no consensus on these or other relevant questions raised in the essays, but they do share the opinion that a clearer understanding of the basic relationships underpinning the contemporary Chinese state is needed. From differing perspectives, they have joined in a search for the building blocks requisite to that understanding.

A fundamental theme that runs through this volume, addressed more specifically in some essays than in others, is the inadequacy of attempts to comprehend the social history of the People's Republic in terms of China's bureaucratic heritage or the concept of totalitarianism. Comparisons with the imperial past or with Stalinist practices indeed come to mind; upon closer examination, however, the apparent similarities tend to dissolve in the light of the distinctive, if not unique, forces at work in contemporary Chinese society. The contributors generally found neither the bureaucratic nor the totalitarian models useful tools to explain how state-society relationships have evolved since 1949.

Party and State

In the analysis of the contemporary Chinese state a key question is the role and position of the Chinese Communist party. A Leninist party, emphasizing iron discipline and subordination of lower- to higher-level decision making, did become the instrument through which the central leaders imposed their will on both the state and the society. And an organization was formed that seemingly enjoyed a monopoly of power. To some Western scholars, especially in the period before the Cultural Revolution, this view of the party's dominant place in society seemed plausible. The essays in this book, however, to varying degrees, take a different view of the party. They generally see the party as having been forced to share power with such other organizations as the bureaucracy and the army. The interests and goals of these organizations tend to come into conflict with that of the party, and the party does not always emerge victorious, as the totalitarian model predicts. At the formal level, the party appears to command the full state apparatus. In practice, the mutual interpenetration of party and government organizations makes it difficult to distinguish between realms of the party and of the state. As Gordon White argues, this blurring of roles occurs because of the vast government apparatus involved in the management and organization of virtually all aspects of social and economic life. It is so vast that autonomous centers of power tend to come into existence within the state despite the party's efforts to maintain hegemony. In turn, the potential for autonomous power within the state, and the competition among different components, work to limit the party's practical ability to command the state machinery.

Indeed, there is growing evidence that, in the post-Mao era, the characteristics generally associated with the totalitarian model do not conform to conditions in contemporary China. Tang Tsou's essay points to the breakdown of totalitarian features of the Chinese state under the pressures exerted by the post-Mao reformers. He identifies this trend as a historic turning point in China's modern revolutionary experience. There are signs of a retreat from the previous emphasis on "politics in command" over all aspects of social and

18

political life and a growing recognition of areas of autonomy from political controls and state intervention. Although more evident in the policies governing intellectual life and the role of experts and specialists, this change in emphasis is also reflected in trends toward more freedom and participation in other areas of collective and personal life. According to Tang Tsou, the trend toward greater autonomy within Chinese society is a natural outgrowth of the commitment of the post-Mao leadership to a moderate program of modernization.

Whether the party, in fact, ever achieved effective total command over the state apparatus, as implied in the Leninist-Stalinist model, is questioned by David Mozingo in his analysis of the relationships between the army and the state. According to Mozingo, attempts to establish the party's monopoly of power over the state were repeatedly thwarted in the post-1949 period by military opposition within the revolutionary movement to the concept of the party-state. For this reason, no group of central leaders could gain or hold totalitarian power at the center, at least not for long. Mozingo traces the inability to erect a centralized party-state along the Soviet model to the character of the Chinese revolutionary movement. The army developed as the earliest center of political and administrative power during the long years of revolutionary warfare in the countryside. The strictly party apparatus, on the other hand, largely developed strength in the areas where the army had first succeeded in establishing and securing base areas and in proportion to the military's success. In the urban centers, where Communist military power could not extend, the party remained extremely weak until the final conquest of power in 1949. This early history of party dependence upon military power was perpetuated in the system of power erected under the PRC. From the very beginning, top military leaders penetrated the entire state apparatus and, through continuing intervention in political crises, helped to determine the outcome of the decisive inner party struggles.

State and Society

Another central issue in the analysis of the state is the nature and character of relations between state and society. According to Marxist theory, the emergence of the state is rooted in the basic divisions within society, and the state, as a product of social division, functions as an instrument of class domination. Although the state serves the interests of the dominant class, Marx also believed that during certain historical periods the state itself could emerge autonomously to dominate society, as in the case of the Bonapartist state. On the other hand, most Western theorists have assumed that the state was largely a natural outgrowth of the need for mechanisms of order and regulation, a form of social contract between the state and the citizenry.

Maurice Meisner details the evolution of Marxist writings on the relationship

19

between state and society through an analysis of the varying interpretations of the concept of the dictatorship of the proletariat. The potential autonomy of the state vis-à-vis society that Marx had acknowledged was denied by the Stalinists. Stalin transformed the original Marxist theory of the state into an ideology legitimizing bureaucratic domination of society. Chinese Marxists also believed that a strong centralized state was necessary to organize and direct China's economic and social development. Meisner documents how the concept of the dictatorship of the proletariat became associated with Mao Zedong's critique of bureaucratic domination. In the Maoist view, echoing Djilas's formulation of the "new class," the party-state bureaucracy gave rise to a new privileged elite in China and hence made necessary a continuing class struggle in the socialist era to prevent termination of the revolution. Although the Cultural Revolution failed to develop institutions that could replace the bureaucratic features that had given rise to this "new class," the Maoist attack did underscore the great importance of the state bureaucrats in any analysis of socialist societies.

Richard Kraus explores this question in his analysis of the social position of China's bureaucrats. Kraus cautions against the tendency to reify the state, that is, to view the state as an entity separate from society; he maintains that the result is a perception of an activist state "pitted against a passive society, thereby masking the interests and actions of state bureaucrats." Drawing on the recent Western neo-Marxist literature on the capitalist state, Kraus attempts to locate the social position of state bureaucrats within the context of a changing Chinese class system. In this analysis, China's state bureaucrats share a common relationship to the means of production, which they do not own but nonetheless control as a group and from which they derive concrete benefits and privilege. Rejecting the "new class" formulation of Djilas and Mao as overdrawn, Kraus views state bureaucrats as a "class-in-formation," rather than as a stratum or status group as Marxists maintained. A class analysis of China's state bureaucrats, however, is complicated by certain similarities between the present-day socialist officeholders and the bureaucrats who administered the imperial bureaucracy. For this reason, as Kraus suggests, Weber's concept of patrimonial rule is useful in identifying those characteristics of China's socialist bureaucrats which uphold the traditions of her bureaucratic past.

To what extent China's bureaucratic legacy molded the development of socialism in the PRC is of central importance to Western scholars and to Chinese Marxists. During the Cultural Revolution, a bitter debate unfolded among Chinese Marxists on the nature of the obstacles confronting China's development as a socialist society. Edward Friedman provides an in-depth analysis of this debate which characterizes the main protagonists as "Marxist idealists" and "Marxists materialists." The materialists argued that China could not develop genuine socialist institutions until economic development transformed its backward economy and thus the conditions that had given rise to "feudal fascism." On the other hand, the idealists (Maoists) contended that the real danger facing Chinese socialism was not so much rooted in the past as in the emergence of a new capitalist class strategically positioned in the party and the state. The principal task was thus to prevent the state capitalists from sabotaging the socialist revolution.

The debate over the nature of China's socialist state subsided following the conclusion of the Cultural Revolution period. Nevertheless, the historical problem it raises remains important, as suggested by recent events in China, namely, Deng Xiaoping's campaign to reform China's massive bureaucracy.

State and Economy

Nowhere has the vision of socialist development been more endangered, or debated, than in the area of the state's role in shaping the economy. For the concentration of the state's power in support of socialist economic goals has seemingly brought forth contradictory results. On the one hand, through the techniques of the command economy, the Chinese leadership halted the social hemorrhage that was the China of 1949 and, in a remarkably short time, restored production, employment, currency, trade, and essential national services — an astonishing achievement by any criteria. On the other hand, command economy techniques have proven to be defective, if not detrimental, to the attainment of levels of economic growth requisite to satisfying the needs and expectations of the population. In a word, the economic system that successfully manages poverty is unable to generate wealth.

Benedict Stavis sees this paradox as arising from the dual character of the basic goals that have motivated Chinese nationalism in the twentieth century. One of these goals has been to acquire economic and technical power enabling China to become an advanced and powerful industrial society. The other goal has been to create a society based on values that conform to the Chinese tradition as well as to modern concepts of social justice. The state, and especially its bureaucratic class, has been the main instrument in the pursuit of these goals. But, as Stavis points out, the concentration of such power in the state tends eventually to serve parochial bureaucratic interests at the expense of broader goals of economic development and social justice.

The Chinese state's inadequate performance in building the economy is also revealed in the attitude toward the promotion of trade and commerce. In traditional China there had been a deep-seated, philosophically based resistance to capitalist methods of stimulating the economy or allowing the free play of market forces. Dorothy Solinger explores the Marxist attitude toward trade and commerce and its impact on the policies of command economy socialism. In

21

general, she finds that three tendencies have coexisted and contended for influence: the "bureaucratic" tendency, which supports policies based on state control of the planning and management of all trade and commerce (and has been the dominant trend since 1949); the "radical" tendency, which wants all trade and commercial activities carefully monitored to ensure conformity (egalitarian, proletarian, values, as opposed to growth or other criteria, which was the position adopted during the Maoist and Cultural Revolution phases); and the "marketeer" tendency, which wants maximal growth and thus favors liberalizing policies designed to stimulate both production and consumption (the line that has been in ascendance since 1978). Given the embedded position of the "bureaucratic" and "radical" tendencies which have vested, though different, interests in the continuance of the planned command economy, however, Solinger suggests that the marketeer approach advocated by the supporters of Deng Xiaoping may rest on unstable foundations.

Center and Locality

One of the major organizational achievements of China's socialist state was the extension of the organs of state power into the villages, which has enabled the state to maintain a permanent presence at a level of society unapproached by previous Chinese state systems. In the imperial state, power was mediated at the local level by the gentry, who provided a go-between service linking the district magistrate in the county seat (the lowest level of government) to local society. The inability of the imperial state to extend its power directly into local society rendered center ties to local regions a weak link in the imperial system and permitted considerable scope for local autonomy. The socialist state has, in part, overcome this historic vulnerability by establishing an impressive network of organizations, linking the state directly to the social and economic processes of village society. Organizational penetration of the village provides the state with the capability for a sustained mobilization of village human and productive resources. More important, it provides channels through which to push state-initiated social change.

Despite this remarkable expansion of state power, center and local tensions characteristic of China's earlier political order were not eliminated. Victor Nee's essay analyzes center and local linkages through an institutional study of China's militia system. He shows that the militia is a key institution through which the state and local society are linked and through which the state extends its power directly into village society.

Yet, despite the tremendous potential for state control implied by the formal structure of China's militia system, Nee argues there is real localist potential for autonomy built into the militia system and into the staffing of local government. The militia command at the local level is largely staffed by former People's Liberation Army soldiers returning to their home county after years of service. As in other areas of county and commune government, the strong presence of local cadres builds into the militia system informal social networks deeply rooted in local interests and society. This aspect of local government, which stems from the practice of staffing the bureaucracy largely with local cadres, in effect, permits local interests and concerns to exert effective countervailing power within the local government. Thus Nee argues that when the policies of Beijing run counter to strongly felt local interests, local bureaucrats are in a position to blunt the effect of such policies, or water down the content of unpopular policies while, formally, seeming to carry them out.

Another feature of the militia system is its capacity to channel the energies of youth in the villages for the purposes of economic development and social change supported by the state. Richard Madsen provides a case study of militia mobilization of youth in a South China village. The focus is on the manner in which the state's interest in mobilizing villagers for political projects intersects with the natural rhythms of village life and economic processes. The case study of Chen Village reveals how village youth in the militia were mobilized to a pitch of political activism that provided state power holders extraordinary leverage to push political objectives in the village.

Madsen also points to the limits of state-initiated mobilization. City youth sent down to Chen Village were easily mobilized to attack village cadres because they lacked roots in the village. Youth from the village, on the other hand, were more moderate and thus less willing to participate in a radical shake-up of the village social and political structures. Thus village youth, who were key elements in the militia, organized the conservative Red Guard group that defended village cadres from the attack of city youth during the Cultural Revolution. Similarly, Madsen's study shows that periods of intense political pressures, transmitted through militia mobilization, were followed by periods of laxness and political passivity on the part of village youths. It may be that the fluctuations between mobilization and passivity can be understood as a reflection of the inability of the state to sustain, except for brief periods, political projects that conflict with strongly felt local interests.

As the diversity of themes and interpretations offered in this volume indicates, the authors did not intend a unified, all-encompassing statement. They did believe it was possible to identify the fundamental state-society relationships shaping the evolution of contemporary China. A certain unity of purpose, therefore, emerges from the contributions in that, taken as a whole, their common thread is the search for the sources and the character of the social forces contending for expression in China today.

The exploration of the major themes addressed in this volume — party and state, state and society, state and economy, center and locality — reveals a consistent and recurrent pattern of competition and conflict. It is worth remembering this characteristic feature of the PRC's history over the past thirty years as concerned observers of events in China stand witness to the revolution's fourth decade.

PART ONE

Party and State

1

The Postrevolutionary Chinese State

GORDON WHITE

My main aims in this essay are to analyze the origin and the form of the postrevolutionary Chinese state and to assess the extent to which the contemporary Chinese policy can be characterized as "authoritarian" or "democratic." The chapter has three broad sections. The first discusses the context within which the state emerged immediately after liberation and its specific form and composition during this crucial period. The second section focuses on the distribution of power within the state and between the state and society. The third section describes and evaluates the impact of three alternative forms of democratization proposed and practiced since 1949: "conservative," "liberal," and "radical leftist." The chapter is an attempt to contribute to a more precise understanding of the relationship between "dictatorship" and "democracy" in China and to provide some empirical and theoretical framework for assessing the potential for democratic change.

The Genesis of the Proletarian State

Though the beginnings of a state machine had existed in the liberated areas before 1949, the key formative phase was between 1949 and 1956. During this period the basic system of organizations was constructed, institutionalized patterns of attitude and behavior were established, and certain problems of recruitment to positions of authority were developed. Each of these processes determined the basic contours of the state and the behavior of its personnel over the next three decades. What were the conditions that influenced the specific state form which emerged in the mid-1950s and what were the major dimensions of the state-building process during this initial period of "socialist transformation?"

27

The Political Heritage

After assuming national power in 1949, the Chinese Communist party (CCP) leadership faced the need to consolidate and expand the political forces of the revolution to construct a socialist state. An administrative system had to be established to handle the burgeoning responsibilities of social organization and economic management. And the forces of order had to be strengthened to confront the imperialist enemies without (notably during the Korean War) and the "counterrevolutionaries" within, most notably the remnants of Guomindang opposition. The task of state-building was undertaken against the background of a millennial tradition of strong imperial rule and a brief experience of revolutionary administration in the Communist-led base areas before 1949.

The long tradition of the imperial Chinese bureaucracy was firmly rooted in political authoritarianism. Within the state apparatus, the hierarchical distribution of power was legitimized by both Confucian and Legalist norms; the system of bureaucratic ranks was reinforced by complex differentiations in modes of address, dress, rank, and other symbolic attributes. The relationship between the state and the general population was both distant and hierarchical, expressing a sharp distinction between superior officials to whom deference and unquestioned obedience were due and a populace that had no formal rights to influence the decisions of the official stratum. A position in the state apparatus enabled officials to appropriate resources, both public and private, to improve their position within the bureaucracy, and to spread the benefits of power to their relatives, friends, and clientele.

This pattern of state power created authoritarian predispositions that were to reappear, albeit in new forms, in postrevolutionary politics, whether these be "radical" (the adoration of Mao in the 1960s and the 1970s was often redolent of the emperor cult) or "conservative" (the resurgence of traditional forms of bureaucratism).[1] This heritage did not augur well for the establishment of participatory political institutions, responsive bureaucracies, or egalitarian power relationships.

The Marxist-Leninist theory of the state which percolated into China in the 1920s through the 1940s was ambiguous: a Saint-Simonian strand of rational administration by experts coexisted with Marx's conception of the participatory proletarian state based on the Paris Commune (a theme later to appear in Lenin's uncharacteristic *State and Revolution*) and Lenin's conception of the leading role in the state played by the elite party of professional revolutionaries. But the main theory of "party" and "state" transmitted to the CCP was Leninism in its Stalinist form. Indeed, as T. H. Rigby points out, "Leninism was the invention of Stalin."[2] This Bolshevik model was elitist in conception (notably the notion of the vanguard party) and authoritarian in operation, with very limited provisions for intraparty democracy. It advocated a tight concentration of decision-making power in the hands of a supreme leader and his cohorts and offered scant provision for effective mass participation in or control over the state machine.

As numerous Western writers and Chinese radicals have pointed out, the prerevolutionary experiences of Mao Zedong and other leaders during the guerrilla struggles of the 1930s and 1940s brought certain theoretical and practical innovations in the process of adapting foreign theory to the realities of the Chinese countryside. Analysts have highlighted the democratic and egalitarian character of the "mass line" style of leadership derived from the CCP's experience in mass mobilization during the Jiangxi soviet and in the wartime base areas, notably the Shanxi-Chahar-Hebei border area and in the Shaanxi-Gansu-Ningxia border region, especially Yanan, central CCP headquarters during this period.[3] The mass line was a set of prescriptions for government officials and party members designed to break down hierarchical barriers between leaders and masses thought to impede communications and effective policy implementation, as well as to stifle unwanted bureaucratic patterns of leadership behavior and to involve the masses of the population in processes of social, political, and economic transformation and construction.

Yet these egalitarian and democratic components of the mass line and the guerrilla ideal operated within strict limits. Though we can agree with Mark Selden that the CCP's revolutionary struggle was "built on foundations of participation and community action" and that "for the first time the peasantry as a group was integrated into the political process,"[4] the mass line was premised on a clear difference in power and authority between cadres and masses, party and nonparty. A massive upsurge of community participation in villages throughout North China was a vital component in the strength of the revolutionary movement. Yet mass participation had to be channeled to be effective, and mass organizations had to be subordinate to party control. Party and government cadres may have made considerable progress in democratizing their work style and eradicating traditional barriers of status and deference, but basic structural inequalities of power remained. Mass participation was not allowed to develop into autonomous political forces capable of checking or supervising the institutions of state power.

Greater flexibility for democratic experimentation was possible in the base areas than in the cities or areas dominated by the enemy. Such patterns, indeed, would have been self-defeating, if not suicidal, for party members working in the "white areas," those controlled by the Guomindang or the Japanese. The white areas seem to have developed a political style much closer to that of Lenin's conspiratorial revolutionary elite, forced by hostile circumstance to be secretive, hierarchical, strictly disciplined, and politically separated from the masses.[5] Communist leaders in both the guerrilla and the white areas were true to Leninism, however, which they regarded as a political methodology attuned to the needs of the revolutionary struggle. They carried this conviction with them into the new area of postrevolutionary socialist construction.

The Establishment of the State Apparatus, 1949–1956

The principles and practice of Leninism were equally appropriate after 1949. Even if the Yanan legacy embodied a significantly more democratic and egalitarian form of Leninism than that practiced in the Soviet Union, its ideological assumptions and operational guidelines were challenged and eroded after 1949. The immediate need to stabilize society and to maintain basic services required considerable reliance on administrative and technical personnel of the former Guomindang government. Because the CCP lacked experienced and skilled cadres, large numbers of former Nationalist officials were retained in office until they could be replaced by more reliable counterparts. By 1955, retained officials had mostly been replaced or moved to less responsible posts, but it is probable that some of their elitist outlook and authoritarian work style rubbed off on their colleagues in the new government. Indeed, in 1958 Mao accused many Communist cadres of behaving like their Guomindang precursors.[6]

In the cities, party leaders encountered problems of mobilization, management, coordination, and control far more complex than their experience in the base areas had prepared them to tackle. In establishing a complex organizational system to cope with an increasingly wide range of state functions, they adopted Soviet institutions as the primary models for imitation and, in some cases, wholesale transfer. This choice of models meant that China was importing many of the inegalitarian, hierarchical components of the Stalinist system. In addition, there was increasing skepticism about the continued relevance of the "rural work style" and the "guerrilla communism" of Yanan.[7]

The influence of the egalitarian revolutionary tradition was further weakened in the early 1950s with the expansion of the state mechanism and the recruitment of a large number of new functionaries who had not participated in the revolutionary struggle. New cadres lacked the experience and often the commitment of their mentors and tended to perpetuate prerevolutionary patterns of political relationship and bureaucratic behavior. The party expanded from 4,488,000 members in 1949, to 10,734,384 in 1956, and by 1961 had reached 17,000,000. By 1961, only 20 percent of total party membership had joined before 1949, and 70 percent had joined after 1953. The ranks of preliberation party members were thinned by death and expulsion, particularly during the political campaigns of the early 1950s. The number of cadres in the government bureaucracy expanded dramatically in the early years. In 1949, the CCP could claim only 720,000 qualified cadres, a figure sufficient to cover about one-third of the posts that needed filling. Thus three million new cadres had to be recruited between October 1949 and September 1952. They came from three sources: 57.7 percent were worker-peasant "activists" mobilized during successive campaigns; 40.1 percent were members of the party and the People's Liberation Army (PLA) and "progressive" retained personnel; and 2.2 percent were new university graduates.

The expansionary momentum continued through the 1950s in spite of attempts by some party leaders to stem the bureaucratic tide through a policy of "curtailment and adjustment" (1954−1955) and the more thoroughgoing measure of "bold retrenchment and reduction" (1956−1957). These measures were not very successful, as Table 1.1 shows.

Table 1.1 Growth of the State Cadre Force, 1949−1958

Year	Number of Cadres	State Cadres as Percentage of Population	Average Annual Growth
1949	720,000	0.13	863,333
1952	3,310,000	0.58	653,300
1955	5,270,000	0.86	883,333
1958	7,920,000	1.21	

Source: Ying-mao Kau, "Patterns of Recruitment and Mobility of Urban Cadres," in John W. Lewis, ed., *The City in Communist China* (Stanford: Stanford University Press, 1971), p. 106.

Ying-mao Kau, who has studied this process in detail, concludes that the inexorable bureaucratic expansion was caused by tremendous pressures for upward mobility arising from the traditional aspiration to become an official (*dang guan*), the income disparity between the urban state sector and the agricultural sector, and the prestige and perquisites of government office. Given such motives, it is not surprising that the phenomena of bureaucratism and careerism became widespread.[8] By 1955, government cadres were eating up 9.6 percent of the national budget, almost double the originally planned figure of 5 percent. Gone were the preliberation days when an official in the revolutionary state faced physical danger, an uncertain future, and material deprivation.

These strong trends toward bureaucratization were reinforced by the comprehensive "regularization" (*zhengguihua*) of all sectors of the state apparatus. In each case, the rules and regulations introduced relied heavily on Soviet exemplars. Regularization was to provide order, responsibility, efficiency, and discipline in the new bureaucratic maze. To tighten the organizational nexus of party and government, a cadre ranking system was introduced in 1955−1956, based on a complex hierarchy of wage and job grades — in sharp contrast to the relatively egalitarian "supply system" and the ad hoc methods of work assignment in the early postliberation years. Recruitment criteria were standardized, cadre responsibilities became more circumscribed, and lines of assignment and

31

promotion more predictable, usually within the confines of a single organizational system (*xitong*). A similar process accompanied the "modernization" of the PLA, heavily influenced again by the Soviet precedent. Modernization involved the conscious attempt to create an elite corps of professional officers, the introduction of a complex system of ranks, decorations, and regulations, and the standardization of systems of pay and promotion. In sum, the socialist state that emerged in the 1950s was a highly bureaucratic, swollen, and complex organism that was to prove singularly resistant to reform in succeeding decades.

One could argue strongly, however, that in these early years, the new state was both socialist and revolutionary. It redistributed power and resources through sweeping programs of structural change in both industry and agriculture. These changes benefited the majority of the working population. Unlike its imperial and Nationalist predecessor, it largely recruited its authoritative personnel from laboring class backgrounds. It was authoritarian in at least two senses. First, it increasingly concentrated political power as the party consolidated its hold over the state machine and the state machine consolidated its control over society. Formerly autonomous political organizations were deprived of genuine independence as they were replaced by wholly or partly autonomous organs of mass participation which could exercise checks over the party and the state generally or play a significant role in decision making at all levels. Although institutions of popular representation were written into the 1954 state constitution (and in the 1975 and 1978 constitutions), in fact they were not permitted any significant political autonomy. The party's ancillary mass organizations were to be, first and foremost, tools for political education, mobilization, recruitment, and control and therefore were allowed only a narrow, residual realm of decisional initiative. If they stepped beyond this limit, the party reacted strongly to bring them back into line.[9] Second, power and authority within all systems of the state machine were organized and exercised in a hierarchical fashion, with the official strata, chains of command, and precise differentiation of functions typical of bureaucracy in all societies.

Yet a historical "Catch 22" has so far frustrated the realization of democratic, participatory forms of socialism in China and other socialist countries. On the one hand, the initial circumstances and challenges — external threat, economic backwardness, social heterogeneity, and political opposition — squeeze the parameters of democratization and justify the logic of the vanguard party and of the communal state. On the other hand, the apparatus created to meet these challenges during the crucial "genetic" phase lives on to become a megastate that reproduces the conditions for its continued existence, clings to obsolete justifications, and resists any significant devolution of power or privilege. Once the mold of the megastate was constructed in China, it proved impossible to break or even to crack, as was to be demonstrated in the following two decades.

The Chinese State: Institutional Structure and Distribution of Power

The state is a complex of interlocking institutions and power relationships that perform vital ideological, political, administrative, economic, and coercive functions. In Communist states, including the People's Republic of China (PRC), the key institution is the party, which is the concentrated political expression of both the partial will of the "proletariat" and the general will of the "people." The party is not above or outside the state — it is, in theory at least, the essential dynamic component, exercising political leadership: decision making, socialization, social coordination, mobilization and control, and conflict management. The party is society's ideological agent within the state, charged with the task of controlling the bureaucratic and coercive organs of power. In reality, of course, the party's focal position as part of the state extends its power over society at large.

The second major sector is the government (or "state"), a vast apparatus of administrative power engaged — formally at least — in everyday policy implementation and organization of social and economic life. Although this complex hierarchy of systems, ministries, bureaus, commissions, and departments is formally — according to successive constitutions[10] — responsible to a system of peoples' representative congresses at local, regional, and national levels[11] — it has been the party which has called the bureaucratic tune (or at least written the music). The power of the party aside, however, the government machine is a formidable locus of potentially autonomous power of three varieties: bureaucratic power based on the possession of formal administrative authority and embedded in a complex network of "state organs" (*guojia jiguan*) stretching down to city districts and rural counties; managerial power exercised at the point of production in state enterprises engaged in the production and circulation of goods or the provision of services such as education and culture; and technical-professional power based on the possession of expertise deemed important to the efficient achievement of government objectives.

The third crucial state institution includes the army and other coercive organs, notably the public security bureau. The People's Liberation Army has exercised a variety of functions since 1949, such as handling political and administrative tasks in the immediate postliberation period and during the power vacuum resulting from the Cultural Revolution in the late 1960s and running various productive enterprises. Yet its main raison d'etre and its source of power are its control over the main instruments of coercion in society. Although the armed forces, like the government, are subordinate to party supervision and control, recent history — notably the Lin Biao affair — has demonstrated the dangers posed by their real though partial autonomy.

33

The Chinese state also contains distinctly different loci and forms of institutionalized power. The distinctions are important for two basic reasons. First, different forms of power based on different functional attributes create the potential for competition among power sectors and, in particular, pose constraints on the party's ability to exercise effective supervision over the government machine and the bureaucracy's ability to manage basic-level units. Second, different forms of power imply different forms of relationship between power holders and masses. Inequality of power is not merely a narrow political question of the relationship between the party and the population. It also involves the exercise of superior authority and power by administrators, managers, professionals, policemen, and army officers, the relative influence and impact of each group having varied over time.

It is argued that the basic patterns of the distribution of political and administrative power in Chinese society have remained virtually unchanged throughout the fluctuations of the late 1950s, 1960s, and 1970s and that their continuity over three decades is rooted in the theory and practice of the Leninist (that is, Stalinist) state.

The Role of the Party

According to the Leninist theory of the vanguard party, the CCP controls all significant levers of the power throughout the state machine and in society at large. This political monopoly was not formally recognized in the first state constitution of 1954, which contained the fictional stipulation (Article 2): "All power in the People's Republic of China belongs to the people. The organs through which the people exercise power are the National People's Congress and the local people's congresses at various levels." Later constitutions repeated this fiction but were more realistic in acknowledging that the true location of political power was the special role of the party. Article 2 in the 1975 state constitution, for example, drafted under heavy Maoist influence, reads as follows: "The Communist Party of China is the core of leadership of the whole Chinese people. The working class exercises leadership over the state through its vanguard, the Communist Party of China." This wording, which is retained in the 1978 state constitution,[12] was drawn up by a different leadership and thus indicates no disagreement over this principle regardless of other differences between sections of the party leadership.

Formal party documents are more precise about the range of party dominance. The party constitution of 1973, for example, stipulates that "state organs, the People's Liberation Army and the militia, labor unions, poor and lower-middle peasant associations, women's federations, the Communist Youth League, the Red Guards, the Little Red Guards and other revolutionary mass organizations must all accept the centralized leadership of the Party."[13] In accordance with these principles, the party gradually extended its organization throughout society and state after 1949: "Of the seven sectors — industry, agriculture, commerce, culture and education, the army, the government, and the Party — it is the Party that exercises overall leadership.[14]

Nevertheless, the party's ability to direct all events in state and society has not been as great as many analysts of the "totalitarian" school assume and has been challenged from various ideological viewpoints.[15] Moreover, countervailing forms of power — notably administrative, managerial, and technical, each rooted in a vital social or economic function — have threatened the party's autonomy and limited its influence. The very size and complexity of Chinese society, and the direct or indirect influence exerted by the interests and demands of a multiplicity of social classes, strata, and groups have kept the party under constant pressure. There is also the danger of penetration by external groups and interests that might influence the process of intraparty decision making. Thus, though party leadership is a basic structural element of the distribution of power in Chinese society, its absolute status is not unquestioned; it requires constant effort to maintain.

The Distribution of Power within the Party. The flow of power within the party is governed by the Leninist principle of "democratic centralism," as spelled out in the party constitution promulgated by the Eleventh National Party Congress in August 1977:

Article 8: The Party is organized on the principle of democratic centralism.

The whole Party must observe democratic centralist discipline: The individual is subordinate to the organisation, the minority is subordinate to the majority, the lower level is subordinate to the higher level, and the entire Party is subordinate to the Central Committee.[16]

Ordinary party members are guaranteed "the right to criticize party organizations and working personnel in leading posts at all levels, and to make proposals to them, as well as the right to bypass the immediate leadership and present their appeals and complaints to higher levels, up to and including the Central Committee and the Chairman of the Central Committee." But the principle of democratic centralism is clearly more centralist than democratic.

The central party leadership has paid more than lip service to the principle of intraparty democracy by allowing limited diversity of opinion, opportunities to criticize and to make suggestions to superiors, provision for discussion of alternatives, and some residual role for representative elections. In part these concessions reflect a pragmatic view of democracy as functionally essential for the efficient operation of any complex organization, as Mao explained in his talk on democratic centralism to a meeting of party cadres in 1962:

35

If there is no democracy we cannot possible summarize experience correctly. If there is no democracy, if ideas are not coming from the masses, it is impossible to establish a good line, good general and specific policies and methods. Our leading organs merely play the role of a processing plant in the establishment of a good line and good general and specific policies and methods. Everyone knows that if a factory has no raw material it cannot do any processing. If the raw material is not adequate in quantity and quality it cannot produce good finished products. Without democracy, you have no understanding of what is happening down below; the situation will be unclear; you will be unable to collect sufficient opinions from all sides; there can be no communication between top and bottom; top-level organs of leadership will depend on one-sided and incorrect material to decide issues, thus you will find it difficult to avoid being subjectivist; it will be impossible to achieve unity of understanding and unity of action, and impossible to achieve true centralism.[17]

In other words, democracy within the party is crucial for political communications: properly channeled, it should provide information that can be "concentrated" by leadership organs at each level and either transmitted upward or converted into policy at that level. This is what party manuals mean when they stipulate that "all decisions must be made by the leading organs of the party through concentrating the opinions of the masses.[18]

In practice, however, this process depends for its success on the leadership cadres of each level, whose job is to solicit the opinions of the rank and file in a flexible and democratic fashion. It is difficult for ordinary party members to enforce this process of consultation in spite of their formally guaranteed democratic rights. Members who raise criticisms can easily be defined as a nuisance and silenced by the leadership's invocation of the principles of party discipline. If they persist, they can be tarred with the brush of advocating "ultrademocracy" or accused of "wearing antlers" (being irrationally combative). The appeal process exists on paper but is often too risky to be anything but a last-ditch option. Since power is highly concentrated at each level of the party apparatus, obedience and acquiescence become more sensible strategies than criticism and disagreement on matters of more than mundane importance. Thus although party leaders are formally forbidden to suppress criticism or retaliate vindictively, the norms of democratic centralism, the structural constraint of hierarchical power, and the weakness of effective institutionalized methods of democratic control make expression of opinion relatively exceptional. During periods of intraparty tension and conflict, moreover, the exercise of democratic rights becomes even more difficult and risky — take, for example, the retrospective critiques in the late 1970s of the lack of democracy in party life during 1966 – 1976. There have been centrally initiated campaigns for intraparty democracy in various periods (most recently, 1978 – 1980),[19] but one can argue strongly that the unchanged reality of hierarchical power within the party inevitably stifles much of the impetus for reform.

The same organizational logic has been operative in relationships between levels in the cadre hierarchy. Regional and local party committees and party branches at the basic level must be granted some decisional autonomy because general directives emanating from Beijing must be increasingly specified at each descending level in order to achieve flexibility. Local party committees have been granted greater decisional power during periods of general administrative decentralization (notably in 1957–1958 and after the Cultural Revolution), when the branch system of vertical rule was partially displaced in favor of horizontal coordinative leadership exercised by local party committees.

The contradiction between central policy directives and specific local requirements, as well as the "leaky" quality of power in a complex hierarchy, have also led to informal decentralization within the party, notably the phenomenon of "independent kingdoms" under local party "bosses." These are bureaucratic bunkers designed to deflect, reshape, or rescind central directives. Valid reasons for their formation include the desire to defend regional or local interests against central policies deemed deleterious, or to restrain central leaders deemed threatening, or to amass patronage power to strengthen the political base of a particular local "boss." The great size and variability of China, difficulties in communications, and the complexity of the party command structure make such "kingdoms" a constant headache for the strategic chess players in the Politburo.

Although more power may "leak" to lower leadership levels than the central leaders would prefer, there is little doubt that the crucial policy decisions are made in Beijing. The Central Committee meets infrequently and tends to ratify rather than to initiate policy. Real power is concentrated in the Politburo and, more particularly, in the Standing Committee of the Politburo, the supreme figures being the party chairman and vice-chairman. Until the mid-1970s, Mao Zedong, as chairman of the party and supreme leader of the nation, dominated party decisions.[20] After his death, the mantle of personal predominance — de facto if not de jure — passed to his erstwhile opponent, Deng Xiaoping. Deng's power over central decision making as a party vice-chairman clearly exceeded that of the party's nominal chairman, Hua Guofeng. Thus the mixture of supreme personal leadership combined with the collective leadership of central party institutions has been a constant feature of CCP politics since liberation. It has also been a source of tension and discontent, as the criticisms of Mao's "leadership cult" after his death made clear.[21]

Policy-making power is highly concentrated in this small group, but it cannot be exercised *in vacuo*. The top leadership relies on a variety of mechanisms, both inside and outside the party, to gather information and solicit opinions; examples include the use of central work conferences to summon national and provincial cadres for consultation in the early 1960s and the national conferences on specific areas of policy called by the post-Mao leadership in the

37

late 1970s. The central work conferences, moreover, provide a context within which functional and regional party leaders can press their arguments and interests.[22]

The complex flow of commands and communications also inevitably confers a large amount of power on the specialized offices under the Politburo, notably the Secretariat and the crucial departments of Organization (personnel recruitment and control) and Propaganda.

Politburo decision making is also influenced by institutions and social groups outside the party. First, since many top party leaders have important jobs in other sectors of the state machine, the balance of sectors represented within the leadership inevitably affects the nature of central decisions. Thus the Politburo, which emerged from the Ninth Party Congress in 1969 heavily influenced by Lin Biao and other military leaders, produced policies granting an important political role to the PLA. After the death of Lin Biao, political power swung back in the direction of Zhou Enlai who, as premier of the State Council, tended to represent the interests of the government. This power shift led to a reassertion of civilian predominance within the party and to policies designed to erase the disruptive heritage of the Cultural Revolution, restoring a situation of stability and unity conducive to bureaucratic operations.

Second, party leaders sometimes act as representatives of key social groups, arguing their interests in Politburo sessions. The clearest example was Peng Dehuai, who in the late 1950s, represented the peasantry by drawing attention to their problems caused by the Great Leap Forward. Deng Xiaoping seems to have played a similar role vis-à-vis experts and intellectuals in the late 1970s.

Third, the central party leaders must take into consideration the actual or potential impact of their policies on sectors of the population who can contribute to the success or failure of the center through apathy, recalcitrance, evasion, and sometimes outright resistance. For example, the negative reactions of the peasantry to the excesses of the Great Leap Forward created strong pressures for a change of policy; similarly, the resistance of many middle-level cadres and intellectuals to the policies of the Shanghai radical group in the 1970s created pressures for, and a social context favorable to, their removal in late 1976.

Despite the pluralist or representative aspects of central party decision making, power is highly centralized in the hands of a small group of men (with the exception of Jiang Qing, women have at no time exerted significant power in this inner sanctum). This group can be replaced, experience suggests, only by the Communist equivalent of palace coups. Thus the pattern of conflict and consensus among this small group is reproduced throughout the party, state, and society at large. Lower levels of leadership or external sectors of the state or society may influence top-level decision making, providing power resources for different individuals or groups within the top leadership, strengthening or weakening their position in the arcane struggles of Politburo politics. As these struggles became more intense in the 1960s and 1970s, the limited formal procedures for restraining conflict and ensuring accountability, personnel changes, and orderly succession (which are written into the party constitutions) became dead letters. The top leadership broke loose from its moorings in the party as a whole. In sum, if we regard the existence of direct or indirect institutionalized controls over the top political leadership by the general population or its representatives as an essential component of democracy, the Chinese power system is clearly not democratic.

The Party in the State. The party exercises its leadership role over other sectors of the state through a hierarchically organized system of committees, branches, and groups, each of which is subject to one of the specialized departments under the Central Committee and the Politburo. According to the 1956 party constitution, the role of each party unit is "to assume the responsibility of carrying out Party policy and decisions, to fortify unity with non-Party cadres, to cement the ties with the masses, to strengthen Party and State discipline and to combat bureaucracy." The party's role in the government administration was defined as follows in the mid-1950s: "The leading role of the Party finds expression in such ways as these: (1) the Party gives exact directives to the organs of state power on the nature and direction of their work; (2) the Party enforces party policies through the organs of state power and other work departments and exercises supervision over their activities; (3) the Party selects and promotes loyal and capable cadres (party and nonparty) for work in the organs of state power.[23]

Control is also exercised through cadres with both party membership and an authoritative nonparty position, or cadre status in both hierarchies. The system of supervision and interpenetration is most intense at the highest levels of the government bureaucracies and gradually decreases from level to level. But the party's organizational grip on the administrative machine, down to and including basic-level units, is tight compared to its hold on the nonstate sector. In the rural areas, for example, party organizations in many production brigades are very weak and some production teams have no party members.

Theoretically, there is a distinction, on the one hand, between political leadership and policy making — the exclusive preserves of the CCP — and, on the other, between administration and policy implementation. In practice, however, this distinction, and the concomitant organizational separation between party and government, have been more blurred in China than in other socialist systems, notably the Soviet Union. The party assumed greater direct administrative and managerial responsibilities, especially after the extension of the principle of dual rule in the late 1950s, which restricted the branch power of the national government ministries, and after the increase in the authority of the party committee in state enterprises, which restricted the monocratic power embodied in the one-man management system.

The virtual fusion of political and administrative roles has created a structural separation between generalist party administrators, often from working-class or poor peasant backgrounds with little formal education, and specialized personnel on the government payroll — engineers and technicians in state enterprises, teachers and academics in the state-run educational system, doctors, journalists, artists, and so on. In the 1950s the distinction was particularly sharp because most of the specialized personnel were from nonproletarian class backgrounds and had been educated before 1949.

The inevitable tension found dramatic expression during the Hundred Flowers movement of 1956–1957. Nonparty intellectuals complained then that outsiders (party-government cadres) cannot lead insiders (specialists), a criticism that amounted to a manifesto for the reallocation of power within the government machine.

The party reacted strongly against this challenge by emphasizing "politics in command," as during the Great Leap Forward and later during the Cultural Revolution. The conflict between these groups is a power struggle between different components of the state, each possessing considerable power resources. Since the party desires rapid economic development and technological modernization, the skills of the specialists have been indispensable. Although political supervision is necessary, excessive intrusion into their areas of professional discretion has proved to be developmentally counterproductive. The record since 1949, therefore, has been fluid, as the extent and effectiveness of party controls have ebbed and flowed.

The leaders of the post-Mao era, however, have called a truce and attempted to inaugurate a new era of relationships among the party, government administrators, and specialists. In relations between the party and the government, principles of functional specialization and organizational separation have been stressed, and the previous tendency of the party to exercise direct supervision over the conduct of government business — administrative, technical, or managerial — has been criticized. Although reducing the tension, such loosening of control implies a reduction of the party's role and the establishment of a more "pluralistic" system of power. In seeking to reallocate responsibility, therefore, the party faces a dilemma. To retain its effectiveness in exercising unified leadership, it must recruit larger numbers of specialists, managers, and professional administrators into the party. With them, however, come their desire for autonomous power and their special interests, which exert unwanted pressures on the direction of party policy. Thus the party runs the risk of becoming both an arena within which strategic state elites jostle for power and an instrument through which they consolidate and extend their dominance over society at large.

Party and Society. Although differing in degree among administrative levels and sectors, the distinction between party members and the masses is important throughout society. The privileged political position of the party and its own internal hierarchy of power differentiate society into distinct political strata — party cadres, ordinary party members, nonparty people, and "class enemies."[24]

Each of these four broad categories contains wide variations: for example, between central party cadres in Beijing and basic-level party cadres in a state enterprise or rural production brigade; between a "higher intellectual" and a poor peasant who are both classified as "ordinary Party members"; between ordinary citizens and special groups receiving party favors at any given time (such as mass "activists," people from "good" class origins, demobilized soldiers, or dependents of "revolutionary martyrs"); between the ordinary "broad masses" and members of political organizations such as the Communist Youth League, or between different varieties of "class enemy."[25]

An illustration is the political distinction between party members and ordinary citizens. Joining the party gives a person political status separate from and superior to that of the rest of the population, who enjoy the relatively limited political rights of the "citizen" (*gongmin*) guaranteed formally in the state constitution but denied to various categories of "class enemy." The party member has access to classified political information and to restricted political meetings; he or she is automatically defined as "reliable" (*kekao*), as worthy of "political trust" (*zhengzhi xinren*) from unit leaders, and thus as cadre material with greater potential access to positions of responsibility in their units. Party membership also entitles one — formally or informally — to certain distributive benefits such as first claim on various allowances and subsidies, welfare benefits, or entertainment opportunities. There is also the prospect of upward mobility within the party, which would bring the individual closer to the core of political power.

Given the social importance of party membership, which sectors of society have access to the party is one rough measure of the relative influence of the different social groups. In the absence of testable, reliable evidence, any firm conclusions on this subject are necessarily tentative and inconclusive. Given the rural experience of the CCP before 1949, it is probable that the vast majority of the 4.5 million party members in 1949 were of peasant origin. The party's social composition shifted in the early and mid-1950s as the leadership recruited more urban workers and intelligentsia.[26] Party membership swelled to 35 million (about 3.5 percent of the population) by the mid-1970s, but no comparable figures on social composition are available. It is unlikely, however, that the earlier priority to recruiting intellectuals, particularly higher intellectuals, was strongly pursued in the 1960s. On the contrary, the Cultural Revolution stressed the recruitment of "workers, peasants and soldiers" and castigated intellectuals as "bourgeois"and in need of "reeducation," a stigma that probably made their access to the party difficult, except for younger intellectuals with "pure" class backgrounds. The post-Mao leadership has berated its predecessors for failing to recruit enough intellectuals into the party, and it has taken

41

steps to recruit more of this class as part of the drive to spur the "four modernizations."

If the percentages of delegates to the Eleventh Party Congress in 1977 reflect
the social composition of the party, the following results would appear likely:
72.4 percent "workers, peasants and soldiers," 20.9 percent "revolutionary
cadres," and 6.7 percent "revolutionary intellectuals." Such a distribution reflects a fall in the percentage of intellectuals compared with the mid-1950s,
even though they are still overrepresented for their percentage in the general
population (about 2.5 percent). As one would expect, cadres are greatly overrepresented, though it is difficult to estimate this ratio precisely. More generally,
urban groups enjoy greater representation in the party (the last precise statistic,
from 1959, suggests that 4.4 percent of urbanites were party members compared with only 2.2 percent of the general population).[27] Only 19 percent of the
delegates to the Eleventh Party Congress were women, an indication of gross
underrepresentation yet still an improvement over the mid-1950s when only
about 10 percent of party members were women. In sum, if we use percentage
of party membership as an index of the political influence of different groups in
Chinese society, the "winners" in the late 1970s would be urbanites generally
and cadres specifically and — increasingly after the Eleventh Congress — intellectuals, while the "losers" would be the rural population and women.

The Cadre Structure and Bureaucracy

The Chinese state is a multicolumn edifice of hierarchically organized offices occupied by cadres, the key representatives of institutionalized power.
Judging from discussions with Chinese citizens, the popular meaning of the
term "cadre" is ambiguous, resting on three different attributes: people who
draw state salaries, people who do mental work, and people who occupy positions of formal authority. One former resident of the PRC argued that the key
criterion was holding authority; thus there are political cadres, administrative
cadres, military cadres, and technical cadres[28] distinguished by their prime area
of job responsibility or institutional affiliation. Though cadres exist at all levels
of society and in all institutions, there is an important distinction between state
cadres and local cadres, the latter employed in and paid by collective institutions such as production brigades and teams. We are primarily concerned with
state cadres.

State cadres, whether in the party or government, are organized in a complex
system of job and salary grades established in the mid-1950s. Not every person
in the administrative salary – grade system is a cadre. Those engaged in routine
clerical work are referred to merely as "administrative personnel" (*xingzheng
renyuan*), — the implication being that they have virtually no authority. According to interview respondents, there is a semiformal distinction between differ-

ent cadre strata based on their salary grades: high-level, middle-level, and ordinary cadres. Within these broad categories, cadres are ranked either according to their salary grade or their job level (such as ministerial-level cadres or section-chief level cadres). Within each type of state unit, moreover, there is a formal distinction between leading cadres and ordinary cadres; a leading cadre in a factory or school might be a middle-level or even an ordinary cadre within the full hierarchy of state cadres. At the bottom of the hierarchy is the basic-level cadre and the interface between people with authority (whom one interview respondent referred to as officials, *guan*) and the masses, those without authority. This gap is a second important expression of power inequality in China, overlapping to a considerable extent but not coinciding with the gap between party and masses.

The hierarchy of power embodied in the cadre system has created and reproduced structural inequality and behavioral authoritarianism. First, differences in power and authority between party members and masses, between cadres and masses, and between different levels of cadre lead to inegalitarian psychological distinctions between levels of social prestige. Second, the cadre system creates tendencies toward what Western sociologists call the "crystallization" of status attributes, that is, people using the power implicit in party membership or a cadre position or both to gain privileged access to scarce goods and opportunities for themselves and their relatives or friends — special consideration in housing, working conditions, education, economic subsidies, entertainment, travel facilities, medical treatment, and so on. These forms of privilege were attacked during the Hundred Flowers and the Cultural Revolution but persisted through the 1970s. Indeed, critiques published during and after the Democracy movement at the end of the decade implied that special privilege had increased since the Cultural Revolution. Third, inequalities of political and administrative power have tended to harden into an enduring pattern of stratification as state elites pass on their privileges to their offspring, most notably through access to higher education, party membership, and cadre positions. These processes represent class formation and have been identified as such by Chinese critics, both left and liberal. Neither critical tendency has succeeded in producing a systematic class analysis of the state, and terminology has varied, some critics referring to "a special power stratum" (*tequan jieceng*), others to a "new bourgeoisie." Party leaders of various political hues have regarded these trends with concern and have tried to tackle them in a variety of ways.

Critiques and Countermeasures

For both ideological and developmental reasons, all sections of the CCP leadership have paid considerable attention to problems arising from the unequal relationships between layers of political and administrative power: the gaps between party and masses, between basic-level cadres and masses, between middle and upper-level cadres and the masses, and between different layers of the government bureaucracies. All sections of the leadership have castigated authoritarian bureaucratism and privilege-seeking as immoral and inefficient and have introduced various institutionalized methods to make the party and the state cadre machine more flexible, responsive, and democratic. I have categorized these approaches as conservative, liberal, and radical leftist.

The Conservative Approach

I am describing certain techniques of democratization as conservative, first, because the methods adopted are basically "in-house" and are conducted in predictable ways according to institutionalized rules that pose no threat to the stability and integrity of the party; and second, because I believe these methods reflect the outlook and interests of the Leninist core of the party. To some extent, the notion of Leninist core is hypothetical and abstract — it is difficult to measure. It is an attempt to identify that dimension of the party as a whole — its leaders and members — which embodies the realities of institutionalized party dominance: the normative reality of democratic centralism, the structural reality of concentrated and unequal power, and the behavioral reality characteristics of hierarchical bureaucracies. It represents the most concentrated imprint of the institution on its members and is thus conservative by definition, loyalty eclipsing voice or exit.

Conservative methods have been discussed extensively by Western scholars, though some of them have been mistaken for "radical" innovations. Such methods concentrate on the behavior of cadres and party members, with only subsidiary attention to limited structural reform. Chinese organizational theory has tended to assume that highly unequal power can be exercised in an equal and democratic fashion if the cadre's work style is "correct." The targets of corrective action are deviations: sectarianism, the tendency for party members or cadres to become too remote from the masses or from their nonparty cadre colleagues; commandism, the tendency to issue arbitrary orders in a high-handed way without sufficient explanation or preparation for their acceptance through democratic discussion and consultation; bureaucratism, a term that denotes a large variety of deviations, many of them familiar to students of Western bureaucracies and others more redolent of the Chinese imperial tradition.

Chinese leadership doctrine has laid down the principle of the mass line (*qunzhong luxian*) as an institutionalized standard for a correct cadre workstyle, applying equally to relations between the party and the masses, between state cadres at different levels, and between cadres and masses. Thus, for example, the 1977 party constitution enjoins the entire party to "keep and carry forward its fine tradition of following the mass line," "to maintain close ties with the

44

masses, constantly listen to their opinions and demands and faithfully report these to higher Party organizations and be concerned about their political, economic and cultural life." Party members and cadres are called on to cultivate "the style of modesty, prudence and freedom from arrogance and impetuosity" and "wage a resolute struggle against bourgeois ideology and the bourgeois style of work."[29] Likewise, the 1978 state constitution instructs government cadres "constantly to maintain close contact with the masses of the people, rely on them, heed their opinions, be concerned for their weal and woe."[30]

To these ends, cadres and party members have been involved in regular programs of theoretical study and intensive discussion designed to promote a flexible and self-aware work style through criticism and self-criticism. Intraparty rectification movements, the first of which took place in Yanan in the early 1940s and which have recurred frequently in the three decades after liberation, have sought to shake up the party and state apparatus by intensifying the normal processes of study and discussion.

These methods have been characteristic of ruling Communist parties in other state socialist societies. But the Chinese have gone further in devising methods to achieve the mass line. To meet the threat posed by the overburgeoning and overcentralized state bureaucracies that arose in the mid-1950s, the practice of "sending downward" (*xia fang*) was instituted. This policy requires higher- or middle-ranking cadres to spend time at the basic levels of their specific institutional hierarchies and is designed to improve communication between bureaucratic layers and to familiarize higher cadres with problems at the grass roots. In the armed forces, this practice took the form of sending officers to the ranks. Cadres at all levels who are divorced from production in their ordinary jobs have also been required to participate in productive manual labor for a prescribed portion of their working week or year. The Cultural Revolution extended this practice by dispatching urban cadres to do manual labor in rural May Seventh cadre schools.

These methods may have alleviated but clearly have not removed the problems they were designed to tackle, as the criticisms of widespread bureaucratism and special privilege in the late 1970s testify. This lack of success is not surprising for two reasons. The first problem derives from the age-old dilemma of who will guard the guardians. The conservative approach has defined the responsibility for keeping party cadres and members up to the mark as an intraparty affair rather like a police review board run by police. Similarly, the measures designed to control bureaucratism have been mainly intrabureaucratic, with one bureaucracy (the party) attempting to rectify others (in the government). Thus the various techniques — *xia fang*, rectification campaigns, obligatory manual labor, political study, or criticism and self-criticism sessions — have become routinized and submerged in a tangled network of bureaucratic opposition or inertia.

Second, the problem of power inequality and democracy has been treated

45

primarily as behavioral and attitudinal rather than structural. The underlying assumption that cadres can be trained to act in ways that transcend the objectively unequal distribution of power is dubious. As Benjamin Schwartz has pointed out, this is a new version of the traditional Chinese conception of "moralizing the holders of power."[31] But both moralizers and moralized are enmeshed in the same state apparatus and subject to the same logic of hierarchical stratification. To hope for any significant democratization of the state by such institutionalized methods would thus seem naive.

Alternative Modes of Democratization

The Liberal Alternative. Certain party leaders who, since the mid-1950s, have viewed economic development as the major task of Chinese socialism — including Deng Xiaoping, Zhou Enlai, Peng Zhen, Chen Yun, and Li Xiannian — have argued that a degree of freedom of discussion and "mental emancipation" should be encouraged as an essential prerequisite for a successful development program. Excessive control, they say, causes apathy, stifles creativity, and limits the range of choice among options, resulting in losses in microlevel efficiency and social productivity. They have been particularly aware of the need for such measures to gain the energetic cooperation of intellectuals and professionals, who have pressed for decisional autonomy in their work and greater freedom in their social, political, and cultural life.

Each period when modernization was defined as the strategic goal — the mid-1950s, early 1960s, and late 1970s — has been accompanied by moves toward liberal forms of democratization: more opportunities for public criticism and free expression without fear of suppression or reprisal; greater stress on the need to guarantee individual rights against arbitrary victimization through a strengthened legal system, as free as possible from direct political interference; and the use of elections — preferably direct and through secret ballot — in the choice of cadres in the government and party apparatus, thus giving the relevant masses in each case (ordinary party members in choosing party cadres, local inhabitants of a city or county in choosing representatives for people's congresses, or factory workers in choosing workshop cadres) more control over their political or administrative superiors.

Party leaders sympathetic to democratization, however, have faced opposition from their colleagues and opponents in the party. During the 1960s and 1970s, leftist party leaders and members opposed liberalization as a betrayal of the masses and the revolution. The more conservative Leninist core has been skeptical about liberalization as a potential threat to its power. Liberalizing party leaders have faced a difficult task in reconciling liberalization — in theory and in practice — with the basic structural principles of Leninist socialism. These leaders — notably Mao Zedong in 1957 and Deng Xiaoping in 1979 —

have been vulnerable to charges from their more conservative colleagues that they are undermining the supreme authority of the party, compromising the ideological principles of Marxism-Leninism, encouraging ultrademocracy, anarchism, and social disorder, and allowing the enemies of socialism scope to vent their spleen. In 1957, the party conservatives won the day and organized a massive counterattack; in 1979, the party leadership was divided and for a time opened and closed the tap of liberalization like ambivalent plumbers before a decisive clampdown was eventually imposed.

Party conservatives have been aided in their attempts to stymie liberalization by the activities of extraparty forces whom they could accuse of going too far. During the Hundred Flowers and the Peking Spring of 1978–1979, certain individuals and groups arguing for human rights extended their criticism and activities outside the bounds which party leaders regarded as legitimate: for example, attacking the basic principles of state socialism, calling for major institutional changes (such as demands for the end of censorship or the dissolution of the communes), or attacking the "wrong" members of the central leadership. A minority of critics in each period even advocated the abolition or severe restriction of party leadership and, in some cases, its replacement by a multiparty, representative democracy based on Western models.

Experiments with liberalization have tended to be short-lived or unstable. So far, liberalizing party leaders have found it difficult to secure the social constraint and political support necessary for a balanced fusion of a Leninist polity and a system of effective democratic liberties. From a popular point of view, moreover, the normative and structural imperatives of Leninism impose strict limits on the real political scope offered by ostensibly democratic reforms. Though "emancipation of the mind" may be effective in insulating certain nonpolitical fields of thought from direct politicization (notably scientific research), it can make little headway in the area of political discourse in the face of an official ruling ideology. Similarly, though legal institutions might provide some marginal protection to individual citizens, laws still reflect party priorities, and there is a danger of replacing arbitrary political victimization with systematic juridical suppression.

The Leftist Alternative. To be accurate, this category should be called leftist or "radical" alternatives because Chinese radicalism has produced a variety of spokesmen, and no dominant, systematically articulated ideological position has emerged. The left critique of the state system which emerged in the 1950s and early 1960s was spearheaded by Mao Zedong, who changed his definition of the "principal contradiction" in Chinese society from economic backwardness to new "class struggle" between the "proletariat" and the "bourgeoisie," each "class" category based on political rather than economic criteria. He received ideological agreement and political support in this analysis from key

47

institutional leaders such as Lin Biao and Kang Sheng and ideologues such as Chen Boda and Zhang Chunqiao.

The left wing of the party leadership perceived the Cultural Revolution as embodying a new form of revolutionary mass movement, involving "extensive democracy" and the "four big freedoms" (big contending, big blooming, big debate, and big-character posters). The movement was a radical break in two basic aspects: it encouraged the formation of partially autonomous mass organizations and it was directed at "enemies" inside the state machine. But it is important not to exaggerate the political implications of these innovations. The official definition of the movement, laid out in the Central Committee's decision of August 8, 1966, did not herald any significant structural changes in the state system. The movement was to be directed at a small minority of officials, "those in authority who have wormed their way into the Party and are taking the capitalist road," not at the party-government machine as such. In fact, the campaign was placed squarely under party leadership, although party officials were instructed to allow the masses as much scope as possible. The original mass Cultural Revolution groups and committees that emerged in some institutions in mid-1966, the first stage of the mass movement, were hailed as "excellent new forms of organization whereby the masses educate themselves under the leadership of the Communist Party . . . an excellent bridge to keep our Party in close contact with the masses." These new organizations, dubbed "the power organs of the Proletarian Cultural Revolution," were to be "permanent, standing mass organizations," elected on the model of the Paris Commune.[32] Thus, although these new mass organizations were originally envisaged as permanent features of the political system, the nature of their role as "bridges" was left unclear, as was their relative autonomy vis-à-vis the party.

These initial prescriptions went by the board in late 1966 and early 1967 when the mass organizations increased their power and the party lost control over the movement. This radical phase culminated in the January Revolution in Shanghai in January 1967, when the established party-government apparatus was replaced, by means of power seizures, by a coalition of mass organizations welded together under the leadership of Zhang Chunqiao into a Paris-style Shanghai People's Commune.[33] Mao Zedong, however, rejected the Commune form as "too weak when it comes to suppressing counter-revolution" and too factionalized and narrowly based to exercise significant administrative and political powers.[34] Mao had clearly been surprised by the force of the mass movement and its devastating impact on the party machine.[35] Consequently, from January 1967 onward, Mao and other key central leaders devoted themselves primarily to reining in the mass movement and reducing its internal dissensions through the direct intervention of the PLA and the imposition of the "three-in-one" combination of the revolutionary committees which brought mass representatives into uneasy — and increasingly subordinate — juxtaposition with former cadres and PLA organizers. In retrospect, it appears that the Maoist leaders had no revolutionary redistribution of institutional power in mind, even though they were apparently swept away by their own rhetoric at times. The principle of party leadership and the organizational reality of the state machine were not to be deposed. In essence, the Cultural Revolution was an attempt to remove certain key officials from power and, in general, to shake up the party-government apparatus through a hitherto unprecedented form of mass mobilization — a combination of reformist goals with radical methods.

This contradiction between limited goals and radical methods led to tension and conflict between the Maoist leaders and their mass base. Organized groups — mostly composed of young people with high-school education and above — had expected more of the Cultural Revolution and had taken some of the more radical pronouncements of Maoist leaders at their face value. Inspired by the tradition of the Paris Commune and the initial rhetoric of the Cultural Revolution, they called for a real political revolution that would abolish the state machine and replace it with organs of mass power. The clearest expression of this position was provided by the Hunanese mass organization Sheng Wu Lian in its programmatic document *Whither China?* published in early 1968. Sheng Wu Lian called itself an "ultra-left faction commune" and identified 90 percent of the nation's senior party-government cadres as a "red bourgeoisie," which was to be swept away by revolutionary action. Professional bureaucrats, Sheng Wu Lian declared, were not necessary for state administration:

> The storm of the January Revolution suddenly turned all this [power] from the hands of the bureaucrats into the hands of the enthusiastic working class. People suddenly found that without the bureaucrats they could not only go on living, but could live better and develop quicker and with greater freedom. . . . [Without] the bureaucrats and bureaucratic organs, productivity was greatly liberated. After the Ministry of Coal Industry collapsed, production of coal went on as usual. The Ministry of Railways collapsed, but transportation was carried on as usual. All departments of the [Hunan] provincial Party committee collapsed, but work went on as usual. . . . The management of industrial plants by the workers themselves after January was really moving. For the first time, the workers felt that "it was not the State which managed them, but they who managed the State." . . . The storm of the January Revolution told people that China would head for a society free from bureaucrats and that 90% of the high-ranking cadres had formed a special class . . . the Cultural Revolution is not a revolution to dismiss officials or a "drag-out" movement, nor is it a purely cultural revolution, but "a revolution in which one class overthrows another."[36]

Thus Sheng Wu Lian opposed the reformism implicit in the moves toward revolutionary committees and demanded "the total smashing of the old state machinery" to create "the embryonic form of a Paris Commune-style new society." It also called for an organization of "armed mass dictatorship" to oppose and replace the PLA. The party was to be replaced by a genuine "revolutionary party," called the Mao Zedong Doctrine party, which would lead the struggle against the "red bourgeoisie."[37]

Clearly, in the political deadlock that emerged during the Cultural Revolution, such comprehensive solutions were not on the agenda — indeed the central leadership saw them as subversive. It is very likely, moreover, that Sheng Wu Lian represented the views of only a small section of the mass movement and owed much of its support to social groups who were more interested in promoting section self-interest than in smashing state power.

Though the main concern of central Maoist leaders seems to have been directed toward the removal of party opponents and a reorientation of party policies, one can argue that they wished to bring about some limited changes in the political relationship between state and society. Accordingly, they hoped that the Cultural Revolution would create some form of partially autonomous mass power which could act as a check on the state bureaucracy and form an important part of their own political base.[38] But the fragmentation of the mass movement — reflected in what radical leaders referred to in exasperation as the "small-group mentality," "mountain-toppism," and the "personal limelight mentality" — reduced this initiative primarily to the principle of direct mass representation in the new revolutionary committees. The resulting distribution of power was hardly democratic, since the very fragmentation of the mass movement had led to the imposition of organizational control by the military and ideological control through an irrational cult of leadership. Thus radical democracy created its opposite, paving the way for the domination of the state apparatus between 1967 and 1971 by its most authoritarian component, the army, and exchanging subordination to the institutionalized party for obeisance to the infallible leader.

Political fragmentation was just one of the basic problems of the leftist concept of democracy put into practice during the early stages of the Cultural Revolution. In practice, many mass organizations did not support the leftist cause. In fact, it seems likely that the membership of "conservative" organizations far outweighed that of "rebel" organizations. Radical leaders and rebel organizations therefore had to acquire power through factional struggle and defend it through political suppression. Many rebel groups, moreover, cloaked sectional demands under a mantle of Maoist rhetoric and, with a few exceptions such as Sheng Wu Lian, rebel ideology and objectives were poorly defined, partly as a result of the lack of clear and systematic ideological guidance from Mao and his colleagues. Moreover, the very context of "revolutionary" mass mobilization — the Manichean imagery of "class struggle" between "proletarian" and "bourgeois" combined with the vagueness and malleability of these categories — fostered a tendency to intensify the climate of political antagonism by artificially polarizing all issues and thus creating an atmosphere conducive to violence. This form of struggle also required the elimination of dissident forms of expression outside the limits of a narrowly defined orthodoxy and led to a climate of fear and mute resentment. The breakdown of centralized control and institutionalized procedures, moreover, opened the way to a decentralized, arbitrary use of power which inevitably led to extensive victimization of individuals and groups.

In sum, one can argue that, though the Cultural Revolution was originally based on authentic forms of mass democracy, it led to authoritarianism, arbitrary suppression, and enforced conformity, which violated alternative (notably liberal) norms of democracy and antagonized many people, particularly but not exclusively among the movement's key target groups. The blatant contradictions between the initial ideological premises of mass democracy and their subsequent submersion alienated many young idealists who had formerly supported the movement. Their sense of disillusionment and demands for democratic rights to counter the authoritarian abuses of the Cultural Revolution found eloquent, if unsystematic, expression in the document by Li Yizhe, published in Canton in 1973 and 1974, "Concerning Socialist Democracy and Legal System."[39] This article lamented the failure of the Cultural Revolution ("because it has not enabled the people to hold firmly in their hands the weapon of extensive people's democracy"), attacked the arbitrary and authoritarian use of power under "the Lin Biao system," and demanded "democracy and a socialist legal system" with the added right of "revolutionary supervision over the leadership at various levels in the Party and the State." Though many of these criticisms and demands are valid, it would be a mistake to condemn the Cultural Revolution one-sidedly as a form of social fascism. The movement was contradictory in its execution and in its results. It loosened the arthritic political and administrative structures forged in the 1950s and pioneered radical ideas and forms of mass action which became part of the political culture of the 1970s. Though the repressive aspects of the Lin Biao system established in the late 1960s were undesirable, the Cultural Revolution also led to a greater propensity for the broad masses without power or position to challenge the forces of authority in ways that recalled the heady days of 1966 — through demonstrations, unofficial publications and organizations, or big-character posters. To this extent, the movement had a beneficial effect on the quality of democratic life. From this point of view, one can argue that the antiradical Tiananmen incident in April 1976 was as much an expression of the legacy of the Cultural Revolution as a demonstration against it.

In sum, one can argue that all three alternative forms of theory and democratization — the conservative Leninist, "liberal," and "radical leftist" — have proved problematic in practice. Perhaps a utopian pragmatist would call for the establishment of a political system that embodies the best in each tradition. But each form of democratization expresses competing beliefs and values: the radical conception stresses class justice and direct mass control over the state; the Leninist conception defends an orthodox Stalinist view of democratic centralism; the liberal conception stresses liberty and the rights of individuals. In their pure forms, each is immoral to the others. Each concept of democracy, moreover, reflects the interests and aspirations of different groups and strata.

The debates over democratization in China over the past three decades can be seen as a contest between three sets of social forces, each combining a fraction of the state with a specific set of wider social interests. The conventional party definition of Leninist democracy has sought and received support outside the state, notably among the laboring classes generally and the industrial working class in particular, as was visible in the widespread mass support for embattled party and government cadres during the Cultural Revolution. Liberalizing party leaders have paid particular attention to mobilizing support among technocratic elements within the state apparatus and various intellectual and professional strata in society at large; leftist party leaders have appealed to a complex patchwork of social interests, both idealistic and opportunistic, and have thus faced great difficulties in piecing together a stable political base.

The coalitional nature of both "liberal" and "radical" projects explains the diversity of each movement (particularly the "extremism" of advocates outside the state apparatus) and is a major source of their political weakness. Moreover, the sponsorship (and domination) of both movements by a fraction of the party-state has inevitably limited their potential for a real shift of power toward the people. When the official sponsors saw each movement getting out of hand, they stepped in to control it — hence the rejection of the Paris Commune alternative by Maoist leaders in 1967 and the emasculation of the human rights movement by Dengist leaders in the late 1970s. Since the cardinal political force in each alternative lies within the state mechanism, none is able to transcend the structural limitations which this fact imposes.

2

Back from the Brink of Revolutionary-"Feudal" Totalitarianism

TANG TSOU

An Historic Turning Point

The Third Plenary Session of the Eleventh Central Committee of the Communist Party of China held in December 1978 may turn out to be the landmark of the beginning of a new historic era in China. For the Chinese Communist movement, it may prove to be as important as the Zunyi Conference of January 1935, which made Mao Zedong the head of a three-man group to handle military affairs and paved the way to Mao's leadership of the party. For the political development of China, it may signal the end of nearly three-quarters of a century of revolutionary ferment and upheaval. In a low-key manner, the communique called on the party to "shift the emphasis of its work to socialist modernization" and to "integrate the universal principles of Marxism-Leninism-Mao Tsetung Thought with the concrete practice of socialist modernization and develop it under the new historical conditions."[1]

But what was the earlier emphasis from which the call for socialist modernization represents a shift? The communique did not address itself to this question in a forthright manner. But it did state that "as Comrade Mao Tsetung pointed out, the large-scale turbulent class struggles of a mass character have in the main come to an end."[2] More important, other official statements and numerous articles, as well as the programs and policies adopted and implemented afterward, have made it clear that this "shift of emphasis" may mark the end of

This essay was prepared as a framework for analyzing politics and social change in twentieth-century China. The support of the Endowment for the Humanities is appreciatively acknowledged. The first draft was completed in early January 1980. It was presented on May 30, 1980, at the Luce Seminar, University of Chicago. The essay was updated in the summer of 1982. In the process of revision, I was greatly benefited by the comments of Professors Ira Katznelson, Adam Przeworski, Philippe Schmitter, Michel Oksenberg, Mark Selden, Edward Friedman, Ross Terrill, Lowell Dittmer, Hong Yung Lee, Mark Blecher, and Brantly Womack.

a prolonged period of revolutionary transformation of the Chinese Society and the beginning a new era of consolidation, adaptation, and modernization. Thus Richard Lowenthal's insight on "the existence of a long-term trend toward the victory of modernization over utopianism"[3] in Communist regimes may be proved correct by events unfolding in China. Or in Samuel Huntington's terminology, the "revolutionary one-party system" in China has now been developing into an "established one-party system."[4]

Lowenthal makes clear that his analysis is based on a "version of the much criticized totalitarian model of Communist Party dictatorship."[5] He concludes that a postrevolutionary Communist party regime "is neither totalitarian nor democratic, but *authoritarian*."[6] The thrust of his argument agrees generally with Juan Linz's conclusion, which is based on an examination of both Communist and non-Communist regimes whether they are totalitarian or authoritarian.[7] In contrast to the "much criticized totalitarian model," however, "totalitarianism" is defined in this essay not in terms of those fixed institutional traits enumerated by Carl J. Friedrich or reconceptualized by other theorists with great sophistication in the light of their improved understanding of developments in totalitarian regimes. Rather, it is simply defined as a central dynamics in the relationship between political power on the one hand and civil society and the economy on the other. As such, "totalitarianism" connotes, to use the words of N. S. Timasheff, "unlimited extension of state functions"; it designates "a trait isolated by means of abstraction and apt to appear in society of various types."[8] But it is a particularly salient feature in a society undergoing a social revolution. One can even suggest that all social revolutions contain within themselves totalitarian tendencies in different degrees. A total social revolution is by definition totalitarian in the full sense of the word. Therefore, we can speak of "the degree of totalitarianism" or "totalitarian-ness" in a continuum, measured by the penetration of political power into other spheres of social life. In a totalitarian society, political power may find concrete embodiment in the state, the party, or a charismatic leader supported by mobilized masses or a combination of all three forms of political power in various proportions.[9]

The Rise and Fall of Revolutionary-"Feudal" Totalitarianism, 1966–1976

Informed by the specific concept of totalitarianism just noted, this essay puts forward the following simple but probably controversial argument. Political developments in the three years from 1978 to 1980 marked an exceedingly rapid retreat from the brink of what I call "revolutionary-'feudal' totalitarianism," which the ultraleftists and Lin Biao with powerful but qualified support from Mao advocated and endeavored to put into action during the Cultural

Revolution of 1966—1976. At the same time, there was an attempt to find a proper and flexible limit to this retreat. By 1981, the tempo of retreat had slowed down. In such areas of civil society as literature and art and the expression of dissent, there has been some retrogression from the high-water mark of 1980, although in other areas such as the relations between the peasants and the state, the trend has continued to move forward. Taken as a whole, the ongoing course of development has been stabilized. Specific reforms and incremental changes reflecting a retreat from the brink have continued to occur.

From a larger historical perspective, the great leap backward in the first three years and the continuing program of reforms mark the reversal of a fundamental trend in China in the twentieth century toward increased penetration of politics into other spheres of society, culminating in the revolutionary-"feudal" totalitarianism of the ultraleftists. Their ideas and programs were "revolutionary," first, because they called for the overthrow of the "new bourgeois class" that had allegedly emerged within the Chinese Communist party; second, because they endeavored to effect fundamental change in the relations of production; and third, because they envisaged the use of both violent and nonviolent methods, bypassing the hitherto officially sanctioned channels and organizations. These ideas and programs were totalitarian because they pushed to the extreme the long-existing tendency of extending political control over every sphere of social life. The concept of "all-round dictatorship over the bourgeoisie" meant, among other things, complete, dictatorial control over all professions because the professionals and the intellectuals were considered by the ultraleftists to be members of either old or new bourgeois class. In the ultraleftists' program, political control over thought, expression of ideas, family life, and individual behavior became even more extensive, penetrating, and repressive, even though this program was not effectively and fully implemented during the chaos of the Cultural Revolution.

In contrast to their revolutionary program and rhetoric, their political actions paralleled the "feudalistic" pattern in the sense that the Chinese Communists use the term, because they derived implicit and in some cases explicit support from the cognitive, evaluative, and emotive orientations of the "feudal" political culture. The notions that "politics can decide everything" and that "with power in one's hand, one has everything" were suggestive. The cult of personality, which the ultraleftists pushed to the extreme, derived implicit support from the previous long history of worship of emperor. Loyalty toward the leader rested on the traditional concept of loyalty toward one's superiors in all political and social ranks. The injunction, "every directive issued by Chairman Mao must be obeyed whether you understand it or not, agree with it or not," drew on the traditional virtue of obedience. The ideas of the Legalist school were revived by the leftists who used historical analogy and allusion as a basis for attacking the veteran leaders and their moderate program.

Thus the revolutionary-"feudal" totalitarianism of the ultraleftists represented a more extreme form of the totalitarian tendency than that which had occurred under the auspices of the organized party. It was first developed in the early phases of the Cultural Revolution when the overwhelming majority of the party organizations were destroyed or paralyzed by the combined action of the leader and the masses. Its fluctuating fortune thereafter varied inversely with the degree to which the party was rebuilt. This totalitarianism of personal leadership plus mass action — an organizational form that existed not exclusively at the highest level but at all levels — is different in principle from the totalitarian tendency of the party. It was much less restrained by any formal rules or norms, and it paid little heed to party traditions. To fill these normative and organizational vacuums, the ultraleftists and their allies fell back on "feudal" values, norms, ideas, and attitudes. To the extent that a party organized along Leninist principles is a modern phenomenon, the totalitarianism organized around Mao's arbitrary personal leadership represented a regression into China's distant past.

But the ultraleftists never achieved total domination. Their increasing influence was opposed by an overwhelming majority of other leaders in the party, army, and government, who received encouragement and support from various social groups and from the unorganized masses in many subtle and unobserved ways. They succeeded only in establishing small enclaves of power. Toward the end of the Cultural Revolution they had little influence over the military, and their effort to build up an urban militia as a second armed force further antagonized the army without achieving any real countervailing power.

Paradoxically, the program of the ultraleftists, which marked the culmination of the totalitarian tendency in the Chinese Communist movement, soon led not only to its total repudiation but, more significantly, also to sweeping historical reexamination by the current leaders. Mao's successors were forced to ask the fundamental question why a movement for class and human liberation had developed into one of the most oppressive systems in Chinese history — what the Chinese Communists call "feudal fascism." This self-examination was undertaken by those who in their youthful and idealistic days joined the revolution to fight against political oppression; who in their middle age became themselves the oppressors, the inquisitors, and the denunciators in an attempt to achieve a revolutionary transformation of the society; who in their late middle or old age were oppressed, condemned, and denounced by others in the name of still another revolution; and who in the remaining few years of their lives regained power and authority. They have indeed been reeducated by the Cultural Revolution but not in the way intended by its originator. The diametrically opposite positions they occupied before and during the Cultural Revolution forced them to view the political system from the bottom as well as from the top, from the outside as well as from the inside, and in their capacity as its victims in contrast to their earlier role as its beneficiaries. Indeed, the pre-1966 oppressors suffered during the Cultural Revolution more grievous harm than those whom they had oppressed. Now they are seriously concerned with their own place in China's history. It is this "second liberation" and the personal experience of the "reborn revolutionary" which give extraordinary poignancy to their reexamination and soul-searching.

Not long after those who before 1976 had been both the oppressors and the oppressed had been rehabilitated by the post-Mao leadership, one witnessed the deeply moving scene of the erstwhile oppressors recently restored to leading positions of power and influence apologizing publicly to their victims and permitting them to publicize views for which they had been punished before 1976. In October–November 1979, at the Fourth Congress of Writers and Artists, which met for the first time in nineteen years, Zhou Yang publicly apologized to those whom he had unjustly persecuted. By this act of self-criticism, he mollified his critics and was even elected chairman of the All-China Association of Writers and Artists.[10] He and other party leaders have been forgiven by at least some of their victims, in the charitable spirit that, as individuals, "they know not what they do." As Ding Ling observed, what happened in the past was not a question of receiving favors or suffering from personal enmity; what she went through involved the entire society; there was no single person who struck her down.[11] These leaders had not known the harmful effects of the more radical principles and policies they had initiated or implemented for the purpose of strengthening revolutionary power and transforming man and society. The full implications of these ideas and practices were realized only when, pushed to their logical conclusion by the ultraleftists, they were used to persecute many of their originators, champions, and advocates.[12] As Ding Ling saw it, the basic source of these errors was a combination of political power and small group mentality, that is, "sectarianism," which was a concrete expression of "feudalism."[13] At that juncture of history, many though by no means all of those who had been disgraced before 1976 found some common ground in raising fundamental questions about some of these erroneous principles and practices or at least in searching for ways to modify them.

Many of the influential figures probably shared Ba Jin's feeling of deep regret that he did not perceive the disastrous consequences of the regime's policies toward literature and the arts in time, that he agreed with or at least acquiesced in their implementation, and indeed sometimes even voluntarily helped further them. In the initial period when he himself was victimized, he truly believed in his persecutors' argument. Only later, he discovered that he was being deceived. This discovery led to a feeling of emptiness and total disillusion.[14] For a brief period, the thought of suicide crossed his mind. Finally, he began to analyze both himself and his persecutors objectively. In his account of his own thoughts, past and present, he tells himself with a profound sense of remorse and guilt that the days of political persecution must not be allowed to return.

Self-doubt and the gnawing feeling that the regime's overall policies might be correct were a major subjective factor in the failure of other writers, such as Liu Binyan, to resist. After being labeled a rightist in 1957, Liu spent the next three years trying piously to reform himself, to criticize his own class and rightist viewpoint, and to place his trust in the party's words. Only the stark realities of life in the countryside gradually convinced him of the falsity of official propaganda and the errors of the policies of the superior authorities. Still, Liu confided his doubts only to himself and his diary. He continued to perform his assigned tasks obediently. His rightist label was removed in March 1966. Less than three months later, the Cultural Revolution began, and he was again attacked when his diary, which had been copied stealthily by one of his colleagues, was used against him. In 1979, he declared that he would continue to write and speak his mind, come what might, because for him and people like him there was no route of retreat. [15]

The amazing fact that a large number of purged leaders not only survived the Cultural Revolution but have been restored to positions of authority must be attributed to the principle gradually developed during the period of civil and foreign wars that top party leaders who lost out in inner party struggles should not be executed. [16] The practice of sparing these leaders reflected the only norm governing inner party struggle and rectification campaigns which was not openly violated during the Cultural Revolution, although not a few prominent leaders are known to have been hounded to their deaths or driven to commit suicide. This longstanding norm turned out to be the saving grace of the system and has given it a second chance to reform itself at a crucial time in the nation's history.

Because the self-examination was undertaken by veteran political leaders who had deep personal experience of the hopes and promises of the revolutionary movement in its early years and their utter betrayal in the recent past, it seems likely to have lasting significance. For the rehabilitated leaders have seen that the system they built could lead to a disastrous outcome and that certain underlying principles and actual practices, which they had strongly advocated or supported at various times, could have devastating consequences for Chinese society as a whole. [17]

The self-examination and soul-searching by many survivors of the Cultural Revolution has also led to a reconstruction of institutions and to a restatement of basic ideological and sociopolitical principles. These changes mark China's transformation from utopianism to development, as Lowenthal foresaw, and from a revolutionary one-party system to an established one-party system, as Huntington suggests. But the true, historic significance of the reevaluation and resulting changes lies in the reversal of the profound trend that began after the May Fourth period and was characterized by increasing penetration of politics into all spheres of social life. This reversal signifies the retreat of politics from the control of society. In other words, the relationship between political power and society in China is beginning to undergo a change in direction. In attempting to sketch an overall view of the post-Mao era as a step toward a larger interpretation of twentieth-century Chinese politics, I can only describe these changes in broad outline. I have not been able to give even preliminary answers to the basic question: What are the larger factors in the Chinese economy, social stratification, relative power among the various social groups, and the international environment which can be induced to account for the rapid collapse of the totalitarianism of the ultraleftists and hence for the current retreat? Description is the first step toward explanation, which will involve difficult theoretical questions and a diligent search for adequate historical data.

The Retreat of Politics as Reflected in Ideological Discourse

The changing relationship between political power and society can be most easily detected in the sphere of ideology, more specifically in a reinterpretation of Mao Zedong Thought. Ideological discussions still fill many pages in the official newspapers and various journals, although the proportion of articles on practical problems, factual reports, and empirical studies has sharply increased. Given the salience of ideology and its function as a template for political action in twentieth-century China, the downgrading of ideology must be, as Brantly Womack perceptively noted,[18] the task of ideology. The reversal of many concrete programs, strongly or partially justified by Mao's ideas, as well as the abandonment of many of his explicit directives or policies, is rationalized on the basis of a reinterpretation of Mao Zedong Thought by giving primacy to his theory of knowledge. This rationale basically implies a shift from the emphasis on the substantive conclusions of Marxism-Leninism and Mao Zedong Thought to a stress on their use as a method of analysis; it also implies a transition from the stress on utopian goals to an emphasis on the concrete conditions confronting China. Specifically, the epistemological postulate that "practice is the criterion for testing truth" has been elevated to the status of the most fundamental postulate of Marxism-Leninism and Mao Zedong Thought, thus reversing the emphasis given by Mao in his later years to the decisive role of theory. These ideological shifts explain the formulation adopted by the Third Plenum on the need to "integrate the universal principles of Marxism-Leninism-Mao Tsetung Thought with the concrete practice of socialist modernization and develop it under the new historical conditions."

In an article published in September 1977, I pointed out that the emphasis on practice can be understood as a principle of prudence in decision making, a criterion to judge the correctness of policies, a basic justification for the Sinification of Marxism and the development of a revolutionary program suitable to

Chinese conditions. From the perspective of the present analysis, we can now see that this slightly reformulated epistemological postulate on "practice" obliges the party, the state, and leaders at all levels and in all spheres to take heed of the social practices of the masses, that is, the needs, the interests, the demands, the life situations, and the behavioral patterns of various social groups and individuals. It gives greater weight to the perceived interests and demands of the various social groups and individuals as they impinge on the party and the state, especially the party's ideas about these interests and demands. To be sure, China still has a system in which the party and its leaders guide the national development, coordinate its interdependent parts, and ultimately control its multifarious groups and individuals. But the inputs and feedback from the society to the party and the state are more direct and have more discernible effects than before.

The process through which the elevation of "practice" to the status of a basic principle was accomplished also suggests that in post-Mao China, the source of new ideological formulations has become more pluralistic and can be found at a much lower level of the party hierarchy. The article, "Practice Is the Sole Criterion for Testing Truth," published on May 11, 1978, in *Guangming Ribao*, was given credit for starting the nationwide public discussion on the theory of knowledge. It was written by Hu Fuming, the vice-chairman of the Department of Philosophy at the University of Nanjing and concurrently the deputy secretary of the party branch of that department. It came about as the author's response to the charge that he was defending "revisionist viewpoints" when he noted the disastrous consequences of the educational program of the ultra-leftists and when he reaffirmed the "theory of forces of production," which had been declared to be a proper subject of criticism in a document previously adopted by a general meeting of the party. He came to the conclusion that the criterion for judging any idea, theory, law, or decree can only be "practice" — the basic point of departure of the Marxist theory of knowledge.[19] Publication of the article met with widespread positive response form the readers. On June 2, Vice-Premier Deng Xiaoping used the important occasion of a conference on political work of the People's Liberation Army (PLA) to drive home its major theme in a speech that called on everyone "to use the method of seeking truth from facts, proceeding from reality and integrating theory with practice."[20]

The nationwide discussions that followed were undoubtedly organized and promoted by the moderate veteran leaders at the top, particularly Deng and Hu Yaobang. They provided strong ideological support for the innovative policies of the pragmatic leaders and showed up the theoretical hollowness and practical absurdity of the position of standpatters. From then on, the latter's argument advanced as late as March 1977 in the party's theoretical journal, *Hongqi*, that "whatever the decision made by Chairman Mao was, we will resolutely support; whatever Chairman Mao's directive was, we will unswervingly obey,"[21] became a subject of ridicule and contempt. The endorsement of the national discussions on criterion of truth by the Third Plenum in December 1978 paved the way for a series of articles demystifying and demythologizing Mao. After intensive soul-searching and internal debate, this process of de-deification of Mao culminated in the "Resolution on Certain Questions in History of Our Party since the Founding of the People's Republic of China" adopted by the Sixth Plenum on June 27, 1981. This historic document reaffirmed Mao's theoretical and practical contributions to the Chinese revolution, particularly his role in leading the CCP from defeat to victory. But it also noted that "chief responsibility for the grave 'left' error of the 'Cultural Revolution' . . . does indeed lie with Comrade Mao Zedong."[22] The "theory of continued revolution under the dictatorship of the proletariat" which incorporated Mao's principal theses justifying the Cultural Revolution was specifically repudiated.

The central ideal of this first systematic and most widely known article on the criterion of truth in the post-Mao era is simply Marxist common sense, as its author emphasized. From the perspective of the philosophy of science, it raises more questions than it answers. More specifically, the criterion of truth for formal logic, mathematics, and all analytic propositions is not "practice." Partly for this reason, the term "sole" has frequently been dropped since 1981 and Mao's phrase "seeking truth from facts" has once again become the standard formulation.

This new epistemological postulate on practice as the criterion of truth which is supposed to inform all decisions and actions is reinforced by a sociological postulate that can be reconstructed as follows. Every sphere of social life has its special characteristics (*te dian*) and is governed by objective laws. Political leadership can and should create the general conditions and framework that are favorable to the operation of these laws and that promote desired development. But it cannot violate these laws without suffering serious consequences.

This restatement of the relationship between politics and other spheres of social life and the reinterpretation of the principle of "politics in command" can be found in the authoritative article by Hu Qiaomu, then the president of the newly created Academy of the Social Science. Hu reemerged as one of the regime's leading theoreticians and powerful figures after a long period of obscurity during the Cultural Revolution.[23] In February 1980, he became a member of the reestablished Secretariat, and since September 1982, he has been a member of the Political Bureau.

On the basis of a selective quoting or paraphrasing of Marx, Engels, Lenin, and Mao, Hu made the following points: Economic laws are like "natural laws," and "natural laws" cannot be dispensed with; they cannot be altered at the will of the society, the government, and the authorities. "Over and above the economic laws in objective existence, politics itself cannot create other laws and impose them on the economy. In fact, insofar as the laws of economic developments are concerned, the mission of correct political leadership lies precisely in making the maximum effort to see to it that our socialist economic work operates within the scope of these objective laws." In a socialist society, political power can bring "enormous damage to economic development" if it is misused.[24] Similar views have been expressed by the current leaders in all spheres of social life, particularly those in the areas of science, education, and literature and the arts who had suffered from various forms of persecution and attack dating back to the beginning of the Cultural Revolution in most cases but to the Yanan period in some cases.[25]

The significance of this postulate lies not alone in the impetus it has given to the restoration of a measure of rationality in economic and other policies. Its fundamental meaning is that there exist certain areas of autonomy in economic and social life into which political power cannot and should not intrude. It thus symbolizes and legitimizes the reversal of the historic trend toward the increasing penetration of politics into all social spheres. It may also mark a new beginning in the relationship between political power and society. For it opens up the possibility for the professionals and specialists in various spheres to show what these objective laws are. Hence, the official acceptance of this postulate has coincided with the reemergence of the economists, educators, natural and social scientists, writers, and artists in positions of authority and influence in the political system. "Listen to the views of the specialists" is now a constant refrain. An article in *Hongqi* declares that the term "authority" has two meanings:

> What we commonly call theoretical authority, academic authority, technical authority, . . . etc., is in essence a synonym for truth. The reason why authority is called authority is that it represents truth, represents the objective laws of natural and social development, represents correct opinions, and thus also represents the interests of the majority. . . . The other meaning of authority refers to the laws, discipline, rules and regulations, order, directives, etc., which are indispensable in class struggle, struggle for production and scientific experiment.[26]

This postulate also changes the terms of the debate on the question of the relationship between the party and the specialists and between politics and other vocations. To be sure, that relationship was and still is defined primarily as involving "redness" and "expertise." Although it was and still is frequently affirmed that officials and cadres in professional work should be both "red and expert," the debate almost always gave redness an easy victory whenever redness came into conflict with expertness. The salience of ideology in modern China, and the highest priority given to moral values in the Chinese cultural tradition,[27] made the outcome nearly inevitable — quite aside from the question of who had actual political power in the society.

Now the sociological postulate marks out spheres of social activities, supposedly governed by special laws that can be discovered by the experts and cannot be ignored by the politicians without doing damage to the entire society. Thus it bolsters the experts' claims of authority even when the traditional formula is used. In other words, the traditional formula has taken on a new meaning within the changed context of discourse.

The social standing of all specialists in China in all fields is now higher than at any time since 1949, and their impact on policies is also much greater. Western social scientists can legitimately ask what the objective laws governing each sphere of social life are and whether such objective laws can be discovered. From their own experience with "the best and the brightest" in government, they rightly question whether the Chinese are entertaining an illusion. But for the moment, we can leave these questions aside and merely note the significance of this sociological postulate as a signpost of the change of direction in China's political development.

The affirmation of these existential objective laws and the implicit grant of a certain degree of autonomy to various social groups also imply a recognition of the positive functions performed by the various professions and occupations. It represents a reversal of the analysis made by the ultraleftists on the basis of many remarks by Mao on the functions of the various groups in the society. In Maoist analysis, the emphasis was placed on what social scientists in the West would call the latent dysfunctions[28] of the various professional and occupational activities, particularly as they affect social stratification and political conflict. For example, the latent dysfunction of education, development of science and technology, and economic management in creating a new bourgeois class and a new intellectual aristocracy was stressed by the ultraleftists, whereas the manifest functions of these professions in the transmission of culture, in economic and technical development, and in the achievement of other aspects of modernization were ignored or given a subordinate place. The ultraleftists were accused of propagating the view that it is better to have workers without culture than a bourgeoisie with culture. The stress on the latent dysfunction of education, science, knowledge, and culture in creating a new class legitimized the intrusion of politics on these spheres as a necessary form of class struggle. Thus the Chinese case provides one more example that functional analysis can be placed in the service of radicalism as well as conservatism. In some cases, the latent dysfunction as seen from the viewpoint of the ultraleftists was interpreted by them as a conscious purpose of those engaged in these activities. Their theory of conspiracy had one of its sources in their functional analysis.

This misuse of functional analysis as a political weapon contributed to the loss of a generation of educated youth, scientists, engineers, physicians, humanists, social scientists, writers, artists, and other specialists. Now the tables are turned, manifest functions are stressed, and latent functions or dysfunctions are deemphasized. Will the Chinese hang themselves on the other horn of the dilemma by creating a new meritocracy? They may do so eventually. But at the moment, the intellectuals and specialists in other fields are only beginning to be liberated from the overcentralized control of the party and government bureaucracies, which generally lack staff sufficiently informed in fields of science, technology, education, and culture. The urgent task is to tame bureaucratism (which is also a legacy of what the Chinese call feudalism) rather than to counterbalance the influence of the intellectuals.

There has also been a deemphasis, reinterpretation, and even repudiation of Mao's reformulation of historical materialism to the effect that in certain conditions theory and the superstructure rather than productive forces, practice, and economic base can and do play the principal and decisive role in social change.[29] Some Chinese theorists assert that Mao's formulation is still correct, but they immediately add that the conditions which make it possible for theory and superstructure to play the principal and decisive role are themselves created by the development of productive forces and the economic base. In the writings of other theorists, Mao's formulation was implicitly but directly challenged and the ultra-leftists' interpretation of Mao repudiated, usually without naming Mao.

The following passage from an authoritative article from *Hongqi* reveals the degree of change in official Chinese thinking within the party.

> In studying the forms of economy and the laws of economics, many comrades often try to recruit the help of such non-economic factors as ideas, politics, violence, instead of beginning their study with the mode of production. They have been accustomed to use the expressed wishes of certain persons, the [ideological and political] line of a certain period, and certain guiding principles and policies in their efforts to explain the formation, development, and transformation of economic relations and to elucidate the movement and functioning of economic laws. Take a few examples. To explain the coming into being of the socialist relations of ownership, they do not attribute it to the objective needs of the developing productive forces, but instead name the role of the proletarian organ of power as the most fundamental and decisive factor. [For them] whether the nature of ownership is socialist or capitalist depends entirely on what leadership it has and is not to be judged by an actual analysis of the form of ownership; the transition of a form of ownership from its lower level to its higher level is to be decided by the ideological and political levels of the masses and cadres, and not to be decided by whether the level of economic development is favorable to the transition; the law of economics has become something people can dispose of at will and can be utilized and restricted in accordance with all sorts of needs, including political needs. Furthermore, it can be put under the "rule of man."[30]

In short, the economists have replaced the revolutionaries as authoritative interpreters of social change. The central message is that economic considerations cannot and should not always be overridden by the political line and the government's action.

But the return to the classical Marxist formulation of historical materialism must be understood in the broader context of the political-economic development in twentieth-century China. The original Marxist thesis reflected the situation in early capitalist society in which the free market and economic forces played the primary role in the transformation of other aspects of social life. In contrast, Mao's formulation asserted that in the revolution and social changes of twentieth-century China, politics (including ideology, state, party, personalized leadership, and the masses) played the primary role in transforming society. But as capitalism developed, especially in mature capitalist society in the West, politics intervened to ameliorate many undesirable consequences of the free market. Political participation of the lower classes and the labor union movement constituted one of the factors in disproving Marx's prophecy of increasing misery of the proletariat under capitalism. The gap between the classes at the top and the bottom narrowed rather than widened.

In China, the reinterpretation or abandonment of Mao's formulation took place after the attempt to push the transformative role of politics to the extreme had created many serious problems in the economy and other areas of society. The practical and operational consequences of the current ideological discourse are to allow economic forces and other social groups a degree of autonomy in order to ameliorate many of these adverse effects of politics. Politics is still given a primary role to play in economic development, but the market and other social forces will also be allowed to play their own roles in the economy and the society. In other words, the real significance of ideological theses in China can be detected only when they are understood both in their theoretical context and in the light of the real situation confronting the political actors and the society. Thus the restructuring, reformulation, and reinterpretation of the ideological theses frequently signify a change in the rules of the game at the most abstract level and provide the broad framework for decision making. The current theoretical discourse in the various journals and newspapers on matters of ideology can best be understood within this context.

The Reversal of the Position of the Intellectuals and the New Perception of the Class Structure

Of the various groups in the society, the broad class of Chinese intellectuals undoubtedly have gained most in the reversal of the trend in the politics-society relationship.[31] During 1968, the term "stinking number nine"[32] emerged as a characterization of the intellectuals as a social group, placing them last on the list of disreputable social groups, the others being landlords, rich peasants, counterrevolutionaries, bad elements, rightists, renegades, special agents (of the enemy), and capitalist-roaders. All were subjected to attacks and discrimination. Now they are classified as "a sector of the working class"[33] engaging in "mental labor." Peng Chong, the former first secretary of Shanghai municipality, stated the matter even more strongly: "The intellectuals in our country are that section of the working class which grasps advanced scientific and cultural knowledge earlier than any other sections. They are the treasure of our nation and our state."[34] The policy of remolding the intellectuals adopted shortly after 1949 is considered to be "no longer applicable in regard to the overwhelming majority of the intellectuals."[35]

The state, the party, or any political leader, however eminent he is, no longer has any automatic and special claims to truth. Formerly, the idea that the natural sciences have no class character had been only intermittently heard. Now it is part of the accepted orthodoxy. The view that the social sciences have class character, however, is still prevalent. But many influential writers assert that truth in social sciences has no class character — undoubtedly a tautology but a tautology with important political implications. The role of the intellectuals as social critics is being recognized. The symbol of this recognition is Ma Yinchu, whose advocacy of population control in the years of 1955 – 1957 had been vehemently attacked in 1958 and had cost him his job as the president of Beijing University. In his late nineties, Ma was appointed as the honorary president of that university, an accolade given nationwide publicity. Virtually all the disgraced scholars and writers in the original Department of Philosophy and Social Sciences in the Academy of Sciences ranging from those condemned as "counter-revolutionary revisionists" to those labeled as "intellectuals with unreconstructed bourgeois world views" have been rehabilitated and given high positions in the academic world.[36]

The once condemned view that literature must "intervene in life," that is, must be "concerned with and involved in the lives of individuals and groups" and must reflect the dark side of the society as well as its bright spots, has been heard once again. It has been reflected in many loudly acclaimed short stories, poems, journalistic reports, and essays including "Between a Human Being and a Monster,"[37] "The Wounds," "The Son of the Commander of the Artillery Forces," and "From Where Silence Reigns." Its once youthful protagonists such as Liu Binyan are now conspicuous figures in the literary world after many years of obscurity.[38] Although there is still a strong undercurrent of opposition to these ideas, and in many places opinion swung away from them in the early months of 1980, the debate has been conducted in the open.[39] The party is apparently attempting to balance those writing which explore the darker side of the society by an advocacy of writings which reflect the endeavors to correct the past mistakes and to build a modernized society. In spite of the criticisms launched against Bai Hua's *Bitter Love* and Ye Wenfu's poems in 1981 and 1982, the slogan "literature and art serve politics" has officially been replaced by "literature and art serve the people and serve socialism." This change was accompanied by the official abandonment of Mao's famous axiom laid down at the Yanan Forum that "literature and art are subordinate to politics" from which the former slogan was derived.[40]

Research institutes and universities have been strengthened and given greater financial support. The expansion of the Academy of Sciences and the transformation of the Department of Philosophy and the Social Sciences into the new Academy of the Social Sciences are merely the most prominent examples. Economists have been playing a very visible role in formulating economic policies. Scientists, engineers, and other technical experts have been given a greater voice in pursuing their own research and in charting the development of their respective fields. Vice-Premier Deng Xiaoping told a group of scientists that he was willing to serve as the head of the department of logistics for their scientific research.[41] Party and government officials were told that although party leadership in the overall programs throughout the nation and in various units must be maintained, outsiders should not interfere with the work of insiders and in technical matters outsiders cannot lead insiders. Indeed, persons with specialized knowledge should shoulder the burden of leadership in party committees and in professional organizations at all levels.[42] One should not be afraid of the charge that one adopts "the line of experts" and allows "the experts to run the factory and the university."

The elevation of the role to be played by scientists and specialists reached a high point in the speech before the National Congress of the All-China Association for Science and Technology made by Party General Secretary Hu Yaobang. He called on the party and the government to place able research workers in positions where they can freely and boldly use their special talents and to promote those specialists with administrative and organizational ability to positions of leadership in the party, government, economic, scientific, and educational works. As a symbolic gesture, he told the assembled scientists that he and his colleagues in the Secretariat were prepared to invite some of the scientists to hold symposiums and seminars on special subjects for their benefit and to invite the scientists to be their "teachers" (*laoshi*).[43]

Almost all the professional and academic associations that existed before the Cultural Revolution have been reestablished. The first meetings of these associations furnished the occasion for the tearful reunion of old friends and colleagues for the first time in more than ten years and, in some cases, more than twenty years. A participant in the Fourth Congress of Chinese Writers and Artists used the metaphor of "hospital for wounded soldiers" to describe the assemblage of writers and artists.[44] Not only were the participants old and sick, or had suffered physical injuries at the hands of the Red Guards during the Cultural Revolution, they were also spiritually "wounded." The meeting was

67

an occasion for treating these wounds. Xiao Jun, the Manchurian writer who had lived in obscurity after his attack on the behavior of the Soviet Union and the Red Army in his native region, called himself "a cultural relic" recently unearthed. Liu Shaotang, who at the age of twenty-one had been labeled a big rightist in 1957, declared that he would begin his life and writing career again as if he were twenty-one.[45]

In addition, new professional and academic associations have been established as a result of the tendency toward increasing specialization. Local associations have been set up in various provinces and cities to mobilize all human resources to achieve a more decentralized pattern of organization and to take advantage of special talents and conditions in these localities. For example, Nanjing is the center for the study of the Taiping Rebellion, Wuhan for the study of the 1911 Revolution, and Guangzhou for the study of the life of Sun Yat-sen. Most significantly, academics and professionals have been encouraged to take the initiative in organizing specialized associations.[46] These associations are not merely transmission belts. They are beginning actively to promote the interests of their members. The Association of Chinese Writers recently adopted a decision to organize a committee to protect the rights and interests of the writers under the chairmanship of the highly respected veteran writer, Xia Yan.[47] At the National Congress of Associations of Scientific Workers held in March 1980, the veteran scientist Zhou Peiyuan declared that the association must resolutely struggle against any attempt to attack and oppress scientific workers or any action that violates their rights and interests.[48]

The *fanshen* or the reversal of the position of the intellectuals and the reverse flow of their influence to the state and the party on basic policy decisions and institutional reconstruction constitute only one of the many manifestations of the changing relationships between political power and society. Former capitalists, landlords, and rich peasants are also being given a different position in the political system. The then premier and party chairman, Hua Guofeng, solemnly declared at the second session of the Fifth National People's Congress in June 1979 that, as classes, the landlords and rich peasants had ceased to exist. As for the capitalists, Hua said that "the great majority of these people have been transformed into laborers earning their own living in our socialist society" and that "the capitalists no longer exist as a class."[49] An effort has been made to return or replace personal and real properties confiscated or requisitioned during the Cultural Revolution. Former capitalists are again placed in enterprises in accordance with their technical and managerial ability. They are being given a major role in programs to attract foreign and overseas Chinese investments in joint enterprises.

Of great importance for our purpose is the new status conferred on former landlords and rich peasants in the countryside. In early 1979, the Central Committee adopted a decision to remove the designations of those landlords, rich peasants, counterrevolutionaries, and bad elements who had, over the years, abided by state laws and decrees, worked honestly, and done no evil and to grant them the same rights as enjoyed by rural commune members.[50] They have been reclassified as commune members.[51] It was also decreed that there should be no discrimination against the descendants of the landlords, rich peasants, and members of the national bourgeoisie in the future regarding education, work, and admissions to the Youth League or the party.

The significance of this change is apparent when viewed against the earlier policy. Up to that time, the alleged existence and continuing influence of these two rural classes were used to justify the increasing penetration of state power into the rural society to bring about the dominance of the poor and middle peasant class in the countryside. The repressive measures against the landlords and rich peasants and the discriminatory treatment of their descendants had the latent function of demonstrating the absolute authority and unchallengeable power of the local cadres, which cowed all social groups and individuals, including the poor and lower-middle peasants, into submission to the state's demands for further social change and economic reconstruction. These practices helped stifle the peasants' expression of demands based on felt needs and perceived interests and give the cadres scapegoats for their own errors and shortcomings. Overall they raised tensions in the countryside which prevented the development of a regularized and predictable relationship between the state and society.[52]

The redefinition of the class situation in society was accompanied by a reassessment of the seriousness of class struggle. It is said that although class struggle has not died out, the period of large-scale and turbulent class struggle is over. "Class struggle in the days to come will no longer be a struggle between *classes as a whole*."[53] It is no longer the "principal contradiction" that needs to be resolved at the present time. Vice-Chairman Ye Jianying declared in his historic speech on September 29, 1979, that "we must oppose the view that magnifies it [class struggle], to say nothing of creating so-called class struggles out of the void."[54] Even more significantly, it is asserted that "at all times class struggle is a means; the basic goal of revolution is to liberate and develop the social productive forces."[55] These statements represent a reaffirmation and an extension of the conclusions adopted by the Eighth Party Congress in September 1956, which of course were repudiated during the decade of the Cultural Revolution. Just as the ultraleftists' totalitarian program rested on a special definition of class struggle, the new definition points to a decision not to change the existing social stratification by direct political action. Inputs and feedback from the society to the party and the state will be allowed to have greater impact than before.

Restructuring the Economy and Rediscovering the Importance of the Immediate Material Interests of the Individual

The retreat of politics finds no more concrete expression than in the field of economics. The former trend toward increasing the scope of planning, restricting the use of the market, limiting the function of price, attacking the use of profits, and disparaging material incentives has been reversed. Now, the limitations of planning are underscored. Xue Muqiao, the noted economist who serves as an adviser to the State Planning Commission and the director of the Economic Research Institute attached to it, has observed that the state economic plan should not be all-inclusive and impose many precise targets on grass-roots units because the more specific the terms laid down by the state organs at the top become, the more difficult it is to strike a balance between the supply and demands for products.[56] Xue suggests that on the contrary, most of the final plans of the state-owned enterprises in production and marketing should be decided on by the enterprises themselves after consultation with the upper-level units. Enterprises should be given certain rights over their own incomes and expenditures. Xue also proposes the abandonment of the present procedure of making state plans under which purchasing plans are worked out according to production plans and marketing plans are in turn worked out according to the purchasing plans. Instead, he urges that purchasing plans should be drawn up on the basis of market needs and production plans drawn up on the basis of purchasing plans. In other words, sales in the market should determine production plans. Concrete measures to implement these suggestions are being discussed. Experiments giving the enterprises a large degree of autonomy have been undertaken.[57]

In agriculture, rural free markets have been reopened and expanded.[58] Private plots and sideline production by peasant households have been given added protection. The use of price policy in the promotion of economic growth is nowhere more obvious than in agriculture. In 1979, the state purchase price of grain was increased 20 percent with an added 50 percent for above quota purchases. The prices paid by the state for edible oil, pigs, and eggs were also raised. According to the government's calculations, these changes in prices would increase the peasants' per capita income from the collective unit by 8 *yuan* a year — an increase of more than 10 percent from their average per capita income of 73.90 *yuan* in 1978.[59]

The autonomy of the basic grass-roots units in the countryside — the production teams — has been given greater protection by the regime. In 1978, it publicized criticism of the cadres in Xiang Xiang County in Hunan Province for their indiscriminate attempts to use, without compensation, the labor power and material resources of the production teams for projects undertaken at the higher levels and for their misappropriation of state funds intended for the benefits of the teams.[60] Soon thereafter another campaign publicized the arbitrary use of power by the cadres in Xunyi County in Shenxi Province.[61] Many of the specific examples of abuses reported in the press were related to the attempts of brigade, commune, and county level cadres to use their political authority and influence to restrict the permissible private economic activities of the peasants.

More significantly, since 1979 the regime has promoted the adoption of the responsibility system in agriculture production, under which the contract relation has been given a progressively larger role while authority over work assignment and distribution of rewards has been transferred downward.[62] A primary feature of this system is the linkage between yield and reward received by the peasants. In December 1981, it was reported that more than 90 percent of the 5,870,000 production teams had adopted one or another of the many forms of the responsibility system, 16.9 percent of them were using the household responsibility system (*baochan daohu*), and 11.3 percent had adopted the household total responsibility system (*baogan daohu*).[63] By April 1982, it was reported that about half of the teams had adopted either the household responsibility system or the household total responsibility system; that is roughly 21.8 percent more than the figure given in December 1981.[64] The draft constitution published on April 28, 1982, provides for the reestablishment of the *xiang*-level government,[65] which was eliminated when the commune system was established as both an economic and a government unit. The communes would presumably be retained as a collective economic unit to manage small industrial and other enterprises. In the three *xian* in which experiment with the reform of the commune system had been undertaken, the production brigade as a level of economic organization was abolished and replaced by a unit with the traditional name of *cun* for the purpose of administration.[66] Thus the plan to divide political and economic functions and assign them to separate organs has been tried out at the lowest level in the countryside. The purpose is to minimize direct political interference in the management of agricultural and other economic activities at the grass roots. The state is to retreat a step further in its control over society.

Urban residents, particularly urban youth seeking employment, are being encouraged to organize themselves into small cooperatives to engage in small industrial and handicraft undertakings and service trades. Licenses for individual traders and handicraftsmen in some activities are again being issued. This decision reverses the political trends since the mid-1950s toward absorbing all family- and individual-owned stores and trades into ever larger state-owned and operated enterprises and cooperatives.

In other words, the state is increasingly relying on indirect methods to control

71

China's economy. This new system is helping to replace, to some extent, centralized bureaucratic measures by the use of market forces and price mechanisms to create a structure in which basic-level units and individuals are given a much larger measure of autonomy than before to respond to economic incentives.[67] Individuals, collective units in both urban and rural areas, and state-owned enterprises are encouraged to play a more active role and to take greater initiative in increasing their own earnings and thus in promoting economic development of the society. At the height of the trend toward economic liberalization, the slogan that China's economy was based on an integration of planned and market economies was frequently heard. Since then, it has been replaced by the formula that China's economy is primarily planned and market economy is to be used as a supplement.

Such changes in economic thinking and practice took place in the larger context of renewed attention to the immediate material interests and pressing needs of the masses, as distinguished from supposedly objective, long-term interests and needs as defined by the party and the state. The party repeatedly noted in its analyses that during the periods of the revolutionary wars, the relationship between the party and the masses was analogous to that between fishes and water.[68] The party survived because it received wholehearted support from the masses. According to the party's own estimates, this support was given because the party attended to the masses' material interests and felt needs and advocated programs designed to link its historic mission to everyday questions of people's livelihood and to their hopes and demands. This relationship gradually eroded after the party came to power. Now wide gaps existed between the party and the masses. The masses kept the party at a distance and did not express their real views and true feelings in the presence of party and government cadres, for they no longer trusted the cadres and they had no confidence in the party. Moreover, they were in constant fear that no matter what policies the party should adopt today, they will be changed after a little while. The party's statements no longer had any credibility; its promises no longer inspired confidence. In other words, the party recognized realistically the existence of a profound crisis of confidence and authority. It was taking steps to overcome this crisis.

To this end, the material interests of individuals are being given a prominent place in ideology and policy decisions. A *Renmin Ribao* special commentator asserts: "Personal interests are the base on which class interests are concentrated; without this base there are no such things as common class interests. Moreover, the common interests of a class will eventually find expression in terms of its members' personal interests. ... To deny personal interests means also to deny common class interests; the so-called 'common interests' divorced from the laborers' personal interests, in fact, can only mean the interests of a few. ... In building socialism, we must not ignore the laborers' personal inter-

72

ests; on the contrary, we must pay close attention to their material interests; otherwise it will be impossible to bring about socialism."[69] In effect, the material interests of individuals are being given a larger place in the traditional formula that the socialist economy should integrate the material interests of the state, the collective units, and the individuals in various fields.

"Socialist Legality" and "Socialist Democracy"

The relationship between the individual and the state is also changing. The direction is toward granting the individual a limited sphere of immunity in which he can be assured of some degree of regularity and predictability in his daily life. The full significance of this new direction cannot be found by an examination of the slight changes in the provisions in the draft constitution for individual rights, or in the reaffirmation of such principles as "all citizens of the People's Republic of China are equal before the law," and the independence of the judiciary. It can be understood only as a profound reaction against the arbitrary use by a minority group of political leaders of the authority of the state and the power of the mob to harass, attack, detain, arrest, and incarcerate a large number of other leaders and to oppress most social strata.[70] The ability of the ultraleftists and the Lin Biao group to grasp a share of power with the support of the mob is attributed, among other things, to the nonexistence of a legal framework that limits the authority of the state and protects individuals from mob actions. The current emphasis on "socialist legality" is intended to prevent the recurrence of the terror unleashed by the Cultural Revolution, which is now regarded as a "catastrophe."[71]

China's basic criminal code, which had gone through more than thirty drafts before the Cultural Revolution, was finally adopted, together with a law on criminal procedures. However imperfect these laws are, they give the Chinese a structure of expectations in their daily life, or at least a set of standards to measure the actions of government organs and officials when these impinge on their personal freedom and physical security. In the legal provisions on the relationships among the police, the procuracy, and the courts, the Chinese now underscore more strongly than before the principle of checks and balances. The powerful political force behind this drive toward socialist legality finds institutional expression in the Committee on Legal Institutions headed by Peng Chen — potentially one of the most important committees of the revitalized National People's Congress.

Notwithstanding the arrest of Wei Jingsheng and the unnecessarily severe sentence of fifteen-year imprisonment imposed on him, the case marks a step forward compared to the judicial behavior of the regime even in the period before the Cultural Revolution. The provisions on counterrevolutionary activities remain highly ambiguous and full of loopholes for arbitrary conviction and punishment. But the recognition of the principle that only overt action plus intent constitute a counterrevolutionary crime is a far cry from the indiscriminate earlier use of the label of "counterrevolutionary."

The legal provisions on perjury and false accusation are also intended to prevent the recurrences of both the use of trumped-up charges and the provision of artificially manufactured testimonies either in political movements or in "special case investigations" conducted by the government and the party.

In a very broad sense, democracy can be understood as comprised of institutions established to facilitate inputs and feedback from the society to the government and, more important, to secure the accountability of the government to the society. Whatever its limitations, "socialist democracy" is supposed to provide the same safeguards. The post-Mao trends stem not only from the tragic experience of most of the current leaders with "feudal fascism" but also from a new appreciation of the positive relationship of a modicum of freedom of person, expression, and association to the major objectives of the regime. Although the slogans "Mr. Democracy" and "Mr. Science" were widely heard during the May Fourth period, in 1979 and 1980 the press publicized the idea that without democracy there cannot be rapid development of science.[72] The relationship between progress in academic research in all fields and political democracy is recognized. Previously, the intellectuals demanded only the drawing of a clear demarcation line between academic study and politics and the grant of freedom of expression on academic questions. In 1979 the view was expressed that, without freedom of speech in the political field as well, there can be no genuine freedom of discussion in science and art. Li Shu, the editor of *Historical Research*, wrote: "To restrict freedom of speech on matters of politics is equivalent to endorsing political autocracy. Once an autocracy is established in political matters, it will definitely not be restricted to politics alone; freedom of speech in the sphere of science and art will also be written off by such an autocracy. This was precisely the case under the cultural autocracy established during the period when Lin Biao and the Gang of Four dominated over the people."[73] To be sure, this is still not the official view, but the fact that it was publicly advocated by an important intellectual is significant.

Although the regime has rejected the slogan of democracy as "the fifth modernization," which was raised by such dissenters as Wei Jingsheng, Ye Jianying in his authoritative speech of September 29, 1979, declared that the reform and improvement of the "socialist political system" and the development of "an advanced socialist democracy and a complete socialist legal system" were "important objectives as well as necessary conditions for the realization of the four modernizations."[74]

The most important reform in the electoral system is the stipulation that the number of candidates nominated through "democratic consultation" should be larger than the number of persons to be elected. An alternative procedure is to have two rounds of voting. The first round is used to adopt a list of nominees. In the second round, this list is voted upon. Both represent a partial return to the Yanan practice. The secret ballot has been reinstituted. The election of cadres at the shop level in factories is being tried. Direct election of local representative bodies has been extended from the basic to the county level, and for this purpose sixty-six counties were designated in 1979 as experimental units.[75] Competition for nomination and election is still subject to many political restrictions in practice. But a small formal beginning has been made. In the new election of provincial governors in several provinces, the first secretary of the party committee of the province is no longer always elected as governor. In some cases, he is elected as the chairman of the standing committee of the Provincial People's Congress, the legislature of the province. The party and the government are in the process of reestablishing their separate identities. Experiments with the use of public opinion surveys to determine the support enjoyed by the cadres and to discover the people's reaction to official policies and decisions are being undertaken, in some cases leading to the promotion and demotion of cadres or modification of policies. In the West, democracy is a system in which the state or the party binds itself or precommits itself so that it becomes impossible or difficult to follow certain options otherwise available to it.[76] Socialist democracy in China may in the end incorporate something similar to this feature but in its own way. Ultimately, the significance of these changes in the institutional structure and rules in China under the rubric of socialist democracy depends on the reciprocal effect between them and the developing institutional pluralism inside and outside the party.

Restructuring the Internal Relations of the Party

The fundamental reorientations mentioned above which, taken together, mark a change in the relationship between politics and other spheres of activities are necessarily accompanied by a restructuring of the relations within the party elite and between party and nonparty elites. Although whether it can be maintained for a long period is unclear, collective leadership has replaced the cult of the individual. When Hua Guofeng was concurrently party chairman and premier of the State Council, he was not the most powerful man in China. Within one year of its announcement, his overambitious program of economic development had been replaced by the three-year program of readjustment, restructuring, consolidation, and improvement of the economy under the aegis of Vice-Premier Chen Yun, with the strong support of the recently rehabilitated economists and the economic, financial, commercial, and trade bureaucracies. Vice-Premier Deng Xiaoping may be the most powerful man, but even he does

75

not dominate all policy decisions. He has found it necessary to change the timetable in the implementation of his policies and to water down some of their content, as in the case of the trial of the Gang of Four, the convocation of the Sixth Plenum and the Twelfth Party Congress, and the reorganization of the State Council and the Party Center.

Neither Ye Jianying, the most senior military leader, Deng Xiaoping, the nominal chief of staff until early 1980, Wei Guoqing, the head of the Political Department, nor Geng Biao, the secretary general of the Military Committee of the CCP can command and control the PLA as formerly Mao or even Lin Biao did. Hu Yaobang, the general secretary of the Secretariat reestablished in February 1980, does not exercise the same control over the party apparatus that Deng Xiaoping did. His promotion to party chairmanship in June 1982 enhances his authority and power, but he cannot dominate the party as Mao did. The post of chairmanship was abolished altogether in September 1982. The State Council under Zhao Ziyang is today a more collegiate body than under Zhou Enlai, although the system of decision by the premier provided by the draft constitution published in April 1982 will undoubtedly strengthen the institutional authority of the premier. Premier Zhao's relationship with Hu is no longer that between a chief lieutenant and a supreme leader. The revitalized and increasingly influential Standing Committee of the NPC represents a new institutional force, the symbol of socialist legality and socialist democracy. The plenary session of the Central Committee now takes place regularly, as it did from 1949 to 1959. The tendency to decentralize power and functions to the provincial-level units to deal with variations in local situations to speed up the four modernizations is likely to loosen up the elite structure still further.

The process of de-deification of Mao has gone so far that it is difficult, if not impossible, for another cult of personality to develop. In the important document adopted at the Fifth Plenum in February 1980, "Guiding Principles for Inner-Party Political Life," Article 2 is concerned with the problem of "firmly upholding collective leadership and opposing arbitrary decision by one individual."[77] A significant editorial in the Renmin Ribao noted that although the top leader in a unit bears the principal responsibility for any departure from "collective leadership," the blame must be shared by those who always agree with the top leaders on questions of principle. The latter are encouraged to think independently and to uphold principles firmly.[78] The promotion of Hu Yaobang and Zhao Ziyang to the Standing Committee of the Politburo, the reestablishment of the Secretariat with eleven new members under General Secretary Hu, and the removal of four of the seven top leaders who had risen to prominent positions during the Cultural Revolution were important steps to prepare for the establishment of a new collective leadership and a repudiation of Mao's practice of cultivating or designating a single successor by the supreme leader.[79] No less important is Article 37 of the new constitution of the CCP to the effect that

"Party cadres at all levels, whether elected through democratic procedure or appointed by a leading body, are not entitled to lifelong tenure."[80] This provision, together with the policy of promoting young and middle-aged cadres with specialized skills to responsible positions and the growing practice of more frequent transfers of cadres from one post to another, will help solve the problem of the increased rigidity of the party and government bureaucracies at all levels.[81]

Equally important, the party and the government, which during the Cultural Revolution were fused to a very large extent particularly on the provincial level and below, are now being separated from each other. In many units, the party leader no longer serves as the head of the administration. More specifically, many articles criticize the past tendency for the party committee, particularly the party secretary, to substitute itself or himself for the administrative leadership not only in the government, economic, educational, and other units but also in collective units down to the level of the brigade.[82] A certain degree of institutional pluralism with checks and balances has been restored.

Bureaucratism and the patriarchal style of administration, which had been deeply rooted in the traditional Chinese sociopolitical system and reemerged in the Communist Chinese political system and command economy, will prove to be the most intractable problem. These two evils are considered by the current leaders as a legacy of "feudalism." As a lead article in *Hongqi* put it, the bureaucrats in economic management do not follow economic laws "in making decisions" but act "according to the will of their senior officials."[83] The gradual abolition of the practice of being a lifelong cadre will be helpful in combating this tendency. The special privileges of the high officials are a frequent target of attack both inside and outside China. Serious as this problem is, it is merely a reflection of the more fundamental problem of the arbitrary power held by the bureaucrats at all levels, which is used to control the life of the individuals. All these problems are recognized by the Chinese leaders. But whether they can be resolved or mitigated by the new reforms discussed herein remains to be seen.

The redefinition of the class situation in China, the recognition of the positive, manifest functions of the various social groups, and the reestablishment of professional and academic associations inevitably imply a restructuring of the relationship between the party and nonparty elites. The party's united front policy has been refurbished. The machinery of China's People's Political Consultative Conference at the national and provincial levels has been revitalized. The eight democratic parties have been revived. All these institutions serve as channels for the nonparty elites to influence party and government policies and decisions. It is likely that the eight democratic parties and groups will soon die out as their aged leaders pass from the scene, unless the regime adopts new policies to give them a permanent position in the political system and to attract younger persons. But as the economy grows in complexity, science and technology become increasingly sophisticated, and the links with the world market multiply, the professional, academic, and economic associations will gain strength and reinforce the structural foundation of social pluralism in China.

The Limits to Changes

It is important to remember that the repudiation of the features associated with revolutionary-"feudal" totalitarianism has occurred under the sponsorship and indeed the direction of rehabilitated leaders who spent their entire lives revolutionizing Chinese society. Their leadership accounts for the relative success of the reversal thus far undertaken but also sets a limit to how far the reversal will go. In their view, the sociopolitical system built by them during the revolutionary wars and after the capture of power had functioned effectively for long periods of time and had achieved great successes in various fields of endeavors until it was deranged and the fundamental principles underlying it were perverted. The program of rebuilding the institutions, shifting the focus of work, reinterpreting Mao Zedong Thought, and adopting new ideological, political, and organizational lines is considered partly an endeavor to meet new conditions brought about by the achievements as well as the errors of the past.

Thus the process of reversal and the new trend toward institutional and social pluralism have definite limits. This is the meaning of the reaffirmation in March 1979, of the four fundamental principles which are to guide Chinese political and social life. These four principles are: upholding socialism, the dictatorship of the proletariat, the leadership of the party and Marxism-Leninism, and Mao Zedong Thought. Deng Xiaoping, the single most important leader responsible for most of the fundamental changes before that time, played a prominent role, at least in public, in setting these limits at a time when the new changes threatened to get out of hand. Such limits were perhaps thought to be necessary to preserve the unity of the party elite and the stability of the sociopolitical system.[84] It is clear that even the Cultural Revolution did not shake the faith of the veteran leaders in the most basic ideological principles, and they cannot envisage an alternative system that will better perform the tasks of modernizing China. They have too much at stake. For many years to come, the question will be whether a political system set within these limits can perform effectively the function of promoting controlled social change fast enough to satisfy the demands and pressures originating inside China while enabling the state to cope successfully with a threatening international environment.

But for the moment let us observe that the consequences of this reaffirmation of the four principles bear only very superficial resemblance to those that followed Mao's retroactive statement in June 1957 on the six criteria for distinguishing "fragrant flowers" from "poisonous weeds." The present trend toward liberalization in such spheres as the economy, education, science and technology, and relationship with nonparty elites not only continued but further developed in spite of the arrest, trial, and imprisonment of Wei Jingsheng. A careful reading of Ye Jianying's September 29, 1979, speech shows that the four principles are discussed in the context of stressing the role of the people. Ye concludes, "Thus, the source of strength of the four fundamental principles is the people and to give them full scope it is necessary to rely on the people."[85] This familiar and seemingly meaningless rhetoric takes on new significance within the changing framework of current ideological discourse and the shift in the relationship between politics and society noted above. Moreover, the Chinese notion of socialism is vague and broad. To some Chinese leaders, it had only two concrete meanings: first, ownership of the means of production by the state or by collective units; and second, the principle of distribution according to work. Later, a third element, a planned economy was added. The experiment of granting autonomy to the enterprises and the expansion of the use of the market mechanism as a supplement to planning point to the loosening of the system of planned economy. The principle of the dictatorship of the proletariat is a necessary reaffirmation of the CCP's link to Marxism-Leninism. Its main function is to legitimize the leadership of the party, defined as the vanguard of the proletariat. In the draft state constitution, the phrase "the people's democratic dictatorship" replaces the words "dictatorship of the proletariat" in crucial provisions although in one sentence in the Preamble the latter is used as an appositive of the former. The principle of upholding Marxism-Leninism and Mao Zedong Thought also, however, may pave the way to a return to dogmatism and fundamentalism in the future. Alternatively, these principles can all be reinterpreted under the formula of integrating "the universal principles of Marxism-Leninism-Mao Tsetung Thought with the concrete practice of socialist modernization and develop it under the new historical conditions."[86]

Undoubtedly, the leadership of the party is the "most basic of the four fundamental principles," as Deng Xiaoping emphasized on January 1, 1980.[87] The theme of the Fifth Plenum held in February 1980 was "to strengthen and to improve the leadership of the party." To strengthen the leadership of the party may mean the strengthening of a "monistic center of power"[88] in the society. But this tendency must also be seen in the context of the granting of a greater degree of autonomy to the various social groups in the society, the elevation of the status of the scientists and specialists, and the growing complexity of the economy, which necessarily strengthens the indispensability and thus the influence of the professional and occupational groups. In other words, the "monistic center of power" will probably be increasingly restrained, influenced, and, indeed, penetrated by the social forces. The recent recruitment of scientists and technicians into the party is an indication of this possibility. In turn, it may be hoped that this possibility may lead to an increase in intraparty pluralism under collective leadership with renewed and widespread popular support.[89]

Yet the strengthening of the leadership of the party still raises the question whether there will be or can be any independent check on the party's power. This question has been underscored by the decision made by the Fifth Plenum to recommend the elimination of the provision in the 1978 State Constitution guaranteeing "big contending, big blooming, big debate and big-character posters" — the so-called "four big freedoms."[90] Later a constitutional amendment was adopted to implement this recommendation. This decision has been criticized even by many sympathetic observers outside China as a sign of a reversal of the trend toward liberalization and as a step to curb popular criticism in order to protect the interests of the party cadres.[91] To be sure, the use of big-character posters and popular protests, particularly in the Tiananmen incident of April 1976, did help the moderate, veteran party leaders first to oust the ultraleftists and later to curb the influence of the standpatters. But it is a practice incompatible with the emergent pattern of politics in which the party has reasserted its primacy and the state is becoming a more and more important mechanism of regularized control through its new legal codes and revitalized institutions.

In early 1981, in another reversal of the trend toward liberalization, the party suppressed the publication of periodicals and journals by unauthorized groups and organizations. "Bourgeois liberalization" itself has been subject to increasingly harsh attack. It is important to watch whether the party will continue to allow or expand the areas of permissible criticism through the regularized channels such as letters to the editor of the numerous newspapers, the journals published by various associations, the meetings of the masses at basic-level units, the "legislative" organs at all levels, and finally the discussion within the party and government bodies. It is impossible to foresee how far the retreat of politics and the reversal of the trend toward totalitarianism will go. We do not know when the limits imposed by the four fundamental principles will be reached. Nor can we tell whether they will be reinterpreted in such a way that the areas of permissible changes will be enlarged or shrunk. But short of a sharp deterioration in China's international environment, it is possible to suggest that the current formula and the pattern of emergent institutions and policies will permit China to go a long way in the direction of growth and modernization before these limits are reached or before an impasse, and perhaps another upheaval to break it, will occur. The more immediate question, one impossible to answer, is what will happen with the passing of the remaining leaders of the Long March generation and their replacement by the generation of the anti-Japanese war.[92] Can the new generation of leaders, particularly those who had their roots in modern large cities and others who hailed from the rural areas and small county seats, maintain enough unity and cooperation to carry on the work and avoid an irreconcilable split such as overcame the Long March generation and lay at the root of the Cultural Revolution?

In sum, the CCP has been trying to incorporate a carefully limited degree of democracy within the restrictive framework of the four principles that form the foundation of a Leninist party-state. Apparently, it hopes that this limited change will provide a measure of mediation between the party-state and the various social groups, thus strengthening that linkage and enhancing the legitimacy of the regime. Allowing the civil society greater autonomy yet retaining the state's absolute control and leadership over it is one of the most difficult feats of statesmanship.[93] Equally difficult is the task of maintaining the delicate balance between two current requirements: first, strengthening all the political institutions to enhance the capability of the state, and second, establishing a system of checks and balances and decentralizing political authority to provide for a higher degree of institutional pluralism and to make government organs more responsive to the multifarious social interests. Most of the political reforms in modern China up to 1977 aimed at satisfying the first requirement. Now the second desideratum must also be on the agenda. These two interrelated feats of statesmanship can meet with success only if necessary structural conditions obtained inside China and the international environment are favorable. Conditions inside China seem at the moment not to be adverse to their success, but a sharp setback in Sino-American relations may have totally unpredictable consequences.

Total Crisis and the Advance and Retreat of the Totalitarian Tendency in Twentieth-Century China

My purpose in this analysis of the post-Mao years is not to answer the questions raised in the last two paragraphs. Instead, I perform this task to seek a new perspective, to look back on political development in twentieth-century China in its entirety, to raise some fundamental questions of interpretation, and to sketch some tentative answers to guide our thinking and research.[94] These questions may be stated as follows: What was the origin of the totalistic response on the part of many intellectuals and political actors to the human conditions in China in the twentieth-century which, after a long period of fluctuation, finally culminated in the revolutionary-"feudal" totalitarianism of the ultraleftists? What were the differences between the totalistic response of the Chinese Communists and that of other Chinese intellectuals which led the former but not the latter to develop a totalitarian program? It is obvious that certain elements of the Soviet version of Marxism or Marxism-Leninism-Stalinism provided the seed for a full-fledged totalitarianism in China. But why did this seed fail to grow into a mature plant during the era of revolutionary and foreign wars? Instead, it was precisely during the Yanan period when the CCP succeeded in establishing relatively secure base areas and rapidly expanded its power and influence that the party made important concessions to the social forces, perfected the united front policy, and developed a moderate pattern of inner party struggle.[95] Why did totalitarian tendencies manifest themselves with accelerated speed after 1949, particularly after 1957? Why did the resistance by various groups and strata prove to be so weak and so easily crushed? Why did the culmination of these tendencies take the form of the revolutionary-"feudal" totalitarianism of the ultraleftists? And yet why did even this species of totalitarianism never find complete fulfillment? Why was it discredited without too much difficulty? Why has the reversal after 1978 of the trend toward full-fledged totalitarianism been achieved with relative ease?

The answers to these questions take only very tentative and schematic form and are based on a series of simple propositions. In my opinion, the totalistic response developed by many of the foremost intellectuals and political actors in twentieth-century China was not primarily the product of the "persistent Chinese cultural predisposition toward a monistic and intellectualistic mode of thinking" or "intellectualistic, holistic, mode of thinking."[96] Although this cultural predisposition facilitated the emergence of the totalistic response, the decisive condition was the total crisis that confronted Chinese society in both domestic and international affairs.

For our purpose, the point to be emphasized is the obvious fact that a totalistic response does not necessarily give rise to the totalitarian tendencies which are a major feature of twentieth-century China. Hu Shih's totalistic iconoclasm and the idea of total Westernization briefly accepted by him could not have resulted in a totalitarian movement even if they had become the ideology of a party or regime. For the totalistic change he sought was supposed to come about through the development of a pragmatic-scientific attitude and habit of thought leading to a change in research, discussion, debate, methods of conflict resolution, behavior, and institutions. For him, politics did not figure prominently as a means; it was a product rather than a determinant of social and cultural change. Roughly speaking, the same was true of those programs that sought the salvation of the nation through the development of science, or industry, or education, or rural reconstruction advocated by various individuals and groups.

In contrast, the CCP's totalistic response contained two elements that turned it into a potentially totalitarian movement and regime. These two elements are the decisive and central role given to political power and the use of violence as a component of political power by a tightly organized elite that regards itself as the vanguard of a particular class. The CCP tried to overcome the total crisis by capturing total power and to reestablish effective political authority in order to bring about a fundamental transformation of the social structure, to establish a new economic system and a new society, and to inculcate new values and attitudes espoused by new men. This approach appealed to many Chinese because it made sense to them. For events in twentieth-century China proved to their satisfaction that education, science, industry, and a new culture could not be developed fast enough to preserve China as a national entity and that they could not be developed without first establishing an effective government. At the same time, an effective system of political authority could not be established without at the same time solving some of the most pressing social and economic problems. Because the approach seemed sensible, its inherent and submerged totalitarian tendency, as well as its many potentially devastating consequences, was overlooked or minimized and rationalized if they were recognized.

The size and fragmentation of China that had made warlordism possible also facilitated the establishment of base areas by the CCP. The Sino-Japanese War of 1937 – 1945 saw the establishment and expansion of new base areas. In these base areas established before and after 1937, the totalitarian tendency began to raise its head. In various places and units, the ideological remolding campaign of 1942 – 1944 took a radical turn and threatened to get out of hand in its later phase. Mao's "Talks on Literature and the Arts at the Yenan Forum" was the first systematic statement legitimizing the control of political power over a sphere of professional activity.[97] It was not an accident that what happened in literature and the arts became the harbinger of things to come for other professions and occupations from 1949 to 1976. For literature and the arts bore a direct relationship to ideology, and they were the most effective instrumentality to influence the thinking and attitudes of the reading public and through them the masses. Moreover, during the Sino-Japanese War, writers and artists constituted the largest and most powerful profession in the base areas, which had almost no regular institutions of high learning or modern industry and commercial enterprises.[98]

But the totalitarian tendency was confined to a small sphere. It was submerged and balanced by other, more powerful currents. Under the policy of the united front, accommodation with various social classes and groups both inside and outside of the base areas reached its highest point since the destruction of the alliance with the Guomindang in 1927. The material interests and felt needs of the people and groups were seriously taken into account in policy decisions and political actions. Persuasion rather than coercive methods were generally used to push reforms in an incremental rather than revolutionary manner. A moderate pattern of inner party struggle emerged, and a set of norms governing it was formalized and practiced under the joint auspices of Mao and Liu Shaoqi. Surrounded by powerful enemies, this was the only feasible way of resolving difference within the party. Otherwise defection to the other side was an alternative readily available to dissenters and opportunists, and a decline in the morale of its members would doom the party to failure. This moderate pattern of inner party struggle was made possible by the establishment of the recognized leadership of Mao.[99] But it is important to remember that the CCP was a minority party leading a minority movement which had to maintain the solidarity of its own rank and to gain the support of various social classes and groups in order to survive and to gain power. This distribution of power within China and the checks and balances among the various political and social forces account for the moderation of the CCP and for the lack of rapid development of the totalitarian tendency inherent in the ideology, the objective to transform the whole society, and the revolutionary use of political power and violence in the CCP's totalistic response to total crisis.

The nationwide victory of the People's Liberation Army brought about a fundamental change in the configuration of political forces. After 1949, the CCP had the monopoly of power. There were no longer any effective external checks and balances. Thus the totalitarian tendency gradually and over a period of years asserted itself and finally culminated in the revolutionary-"feudal" totalitarianism of the ultraleftists, which aimed at the removal of any internal party opposition and at another revolutionary transformation of the society. The Chinese now frequently used the term "feudal fascism" to characterize their program. A Chinese writer went a step farther and charged that they exercised "supra-feudal, supra-fascist 'all-round dictatorship'" over numerous cadres and masses.[100]

Moreover, the nationwide victory was achieved by a strategy of surrounding the city from the countryside in a protracted struggle lasting twenty-two years. This struggle relied on the revolutionary momentum of the peasantry, a peasant-based army, and a party and government administration in base areas staffed by a large number of middle and lower-level cadres of rural origin with very little knowledge of urban life and still less of the world outside of China. Many top leaders, particularly Mao, took the peasantry, particularly what has come to be known as the poor and lower-middle peasants, as their responsibility reference groups. At different times, this rural orientation exerted its influence in different ways on the policies and programs adopted by these leaders toward various groups in the urban sectors.

Chinese peasants are very practical persons. But their attitudes and habits have been influenced by the long Chinese traditions rooted in the patriarchal Chinese family structure, such as the custom of sharing though not equality among family members and relatives, arbitrary decisions made by the patriarch, and respect for the aged. Although they welcome the practical benefits of modernization and mechanization, they have no conception of the requirements and consequences of rapid change. They desire their children to move upward in the social ladder, but they have little knowledge of modern culture, science, and technology. Many middle and low-level cadres who dominate the party and government at lower levels and even some top-level leaders have little or no scientific and technological knowledge and little education. A rapid program of modernization oriented toward the urban sector would inevitably undermine their position and render them useless. Yet any policies or measures that jeopardize their vested interests can be opposed or resisted as attacking the interests of the poor and lower-middle peasants and as forgetting their revolutionary contribution.

But there is another paradox. The CCP is a peasant-based party but not a peasant party. It is supposed to be the vanguard of a small, weak, disorganized, and uninformed proletariat — a class that can provide neither strong leadership nor the proper orientation for the entire society. The vanguard is to decide what is good for the nation without any immediate and direct political restraints from the various social forces. Thus the party can take steps that run counter to the immediate perceived interests and the desires of the peasantry, as it did in the acceleration of the program of cooperativization and communization and the abolition or restriction of private plots and rural markets in two different periods and in various localities. The party, or its radical leaders, is perhaps justified in thinking that the transformation of the peasants as a class of small producers is a necessary step in the transition to socialism or modernization. Even so, a proper sense of limits imposed by objective conditions can be, and was, overwhelmed by a desire for haste, by a sense of the omnipotence of political power it monopolizes, by the effectiveness of the organization it built, and by the popular support it once enjoyed.

Viewed from this perspective, political development since 1949 can be understood as a conflict between the inherent totalitarian tendency cum rural orientation and the need to recognize the indispensable roles played by various functional groups in the urban sector in achieving economic growth and modernizing the society and the state. The traditions established in the Yanan period would incline the party to respect a measure of autonomy and preserve the influence and limited authority of these functional groups, but the monopoly of power and the ardent desire to effect a total transformation of the society favored the totalitarian tendency. In the years before 1957, all party leaders, including Mao on one side and Zhou Enlai on the other, were ambivalent about the role of these functional groups, particularly the intellectuals. The party achieved a historic, unprecedented success in handling "national-capitalists." It destroyed them as a class but retained them in their managerial and technical positions and allowed them to perform their necessary functions in the economy. This innovative and ingenious solution now informs its handling of all functional groups in the society.

But in dealing with the intellectuals, who constitute one of the most important functional groups in any modern society, the party instituted a series of policies which finally led to disastrous results in the Cultural Revolution. The party reorganized the system of higher education after the Soviet model, amalgamating some of the universities and dismantling others, destroying their individuality and setting up a highly centralized and uniform system. The principle of party leadership overwhelmed and discredited the principle, advocated by some intellectuals, that professors should run the university. The dissatisfaction of the intellectuals, educators, and scientists which surfaced during the Hundred Flowers period soon brought about the antirightist movement. A similar process of tightening political and ideological control followed by resistance and protests and then by drastic repression of dissent occurred also in literature and the arts.

The rapid collapse of the resistance of these groups and the easy victory of the party were the almost inevitable result of the party's monopoly of power, the weakness of the intellectuals and the professional groups in the underdeveloped economy, and the imponderable might of the peasants and workers who formed the social basis of the party. But in retrospect, one important dimension in this development seems clear. It was that the party leaders did not have sufficient appreciation of the indispensability of the functions performed by the intellectuals and the various professional groups as political and social critics and as constructive forces in economic development. Thus 1957 marked a turning point in the relationship between the state and society. From that time to 1966, no social groups outside the party would offer any active resistance to the party. The penetration of politics into other spheres of society broke through all nonparty barriers. Only internal party restraints existed.

By breaking most of the internal party restraints and suppressing with some success whatever institutional and political pluralism existed within the party, the Cultural Revolution of 1966 – 1976 marked the culmination of the totalitarian tendency that found expression in the program and actions of the ultraleftists. Political actions undertaken by the Red Guards or mobs mobilized or encouraged by a group of leaders or simply permitted and protected by them broke through almost all restraints, legal, political, civic, social, and traditional, in utter disregard of common decency in an attempt to change man and society. "Politics takes command" degenerated into "politics may assault or overwhelm everything."[101]

The ultraleftists' understanding of the role of political power reflected a nonsensical reductionism that can be reconstructed as follows. From the not totally incorrect proposition that there is a political aspect to every event and to every relationship in society, the absurd conclusion was drawn that politics is everything and power constitutes the only relationship that counts. Thus the ultraleftists urged the workers "not to produce for the wrong [ideological and political] line," "not to produce for the faction of those taking the capitalist road." "We would rather have socialist low ratio of growth than capitalist high rate of growth." "We would rather stop production for two years than stop class struggle for one moment." Zhang Chunqiao was charged with having declared that "I would rather have a laborer without culture than to have an exploiter with culture" and that "it is useless to study."[102]

The general theory of class developed by the ultraleftists was based on a superficial and fundamentally incorrect interpretation of Marx's ideas. Yet many of its political slogans bore a close resemblance to traditional Chinese ideas and practices. It could not have been otherwise. For in attempting to destroy or weaken the party organization and government bureaucracy controlled by their opponents, the ultraleftists had to act in a fashion contrary to the modern organizational norms, rules, and ideas embodied in these establishments. The cult of personality derived strong implicit support from the cult of the emperor although the new cult was attached to a charismatic, revolutionary leader and used to effect revolutionary changes, whereas the traditional cult was an institutionalized practice to preserve the political system. Loyalty to the leader and absolute obedience to him found expression in such ludicrous practices as "asking for instructions in the morning and making a report in the evening," and "loyalty dances." More significant and sinister were such statements as "Every sentence said or written [by Mao] is the truth," "One sentence [by Mao] is equal to ten thousand sentences by us,"[103] "One must obey Chairman Mao's instruction whether one understands it or not." Taken together, such utterances paralleled the leadership principle practiced by Nazi Germany.[104] Chinese Legalism, which had formed the basis of many autocratic and tyrannical practices in the traditional states, was revived by the ultraleftists as the justification for their political program and as an ideological weapon to attack the moderate veteran leaders.

Moreover, one can perhaps justify the proposition that it was precisely the Chinese political tradition which facilitated the development of the tendency for politics to penetrate into all spheres of social life. It can also be said that in the traditional society of China, "politics take command." The system of examination was a more important constituent of the system of social stratification in China than any single political institution was in other societies. It was perhaps as important an element as the ownership of land in the formation of the landlord class. The political bureaucracy had always dominated the merchant and other classes and groups; its belief system achieved ideological hegemony. When the total crisis in the twentieth-century demanded total solutions, when a revolutionary party monopolizing power was determined to transform the whole society, and when modern means of communications and control and modern organizational forms and techniques were available, the tradition of politics in command easily and imperceptibly slid into the trend toward totalitarian control.

Thus after a protracted revolution of half of a century to eliminate "feudal" ideas and practices, the CCP found that these very ideas again erupted at the very top of its political system and threatened to overwhelm everything it had fought for. No wonder "feudalism" is now considered by many to be the main source of errors committed in the past and the main obstacle to modernization at the present time.

Nevertheless, the revolutionary-"feudal" totalitarianism of the ultraleftists

87

did not achieve dominance in the Chinese political system. It had the strong but not complete support of Mao. More important, it was subtly opposed by most veteran leaders, whose outlook, style of work, and institutional commitments were formed during the periods of revolutionary and foreign wars in which ultraradicalism and totalitarian attempts to suppress violently various social classes and groups led to defeat while moderation and accommodation with these groups in a program of incremental and induced change through persuasion produced success. This common experience in the period when the inherent totalitarian tendency in the Chinese Communist movement was held in check by the internal distribution of power in China was strengthened by the urban origin or orientation of some of the leaders, inclining them to appreciate the complexity of the economy, the need for specialization, the imperatives of scientific and technological development, and the importance of the international environment.

This common experience and outlook form the foundation of their alternative program, which they carried out after Mao left the scene. Above all, their personal suffering and difficulties as well as the deepening crisis of authority in the last years of the Cultural Revolution made them fully realize the dire consequences of certain, but not all, ideological and institutional principles endorsed and practiced by them at one time or another when these principles were carried out to their logical conclusion, or, in their view, were perverted by the leftward thrust. The result was a rapid, decisive reversal of the trend toward totalitarianism. China now may be approaching the post-totalitarian stage of her political development without having gone through a period of full-fledged totalitarianism. She has come back from the brink of revolutionary-"feudal" totalitarianism.

3

The Chinese Army and the Communist State

DAVID MOZINGO

Transformation of the system of revolutionary power which created the People's Republic of China (PRC) into the centralized bureaucratic order characteristic of Communist states elsewhere remains incomplete in postliberation China. In Chinese Marxist theory such a state already exists; the PRC is an instrument of class dictatorship — the worker-peasant alliance — led by the unchallenged supremacy of the Chinese Communist Party (CCP). In fact, this theory does not square with China's turbulent history. That history shows that the Communist party has been unable to generate within its own ranks any durable consensus on the basic principles through which to effect the transformation. Nor has the party been able to supply an enforced cohesion in the form of a dominant personality or faction capable of pushing through its vision of the transformation.

For more than thirty years the senior leaders of the Chinese revolution have argued about the basic questions of how the state was to be organized and what form of socialist society the revolution would build. Four organic laws have been laboriously drafted and promulgated — the 1949 Common Program and the constitutions of 1954, 1975, and 1978. This need to alter the structure of the state periodically is ample testimony that the passage from revolutionary upheaval to socialist order is incomplete and that the vision of the future seldom has been unanimous.

Other Communist-led revolutions seem to have made the transformation more completely. Despite the imprint of nationalism and the charismatic personalities that have given different communisms their special character, for example in Cuba and Yugoslavia, the ultimate triumph of the centralized party-state is everywhere apparent. Special forms of economic decentralization, or cultural autonomy for minority nationalities, exist throughout the socialist world. But even in Hungary and Yugoslavia, where liberalization under communism has most fully evolved, the central party apparatus totally commands the machinery of the state, and its authority is beyond question. The compatibility of liberalization with central party control has been challenged recently in Poland. The intervention of the Polish army, the party's apparatus, has prevented victory by the Polish dissidents. But the Soviet Union, having on four previous occasions intervened in Eastern Europe to check the growth of liberalization, seems poised to intervene again if necessary to preserve centralized Communist power in Poland or elsewhere within Moscow's geopolitical domain.

A unique feature of China in comparison to other socialist countries is the inability of the centralized party-state to consolidate itself during the postliberation period. For many years, of course, it was thought that China represented the most extreme form of centralism yet to appear, indeed "Asian totalitarianism." Given what was thought to be known about the relationships between Mao Zedong, the main revolutionary leaders around him, the Communist party and its organs, and the military and security forces at the disposal of the Communist leaders, the notion of a Chinese totalitarian state was entirely credible to the Western scholarly community, especially in the United States, which had accommodated itself to the prevailing Cold War ideology. As the presumed Chinese Stalinist regime crumbled in the mid-1960s, and, within a few years, American geopolitical interests no longer required a "Chicom threat," it became possible to reexamine on a more objective basis why the totalitarian state had broken down and whether, in fact, this model had ever really existed in China.

If the formation of the present Chinese state is viewed as a cumulative process beginning in the 1920s, the main reasons why a centralized bureaucratic regime failed to establish itself are apparent. Fundamentally, the revolution was made by a heterogeneous Communist movement consisting of dispersed, long-established, and largely autonomous military-political base areas positioned in many parts of the country. The largest centers of revolutionary activity were located in three geographic regions: the liberated zones around Yanan; the base areas of the central and lower Yangzi valley; and the underground movement in the cities of the East China Coast, which were occupied by the Guomindang or the Japanese for nearly the entire period down to 1949. In effect, there were many separate political-military components in the Communist movement, not one revolutionary center expanding from Yanan and led solely by Mao Zedong.

Communist leaders were everywhere paramount in the various geographical spheres of the movement. But the role played by the party's control and organizational apparatus was much less than that of local military commanders, peasant, worker, and guerrilla leaders, whose power, prestige, and contributions to the movement in their province depended minimally on their specifically party roles.[1] This primacy of small group loyalties and ties within the dispersed revolutionary movement was unavoidable. It reflected both the deeply entrenched feudal practices of Chinese social organizations and the hard realities of making revolution. The creation of a power system along the lines of the Leninist-Stalinist party was inapplicable, if not impossible, under the conditions that prevailed in war-torn rural China. The genius of the Communist leaders, especially Mao, lay in their ability to forge a coherent instrument of social revolution out of the diverse and largely segmental elements on which it was based.

The numerous strains of the revolution, including the dominant Communist elements, worked effectively to wage war and seize power. They were far less effective as a governing coalition, though in theory unity was assured by Communist party supremacy. In fact, however, the party leadership was unable to reach a consensus on whether the decentralized, semiautonomous power system that won the revolution was to be integrated into the new state or was to be replaced by strictly Communist party organs and mechanisms. Mao Zedong is, of course, the best-known opponent of establishing the regime of the party bureaucrats and technicians;[2] but he was neither the first nor, ultimately, the most successful. The Chinese military class has stood as the most consistent obstacle to the triumph of the party-state.

The military's opposition to the party-state has taken different forms and expressed itself in a variety of political contexts. It has reflected both the army's own internal contradictions and the perceived threats to the interests of its different constituent parts, such as the veteran military leaders in the highest leadership organs, the central army command, and the regional and provincial military commanders.[3]

A common thread nevertheless appears to link all the major instances of military intervention in elite politics: whatever the political character of these interventions, they have been directed against elements in the party whose policies or "line" threatened to establish a monopoly of power within the state detrimental to perceived military interests and values. It is apparent that army leaders with otherwise quite different political and policy preferences nevertheless have commonly perceived a distinction between loyalty to the Chinese revolution and loyalty to communism. The record of military intervention to oppose the party leadership indicates that the officer corps has consistently regarded allegiance to their conception of the revolution as higher than any obligation to communism or the party.

Seen in this light, the six major instances of military intervention in politics down to the present have shown no great resistance on the part of army leaders to challenge the party on the great questions of public order, war and peace, and who shall rule in Beijing.

Military Interventions in Politics

The 1953 attempt of Gao Gang and Rao Shushi to preserve a regional base of power against the extension of the party center's authority is the first known instance of military insubordination after liberation.[4] Although Gao and Rao both held top party posts at the time, these positions had flowed to them as the result of their prominence during the civil war as, respectively, People's Liberation Army (PLA) political commissar in the Northeast and East China regions. They were alleged to have set up an "independent kingdom" when serving as military officers in charge of civilian administration in these regions from 1949 to 1953. At this early stage in the PRC's development, rebellious regional interests had few supporters. With little resistance from any quarter, Mao, the state administration, the party, and the military commanders united to oppose the Gao-Rao tendencies. Gao is reported to have chosen suicide, and Rao disappeared. Whether the charges against them also stemmed from their politically conspiring with Moscow has yet to be proved.

Defense Minister Peng Dehuai's open attack on Mao and the party policies associated with the Great Leap Forward is the most unambiguous assault on party-state supremacy by a faction of the military. The challenge thrown down appears to have extended to questions of PRC military policy, strategy, and relations with the Soviet Union. What is most revealing about the Peng episode, however, is the evident fact that he (and possibly other officers, judging from the shake-up of top personnel in the army following his dismissal) felt his status entitled him to challenge the leader and the party, even to the point of criticizing them at a time of great domestic and foreign crises.

The Peng affair also shows that senior military officers construed their roles and duties as encompassing all the great issues affecting the nation, not simply those involving the armed forces. Peng's attack on Mao and the party at the Lu Shan Plenum was on the grounds of the failures of the economic policies of the Great Leap, not military matters, and it revealed that the marshal was thoroughly familiar with China's economic situation.[5]

Unlike that involving Gao-Rao, the Peng incident was strictly a conflict within the center, an attack on the state's basic policies by China's then ranking military officer. Whether the regional military commanders saw their interests as vitally affected by the outcome of this dispute can be assumed but has not been proved. It seems certain, however, that the most important regional commanders, as well as other marshals at the center, sided with Mao on the removal of Peng. Fundamentally, the issue was one of allegiance to Mao rather than to the party. In an emotional reply to Peng's attack, Mao is reported to have said he would go back to the countryside to raise a new army if his old PLA commanders deserted him. The dismissal of Peng and his supporters indicates that the regional commanders as well as elements in the central PLA command supported Mao and thus assured his dominance over the party leadership. And this victory over Peng Dehuai was of decisive importance to Mao's continuing political supremacy for a decade thereafter.

The third military intervention in elite politics after 1949 was the army's alignment with Mao in overthrowing the central party leadership in the initial phase of the Cultural Revolution.[6] The process of forging this alignment began with Lin Biao's replacement of Peng Dehuai in 1959; no single event or date conveniently marks the intervention. As minister of defense, Lin succeeded in staffing the central PLA headquarters (though not nearly so thoroughly the regional and provincial commands) with officers supportive of Mao's policies and philosophy. The Mao-Lin association between 1959 and 1965 resulted in a politicized army. During this period the central PLA command and main force units came under the leadership of Mao-supporting officers. Of equal importance, by 1964 army work teams began to duplicate and then replace party organs in the state administration. When the struggle between the "minority" Mao faction and the "majority" Liu-Peng-Deng faction finally broke into the open in 1966, the entrenched position of the army, loyal to Mao, speedily decided the outcome.

In siding with Mao during the opening phases of the Cultural Revolution, the army officers gave a clear expression of no confidence in the leaders then dominating the party center who challenged the chairman's position on the great issue of war or peace. The most important of these issues in the period immediately preceding the 1965 – 1966 intervention of the army on Mao's side was China's strategic response to the landing of U.S. troops in Vietnam. Mao's policy on this issue conflicted with that of the dominant faction in the central party leadership. The main generals sided with Mao in rejecting "united action" with Moscow or direct "forward defense" to support Hanoi, as had been done in Korea.[7] Had China's decision been exclusively up to the party center, the outcome almost certainly would have been a collision with America. But the old PLA marshals decided war was far too important a matter to be left in the hands of China's professional party leaders.

Mao, who had earlier been the principal beneficiary of army intrusions in politics, was himself defeated by the fourth instance of military intervention against the center. Having crushed the party headquarters in Beijing and the "revisionist leadership," the Cultural Revolution forces soon thereafter attempted to carry the purge into the army and the provinces. Resistance was immediate, and its effects were overwhelming. Beginning with the July 1967 army mutiny in Wuhan, the Left current was arrested and then rolled back. Mao, who can scarcely be disassociated from the radicals at that time, had urged the Left's latest advance. When confronted with the open rebellion of the regional commanders upon whom he was politically dependent, however, Mao abruptly sided with the old generals. He subsequently joined the Right in calling for an end to the Cultural Revolution — especially its attack on the veteran PLA cadres — and sought to position himself within the counterrevolution that developed after the Wuhan revolt.

The army's readiness to cooperate in the early purge of the party center is explainable on several counts, an important one being that it believed Mao more truly embodied the meaning of genuine socialist revolution in China than did the party leaders who had challenged him. But the military's willingness to crush the Left, which was strongly identified with Mao, showed that the senior army leaders in the provinces were not deterred from intervention in politics even by the chairman's prestige. Thus it was that army intervention in the Cultural Revolution was the decisive factor not only in the overthrow of the party center and the radical Left but, ultimately, in the diminution of Mao's own authority and power as well. In effect, the balance of power between the center and the provinces shifted to the latter from 1968 on, and even Mao was unable subsequently to reverse this trend.

The events leading up to the Lin Biao affair of September 1971 suggest that what in fact occurred was a preemptive act of self-defense rather than an attempted coup aimed at deposing Mao.[8] Lin Biao's succession to Mao, officially proclaimed at the Ninth Party Congress in 1969, was immediately undermined by the tidal wave of opposition to the Cultural Revolution Left gathering in the provinces and aimed, unmistakably, at Beijing. As the head of the central PLA most identified in the army with the effort to carry the purge into the provinces, Lin and his supporters in the Ministry of Defense were inevitably among the chief targets of the counterrevolution.

Circumstantial evidence indicates that Lin Biao's own base of power in the military was weak, limited to the air force, navy, and possibly special units attached to central PLA headquarters. From 1967 to 1971 he was able to remove none of the powerful eleven military region commanders and only two of the twenty-two military district (province) commanders. On the other hand, by November 1968 (and in response to the Wuhan mutiny) the regional commanders had forced the removal of Lin's chief of staff, Huang Yongsheng, and thirteen political commissars associated with him. When the alleged coup attempt took place, the units involved on Lin's side were small and scattered. Lin is alleged to have planned on retreating to South China to launch a civil war if the coup failed, a contingency that suggests he was preoccupied with thoughts of impending defeat rather than victory. That he did not even control main force units in and around Beijing, after twelve years as minister of defense and heir apparent to Mao, underscores the weakness of his position in the struggle for power.

A contributing factor in Lin's demise, as with Mao's opponents in the central party apparatus in 1965 – 1966, was undoubtedly the radical shift in China's strategic policy during the summer of 1971. Over the objections of the Left, Mao and Zhou Enlai had made the decision to effect rapprochement with the United States. This decision could not have prevailed without the strong support of the regional military commanders and other generals at PLA headquarters, for by 1971 the army was the dominant political force in provincial government organs, the central administration, the Central Committee of the party, and the Politburo. Lin Biao and his supporters were isolated. If they did, in fact, attempt a coup it appears to have been an act of desperation.

The sixth, and to date the last, instance of military intervention in elite politics has yet to run its course. Following the attempted escape and death of Lin Biao and the subsequent purge in 1971 – 1972 of some fifty-six generals linked to him and to the Left, political power in China has been the result of a compact between the main regional military commanders and the veteran cadres of the state administration led, until his death in 1976, by Zhou Enlai and his successor, Deng Xiaoping. The late Premier Zhou emerges as the hero of the Cultural Revolution era. He managed to hold the organs of the state together, protected the old comrades from the terror, fought off the Gang of Four, launched detente with America, and laid down the principles of the four modernizations, which have been the cornerstone of China's national construction policy since 1974.

By the late 1960s, Premier Zhou had already displaced Mao as the one leader in Beijing to whom the main provincial and central military commanders could pledge their allegiance. His self-appointed replacement, Deng Xiaoping, also has strong support in the army but this is thought to be primarily from several key regional military commanders whose base of power is in South and Central China. Mao's self-appointed replacement, Hua Guofeng, appeared to have the support of generals at central PLA headquarters and of several regional military commanders in North China, together with survivors of Maoist elements in the central party apparatus.

Since 1973 a concerted effort has been under way to restore and revitalize the role of the central party and gradually to reduce the military's power in the governance of the country. But observers of the Chinese scene are entitled to question formal proclamations of this or that reduction in the military's position vis-à-vis the allegedly resurgent party apparatus. It is well to remember that such proclamations have been made before and have tended to have little meaning unless the party retained the confidence of the military that the affairs of the Chinese state were in good hands.

Sources of Military Insubordination

The military leaders who have engaged in these political interventions, winners and losers alike, were obviously not constrained by significant feelings that the party center — or Mao for that matter — possessed an inherent legitimacy greater than their own to decide the fate of the Chinese nation. What, then, are the principal causes of this endemic pattern of political insubordination on the part of the Chinese military?

The longstanding debate in the West over the question of whether the Communists won power in China by riding out the tide of a social revolution or by positioning themselves at the head of an essentially antiforeign nationalist movement has obscured the more important fact that the creation of the present Chinese state was the outgrowth of war, a near-continuous process of fighting on a vast scale which lasted for close to thirty years and consumed tens of millions of lives. Although the strategies, tactics, and forces the Communist leaders devised during these years played a great part in their ultimate success, there was nothing distinctively Marxist about their methods, which were frequently adapted to suit changing situations. At each stage from the mid-1920s on, the sine qua non proved to be the capacity to develop sufficient armed forces to ensure the survival of the revolutionary movement.

From the earliest days of its existence, the Communist movement had been able to attract widespread popular support, whether on the basis of anti-feudal or anti-imperialist appeals. Indeed it was the Communists' alarming ability rapidly to generate popular support which determined Chiang Kai-shek's consistent efforts to exterminate them. The CCP repeatedly suffered defeats, its party organs decimated and scattered, until the full-scale Japanese invasion of 1937 provided the strategic environment in which the revolutionary movement was able to develop a series of military base areas in Central and North China. At the time of the Japanese surrender in 1945, the population under the effective control of these base areas was between eighty and one hundred million. In the same period, total Communist military forces numbered more than one million men, a hundredfold increase in the size of the army that had staggered into Yanan at the end of the Long March.

The creation of this essential power structure, which rapidly expanded between 1945 and 1949 to overwhelm the Guomindang, was primarily the work of the military arm of the revolutionary movement in the countryside. The leading men and women who put this structure together regarded themselves as loyal Communists; most were undoubtedly party members. But their most important day-to-day work in those thirty years, of necessity, was building "the gun," not the party. Basically the organization of peasant, youth, worker, and women's associations and the party organs that accompanied the development of the rural base areas grew in proportion to the movement's ability to provide physical security through military control. In other words, the expansion of the party's role in the war-torn society was fundamentally dependent on the success of its military efforts. The truth of this situation is revealed in the feeble performance from 1927 to 1949 of the Communist underground apparatus in the cities, which were effectively controlled by both the Guomindang and the Japanese right up to the moment of their defeat, despite the decades of clandestine and intensive organizational efforts of the party.

The fact that the military-related arm of the movement developed to a far greater extent than the purely party organs in the formative years has exerted the most profound influence on the social composition of the Communist leadership. That most pronounced class characteristic of Communist elites elsewhere — urban intellectuals professionalized in working-class organization and agitation — was not the dominant stratum in the Chinese revolution. This element was, in fact, so underdeveloped in 1949 that it required years of "party building" and the wholesale admission of unproven urban social classes (at the expense of veteran rural peasants) into the party before a more representative, Soviet-style balance was achieved in the mid-1950s. Indeed, until 1953 the People's Liberation Army exercised de facto civilian powers throughout the country. In effect the PRC was governed by the military while the institutions, state and party, of a Soviet-style Communist political system were being built up to replace the unavoidable short-term necessity of military government. But the transfer of power from the party soldiers to the party bureaucrats, essential to the formation of a state on the Soviet model, clearly seems to have been both incomplete and, possibly from the outset, resisted.

As a result of their prominence in all phases of organizational work in the base areas and in the liberated zones, there was a very great lateral and vertical movement of PLA men, both political cadres and field commanders, into civilian institutions immediately after 1949.[9] The longer-term political significance of this shift — in effect the co-opting of key positions in the economic and administrative structure at local, province, and national levels by former military officers — was largely unappreciated abroad. Foreign observers at that time, understandably, gave more attention to the massive demobilization of the PLA in the early 1950s. The reduction of the huge guerrilla armies (from over four million to approximately two and a half million troops) seemed to indicate an overall lessening of the army's role in the new society as China's leaders turned their attention from revolution to national reconstruction. In fact, the key element in the Chinese army, as in any other army — its officer corps — was being transferred to the civilian sectors. But these same officers carried with them attitudes and loyalties formed over many years during which the influence of strictly party organs and concerns had been secondary in their lives.

At local and provincial levels, larger numbers of demobilized PLA men took up positions in the economy, county and city government, and even in the party branches. An even more dramatic accumulation of power by military men took place in 1951 — 1952, when many of the senior political commissars of the PLA were transferred from the headquarters of the five great field armies to key positions in Beijing. National leaders such as Li Xiannian, Bo Yipo, Rao Shushi, and Deng Xiaoping are examples of former PLA political generals who rose to power in this way. The presence of men with this career pattern stood in marked contrast to the underground trade union organizers typical of the Lenin-Stalin party cadres. More important, these high-ranking former political commissars constituted a serious obstacle to the dominance of personalities whose

97

promotion was based on work primarily within the organs of the Communist party. Had the military's role in the movement been less dominant in the 1930s and 1940s, party apparat figures would perhaps have gained a clearer advantage after 1949.

Historical developments in the Chinese Communist movement also indicate why many of the field commanders and political commissars may have, from the beginning, resisted a complete transfer of power to a Stalinist party-state. What has been termed the "Yanan Way" represented a popular and successful experiment in revolutionary social engineering based upon enthusiasm and voluntary participation.[10] The replacement of this ethic by those dictatorial leadership techniques associated with Communist parties modeled after the Bolshevik tradition was alien and impractical to many army men. Veterans of the Yanan tradition rightly understood that the revolution's success, and their own, stemmed from loyalties and ties that could only be undermined by the imposition of foreign control doctrines and methods, however much they might carry an alleged label of "scientific Marxism."

Behind the army's justified skepticism of a state dominated solely by the party lay the uncomfortably close association between the notion of a Chinese party-state and the Soviet Union. Some Western analysts have assumed that after 1949 Russia exerted a strong attraction for the PLA because the officer corps hoped to modernize the army with Moscow's help.[11] Two factors undoubtedly weakened this attraction, to whatever extent it, in fact, existed. First, Soviet aid to Communist allies was rarely given, as the Chinese well knew, unless Moscow could extract political concessions that would have been unacceptable to the veteran PLA commanders. Because the Chinese revolution had triumphed, in part, by a consistent repudiation of Soviet policies and advice, there were no doubt many important army leaders who had reservations about emulating Moscow's prescriptions for building socialism. The fact that leading party figures, such as Liu Shaoqi, later appeared to support just such a development likely fueled the tensions between the PLA and the party in the period of the Sino-Soviet alliance. Second, the Sovietization of the PLA, which took place in the 1950s as a result of the Korean War and the alliance, appears to have caused political friction within the Chinese military. It led directly to the dismantling of the field army system and to the concurrent increase of Beijing's — and the Communist party's — control over the Soviet-equipped main force units, at the expense of the previously dominant field army commanders.

Modernization also meant, in the context of the party's post-1953 efforts to confine the PLA to the status of a professional department of the government (like agriculture and foreign trade), the relinquishment of the army's special role in numerous civic activities, including production, public security, and construction. A number of foreign observers have assumed that PLA officers more or less unanimously approved of changes leading to greater military professionalization at the expense of allegedly onerous social missions.[12] But provincial military commanders in charge of regional forces and the militia were not Chinese versions of West Point graduates, pinning hopes of promotion on the next war with modern weapons. Other attitudes aside, their career projections turned on making a success out of their imperfectly trained and equipped forces in the task of preserving order, security, and the allegiance of the local population — tasks far removed from concerns about armored warfare or strategic nuclear policy. To officers of this persuasion, the efforts of the party headquarters in Beijing to "modernize" the PLA raised issues of power as well as revolutionary social principles and thus constituted another element in their doubts about the wisdom of allowing a Soviet-style party-state to become the reality of communism in China.

Resistance within the army to a political system everywhere monopolized by the party organs might have been overcome, as the rapid growth of its apparatus in the early 1950s indeed suggests, had not Mao Zedong also turned against the party. Whether the chairman's postrevolutionary vision of Chinese society or merely the state as he saw it emerging after 1956 eventually inclined him to oppose the party is a distinction without a difference. For the essential fact is that, however much Mao remained until the close of his life the central personality in Chinese communism, he was more or less continuously at war with one or another faction of the party.

To retain his leadership of the movement, Mao ultimately destroyed the CCP during the Cultural Revolution because he no longer commanded the support of the majority of the members of its central organs. The principal weapon he used to overthrow the party apparatus was the PLA, an instrument he had consciously shaped into an alternative power system to that of the party from the time he replaced Peng Dehuai with Lin Biao. That he was able to do this at the expense of, and over the objections of, the main civilian party leaders shows the weakness of his own and the army's commitment to the principle of absolute party dominance. It is this principle, of course, which most distinguishes Leninist-Stalinist regimes from other political systems. Although Mao's radical brand of upheaval politics was ultimately checked by the regional military commanders following the Wuhan incident, as the outcome of Lin Biao's attempted coup revealed, no concerted effort developed within the army to challenge Mao's right to lead the state, as it had with respect to the party's.

It is thus evident that the convergence of Mao's and the army's opposition to the establishment of sole party supremacy was decisive to the outcome of China's various political crises after 1959. The roots of this alliance reached deep into the history of Chinese communism but centered on two basic concerns. Mao and most of the leading army figures have regarded the principles and values of the revolution, a vague "higher law" ideology, as the paramount symbols of legitimacy; the party was an important institution for the realization

99

of revolutionary values but was not above the revolution or its ideology. In this conception, the central party apparatus is not sacred nor does it possess immunity from challenge or reform, as it does in the Lenin-Stalin tradition.

The second concern that aligned Mao and the PLA in opposition to the party's sole monopoly of power was whether party and Communist leadership would continue to mean that broad, heterogeneous composition of veteran cadres reflecting the realities of the revolution's many tasks and social classes, as it had all during the liberation struggle, or would be transferred to the narrow concept of an elite vanguard of bureaucrats drawn primarily from party headquarters, as was clearly the preference of Mao's opponents from the mid-1950s until he destroyed them in the Cultural Revolution. The latter conception, of course, has prevailed in other Communist states but to date has lacked the power base to triumph in China. It would appear, therefore, that many army commanders shared with Mao, albeit unstated, a conviction that the party was only one element in a broader conception of "Communist leadership," and hence that the state, as such, must be responsive to a variety of societal forces and values outside and above the purely party apparatus.

These same theoretical principles, of course, made eminently good sense from the standpoint of Mao's and the army's selfish political interests. Faced with a party bureaucracy that never fully supported his policies (and after the early 1950s was increasingly disposed to reduce his influence), Mao had reason to foster multiple centers of power so as to build up his allies and undercut his opponents. He skillfully used the PLA for this purpose though, as a consequence, he eventually became dependent on his generals. The army also clearly benefited from the alliance with Mao, whether from the standpoint of curbing the growth of a Soviet-style state system detrimental to many of the officers' conception of revolutionary values and traditions or because the ascendance of the party bureaucracy would have eventually led to the effective political demise of its senior leaders' influence in the affairs of the state.

Organizational Rivalry

The makeup of the forces generally referred to as the PLA reveals yet other sources of military insubordination. Based on what is known about the composition of the Chinese armed forces, it is difficult to escape the conclusion that powerful elements within the Communist leadership have long insisted on a scheme that would prevent the organized violence of the state from being concentrated under a single hierarchy in Beijing. On the contrary, it is apparent that the division and structure of the Chinese military forces are essentially reflections of rival power centers and, consequently, a perceived need to maintain a balance among longstanding political factions and interests.

Military power in China comprises several distinct types of forces. In practice, however, each of these has a different command relationship to the Ministry of Defense and to the Military Affairs Commission of the CCP. The PLA combines three combat arms: army, navy, and air force. By far the largest of these, the army, comprises 3.5 million men in approximately two hundred divisions including ten armored, four paratroop, and fifty-eight local force divisions. The navy, essentially a coastal defense force of 275,000, includes 30,000 marines and is deployed in nine naval bases in the ports of East China. The air force numbers about 250,000 men, including a nuclear and missile weapons service arm.

Before examining the actual command and control relationships of these forces to the central party and government organs, three other military elements — the militia, the public security forces, and the "8341 unit" — must be mentioned, for they have exerted extremely important influences on the political balance of power within the state and thus the behavior of the military as a whole.

China's twenty-eight military district commanders have direct control over a vast militia system comprising about five million active reservists and more than seventy-five million inactive members. Theoretically, main force, local, and militia forces are all part of the PLA and thus under the command of the minister of defense. In practice, however, the local forces in the provinces are responsible for the organization and training of the largely commune-based militia units. This arrangement gives the military district commanders special powers as the key links between the central army headquarters in Beijing and the huge population that could be mobilized in the countryside, independent of orders or support from Beijing, in the event of war or political turmoil. During periods of national crisis, such as the Cultural Revolution and the Lin Biao affair, the militia units were overwhelming responsive to the military district commanders rather than to Beijing, a fact which again points to the limited authority of the central military apparatus in China.

Victor Nee's chapter in this volume examines more fully the question of the role of the militia in Chinese society. Here, mention need only be made of the fact that historically the regime's attitude toward the militia has vacillated between expanding and reducing its role depending on the shifts and turns of elite politics. Mao and his supporters seem consistently to have supported the idea of a large, active militia. The domestic political reasons for this preference are not difficult to see. Strengthening the position of provincial power holders appears to have been one of Mao's tactics in checking the influence of party elements that opposed him in Beijing. Apart from whether a large militia in fact served to deter foreign attacks on the PRC, it augmented the power of those local and regional military commanders who agreed with Mao that the

PLA should retain its guerrilla political traditions at the same time that it developed modern, professional war-fighting capability.

Opposition to the idea of centralized control over the army no doubt also influenced the Chinese Communists' early decision not to create a secret police monster such as pervades the Soviet system. As early as 1949, elements of the regular army were detached to form special public security units to guard the railroads, ports, airfields, and other communication centers. Until about 1967 these and other special units were controlled locally rather than from Beijing. During the Cultural Revoltuion, however, the PLA took charge of most of these functions, a development that probably produced less centralized control over these units than might otherwise appear in view of the army's own internal contradictions at that time.

The role of the national police administration — the Public Security Bureau (PSB) — is another matter. Although police administration is also highly decentralized — to judge from its performance during the Cultural Revolution — the prominence of this force in shaping the outcome of elite factional conflict in Beijing from the late 1960s on can scarcely be ignored. The PSB was the power base of such leaders as Xie Fuzhi, Kang Sheng, Hua Guofeng, and Wang Dongxing, who played crucial roles in the struggles of the late Cultural Revolution, the Lin Biao affair, the rise and fall of the Gang of Four, and the period of the Hua-Deng ascendancy. Whereas the army appears also to have taken over control of PSB units throughout the country as early as the Cultural Revolution, in Beijing a far more complicated pattern of control and intrigue prevailed and may still obtain today.

The close association and political prominence of all the ministers of public security after 1966 with Mao Zedong plainly indicates that the chairman gradually built up and came to rely upon a personal secret police apparatus, a violation of the best principles to which he had earlier devoted his life. Mao's reliance on this group is another reminder of how incomplete was his real authority within the party and how desperate he was to retain power at any cost. For it was the PSB, in cooperation with the Cultural Revolution radicals and the Gang of Four, which was mainly responsible for the massive arrests, intimidations, and other features of the terror that reigned in Beijing during the decade before Mao's death. The subsequent purge of former PSB Minister Wang Dongxing and the apparent removal of this institution from the inner circles of the Politburo in recent years indicate that it was a principal target of those who, so far, have won out in the succession struggle. How complete their victory is remains open to question, however, and surely the precedent has been established for factional elements to create a base of power, as Mao did, in the PSB in order to control the elites in Beijing and through them to influence the allegiances of provincial military and party leaders.

The third armed force that has contributed to the potential for military insubordination is the little-known 8341 unit. Unmistakably a praetorian guard originally formed to provide security for the Central Committee members in Beijing, in the latter part of Mao's reign it clearly functioned as his private municipal garrison and bodyguard. Although armed and trained as a special PLA unit, it was reportedly led by officers unquestionably loyal to Mao — possibly relatives — and was under his command. Apparently the unit was made up of several men drawn from every county in China. On a rotation basis, half were on duty in Beijing, the other half in their native locales. The unit in the provinces was used to undertake all manner of provincial investigations, which were regularly reported to the chairman. The unit in Beijing ensured his physical control over the top leadership of the state, party, and army.

It was the 8341 which dispersed the April 5, 1976, demonstrations and later arrested the Gang of Four shortly after Mao's death, an intervention that quickly sealed the fate of the remaining leftists and averted the possibility of a potentially wider conflict involving the army. But the control and allegiance of this unit in the post-Mao period is open to question. As he did with the PSB, Mao appears to have gradually transformed the 8341 unit from an organ of the Central Committee to a weapon of his own. Whether the party headquarters has in fact regained sufficient authority to control and use its Chinese praetorian guard, or whether the PLA high command has absorbed it, remains uncertain at this time.

These sources of military insubordination — militia, security police, and the 8341 unit — would have served to undermine the PLA's monopoly of violence within the state even if the army leadership had enjoyed unity and remained politically neutral. But in addition to these outside competitors, the PLA's own structure reflects built-in centrifugal forces that have weakened its capacity to act as a unified institution, except in those unusual times when the leadership has spoken with a single voice. For the PLA is fundamentally two armies — first, the main force divisions and special forces such as the border troops, airborne divisions, air force, and navy, under the command of the Ministry of Defense; and second, the local force divisions, mostly light armed infantry, under the control of the regional and district military commanders. The former units are the modern, integrated combat elements whose primary mission is the defense of the state against foreign enemies; the latter forces more closely resemble a territorial guard whose basic function is civil and political, that is, the maintenance of public order and internal control. The regional forces can and have been used to expand and back up the main force units, as they did throughout the revolutionary war years, but their basic task has always been to hold and secure the provinces. The strategic mobile elements of the Chinese army have been the main force units, which alone possess the training, equipment, and transport to act on a national scale. (A number of these divisions were deployed in the campaign against Vietnam in February 1979.)

103

The political basis for conflict within the military arising from these dual missions is rooted in the system of administration and deployment of the army. Whereas the main force units are supposedly under the Ministry of Defense, in fact most of them and the local divisions are administratively controlled through the eleven regional and twenty-eight district military commanders. The Defense Ministry's basic policies are set by the Military Affairs Commission of the party, which is composed of China's most senior military leaders, political commissars, and key Politburo members. The military members of this body appear to have been chosen with a view to representing the interests of the original five great field armies, which in 1947 became the PLA but did not, as a result of that union, entirely give up their regional character or their power.

Inevitably, therefore, the real authority of the Ministry of Defense vis-à-vis the regional military commanders depends upon the degree of unity among China's top political-military elite. Even with Mao's backing and a largely dismantled party apparatus, Lin Biao was unable in twelve years to gain effective control over the military forces in the provinces. Subsequent efforts to rotate the regional commanders in 1974 and 1979 have not notably enhanced the Defense Ministry's position because the network of staff and command officers in the provinces is still deeply entrenched, and it is watchfully protected by the elder military statesmen of the revolution who, in their seventies and eighties, still occupy key positions in Beijing whether they bear military or civilian titles. It will seemingly require a new generation of younger officers, more committed to centralization than their elders are, before the centrifugal forces at work in the PLA might be removed. By that time, of course, young advocates of provincial interests may also have risen to higher posts in the army with the support of the current elder soldier-statesmen and thus serve to perpetuate the present system.

Although "military feudalism" is probably not an apt description of power realities in the PLA, it is fair to say that the influence of the various currents in the army pervades each of the main political factions or groupings that have competed since Mao's death. Generally speaking, these factions are the veteran senior cadres of the state administration who supported Zhou Enlai and, after his death, Deng Xiaoping (such as Nie Rongzhen, Li Xiannian, Chen Yun, Bo Yipo, Zhao Ziyang, and Hu Yaobang); the old central PLA marshals and commanders who have worked as something of a junta in support of Zhou's policies since the late Cultural Revolution and now center around Ye Jianying (such as Xu Xiangqian, Su Zhenhua, Yang Chengwu, Su Yu, and Liu Bocheng); the main regional military commanders, especially in Shenyang, Beijing, Nanjing, Guangzhou, Wuhan, and Jinan (such as Xu Shiyou, Li Desheng, Yang Dezhi, Zeng Suyou); and remnants of the Mao "Left" who were not part of the Gang of Four but have been undermined through previous associations with it (such as Hua Guofeng and Zhen Xilian).

It is the working out of the relationships, harmonious and otherwise, among these groups which will most likely determine whether a truly centralized, nationally directed army is desired or can be brought into being. The regional interests and the old guerrilla marshals represented in these factions, however, are strong enough to raise serious doubt that the PLA will soon undergo any meaningful transformation of its structure and organization.

In the absence of such social engineering efforts, it is difficult to see the logical basis on which the army would, in the 1980s, more easily subordinate itself to the dictatorship of the central party organs than it was prepared to do in the 1950s, 1960s, and 1970s. Largely because the military, regional, and central commanders alike have supported restructuring the party and state apparatus, the coalitions around Deng Xiaoping, Hua Guofeng, and possibly others have a chance to restore the party's supremacy. But it is only a chance, not a mandate. Military insubordination arose because of the divisions within the central leadership. The military is very likely to revoke the party's chance to rebuild its leadership position should new rivalries and conflicts at the center again lead to chaos.

To meet that challenge seemingly requires that the party once again demonstrate the vision and the energy of its revolutionary years, years of achievement which earned it the right to lead and thus to rule. In the post-1949 period, however, the party did not measure up to the challenge of the transformation from revolution to state. The resources available to it today, human and material, do not suggest reasons for optimism that this challenge will be more successfully met. Both the state apparatus and the military apparatus are, as a result of earlier upheavals, now stronger than those of the party. More important, the state and the military machinery are also more essential to the actual governance of China. No figure of the stature of Mao looms on the political horizon, nor is one wanted. Under these circumstances, the Chinese military is likely to remain the very watchful guardian of the state as it matures, just as this army in an earlier period nurtured the revolution in its infancy.

PART TWO

State and Society

4

The Concept of the Dictatorship of the Proletariat in Chinese Marxist Thought

MAURICE MEISNER

Since the late 1950s, the Marxist theory of the dictatorship of the proletariat has loomed increasingly large in the political and ideological life of the People's Republic of China. The prominence of this concept over the past two decades is historically intelligible both on Chinese socioeconomic and political grounds, as will be suggested in this chapter. But before attempting to understand the place and function of the dictatorship of the proletariat in the recent history of the People's Republic, it is necessary to understand something of the nature of the concept in original Marxist theory and its place in the Marxist-Leninist theoretical heritage from which Chinese Communist leaders claim to have derived and developed the notion. This task is by no means easy, for the concept of the dictatorship of the proletariat is not systematically or neatly laid out in the writings of Marx and Engels (in part because of their well-known reluctance to draw "utopian" blueprints of the future), and no aspect of Marxism has been more misunderstood, misinterpreted, and subjected to greater political and ideological abuse, both by its critics and its professed adherents. Yet the task is essential, for the concept lies at the heart of Marxism as a revolutionary theory; it is crucial for understanding the Marxist view of the relationsohip between state and society, crucial for understanding the Marxist view of the transformation of that relationship in postrevolutionary society, and essential for understanding the Marxist definition of socialism and communism.

One often reads statements to the effect that we can never know what Marx actually meant by the term "dictatorship of the proletariat."[1] Although the concept is not set forth as clearly as one might wish, it is by no means as vague and ill-defined as many Marxologists make it out to be. The concept can be reconstructed from various writings of Marx and Engels, and that process of reconstruction must be done in the wider context of the Marxist theory of the state. For the purposes of the present discussion, I can only outline what seem to me the basic propositions of the Marxist theory of the state, focusing on those aspects most directly relevant to understanding what Marx did mean by the concept of the dictatorship of the proletariat.

The Marxist Theory of the State

The first and essential proposition of Marx's theory of the state is that the state, at least in the first instance, is not an independent and autonomous force in history but rather *a product of society* — and thus the origins, nature, form, and functions of the state must be sought in the social class divisions and conflicts of civil society. For Marx, "the state is the active, conscious, and official expression" of "the present structure of society."[2] Here Marx departed from the classical liberal view that the state is an autonomous entity whose power, while perhaps socially necessary, must be restrained through legal and constitutional relationships from interfering with the workings of the "free market." Moreover, Marx rejected the more positive liberal ideal that the state is (or, at least, should be) the impartial mediator of civil conflicts to ensure social order for the natural operation of capitalist forces of production. For Marx, of course, there was nothing "natural" about capitalism, much less the capitalist state. Rather, the state reflects "the unsocial nature of this [capitalist] civil life, this private property, this trade, this industry, this mutual plundering of the various circles of citizens. . . . This fragmentation, this baseness, this *slavery of civil society* is the natural foundation on which the modern state rests, just as the *civil society of slavery* was the natural foundation on which the ancient state rested. The existence of the state and the existence of slavery are inseparable."[3]

At the same time that Marx dismissed the liberal view of the state, he also rejected the anarchist assumption that the state as such is the principal evil in history and responsible for all the evils that afflict society. For Marx, as the passage quoted above indicates, precisely the opposite is the case: it is the evils of society which are responsible for the evil of the state.

Nor did Marx have much use for the Hegelian theory of the state. Indeed, Marx's theory of the state was originally formulated in large measure as an extended critique of Hegel's views that the state embodies the supreme "Idea" or "Spirit" of history, that the state is the subject of history whereas society is its object, that the existence of society is dependent on the existence of state, and that the state represents "univeral interests" as opposed to the "particular interests" of society, with the state resolving the contradiction between the universal and the particular. For Marx, this was indeed a case where Hegel had turned reality upside down. For the state, far from resolving social contradictions, merely reflects and perpetuates them. And rather than embodying universal interests, Marx argued, the state is based precisely "on the contradiction between public and private life, between general interests and private interests."[4]

These views on the relationship between state and society which appear in Marx's early writings remained the essential presuppositions of his mature thought, expressed particularly forcefully in his 1875 "Critique of the Gotha Program." Addressing the notion of "the free state," a phrase he regarded as a contradiction in terms at best, Marx caustically wrote: "The German workers' party . . . shows that its socialist ideas are not even skin deep; in that, instead of treating existing society (and this holds good for any future one) as the basis of the existing state (or the future state in the case of future society), it treats the state rather as an independent entity that possesses its own intellectual, ethical, and libertarian bases."[5]

The general proposition that the state is the product of society is, of course, the basis for what is generally taken to be the primary Marxist view of the origins and function of the state. As classically formulated by Engels: "As the state arose from the need to hold class antagonisms in check, but as it arose, at the same time, in the midst of the conflict of these classes, it is, as a rule, the state of the most powerful, economically dominant class, which, through the medium of the state, becomes also the politically dominant class, and thus acquires new means of holding down and exploiting the oppressed class."[6]

But this familiar general rule is subject to numerous modifications and qualifications which flow from the second major proposition on the state that Marx set forth, namely, the tendency for all states to separate themselves from the societies that produced them and to assume (to greater or lesser degrees) a partial independence. In *The German Ideology*, for example, Marx discussed the state not only as a political organization used and controlled by the economically dominant class to further its own interests but also as "a separate entity, beside and outside civil society."[7]

The proposition that the state tends to acquire a certain degree of autonomy and independence from society does not contradict the original proposition that the state is the product of society, as may appear the case at first sight. For it is the Marxist argument, or at least it was Marx's argument, that the nature and the extent of the independence of the state are determined by the condition of society. From the writings of Marx and Engels, it is possible to identify four general sociohistorical situations conducive to the growth of an autonomous state power. The first is one in which the social structure in general is weak and social classes are ill-formed. As Marx noted: "The independence of the State is only found nowadays in those countries where the estates have not yet completely developed into classes, where the estates, done away with in more advanced countries, still have a part to play, and where there exists a mixture."[8] In the second, the state is likely to assume a relatively autonomous status vis-à-vis society in transitional historical eras when two strong social classes struggle for dominance, with neither able to prevail; in short, when there is a prolonged stalemate in the class struggle. "Periods occur," Engels observed, "in which the warring classes balance each other so nearly that the state power as ostensible mediator, acquires, for the moment, a certain degree of independence of both. Such was the absolute monarchy of the seventeenth and eighteenth centuries, which held the balance between the nobility and the class of burghers."[9] Third, Marx suggested that under certain modern historical conditions the persistence of a large mass of small-holding peasants can form the social base for the rise of a largely independent Bonapartist bureaucratic regime. The major historical example, of course, is mid-nineteenth century France under the rule of Napoleon III. "Only under the second Bonaparte," Marx wrote, "does the state seem to have made itself completely independent."[10] Although the Bonapartist state by no means truly represented the interests of the peasantry—and indeed functionally served to preserve the existing capitalist order—Marx attributed the independence of the state, in large measure, to the political support afforded to Bonaparte by politically gullible peasants. For, as Marx argued, given their mode of socioeconomic life, the peasants are "incapable of enforcing their class interest in their own name, whether through a parliament or through a convention. They cannot represent themselves, they must be represented. Their representatives must at the same time appear as their master, as an authority over them, as an unlimited governmental power that protects them against the other classes and sends them rain and sunshine from above. The political influence of the small-holding peasants, therefore, finds its final expression in the executive power subordinating society to itself."[11]

Finally, the most extreme example of the independence of the state and its dominance over society is suggested in Marx's theory of the "Asiatic mode of production," in which a more or less permanent bureaucratic state apparatus establishes itself on the basis of a society characterized by isolated and self-sufficient communal villages combining agriculture and handicrafts in an unchanging division of labor. Whether the theory fits any known historical reality is of course highly problematic. For the purposes of the present discussion, it is sufficient to note that Marx did not exclude the historical possibility of socioeconomic formations in which the state bureaucracy itself is the ruling class.

These, in brief, are the main sociohistorical situations that foster the independence of the state — and, at the same time, the major modifications (made by Marx and Engels) of what is conventionally understood to be the Marxist theory of the state. Needless to say, Marx did not view the tendency for the state to become relatively independent as desirable or historically progressive. For Marx, the more independent the state is, the more arbitrary and despotic it is likely to be in its relationship with society. For example, in his critique of the notion of "the free state" in the "Gotha Program," Marx sarcastically commented: "Free state — what is this? It is by no means the aim of the workers, who have got rid of the narrow mentality of humble subjects, to set the state free. In the German Empire the 'state' is almost as 'free' as in Russia."[12]

The third, and perhaps most fundamental, proposition of the Marxist theory of the state is that the state constitutes a form of alienated social power. The state, originally the product of society (or, more precisely, the product of the social division of labor and consequent social class divisions and conflicts), once in existence, tends to take on a life of its own, usurping the powers that rightfully belong to society as a whole. The state, in short, is a principal expression of man's alienated "pre-history," both in historical reality and in human perception.

In objective historical reality, the state as an expression of alienated social power takes the very real form of a bureaucratic apparatus that stands above and tends to separate itself from society. Indeed, the very birth of the state is a reflection of mankind's increasingly alienated "pre-history" and marks a quantum leap in that process of alienation. For the birth and growth of the state is, in the first instance, society's admission that it cannot by itself control its internal antagonisms but must surrender that function to a higher power. As Engels put it: "This power, arisen out of society, but placing itself above it, and increasingly alienating itself from it, is the state."[13] And once in existence, the state assumes an increasingly alienated form. For in Marxist theory, the state is not an abstract "ethical idea" but an all too concrete entity: a bureaucratic machine (presided over by flesh and blood bureaucrats) supported by the organized forces of violence of society — the standing army and the police. Moreover, the bureaucrats who operate that state machinery have a vested interest in its perpetuation and its independence. In possession of public power, as Engels notes, "the officials, as organs of society, now stand *above* society."[14] All states thus strive for independence from society and for the power to dominate society. The extent to which they are able to achieve an autonomous status depends on particular sociohistorical conditions, some of which have been noted above. But to greater or lesser degrees, it is inherent in the nature of the state to become something of a Frankensteinian monster, constantly threatening to dominate its social creator. The state as an alien entity that usurps human social powers is strikingly pictured by Marx in his description of the nineteenth-century French state: "This executive power with its enormous bureaucratic and military organization, with its ingenious state machinery, embracing wide strata, with a host of officials numbering half a million, besides an army of another half million, *this appalling parasitic body*, which enmeshes the body of French society like a net and chokes all its pores."[15]

The alienation of state from society finds ideological expression in human perceptions of the state as an independent entity and a higher power embodying universal interests, whereas in reality it pursues particular interests — both its own and those of particular social classes. This "false consciousness" primarily takes the form of patriotism; incapable of recognizing the state as a human-fashioned institution serving particular human social and political interests, people commonly perceive the state as a higher power and worship it through

113

patriotic celebrations, much as they worship their self-created gods through religion. As Marx wrote: "The state is the intermediary between man and man's freedom. Just as Christ is the intermediary to whom man transfers the burden of all his divinity, all his religious constraint, so the state is the intermediary to whom man transfers all his non-divinity and all his human unconstraint."[16] For Marx, the state is an alien power, both in reality and in consciousness.

The Concept of the Dictatorship of the Proletariat

The views of Marx and Engels on the relationship between the state and society discussed above are essential for understanding Marx's conception of the dictatorship of the proletariat, the period defined in Marxist theory as the era of the revolutionary transition from capitalist to communist society — from the time of the political triumph of the proletariat and the establishment of the "lower phase" of communism (or socialism) to the advent of "full communism." The following discussion of the period when the state takes the form of the dictatorship of the proletariat will be arbitrarily divided into two parts: first, the socioeconomic transformations and tasks that are to be accomplished during this transitional era; and, second, the unique way in which political power is to be organized under the dictatorship of the proletariat — and how it is to disappear.

Socioeconomic Functions of the Dictatorship of the Proletariat

Marx, as is well known, refused to draw "utopian blueprints" of the future communist society or to draw up a detailed road map on how mankind was to arrive there — partly as a matter of principle, partly perhaps as a matter of political strategy. Yet Marx was by no means silent on the course of development he envisioned in the postrevolutionary era. He set forth general guidelines — and in some areas suggested specific measures and principles — for the transition from capitalism to socialism and communism. Indeed, as Bertell Ollman has shown, it is possible to reconstruct Marx's vision of communism (and many aspects of his vision of how it was to be achieved) from various descriptions and comments scattered throughout his writings.[17] It is sufficient here to take note of two points. First, the social and economic changes that Marx regarded as necessary in the early phase of postrevolutionary society presuppose the existence of a reasonably strong and effective central governmental power. Second, the establishment of socialism, and even more the transition to communism, presuppose conditions of economic abundance and the employment of the very highest levels of technological knowledge.

The first point is clearly demonstrated in the section of the *Manifesto* in which Marx discussed what likely will take place in the immediate aftermath of a successful workers' revolution. "The proletariat," he wrote, "will use its political supremacy to wrest, by degrees, all capital from the bourgeoisie, to centralize all instruments of production in the hands of the State, i.e., of the proletariat organized as the ruling class; and to increase the total of productive forces as rapidly as possible." He then suggests ten measures that will be "generally applicable" in "the most advanced countries": (1) "Abolition of property in land." (2) "A heavy progressive or graduated income tax." (3) "Abolition of all right of inheritance." (4) "Confiscation of the property of all emigrants and rebels." (5) "Centralisation of credit in the hands of the State." (6) "Centralisation of the means of communication and transport in the hands of the State." (7) "Extension of factories and instruments of production owned by the State; the bringing into cultivation of wastelands, and the improvement of the soil generally in accordance with a common plan." (8) "Equal liability of all to labour. Establishment of industrial armies, especially for agriculture." (9) "Combination of agriculture with manufacturing industries; gradual abolition of the distinction between town and country, by a more equitable distribution of the population over the country." (10) "Free education for all children in public schools. . . . Combination of education with industrial production."[18]

Many of these measures obviously demand a strong central government, and Marx clearly assumed that the state would play a central role in the transformation of society in the early postrevolutionary period. It also would play a partly coercive one. As Marx wrote in his debates with the anarchists: "As long as other classes, especially the capitalist class, still exist, as long as the proletariat is still struggling with it . . . it must use coercive means, hence governmental means; it is still a class, and the economic conditions on which the class struggle and the existence of classes rest, have not yet disappeared and must be removed by force, or transformed, their process of transformation must be speeded up by force."[19]

As society moves to full communism, it is clear that Marx believed (and believed it an absolute necessity) that the process would be based on the very highest levels of modern productive forces and a superabundance of material wealth. In the "Gotha Program," for example, Marx wrote: "In a higher phase of communist society, after the enslaving subordination of the individual to the division of labour, and therefore with also the antithesis between mental and physical labour, has vanished; after labour has become not only a means of life but life's prime want; after the productive forces have also increased with the all-round development of the individual, and all the springs of cooperative wealth flow more abundantly — only then can the narrow horizon of bourgeois right be crossed in its entirety and society inscribe on its banners: 'From each according to his ability, to each according to his needs!' "[20] Marx's insistence on the necessity of economic abundance as a precondition for the new society was reinforced by the enormous emphasis he placed on the need to shorten the working day in the process of the transition to communism, for it is only by the leisure time thus afforded that people could freely develop their many-sided human faculties and potentialities that would characterize the communist future of "a truly human life."

With the movement toward a communist society, Marx proclaimed that the state would begin to "wither away." Since the first proposition of Marxian state theory is that the state is the product of the class divisions and struggles of society, it is only logical to assume that with the abolition of the tyranny of the division of labor and the consequent abolition of social class distinctions and conflicts, the abolition of the state will follow. Yet here one encounters one of the most vexing problems in Marxist theory. For the Marxist theory of the state is by no means confined to the proposition that the state is simply the reflection of society and its antagonisms. As has been noted, Marx also regarded the state as an entity that assumes a relatively independent status, one that strives (with greater or lesser degrees of success) to establish its autonomy in its relationship with society, and, most important, an entity that is an expression of alienated social power, the usurper of the powers that rightfully belong to society and its members. What kind of state then is likely to promote the revolutionary social transformations that will destroy the basis of its own existence? What kind of state will abolish itself on its own accord? The state that is defined as the dictatorship of the proletariat is clearly not a state in the conventional sense. It was to be a state of a very unique political character — and it is essential to understand the unique characteristics that Marx assigned to state power in postrevolutionary society to understand what he meant by the dictatorship of the proletariat, and indeed to understand what socialism and communism mean.

Political Characteristics of the Dictatorship of the Proletariat

It often has been noted that Marx's choice of the term "dictatorship" to characterize the form political power would take in postrevolutionary society has proven to be a most unfortunate one, lending itself to charges by anti-Marxists that Marxism is inherently authoritarian in nature, and perhaps most unfortunately permitting Marxists in power an implicit ideological justification for dictatorial forms of rule. Yet even a cursory reading of Marx's writings on the dictatorship of the proletariat reveals that Marx did not have in mind a "dictatorship" in the conventional sense of rule by an elitist party, a small group of leaders, or a single person. Rather, Marx assumed that the dictatorship of the proletariat would take the form of the democratic self-government of the producers, the vast majority of society. It would be a dictatorship only in the sense that Marx regarded all states and forms of organized political power as essentially dictatorial and repressive, and its dictatorial functions would be directed only against the remnants of the old exploiting classes, a small minority of the population whose properties would be expropriated and who would be reduced to the level of ordinary citizens. Moreover, Marx took it for granted that the proletarian state, far from abolishing conventional bourgeois liberties (such elemental democratic rights as freedom of speech, freedom of assembly, and free elections) would inherit and expand them. The liberties proclaimed in bourgeois constitutions, which can only be partial and in large part illusory under capitalism, would become realities in a newly born socialist society in accordance with the eminently democratic forms and principles of popular self-rule Marx set forth in *The Civil War in France*.

It is, of course, in this analysis of the Paris Commune of 1871 — "the political form at last discovered under which to work out the economic emancipation of labour"[21] — that Marx discussed in greatest detail the political character and forms of the dictatorship of the proletariat. In that celebrated treatise (and one much celebrated by Maoists in China over the years) Marx was centrally concerned with the problem of how to prevent a workers' government from becoming independent of and alienated from society. Thus at the outset Marx emphasized that "the working class cannot simply lay hold of the ready-made State machinery, and wield it for its own purposes."[22] Rather, before new and different forms of political power can be established, the workers must destroy what Marx characterized as "the centralized State power, with its ubiquitous organs of standing army, police, bureaucracy, clergy, and judicature," to ensure that they do not remain or reemerge as parasitic organs standing over society. The point was reemphasized by Engels in his 1891 introduction to the German edition of *The Civil War in France*: "From the very outset the Commune had to recognize that the working class, having once attained supremacy in the State, could not work with the old machinery of government." For, as Engels observed: "Society had created for itself definite organs, originally by simple division of labor, for the provision of its common interests. But these organs, at the head of which is the power of the State, had in the course of time, and in the service of their own separate interests, transformed themselves from the servants of society into its masters." The great historical accomplishment of the Commune was that it was the antithesis of "this transformation of the State and the State's organs from the servants of society into its rulers — a transformation which had been inevitable in all hitherto existing States."[23]

The specific measures undertaken by the Communards to guarantee that the new workers' government would be the servant of society and not become its master — the measures that Marx praised and established as the Marxian principles of the dictatorship of the proletariat — are well known and need only be briefly noted here. To restore political power to society, the standing army was abolished in favor of the "the armed people." The police was "stripped of its political attributes and turned into the responsible and at all times revocable agent of the Commune." The Commune itself was organized as "a working, not a parliamentary, body, executive and legislative at the same time." Such administrative functions as were socially necessary were performed not by appointed officials but by persons directly chosen by the masses through universal suffrage, supervised by the masses, subject to immediate popular recall, paid ordinary workingmen's wages, and not granted any special privileges or status. Educational institutions, "cleared of all interference of Church and State," were open to all, and science was "freed from the fetters which class prejudice and governmental force had imposed upon it." And magistrates and judges, divested of their "sham independence," were "like the rest of the public servants . . . to be elective, responsible, and revocable."[24]

It is thus that the repressive organs of the old state power are amputated and the legitimate functions of government are "wrested from an authority usurping preeminence over society itself, and restored to the responsible agents of society."[25] The constitution of the Commune, Marx wrote, "would have restored to the social body all the forces hitherto absorbed by the State parasite feeding upon, and clogging the free movement of society."[26]

This historically unprecedented form of state power — what Marx termed "the self-government of the producers" and Lenin called a "semi-state" — is the only form capable of carrying out the social revolutionary transformations that are assigned to the era of the dictatorship of the proletariat and is indeed the only form of state that is capable of "withering away." And that process of "withering away" is not the distant end product of communism, much less a gift eventually bestowed upon society by a dictatorial state after a period of authoritarian rule. It is a process that begins at the beginning of the era of the dictatorship of the proletariat; as a state, the proletarian dictatorship begins to wither away on the very morrow of its establishment, as an essential part of the process of both political and socioeconomic liberation. The dictatorship of the proletariat, as Marx conceived it, is above all the time when society as a whole reappropriates the powers which have been taken from it by an alien state power — for, as Marx once put it, "only when man has recognised and organised his own powers as social forces, and consequently no longer separates social power from himself in the shape of political power, only then will human emancipation have been accomplished."[27]

Twentieth-Century Communism and the Marxist Theory of the State

It is hardly necessary to point out that in the orthodox Marxist-Leninist doctrines under which twentieth-century Communist revolutions have proceeded, the Marxist critique of the state has been transformed into an ideology of state

118

legitimation. Marxian state theory and the concept of the dictatorship of the proletariat have been invoked to justify the autonomous bureaucracies that stand above and rule over the societies where successful Marxist-led anticapitalist revolutions have taken place — and, indeed, to celebrate the progressive role of the state in historical development, not only in the Communist present but also in the national past.[28]

The mechanics of this process of ideological rationalization are quite simple. First, there is a rigid insistence on the universal validity of the conventional (or primary) Marxist theory of the state, that is, the proposition that all states in all historical times are instruments in the hands of a dominant social class. Second, there is a denial (usually implicit) of the original Marxist proposition that states strive for independence from society and that under certain historical conditions states do in fact achieve a relatively autonomous status. Third, the original Marxist view of the state as a form of alienated social power is ignored. The illusory conclusion follows that in societies in which the capitalist class has been eliminated the workers (or "the laboring masses") are the dominant class, that therefore the state described as a "dictatorship of the proletariat" can be nothing other than a proletarian workers' state, and that, since the proletariat embodies universal interests, it is therefore a state that represents the interests of "the people." It is thus that the Marxist critique of the state is distorted into an ideology to legitimize a bureaucratic dictatorship which rules over society.

The political and ideological need to mask the autonomous character of contemporary Communist bureaucracies has reflected itself in a historiographical orthodoxy that demands the identification of a ruling class in all historical eras and, correspondingly, a state that is the instrument of that class. The well-known debates on the question of the relationship between state and society during the transition from feudalism to capitalism in western Europe might illustrate the point. The Stalinist orthodoxy on the matter was laid down in 1940: "The view of the absolute monarchy as a feudal landowners' state of the nobility has, as it were, been assimilated by all Soviet historians."[29] The view was also quickly "assimilated" by Western Marxist historians such as Maurice Dobb and Christopher Hill, both members of the British Communist party at the time. When in 1950 the noncommunist Marxist Paul Sweezy suggested that the fourteenth to sixteenth centuries were a transitional period when neither a disintegrating feudalism nor an emerging capitalism constituted the dominant mode of production, thus implying that the absolutist monarchies of the era were relatively autonomous states,[30] Dobb and Hill were quick to reject the view as both historically inaccurate and theoretically impossible. Dobb, on the basis of a reasoned argument, concluded that "the ruling class was still feudal and that the state was still the political instrument of its rule."[31] Hill was content to present the same judgment — "the absolute monarchy is a form of feudal state"[32] — by quoting the "final agreed conclusion" arrived at by a group of

119

English Marxist historians several years earlier: "The Tudor and early Stuart state was essentially an executive institution of the feudal class more highly organized than ever before. . . . Only after the revolution of 1640−49 does the state in England begin to be subordinated to the capitalists. . . . The revolution of 1640 replaced the rule of one class by another."[33] Stalinist historiography, in short, could not entertain the possiblity of any degree of state autonomy in any historical era, lest it raise embarrassing questions about the relationship between political power and social classes in the Soviet Union and thereby cast doubt about the existence of the "dictatorship of the proletariat."

The Chinese History of the Concept of the Dictatorship of the Proletariat

The Marxist theory of the state has, of course, also been put to use in the People's Republic of China to obscure the relationship between state and society. In China, however, the ideological need to define the relationship between political power and social classes in accordance with orthodox Marxist-Leninist formulas has been a particularly difficult task, partly because of the peculiarities of the modern Chinese historical situation and partly because of the peculiar nature of the Chinese Communist revolution. In modern China, where all social classes were weak and consequently where the holders of political and military power tended more to determine the fate of social classes than to reflect specific social class interests, the Chinese Communist party came to power on the basis of mobilizing the forces of peasant revolt in the countryside but without the active support of the urban proletariat, the class the party claimed to represent.

Given the nature of the Chinese Communist revolution, and the historical conditions in which it took place, it was hardly to be expected that the new state established in 1949 would bear any resemblance to the original Marxist concept of the dictatorship of the proletariat. In a country still largely governed by precapitalist socioeconomic relationships, in a land suffering from the most wretched backwardness and impoverishment, in a country that had yet to achieve any real modern national political unity, and in a society so long preyed upon by marauding warlord armies, parasitic landlords, Guomindang bureaucrats, and foreign imperialists, it would have been sheer folly to introduce socialist political forms.

The Chinese Communists had no intention of commiting such a folly. During the revolutionary years, Mao Zedong (for good historical reasons) had insisted on the bourgeois character of the Chinese revolution, and he reaffirmed that view in 1949. Mao defined the new state not as a dictatorship of the proletariat but rather as a "people's democratic dictatorship," which presumably was "led by the proletariat and based on the worker-peasant alliance,"[34] a formula that reflected the revised Maoist version of the Marxist-Leninist concept of a bourgeois-democratic revolution. And while Mao also reaffirmed the commitment of the Chinese Communist party to achieve the ultimate communist goals proclaimed in Marxist theory, including the "withering away" of the state, the immediate task was not to set in motion a process leading to the disappearance of the state but rather to establish "a powerful state apparatus," which (as Mao bluntly put it at the time) would be an "instrument by which one class oppresses another."[35] A strong state was the essential prerequisite for carrying out the two other immediate tasks: the modern industrial development of an economically backward land and the abolition of precapitalist relationships in the country-side. All three tasks were eminently bourgeois (not socialist) and thus were fully in accord with the official ideology of state power as well as with the needs of the postrevolutionary historical situation.

While the term "people's democratic dictatorship" reflected the Maoist insistence on the "bourgeois" character of the Chinese revolution, it was also a political formula that obscured the relationship between political power and social classes. Since the tie between the ruling Communist party and the Chinese proletariat had been severed in 1927 and had not been restored during the more than two decades of rural revolutionary warfare that followed, the claim that the new state was "led by the proletariat" was little more than an ideological fiction, as was the notion of a "worker-peasant alliance."

A new fiction was added to the ideology of state power in 1956, when (in response to Khrushchev's Twentieth Soviet Congress speech denouncing Stalin) the leaders of the CCP proclaimed both the universal historical validity and the particular Chinese historical necessity of the "dictatorship of the proletariat."[36] From that time on, the term "dictatorship of the proletariat" generally replaced "the people's democratic dictatorship" as the more or less official description of the nature of state power in the People's Republic, although the term was not formally canonized until the promulgation of the constitution of 1975.

More than a purely semantic change was involved in the Chinese Communist adoption of the Marxist concept in 1956, and the increasingly strident use of the phrase over the following years reflected more than a need to score ideological points in the emerging polemical battle with the Soviet Union, although the timing of the announcement was no doubt partly determined by a desire to establish Beijing rather than Moscow as the world center of Marxist-Leninist orthodoxy. The invocation of the term "dictatorship of the proletariat" also reflected the Chinese Communist pursuit of radically new socioeconomic policies and significant changes in Chinese social reality. The "people's democratic dictatorship," the political formula for the Maoist version of a bourgeois-democratic revolution, corresponded, from a Marxist point of view, to the es-

121

sentially bourgeois character of social change in the early years of the People's Republic — the unification of China and the creation of a national market under a strong central state power, the eminently "bourgeois" character and results of the Land Reform campaign, and the encouragement of "national capitalism" in portions of the urban sector of the economy. The proclamation of "the dictatorship of the proletariat," on the other hand, followed shortly after the announcement of what was conceived as the beginning of "the transition to socialism," which essentially meant the virtual abolition of private property and private ownership of the means of production through the de facto nationalization of what remained of the private sector of the urban economy and the collectivization of agriculture, both largely accomplished by the end of 1956.

But if the growing prominence of the term "dictatorship of the proletariat" in Chinese Marxist theory was not wholly unrelated to a changing social reality, its use did not signify any change in the nature or exercise of state power or in the relationship between state and society. Just as the CCP's claim to represent the proletariat and incarnate "proletarian consciousness" in the 1930s and 1940s was made in the absence of any meaningful tie between the party and the urban working class, the proclamation of the dictatorship of the proletariat in the late 1950s hardly meant the political dominance of the actual proletariat. The term was invoked as a moral category rather than as a description of a political reality, used (as Benjamin Schwartz has noted) as "a designation of the dominance of the forces of good"[37] — or, at best, as a reaffirmation of the leadership's commitment to the socialist and communist goals which Marxist theory attributes to the proletariat. But political power remained with an autonomous party-state bureaucracy which was the master, not the servant, of society. The term "dictatorship of the proletariat," derived from the inherited body of Marxist theory, was used ideologically to legitimize the existing state apparatus and further obscured the realities of the relationship between state and society.

If Chinese Marxist writings on the state offered only standard Marxist-Leninist ideological justifications for Communist state power, it would hardly be a matter deserving serious inquiry. But while that voluminous body of literature contains its fair share of ideological rationalization for the state as it is, it also offers much which points to a critique of the existing state and its relationship to society. Here, in confronting a vast body of theory and practice filled with contradictions and ambiguities, I can only suggest several tendencies in Chinese Marxist theory over the last two decades of the Maoist era which depart from orthodox Marxist-Leninist dogma — and which perhaps deserve further investigation and more serious attention than they thus far have been accorded.

In reviewing Chinese Marxist theoretical literature over the period 1957 – 1976, one cannot fail to be impressed by the predominance of three overriding themes, all of which are essential for understanding the Maoist conception of

122

proletarian dictatorship. There is, first, the proposition that class struggles inevitably and necessarily continue under socialism — and the more distinctively Maoist notion that such class struggles take a primarily ideological form. "Class struggle is not yet over," Mao proclaimed in 1957, and he then went on to declare that "the class struggle *in the ideological field* between the proletariat and the bourgeoisie will still be long and devious and at times may even become very acute . . . the question whether socialism or capitalism will win is still not really settled."[38] The "class struggle" Mao announced was of course less a struggle between actual social classes than between social class viewpoints, between "bourgeois" and "proletarian" ideologies. The proclamation of the continued existence of class struggle, in any case, established the Marxian socioideological rationale for the necessity — and, indeed, for the necessity of strengthening — "the dictatorship of the proletariat."

A second distinctive Maoist notion — and one far more heretical from an orthodox Marxist-Leninist point of view — is the proposition that a bureaucracy can establish itself as a new ruling class. In a society that has abolished private property and private ownership of the means of production, Mao early recognized that the principal social contradiction is no longer primarily economic but rather political, the elemental distinction between those who hold political power and those who do not, between the rulers and the ruled, between (as Mao put it in 1957) the "leadership and the led."[39] From there he was inexorably driven to the conclusion that China's bureaucrats were becoming a new exploiting class; they were, he charged in 1965, "bourgeois elements sucking the blood of the workers"[40] — in effect, a functional (albeit propertyless) bourgeoisie able to exploit society and appropriate much of the fruits of social labor by virtue of the political power they wielded. The proposition that a bureaucracy can constitute itself as a ruling class, a notion remarkably similar to Milovan Djilas's theory of "the new class," was to receive abundant Maoist theoretical elaboration during the Cultural Revolution era.

A third uniquely Maoist theme heard during the last two decades of the chairman's life announced the separation of the concept of the dictatorship of the proletariat from the institution of the Chinese Communist party. Mao's Leninist faith in the organized consciousness of the vanguard party had always been mitigated by a conflicting populist faith in the spontaneous revolutionary creativity of the masses, especially the peasant masses.[41] But it was not until the Hundred Flowers era that Mao explicitly began to question the revolutionary sufficiency of the party, arguing that the Chinese Communist party and even its highest leaders were not ideologically infallible and were therefore to be subjected to criticism by "the people" from without.[42] If the party was no longer immune to bourgeois ideological corruptions, and if it could no longer be relied upon to rectify itself, as Mao now suggested, the question was raised of where the dictatorship of the proletariat resided.

123

A tentative, albeit abortive, answer was provided in the Great Leap Forward campaign. During the years 1958–1960, Maoist theoreticians, drawing heavily from Marx's analysis of the Paris Commune, identified the new rural people's communes as organs of proletarian dictatorship. In the radical Maoist ideology of the time, the communes were conceived not only as more or less autonomous socioeconomic units but also as political entities "performing the functions of state power." The communes were not only to carry out all the social and economic transformations that Marxist theory assigns to the era of the dictatorship of the proletariat, but they were to "merge" the basic economic organizations of society with the basic "organs of state power" in what was celebrated as the period of "the transition from socialism to communism." In the course of that transition, the internal functions of the state (in theory, now appropriated by the communes) would gradually "wither away."[43] The threat that this utopian vision posed to the power of existing state and party bureaucracies is obvious. And it is by no means fortuitous that the most ardent Maoist exponents of that vision (such as Guan Feng, Wang Li, and Qi Benyu) were to be denounced as "ultraleftists" in the waning phases of the Cultural Revolution, as was Chen Boda several years later.

It was with the beginning of the Cultural Revolution, of course, that the Maoist emphasis on the concept of the dictatorship of the proletariat reached its apogee, accompanied by an enormous stress on the gravity of the class struggle between the "bourgeoisie" and the "proletariat," and a wholesale attack on the Chinese Communist party as the institution where the "bourgeoisie" resided. Implicit in the attack on the party was the Maoist acceptance of the notion that bureaucracies could establish themselves as new ruling classes, for it was made clear that the movement was directed against "those within the Party who are in authority and taking the capitalist road."[44] Socialist China, it was proclaimed, was threatened by a "bourgeois restoration" and the dictatorship of the proletariat was in danger of being transformed into a "dictatorship of the bourgeoisie," the leaders of which were obviously in the highest ranks of the Chinese Communist party and its bureaucratic appendages.

Perhaps the most astonishing feature of the ideology of the Cultural Revolution was the Maoist thesis that the main source and site for the struggle between "socialism" and "capitalism" was the state apparatus itself, that it was organized political forces of state and party which were producing (and reproducing) "revisionist" social and economic relationships taking China on the road back to capitalism.[45] This novel Maoist notion is virtually a total inversion of the conventional Marxist theory of the state, for it is based on the assumption that it is not socioeconomic forces which determine the nature of the state but rather the nature of the state — and the consciousness of those who control it — which determines the direction of social development.

Having thus identified the established political apparatus as the source of bourgeois corruptions, and having dismantled much of the party structure in the process, Maoists were confronted with the question of what constituted the dictatorship of the proletariat and where it was located. Two radically different alternatives presented themselves during the course of the Cultural Revolution. On the one hand, the People's Liberation Army, formally under the command of Lin Biao, early in the upheaval announced itself as "the mainstay of the dictatorship of the proletariat." Nothing, of course, could have been more incongruous with the original Marxist concept than the notion that proletarian dictatorship could be exercised by a standing army. On the other hand, radical civilian Maoists advocated that state power, in the form of the dictatorship of the proletariat, be reorganized in accordance with the Marxian principles of the Paris Commune. A noteworthy feature of the Maoist literature on the topic at the time was an eminently Marxist recognition of the state as a partially independent and alien entity; as one theoretician typically put it, echoing Engels, the Chinese state threatened to "change from the servant to the master of society."[46] And the celebrated principles of the Commune were not wholly confined to theory; abortive attempts to implement those principles were made principally in Shanghai but elsewhere as well. There is no need to pause here to inquire as to why those attempts were flawed from the outset and why they ultimately failed.

Neither of the two alternatives long commended themselves to Mao in any event. However many proletarian virtues Mao may have attributed to the PLA, the prominence of the army in the political arena aroused Bonapartist fears, and the soldiers eventually were to be returned to their barracks. And when Mao concluded, in February of 1967, that Paris Commune-style governments were "too weak when it comes to suppressing counterrevolution,"[47] among other deficiencies, the Shanghai People's Commune (presumably based on the Marxian model) was immediately aborted after an undistinguished three-week history. While the leaders of the Cultural Revolution searched fruitlessly for alternative political forms, China's "dictatorship of the proletariat" could find no other place to lodge itself than in the person and thought of Mao Zedong. The masses who had been called upon to rebel against an alien and established political apparatus at the beginning of the Cultural Revolution now subordinated themselves to the all-embracing wisdom of a single leader, presented and perceived as the embodiment of their collective will. The cult of Mao Zedong was one of history's most extreme examples of the alienation of social power and a grotesque outcome of a movement that had been launched under a doctrine that demanded the restoration to society of the powers usurped from it by the state. At the end, the only solution for the political and ideological chaos wrought by the Cultural Revolution was to resurrect and rebuild the Chinese Communist party. At the Ninth Party Congress in 1969, and more fully at the Tenth Congress in 1973, the CCP was restored to its customary Leninist posi-

125

tion as "the vanguard of the proletariat," and presumably again as the main institutional carrier of the dictatorship of the proletariat.

In the years following the conclusion of the Cultural Revolution until the death of Mao Zedong in September of 1976, during the period that the post-Mao leadership in Beijing now condemns as "the feudal-fascist" reign of the Gang of Four (circa 1972–1976), there was a continuing (and, indeed, an increased) emphasis on the concept of the dictatorship of the proletariat in Maoist theory. "Continuing the revolution under the dictatorship of the proletariat" was the guiding ideological slogan of the time. The stress on proletarian dictatorship, however, now was no longer directly connected with the attack on the Communist party, as it had been during the early phases of the Cultural Revolution. Although the Marxist principle that "the dictatorship of the proletariat is a dictatorship by the masses" was repeated in ritualistic fashion, it was clearly laid down that its functions were to be performed "under the leadership of the Party."[48]

Yet the supremacy of the party was by no means totally guaranteed in the Maoist ideology of the era, for discussions of the dictatorship of the proletariat often were accompanied by the novel Maoist thesis that the class struggles which would continue throughout the era of proletarian dictatorship were essentially directed against "the bureaucratic class." There was of course nothing particularly novel in the notion that a prolonged (and even "acute") class struggle would persist throughout the socialist era until the achievement of the "higher stage" of communism. Indeed, the existence of class struggle is the necessary Marxian theoretical rationale for the existence of a dictatorship of the proletariat. Zhang Chunqiao, for example, began his well-known treatise "On Exercising All-Round Dictatorship over the Bourgeoisie" by quoting Lenin's dictum, "Only he is a Marxist who extends the recognition of the class struggle to the recognition of the dictatorship of the proletariat." Zhang proceeded (again closely following Lenin) to attempt to demonstrate the existence of a bourgeoisie and the social basis of its alleged existence, emphasizing the persisting habits of small-scale production which constantly engender "new bourgeois elements."[49]

There was nothing unduly threatening to the party apparatus as long as class struggle was directed against vaguely defined "bourgeois elements." But Zhang went on to strike, however gingerly, an ominous Cultural Revolution chord, observing that a "bourgeois wind [was] blowing from among those Communists, particularly leading cadres."[50] Other radical Maoist theorists were more candid and explicit in identifying the "bourgeoisie" as a new "bureaucratic class" embedded in the Chinese Communist party. The most extensive theoretical treatment of this thesis appeared in a lengthy treatise entitled "The Bureaucratic Class and the Dictatorship of the Proletariat," published shortly before Mao's death. The authors, using the acronym Ma Yanwen, pro-

126

ceeded on the basis of Mao's statement: "The bureaucratic class on the one side and the working class together with the poor and lower-middle peasants on the other are two classes sharply antagonistic to each other."[51] The origin of "the bureaucratic class" was partly attributed to the ideological remnants of bureaucratism left over from the old society, but it was primarily attributed to contradictions generated from within postrevolutionary society itself, especially the opportunism of Communist revolutionaries who became rulers: "After the Communist party came to power, these persons, having become officials or higher officials in particular, soon turned into bureaucrats . . . subverting the dictatorship of the proletariat, rallying under the revisionist line and forming a bureaucratic class." The bureaucratic class, it was charged, was "worse than the capitalists in sucking the blood of the workers," the Cultural Revolution was described as "a major struggle waged between the proletariat and the bureaucratic class" (not, as conventionally, between the proletariat and the bourgeoisie), and the bureaucratic class was identified, in turn, as "the bourgeoisie within the party," who by virtue of their party positions were appropriating capital and authority.[52] Thus it was proclaimed, "overthrowing the bureaucratic class is one of the basic tasks of continuing the revolution under the dictatorship of the proletariat."

The Chinese Communist party had been restored to its Leninist vanguard position in the wake of the Cultural Revolution, for lack of any other viable political institution to take its place, but Maoist suspicions that all was not entirely well within the party remained. For if one of the tasks of the dictatorship of the proletariat was to overthrow "the bourgeoisie within the party," then the exercise of proletarian dictatorship clearly could not be left to the party alone.

Perhaps the most striking feature of Maoist writings on the dictatorship of the proletariat in the 1970s was an enormous emphasis on the more authoritarian aspects of the Marxian concept, an ideological tendency well suited to the Jacobin and repressive character of the politics of the time. The need to strengthen proletarian dictatorship and centralize state power was of course justified by the alleged gravity of the class struggle. As Zhang Chunqiao typically argued: "The class struggle between the proletariat and the bourgeoisie, the class struggle between the different political forces, and the class struggle in the ideological field between the proletariat and the bourgeoisie will continue to be long and tortuous and at times will even become very acute. Even when all the landlords and capitalists of the old generation have died, such class struggles will by no means come to a stop, and a bourgeois restoration may still occur."[53] Hence the necessity to exercise "all-round dictatorship" and the prospect of an increasingly centralized and oppressive state structure. Indeed, there was also the prospect of increasingly arbitrary practices on the part of the state, for the ideology of the time celebrated violence as both a necessary and a desirable attribute of the dictatorship of the proletariat. As typically put: "Instead of opposing the revolutionary violence which conforms to the direction of historical development, Marxists acclaim it."[54] The necessity of "revolutionary violence" also dominated discussions of the Paris Commune. The Paris Commune model of proletarian dictatorship was still praised in the literature, but more for its repressive functions than for its popular democratic political forms. The model, indeed, was viewed as partially flawed because the Communards had indulged in excessive "benevolence" to class enemies and "the commune failed to display the full power of the proletarian dictatorship."[55]

The general theoretical conclusion Maoist ideologists drew from their considerations of the notion of the dictatorship of the proletariat was a renewed emphasis on the importance of the "superstructure" in historical development in general, and particularly the central role of state power in eras of transition from one mode of production to another. As Zhang Chunqiao formulated it: "The superstructure may play a decisive part under given conditions. . . . Historically, every major change in the system of ownership, be it the replacement of [the] slave system by [the] feudal system or of feudalism by capitalism, was invariably preceded by the seizure of political power which was then used to change the system of ownership on a big scale and consolidate and develop the new system of ownership. This is even more so with socialist public ownership."[56]

The Maoist emphasis on the decisive role of the state (and its repressive functions) in eras of sociohistorical transition was abundantly reflected in the historiography accompanying the anti-Confucius campaign of the early 1970s. There is no need here to inquire into the contemporary political origins and implications of the "Pilin, Pikong" (criticize Lin Biao, criticize Confucius) campaign and its diverse ideological messages, often conveyed through obtuse historical allusions and analogies. Suffice it to note that one of the major themes of the movement was to celebrate the historically progressive nature of the Qin dynasty (which unified China under a centralized state structure in the third century B.C.), its first emperor (Qin Shi Huang), and its authoritarian Legalist ideology; and to condemn as historically reactionary the Confucian opposition who represented the interests of the old slaveowning class and attempted to preserve old political divisions and outmoded social relationships.

Among the initial and more significant historiographical efforts was a 1972 article by Guo Moruo, "The Periodization of Ancient Chinese History."[57] In attempting to identify the time of the transition from "slavery" to "feudalism" in ancient China, Guo argued that the lack of adequate documentation for the period made it difficult to distinguish between serf and slave labor in agricultural production. He therefore advised historians to concern themselves less with the peasantry and more with the question of the presence (or absence) of a landlord class. The significance of Guo's article was to redirect attention

128

from the history of the masses to the history of the ruling classes — and from there, inevitably, to the question of the state and the uses of state power by the ruling class.

In the historical writings produced over the next few years, the focus was indeed on the question of the nature, role, and ideology of the state in ancient China. Crucial to bringing about and consolidating the transition from the relations of production of slavery to those of feudalism, it was argued, was the construction of a new, centralized state structure that represented the interests of the new (and relatively progressive) class of great landlords and was capable of consolidating the new feudal relations of production by employing the necessary forces of violence to suppress the restorationist attempts of the old slave-holding class. Equally important was the doctrine of Legalism, which, however harsh, was to be judged as historically progressive insofar as it represented the interests of the new landlord class and promoted the establishment of a centralized state — and particularly insofar as it countered Confucian ideology, which aimed to restore ancient political forms and social relations. The results of the historical inquiries, as typically popularized at the time, praised the "revolutionary dictatorship practiced by Chin Shih Huang," who, it was said, "followed the trend of the development of history, rejected the doctrine of Confucius and Mencius, applied laws advocated by the Legalists, unified China through war, abrogated the vassalage left over from the slaveowning system and established a centralized dictatorship of the feudal landlord class on the basis of the prefectural system. He used this dictatorship to resolutely suppress with violence the reactionary Confucianists who were vainly trying to restore the slave system."[58]

The contemporary political message conveyed by the "lessons of history" was of course not difficult to divine. Just as the "revolutionary dictatorship" of the Qin state had been necessary to consolidate the transition from a "slave" to a "feudal" mode of production in ancient China, so the dictatorship of the proletariat was necessary to guarantee China's contemporary passage from capitalism to socialism. Just as the Qin state was guided by the historically progressive doctrine of Legalism, so the present Chinese state required the guidance of Mao Zedong Thought. And just as the Qin dictatorship was forced to employ violence to prevent the restoration of slavery, so the contemporary proletarian dictatorship was compelled to use "revolutionary violence" to forestall a "bourgeois restoration." It was thus that the history of ancient China, suitably reinterpreted, was invoked to provide historical justification for the political and ideological imperatives of the present. Perhaps the most remarkable feature of these notions from the perspective of Marxist theory was the enormous importance attributed to the superstructure — the state, its leaders, and their ideology — in determining the course of historical development.

While radical Maoist ideologists in the 1970s drew upon the more author-

129

itarian strands in the Marxist-Leninist tradition (and in the Chinese historical tradition) to promote a repressive state structure formally baptized as "the dictatorship of the proletariat," what actually constituted proletarian dictatorship in the People's Republic remained ambiguous — in theory as well as in reality. In formal ideology, the Chinese Communist party (and the state apparatus over which it presided) was the institutional form of the dictatorship of the proletariat. But since the party was still suspected of harboring "bourgeois elements" — and, indeed, was seen as the source and site of a new "bureaucratic class" — the institutional location of the dictatorship of the proletariat remained in doubt. Proletarian dictatorship, in the view of Maoist ideologists, resided only in those parts of the party-state political apparatus deemed to be guided by Mao Zedong Thought and controlled by those deemed to be its authentic carriers. In light of the bitter political struggles that raged at the highest levels of power at the time, however, the question of what constituted China's "dictatorship of the proletariat" was a most murky and ambiguous matter.

The ambiguities were resolved, or at least buried, with the death and burial of Mao Zedong in late 1976, the subsequent purge of the Gang of Four and their supporters, and the ascendancy of Deng Xiaoping and the policy of the four modernizations. Such political authority and legitimacy as were conveyed by the concept of the dictatorship of the proletariat are now firmly attributed to the Chinese Communist party, which, more fully than ever before, has been established in its sacrosanct and infallible Leninist position as "the vanguard of the proletariat" and "the core of leadership of the whole Chinese people."

In the years since Mao's death, the term "dictatorship of the proletariat" has appeared less prominently in Chinese theoretical pronouncements than it did during the preceding two decades. Nonetheless, it is still regarded in official ideology as "the quintessence of Marxism-Leninism" and remains the formal description of the nature of the Chinese state. As the new constitution promulgated in 1978 proclaimed: "The People's Republic of China is a socialist state of the dictatorship of the proletariat led by the working class and based on the alliance of workers and peasants."

Yet, while still proclaimed, the concept has been shorn of the critical and radical ideas with which it was so intimately associated during the Maoist era. First, the persistence of class struggle, the essential Marxian rationale for the necessity of proletarian dictatorship, has been increasingly deemphasized in favor of "the struggle for production" to be undertaken by a more or less united people. Second, the concept of the dictatorship of the proletariat is no longer used to question the revolutionary sufficiency of the Communist party, for it clearly has been laid down that the party is its sole and true institutional carrier. Third, and perhaps most significant, the theory of a bureaucratic ruling class, which often was closely tied to the question of proletarian dictatorship in earlier years, now has vanished from Chinese Marxist writings. It is acknowledged, to be sure, that bureaucracy and bureaucratism remain problems, which are variously attributed to economic and cultural backwardness, the vestiges of feudalism, and the persistence of a "small producers' mentality." But the notion of a new bureaucratic class is now beyond the pale of acceptable political discussion.

During the Maoist era, the concept of the dictatorship of the proletariat was a Janus-faced phenomenon, on the one hand serving to stimulate radical critiques of the existing state apparatus and, on the other, promoting authoritarian and Jacobin forms of political rule which silenced critics of the existing state of affairs. In the post-Maoist era of the People's Republic, as in the Soviet Union, "the dictatorship of the proletariat" is little more than a ritualized slogan invoked to provide a spurious Marxist ideological legitimation for a state that remains more the master than the servant of society.

5

The Chinese State and Its Bureaucrats

RICHARD KRAUS

Most observers agree that one of the consequences of the Chinese revolution has been the accretion of power to the Chinese state. Yet this postrevolutionary state is far from omnipotent. Successive administrations, both radical and conservative, have encountered significant resistance from various sectors of society to some of their most determined policy preferences. Nonetheless, the socialist state has struck root more deeply in Chinese society than did its predecessors.[1] This essay will examine the relationship between state and society as it applies to China's class system, with special attention to the social position of China's bureaucrats.

Against the Reification of the State

The venerable conceptual pairing of state and society has the great merit of drawing attention to the alienation of the state from the citizens whose lives are shaped by its actions. But this insight bears a price: the analytical separation of state from society can easily beguile us into imagining that the state can somehow stand apart from the society in which it is rooted. Once reified in our minds, an unrealistically abstracted state eludes sociological analysis.

Although there is no easy way of penetrating the mystification of social relationships which the state entails, a common procedure in studies of Western politics has been to examine the relationship between this thing we call the state and the class system. One approach has been to focus attention upon the outcomes of state activity to learn whose interests are aided and whose are damaged by government policy.[2] A second method has been to examine the place

I am grateful to the many people who have offered suggestions for improving this paper. I must especially acknowledge the critiques of Stephen Bunker, Belden Fields, Dorothy J. Solinger, Suzanne Pepper, and G. William Skinner.

of the state within the total structure of capitalist society.[3] Finally (and most simply), some students have looked at the personnel who staff the state, with special attention to the web of social interconnections which binds the personnel to members and institutions of various classes.[4]

Studies of Chinese politics have not yet been especially concerned to employ comparable approaches to give flesh to the abstraction of the state. Attention has focused on the policy outcomes of Chinese state activity, which are among the most arresting features of the People's Republic. But such analyses typically have been content to distinguish elite from mass interests — an opposition that is insufficiently refined to capture the complexity of the connection between class and the Chinese state.

Neither have structural interpretations of the Chinese state been well developed. I do not wish to demean the sometimes rarefied contributions of Charles Bettelheim so much as to acknowledge the difficulty of fashioning an adequate structural theory of socialism.[5] In contrast to capitalism, which has been observed in constant formal variation over five centuries, socialism as a genus of social organization is still a historical novelty. Shared perception of the relationship of the socialist state to its class structure is not likely to come easily.

Finally, attention to the collective characteristics of the personnel who staff the Chinese state has been surprisingly low. The surprise comes in part because socialist China's bureaucrats have provided a quality of leadership in both revolution and economic development which, at its best, has been aggressively efficient and honest. There have been ample hints from China that these bureaucrats bear serious examination as a real or potential class. Mao Zedong, for instance, discussed the new contradictions of socialist China with a keen sense for the central role and collective identity of the bureaucrats: "There are several hundred thousand cadres at the level of the county Party committee and above who hold the destiny of the country in their hands. If they fail to do a good job, alienate themselves from the masses and do not live plainly and work hard, the workers, peasants and students will have good reason to disapprove of them. We must watch out lest we foster the bureaucratic style of work and grow into an aristocratic stratum divorced from the people."[6]

The heart of the problem is that students of Chinese politics have found it easier to talk about than to do class analysis, even though one important tradition of Western scholarship has argued that the state becomes intelligible only when related to the structure of human inequality. I offer here no easy formula for overcoming this difficulty; to the contrary, this essay is intended to raise, not solve, problems. My assumption is that the study of the Chinese state must be joined with a consideration of the location of the bureaucrats who staff it within China's changing class structure. The neat opposition of state to society is a hindrance to this undertaking because it resembles too closely the "worldview of the high administrative official," pitting an active state against passive society, thereby masking the interests and the actions of state bureaucrats.[7] In seeking to locate China's bureaucrats within rather than in opposition to the society they administer, three issues will be considered: the relationship of state officials to the means of production, their levels of class consciousness, and the historical antecedents of a bureaucratic class in China.

A Common Relationship to the Means of Production

Let me be as clear as possible just who these bureaucrats are. I include both party and state bureaucrats: they follow a common organizational model (and salary scale) and are jointly identified by the Chinese as "cadres." But I exclude those cadres at the local level who are paid on the basis of collective work-point values rather than fixed state salaries. The career patterns of Chinese officials provide little basis for excluding military bureaucrats from this group; political conflicts between opposing civilian and military interests are as common as disputes pitting the interests of agricultural against industrial cadres or of commercial against propaganda bureaucrats. Although there are many bases for internal disagreement, China's bureaucrats are bound together in a hierarchical organization that sets them apart from the great bulk of the population.[8]

An immediate objection to this enterprise may well be that bureaucrats have no clearly defined individual ownership of the means of production comparable to capitalists or proletarians in the bourgeois society of Marx's theory. This difference is real but is not an adequate basis for denying the applicability of class analysis. For if socialism is new, one should anticipate unprecedented class relationships to emerge from its organization of production. And the bureaucrats do have a relationship to the means of production distinct from the rest of the population: a collective authority over productive assets. The surplus of the Chinese economy is extracted through the leadership of the cadres, and its disposition is planned by them. The "several hundred thousand cadres" of whom Mao spoke are at the county committee level and above, precisely those officials who oversee rather than actively participate in production (the former Maoist interest in the Xiyang model for cadre labor reinforced this distinction — commune, brigade, and team cadres were expected to engage in agricultural labor for one hundred, two hundred, and three hundred days respectively per annum).

Current Chinese administrative practice treats nonproductive county-level and higher officials as a distinctive group. One illustration comes from the procedures followed in preparing Ye Jianying's important speech celebrating the thirtieth anniversary of the founding of the People's Republic. Ye was among the most distinguished (and powerful) surviving members of the founding cohort of Communist revolutionaries, and his commemorative speech was controversial for its negative assessment of the Cultural Revolution. The formal occasion of this speech meant that Ye's references to the Cultural Revolution as a "calamity for our people" and the "most severe reversal to our socialist cause since the founding of the People's Republic" assumed the flavor of an official verdict.[9] Three months before Ye's delivery of this speech, a draft was prepared by a writing group of the State Council and was distributed to all civil cadres at the county level and above, provincial cadres of section head and higher, and military cadres at the battalion level and above. At least ten million cadres were asked to offer suggestions, which provincial writing groups used as the basis for revisions that were returned to the State Council.[10] This elaborate process no doubt served as much to inform lower-level officials of discussions at the party center as to solicit their opinions for revision, but it also reveals the lines employed by the cadres in demarcating officials from the rest of society.

When I say that the relationship of these cadres to the means of production is a collective one, I mean that the individual bureaucrat possesses no assets beyond state office. Unlike capitalists, who by definition possess property by which social position may be protected, individual Chinese bureaucrats are highly vulnerable to discipline by the greater collectivity to which they belong. This system may well prove in the long run to be as powerful a force for group cohesion as is the market rationality that underpins the calculation of capitalist interests.

The bureaucrats' lack of personal material assets intensifies their dependence upon the state that employs them. This dependence colors Chinese political life in important ways. The cadres' lack of security against political criticism and possible removal from office encourages the elaboration of particularistic social networks for political protection. Administrative position bestows upon the official the right to participate in the collective allocation of economic resources and is an important resource in its own right because cadres can use their positions to manipulate promotion and demotion. Cadres typically seek the security imagined to rest in the patronage of more powerful officials, who in turn weave webs of personal dependence as the clients of still higher-ranking cadres. Socialism thus seems to reinforce ancient proclivities toward factionalism among Chinese officials. Moreover, the commonly noted pattern of purge and rehabilitation politics is strengthened by cadre vulnerability. Without private wealth to sustain fallen officials until new quests for power can be launched, cadres purged in one campaign often collectively press for the public reversal of the center's verdict justifying their disgrace, along with the removal of the label that may restrict them to inferior posts. The successive waves of cadre rehabilitations that have taken place since the early 1970s, culminating in the rehabilitation of the "rightist elements" of 1957, fit this pattern.

Officials use their control of the state apparatus to implement policies that will mitigate the impact of their individual vulnerability. Like other classes

135

without private assets (such as pensioners or salaried professionals in the United States), China's bureaucrats are fearful of inflation. Memories of the difficulties faced by civil employees during the Guomindang inflation of the 1940s may contribute to the zeal with which the People's Republic has pursued policies of monetary stability. A sharper example can be seen in the cadres' use of the state to create regular channels for upward social mobility through the school system. Cadres are unable to pass their social positions to their children through bequests of wealth, so they are motivated to support educational certification as an alternative means for transmitting social standing across generations.[11] Elite preparatory schools for cadre children, along with university admissions based upon formal examinations of prior knowledge (rather than selection by such political criteria as membership in a previously underprivileged class, sex, or ethnic group) have been pursued against strong opposition, suggesting the centrality of education to cadre strategies for upward social mobility.[12]

The possible emergence of a class of socialist bureaucrats was envisioned by Engels: "When the working class comes to power, . . . it must, in order not to lose its newly won supremacy, on the one hand, get rid of the old machine of oppression which had been used against it, and on the other hand, *protect itself against its own deputies and functionaries.*"[13] This problem was also taken up by Marx (in *The Civil War in France*), by Lenin (in *State and Revolution*), and by writers as different as Robert Michels, Milovan Djilas, and Leon Trotsky. These works have often been used by critics of socialism as evidence for the inevitability of oligarchy and the ultimate futility of revolution. How, it is argued, can the blood and suffering of revolution be justified if a new advantaged group is born of the struggle against privilege?

The Chinese case suggests that extreme statements of the "new class" argument are too simple. However powerful the bureaucrats of the Chinese state may seem since Mao's death, they cannot unambiguously be characterized as having established an unchallenged domination over the rest of society. One must recall that Chinese officialdom was subjected to indignities in the Cultural Revolution to which no dominant class would ever willingly submit. To argue that other classes have more often prevailed over bureaucrats than the writing of Djilas would allow, however, is not equivalent to denying the class character of the cadres.[14]

Marxist analyses of Western politics often have tended unsubtly to disregard any independent social basis for bureaucratic power, simply assigning bureaucrats the status of hired gun for the capitalist class. However problematic this approach may be for understanding contemporary capitalism,[15] it cannot be applied directly to the phenomenon of socialist bureaucrats unless one accepts uncritically their self-conception as merely the representatives of workers and peasants in the dictatorship of the proletariat. Two competing approaches may be distinguished which recognize the independent nature of bureaucratic

136

power. One considers officials as a state bourgeoisie, emphasizing their role in the accumulation of capital; the other, developing Marx's analysis of Bonapartism, stresses the autonomy of bureaucrats as a nonclass group that flourishes when true classes are immobilized in conflict.

Discussions of state capitalism are rooted in the question of the existence of a "socialist mode of production." There can be no socialist mode of production, argues Louis Althusser, because socialism is transitional — it is part capitalism and part communism.[16] One response to this line of reasoning is that everything is transitional (including capitalism) and that socialism seems well on its way to becoming a permanent feature of the world political economy. The conceptual weakness of a distinctively socialist mode of production is more cogently argued by Immanuel Wallerstein: the contemporary world system is a capitalist system, and because "socialist" societies participate in the production and exchange of commodities in a world market, they cannot be said to have fully transcended capitalist social relationships. Socialism, argues Wallerstein, demands the abolition of capitalism, although one must note that this formulation does not deny the distinctiveness of "socialist" social organization in a capitalist world.[17]

Perception of Chinese cadres as state capitalists, then, does not equate them with the J. P. Morgans and Rockefellers of the days of buccaneer capitalism in the West. Nor need it posit any common identity among bureaucrats of different socialist societies; just as Nazi Germany and liberal Sweden are subsumed under the common label of capitalist, so are there a great diversity of forms of state capitalism. An extreme argument is that socialism is merely the fusion of the state and the capitalist class.[18] A milder version might emphasize the role of the bureaucrats of China in accumulating capital for industrial investment, planning the expansion of commodity production, and coordinating industrialization in a manner analogous to (but distinct from) the West's bourgeoisie. In either version, bureaucrats as state capitalists exercise power through the control of the economic surplus generated by socialist production, usually retaining a distinct proportion of that surplus for their own personal advantage in such forms as high salaries, servants, and the use of automobiles.

The Bonapartist analysis of socialist bureaucrats draws upon a different Marxist tradition. In attempting to explain the political success of Louis Bonaparte in the aftermath of the 1848 revolution in France, Marx emphasized the new emperor's control over the powerful French bureaucracy and his ability to profit from a stalemate in which various powerful class interests were balanced, thus gaining freedom of political movement and manipulation. Although he had not been propelled to power by the bourgeoisie, Bonaparte provided the stability necessary for the maintenance of the bourgeois state. Bonaparte could represent the bourgeois class as a whole precisely because he represented none of its powerful substrata.

A strength of the Bonapartist model which is less evident in the state capitalist approach is its conception of bureaucrats as a group whose power rests upon the mediation of opposing class interests in society. And it is here, in exploring the opposition of worker and peasant interests and the role of the bureaucrats in constantly adjusting and reconciling them, that a Bonapartist analysis assumes greatest interest.

The exiled Trotsky drew extensively upon this strand from Marx in his analyses of the Soviet Union,[19] as did Livio Maitan in his study of the Cultural Revolution.[20] One of the apparent appeals of this mode of analysis has been that it permits attention to the relative autonomy of the state bureaucrats in the twentieth century while still remaining true to Marx's refusal to count bureaucrats as a separate class. Trotsky, for instance, called Stalin's bureaucrats a "stratum," withholding the weightier designation of class on the grounds that these officials did not yet possess individual rights to property. Maitan similarly refrained from discussing a bureaucratic "class" because he saw political rather than economic exploitation in China.

The deeper issue here is the perception of the relationship between politics and economics in the twentieth century. The Bonapartist analysis permits an old-fashioned insistence upon a clear causal priority to superficially strict economic factors. Yet the relationship of politics to economics does not seem to admit such a rigorous distinction, if one accepts the argument of Wlodzimierz Brus: "Extended state interventionism becomes a source of 'politicization of the economy,' and begins to alter the relations between the economic base and the political superstructure. If ownership in an economic sense is understood as actual and relatively permanent disposition over means of production, the direction of dependence begins to be modified here, since in some areas power no longer stems from ownership, but rather ownership stems from power."[21]

A Class in But Not for Itself

"Class" is characteristically a variable category: the sharing of a material basis is only the initial criterion for inspiring classlike behavior. A common relationship to the means of production merely marks a group in analytical terms as a class in itself; the political action waged by a class for itself requires consciousness and organization. This more-or-less quality of class may be seen in Marx's well-known description of the French peasantry:

> The small-holding peasants form a vast mass, the members of which live in similar conditions but without entering into manifold relations with one another. Their mode of production isolates them from one another instead of bringing them into mutual intercourse. ... In so far as millions of families live under economic conditions of existence that separate their mode of life, their interests and their

138

culture from those of the other classes, and put them in hostile opposition to the latter, they form a class. In so far as there is merely a local interconnection among these small-holding peasants, and the identity of their interests begets no community, no national bond and no political organization among them, they do not form a class.[22]

It is immediately apparent that China's bureaucrats possess significant advantages over the French peasants in regard to consciousness and organization. They work together in a highly social form of activity, and they enjoy access to the national, state, and party administrative structures. Nonetheless, there remain serious limitations upon the elaboration of bureaucratic consciousness and organization in contemporary China.

Both consciousness and organization, for instance, are shaped through active opposition to the interests of other classes. For China's cadres, this has meant that the form of their institutions and the content of their ideology have been developed in protracted revolution against foreign imperialism and domestic landlords and capitalists. Tensions that may have arisen among cadres, workers, and peasants have been subsequent to the origin of the bureaucrats; cadre institutions and ideology thus still bear the heavy imprint of their initial direction against classes no longer active in Chinese society. Over time, of course, both ideology and organization can be reshaped by newer conflicts. In the meantime, one might expect a certain lag in consciousness, with the weight of memory and past orientation perhaps artificially emphasizing bureaucratic solidarity with workers and peasants.

Certainly a powerful legitimation for the authority of the cadres is their leadership of a revolutionary struggle that claimed to reform society in the interests of workers and peasants. And there is ample reason to believe that many cadres take this cause very seriously. The civil war and anti-Japanese struggle produced pain and suffering for all of China, and no group made greater personal sacrifice than the cadres of the Communist party (the complex and tragic history of Mao's family is but one example).

Against this background, the world of the cadres has become an establishment since liberation, and establishment membership does not bear the penalties that once offered protection against careerism. The fact that one-half of the members of the Communist party have joined since the Cultural Revolution suggests that the social processes of revolution (and the memories derived from them) may well become less significant once the Hu Yaobang generation of cadres is no longer active in political life. Similarly, the diverse social origins of this generation may give way to a form of class closure in which bureaucrats are increasingly recruited from the children of bureaucrats, a tendency likely to be exacerbated by the elitist reforms of the education system in recent years.[23]

The party's well-known practice of ideological reform seems to have an am-

139

biguous role in the establishment of a bureaucratic consciousness. Rectification and thought reform are certainly consciousness-raising institutions, and an early milestone in the developing cohesion of the cadres was the shared experience of the wartime rectification movement in Yanan. Martin Whyte has shown that formal small group activities can further solidify the bond among cadres.[24] Yet the content of ideological study in China takes away consciousness which the social experience may inspire. The Marxist-Leninist classics are not texts that readily enhance bureaucratic identity and pride. The slogan "Serve the People" may mask cynical emotions, but such an ideology renders illegitimate public appeals on behalf of bureaucratic class interests. Thus it is not surprising that since Mao's death, China's resurgent bureaucrats have first deemphasized the importance of political study in general and then recast many traditional Maoist ideological formulations in language less threatening to their interests. Perhaps the clearest example of such ideological adjustment is the redefinition of intellectuals as part of the working class, a sociological category that provides office-working cadres their best defense against Marxist criticism.[25]

Finally, both state and party, the political institutions through which bureaucratic interests are expressed, are shared with other classes. My insistence upon viewing bureaucrats as a social group must here give way to recognition that bureaucracies are institutional structures in which social struggles are fought. As an arena for class conflict, state and party organizations contain representatives of workers and peasants as well as cadres who may seek to use the state apparatus to serve their own emerging class interests. Thus Maoists were also to wage cultural revolution from within the state, as these renegade bureaucrats appealed to non-cadre classes in an effort to depress the evolution of bureaucratic consciousness among their fellow officials. It is obvious that the impact of other classes within the state can be diminished by new patterns of recruitment into the bureaucracy. If the question of differential class access to political institutions is viewed comparatively, however, China seems quite open. One finds few workers, for instance, in the central institutions of power in American society: corporate boards of directors, the courts, the stock exchange, or Congress.

A Bureaucratic Heritage

An abstract conception of class is of limited value in explaining concrete social situations. Classes assume particular (often national) forms, revealing the powerful influence of shared historical experience. In studies of class politics in the West, for instance, the capitalists and workers of the United States are often characterized as having a very different consciousness from their European counterparts because North America had no protracted struggle against feudalism.

140

The bureaucrats of the People's Republic are a new social group, a class in formation, whose primary bond is a common position in the Chinese social organization of production. But the existence of a powerful bureaucratized class is no novelty in Chinese political life. How are the cadres of the contemporary Chinese state related to the Chinese bureaucratic tradition?

This question has not found a high place on the agenda for the study of Chinese politics perhaps because it sometimes appears to contain its own unsatisfying response: there was no Chinese revolution, but only another bureaucratic restoration. But to explore the comparability of the styles of such celebrated Chinese bureaucrats as Zhou Enlai and Li Hongzhang is not to dismiss the Chinese revolution's outcome as a mere reconstitution of the celestial empire. The structural reforms introduced in the course of revolution and planned industrialization have altered the character of Chinese society in dramatic ways.

Foremost among these changes has been the establishment of socialist institutions. Li Hongzhang's class was propertied; it joined land ownership to state office throughout centuries of domination of Chinese society. Members of the former ruling class (be they called mandarins, literati, gentry, or landlord-bureaucrats) developed interests distinct from those of the present Communist cadres, whose individual lack of productive assets places them alongside the proletariat (in Chinese, the "propertyless class") whose vanguard they claim to be. In imperial China, the desire of bureaucratic families for private land had a deleterious impact upon the accumulation of capital. China's new socialist bureaucrats, however, denied the option of private purchase of land, have a strong incentive to increase public capital formation as a means of enhancing the foundation of their own power. Among the many divergences of current administrative practice from imperial bureaucratic tradition has been the end of the law of avoidance, by which officials were not allowed to serve in their native areas. The new institutional barriers to the acquisition of private fortunes have diminished the need for this particular check against cadre corruption.

It is easy to dismiss as a parlor game the comparison of elements from imperial and contemporary Chinese society. But after considering the analogy of Marxism to Confucianism and arguing against the superficial notion that nothing has changed in China, Joseph Levenson stated: "Still, the appearance of survivals is by no means just a trick of the eye. Many bricks of the old structure are still around — but not the structure. Fragments may survive because they meet a modern taste, not because (more than the fragments forgotten) they must be conveying the essence of an invincible tradition."[26] Among the fragments of the old social structure which have been cultivated most assiduously in the new one is an organizational sensitivity that was long ago analyzed by Max Weber under the rubric of patrimonialism.[27] According to the gloss of Reinhard Bendix, "Weber used the term to refer to any type of government that is organized as a more or less direct extension of the royal household. Officials originate as

141

household servants and remain personal dependents of the ruler as long as patrimonialism remains intact."[28]

Weber's writings on China were of course based upon secondary accounts,
many of which have been superseded both in detail and in fundamental interpretation by contemporary scholarship on China. But the significance of Weber's
excursion into Chinese historical sociology is not the accuracy of his Sinology
but the enduring utility of the ideal-type by which he sought to capture a fundamental dynamic of Chinese political life. Weber elaborated his opposition of
ruler to royal household into a broader patrimonial characteristic of creative
tension between monarch and officialdom. Levenson's writings are the most
notable contemporary effort to interpret imperial Chinese politics as a mutual
tension between throne and officials, a vital opposition of interests which long
invigorated the culture of Chinese politics.[29]

Many of the characteristics of patrimonial rule, such as the sharp distinction
between the learned and the untutored, have been vigorously combated by the
Communist party. It is equally apparent that the struggle against China's man-
darin past has been strongly colored by that patrimonial-bureaucratic tradition.
As Levenson suggests, the analogs are too common to ignore. Like the former
gentry, the socialist cadres advocate an open, nonhereditary bureaucracy,
staffed by generalist officials. The Maoist opposition of redness to expertise
echoes the Confucian maxim, a gentleman is not a tool. Both literati and cadres
emphasize moral suasion as a device for rule preferable to fixed legislation, and
models of virtue are still propagated as exemplars for the populace. While the
lessons learned from Marx, Engels, Lenin, and Mao surely differ in content
from those contained in Confucius, Mencius, and the dynastic histories, the
assumption that wisdom may be derived from the judicious study of classic
texts remains constant. Contemporary enthusiasm for mass construction projects recalls the ancient corvée; both are within a tradition of state supervision of
public works. Again, the patrimonial model calls attention to the importance of
court intrigue — various groups seeking the attention of the emperor. The demise of Lin Biao or of the Gang of Four was certainly more complex than the
machinations of palace eunuchs, but the parallel demands more serious examination than it typically receives.

There is a temptation to explain such parallels only as cultural characteristics;
after all, the imperial mandarinate's ascendancy endured for many centuries,
and its orientations toward political life are not likely to be obliterated easily.
But Levenson's hint that one must look for structural factors to explain such
survivals demands that we do more than dismiss patrimonial features of the
contemporary Chinese state as vestigial. Weber insists that the "patrimonial
office lacks above all the bureaucratic separation of the 'private' and the 'official' sphere."[30] In drawing a sharp distinction between patrimonial and what he
regarded as "modern" bureaucratic administration, Weber offers a point which

is applicable as well to a socialist state in which officials lack independent material resources:

> In contrast to bureaucracy, therefore, the position of the patrimonial official derives from his purely personal submission to the ruler, and his position via-à-vis the subjects is merely the external aspect of this relation. Even when the political official is not a personal household dependent, the ruler demands unconditional administrative compliance. For the patrimonial official's loyalty to his office . . . is not an impersonal commitment . . . to impersonal tasks which define its extent and its content, it is rather a servant's loyalty based on a strictly personal relationship to the ruler and on an obligation of fealty which in principle permits no limitation.[31]

The first generation of the People's Republic is not merely the initial step through yet another trip around the traditional dynastic cycle. The structural continuities that may sustain patrimonial modes of interaction exist amid structural innovations of enormous significance, chief of which has been the mass mobilization into political life of ordinary citizens. Yet this mobilization has been poorly institutionalized, in part because Mao and his associates were suspicious of the conservative drift that often accompanies permanent institutions. In the absence of "modern" Weberian legal-rational institutions, the ruler-subject bond (in new guises as chairman-masses and sometimes party-masses relationships) has formed a basis for political activity that captures important aspects of a patrimonial model originally fashioned for a state with severely limited political participation.

Patrimonial officials, it must be remembered, do not necessarily relish their dependence upon the state, with its consequent inhibition of bureaucratic autonomy. Classic remedies attempted by unwilling officials include efforts to subvert patrimonialism into a form of feudalism, thereby endowing themselves with the relative security of fiefs, in contrast to the insecurity of their official prebends. Less drastic is a tempering of patrimonial discretion by increased reliance upon formal rules, a pattern found in the frequent recourse to Legalist administrative practices among county magistrates in the Qing dynasty.[32] Another classic defense of the bureaucrat against the demands of the patrimonial ruler was the distinction between officials of the "inner" and "outer" courts. In the late Tang dynasty, the inner court included Hanlin scholars, eunuchs, and other officials with direct access to the emperor, in opposition to the regular civil and military bureaucracies.[33] The former officials were subject to the personalistic pressures and "Byzantine" politics that Weber describes, but the latter group of bureaucrats were less readily incorporated into the patrimonial model.

Resistance to patrimonialism is certainly evident in China today, where a variety of measures have been implemented or proposed to limit what is identi-

143

fied as the "feudal patriarchal" system through which Mao Zedong extended his influence, especially in the last decade of his life. The purge of the ruler's closest personal followers is an obvious step, which included not only the Gang of Four, bound to the chairman by close personal ties, but also rivals of the four. Wang Dongxing, for instance, used his position as head of the 8341 military unit — Zhongnanhai's palace guard — to arrest Jiang Qing and her three allies, only to continue to use his classically patrimonial position to become party vice-chairman. His forced resignation in 1979 was a victory for those who seek to prevent the reestablishment of leftist patrimonialism now that the strong founder of the dynasty is dead. To prevent such a development ambitious schemes have been announced for the extension and strengthening of the legal system, as well as campaigns to regularize administrative procedures. Each of these is a reasonable course of action for intellectuals and for middle and upper-level officials who may be eager to dig in and protect themselves against some future central leader who might use patrimonial methods to appeal to lower-class interests, as did Mao.[34]

Our inattention to questions such as these reflects the decline of scholarly interest in the patrimonial model after Weber's death in 1920. It is only in recent years that American social scientists have been exposed to a reexamination of patrimonialism in the diverse writings of Etienne Balazs, Guenther Roth, Norman Jacobs, S. N. Eisenstadt, Randall Collins, Simon Schwartzman, and Lloyd Rudolph and Susanne Hoeber Rudolph.[35] In different ways, these writers have employed patrimonial concepts in analyzing the politics of certain preindustrial or Third World societies. This renewal of interest in what had become a museum piece of historical sociology coincided with the declining persuasiveness of modernization theory, which had been intolerant of the geographical specificity of patrimonialism — for not all societies have been patrimonial, whereas none was allegedly immune to the process of modernization.

In a related vein, the dead end of Marx's musings about an Asiatic mode of production also discouraged interest in what is distinctively Asian about Chinese society.[36] And finally, for many years after liberation, the novelty of the Chinese revolution overshadowed continuities with past social behavior. Indeed, in this period perhaps the most serious effort to root the new Chinese government in its imperial past was Karl A. Wittfogel's anticommunist *Oriental Despotism*, a work whose insights were obscured for many by the shrillness of its polemic.[37]

The patrimonial model of analysis also fell into the midst of an overdrawn opposition of Marx to Weber. If these two thinkers were at odds, then surely one must either choose class or patrimony as an analytical orientation. The point is given special meaning when we read the China watchers, who are typically disinterested in class yet practice a vulgar patrimonialism from Hong Kong (Who is Mao's niece? Which faction has the upper hand? Look how well veterans of the Fourth Field Army have done, and so on), as if revolution were irrelevant.

But Marx and Weber pose no either-or choice, and a class analysis of Chinese politics must recognize that the Chinese do organize into factions, that Mao often took cues from past leaders of an imperial Chinese state, and that court intrigue is a significant feature of Chinese political life. The problem is not to oppose patrimonialism to class analysis but to integrate the two.

Any society contains multiple axes around which social relationships can be constructed; patrimonial and class structures exercise contradictory influences upon individual Chinese; but there is no reason why these two aspects of Chinese reality cannot be analytically compatible. The work on patron-client ties in Southeast Asia by James Scott, for instance, succeeds in taking account of both class differences and patronage structures.[38] For the study of China, we might examine more seriously the links between Zhongnanhai cliques and the class appeals made in the course of apparently factional politics. That class analysis now has been displaced by power-struggle interpretations in Beijing, as well, should not blind us to the persistent class dimension in Chinese political life.

Failure to develop similar lines of inquiry may in the end deny us insight into what is *Chinese* about Chinese socialism. The tradition that has been inherited (even if sometimes unwillingly) by Communist officials continues to engender a high level of distinctively national organizational sensitivity and occasional bureaucratic brilliance in the face of enormous problems of governance. I do not mean to diminish the role of the revolutionary experience in leading the cadres to acquire new administrative skills. Nor, it should be clear, do I mean to imply that today's bureaucrats are merely landless mandarins. Attention to the past of Chinese officialdom may, however, increase our understanding of the differences between Chinese and Soviet bureaucrats, whose relationship to the means of production seems similiar.

The ambiguity surrounding the phrase "state power" is difficult to resolve without locating the state within a particular class structure. Although this procedure is commonly employed in studies of Western, capitalist politics, it has not been popular in the study of China. One reason may be an unstated assumption by some scholars that discussions of social inequality in the People's Republic are somehow anti-China, disdainful of the revolution. Such an attitude unthinkingly arrogates to Westerners the act of validating the Chinese revolution, which does not need our assistance. Its past achievements will not be sullied nor will its present accomplishments diminish in significance if North American social scientists begin to confront the fact that class tensions are a primary determinant of the nature of the Chinese state.

A second impediment to the development of a sensitive class analysis of Chinese politics has been the awkwardness of fit between a theory of capitalist,

145

Western provenance and a socialist, Chinese reality. The problem is not that class has been completely ignored but that the categories employed have embodied only those classes already active at the time of the socialist transformation of 1956.

The most problematic social group in the class analysis of contemporary China is the cadres. Although there is likely to be little consensus about how this group can be most usefully perceived, the cadres' common position in the social organization of production has clearly given them shared material interests. Students of Chinese politics have understandably been fascinated by the often sharp internal divisions among these bureaucrats;[39] this fascination has perhaps unfortunately sometimes deflected our attention from common interests that encourage bureaucratic cohesion. Intrabureaucratic conflicts have been organized around such divisions as generation, region, and faction; little effort has been spent examining the extent to which these internal conflicts can also be related to distinctions in the *type* of productive assets groups of cadres may control.

These bureaucratic interests are not necessarily inherently in contradiction to the interests of workers and peasants. To the contrary, a primary collective interest of the bureaucrats surely must be the maintenance of institutions of public ownership. Some individual bureaucrats may tolerate limited erosion of socialism, striking deals with a small private sector (including the toleration of agricultural decollectivization, underground factories, and illegal speculation). As a class, however, bureaucrats find in socialist institutions an unprecedented power base. Insofar as socialist institutions have improved the lot of China's worker and peasant majority, there is a coincidence of interests on this fundamental point.

Nonetheless, there remain important areas of potential conflict between bureaucrats and the clients they serve. One obvious point of contention is the distribution of benefits in Chinese society. Public austerity has marked the life style of cadres since liberation — even accounts of cadre malfeasance impress one with the simplicity of behavior judged decadent in China (for example, Deng Xiaoping's fondness for bridge). But it is readily apparent that bureaucrats enjoy often extravagant economic advantages over both peasants and workers. If bureaucrats were to abandon their spartan public image, or even to increase their consumption of the surplus they administer, class tensions would likely increase.

A second critical area is access to the bureaucratic group. Debates over education policy are paramount here because their outcomes may establish regular procedures by which future cadres will be selected. To the extent that cadre children are favored by educational institutions, the bureaucrats may become an increasingly closed class, cut off from the rejuvenating effect of continuous absorption of worker-peasant activists.

146

A third problem area stems from the bureaucrats' position as mediators between workers and peasants, who are themselves only precariously allied. The conflicting demands of industrialization upon an explicitly agricultural foundation, the hallmark of Chinese development strategy, are not easily contained. China's cadres have to date demonstrated enormous skill in reconciling peasants to a lower standard of living than workers and in simultaneously withstanding worker demands for pay raises that would increse the urban-rural gap. Clumsy handling of this delicately balanced relationship could well magnify the level of open class conflict with which the bureaucrats must contend.

6

The Societal Obstacle to China's Socialist Transition: State Capitalism or Feudal Fascism

EDWARD FRIEDMAN

The Solution Is Socialism

China's state power holders remain committed to building socialism. They seek sustenance and inspiration for creatively and humanely grappling with the almost intractable problems and conflicts of their country in the tradition of Karl Marx, V. I. Lenin, and Mao Zedong.

The idea that Chinese leaders seek a socialist answer seems odd to many outside observers of both Left and Right persuasions. Many foreign leftists, including some who once proclaimed themselves ardent supporters of a unique Chinese path toward communism, insist that China's post-Mao rulers have taken an antisocialist road, which actually leads back to capitalism. Many anti-Marxist foreigners, on the other hand, looking at China's two decades of relative rural stagnation and staggering urban inhumanities, contend that the Chinese must now know they have to choose capitalism and stability, instead of continuing a revolution which in fact brings, not progress and liberation, but continued massive poverty and paralyzing, cruel terror.

The foreign consensus, Left and Right, that China has abandoned socialism contains some truth but misses the central point, the issue on which there was little disagreement in China. In addition to power, the ruling groups in China were fighting over *how* to develop a nation that could avoid the exploitation, dependence, and inhumanity of capitalism and imperialism. The answer to the "how" is not obvious. But the dedication to seeking an answer through socialism is total.

In the 1500s western Europe suffered through a century of religious wars. The result for many was a belief in religious toleration. Few took the monstrous bloodletting as proof that one should abandon Christ. Whether the issue is burning witches, carrying out an inquisition, or discovering corruption among

148

church leaders, members of that religious tradition do not respond by abandoning faith in the Gospels. They work within the tradition, to purify it, improve it, and make it relevant so that its assumed truth and humane essence will flourish.

We can learn much about the limits and possibilities of socialism in China by following some of the most prominent Chinese exponents of different answers to "how" to build socialism and remove the obstacles to advancing on that path.[1] There have been two dominant responses to the question of what is the obstacle blocking socialist progress. Some Chinese believe the obstacle is fascist feudalism. Others conclude that it is statist capitalism. There is much diversity and motion within and across the two theoretical approaches to socialism and the Chinese state. I will focus here on a few of the most important positions in this ongoing debate. My purpose is not to take sides but to clarify what is shared or slighted or omitted or exaggerated. I want to begin to learn how prominent socialist thinkers in China, who identify with a tradition of revolutionary Marxism, comprehend and work within the bounds of their socialist tradition.

Feudal Fascism as the Enemy of a Socialist State

On May 16, 1966, a circular from Beijing indicated that Mao Zedong had aligned himself with various power groups who cried that "capitalist-roaders" controlled the levers of state power in China. These power groups closed schools. They urged students and then younger employees, especially in urban administrative centers, to seek out and pull down people with authority who allegedly were "taking the capitalist road." What erupted was dubbed the Great Proletarian Cultural Revolution.

Even in 1966 Mao set strict limits on this struggle, ordering participants not to disrupt production. By early 1967, Mao expressed second thought on the Cultural Revolution. He discouraged Cultural Revolutionaries from trying to implement in China Karl Marx's program for the Paris Commune of 1871, which Marx had once described as a model for a proletariat in power.

By mid-1967, Mao further reined in the Cultural Revolutionaries, ordering them not to invade the military in a search for capitalist-roaders. People who continued the Cultural Revolution, even aiming their arrows at targets perilously close to Mao himself, became Mao's enemies. By 1968, the "516" or May Sixteenth Group, once the ideological heartbeat of the Cultural Revolution, was stopped and its leaders were jailed. Schools were reopened. Millions of youngsters who had participated in the often violent chaos of the preceding two years were sent to live on distant rural frontiers, where they were treated, at best, with circumspection, suspected of being punished as political criminals.

Mao then tried to consolidate what he saw as the gains of the previous two

149

years, projects such as upgrading rural health care. Those who instead insisted on continuing the Cultural Revolution struggle to control levers of state power also became Mao's enemies. Mao moved against Chen Boda, the leading theorist of the danger of state capitalist restoration. Chen had insisted that only extraordinary efforts could avoid the supposed evils of Titoism, of China following Yugoslavia and abandoning socialism for a decentralized, market economy that would eventually turn into capitalism. Mao also began to move against Chen's ally, Minister of National Defense Lin Biao, who had been Mao's major military prop since 1966.

Lin and his closest colleagues tried to preempt Mao. They failed and fled, and in September 1971 Lin died. Lin's leading opponents among China's ruling groups denounced him as a Confucian feudalist and urged upon China's people the need for an antifeudal struggle. But some ruling groups still shared the feudal Lin-Chen persuasion. Their riposte was to turn the struggle against the leader of the antifeudal group, Prime Minister Zhou Enlai.

These upheavals made no fundamental change in China's structure of state power. The problem was not a group of dethroned feudalists but a still powerful feudal system. In 1973 – 1974 in the southern city of Canton, once a Lin Biao stronghold, a group of young, former Cultural Revolution activists, who had earlier been jailed by Lin Biao's Canton allies, launched an attack on the feudal Lin Biao system.[2] They posted a series of pages, which concluded that "feudal fascism" still held sway in People's China. Their essay was published and circulated not only outside of China but also among key power groups in China.[3]

One theorist of the writing group was Wang Xizhe.[4] Wang wanted to understand why, even after the removal of Chen Boda and Lin Biao, so little had actually changed. People closely associated with Lin went unpunished, yet veteran revolutionaries, victims of the Cultural Revolution's mass vigilantism, were still treated as enemies of the people. The writing group concluded that a system, which they called the Lin Biao system, was still in place. Wang Xizhe set out to analyze the inner dynamics of this system, which, he concluded, if left to its natural tendencies, would carry China not to socialism but to fascistic feudalism.

Wang found that the Cultural Revolution had in fact not been a second revolution preventing a capitalist restoration, as its defenders claimed. Instead, it had firmly established the Lin Biao system, which was fascist and feudal. Its army was feudal, infused with patron-client relations. Its political party was also feudal, premised on patriarchal ruler-vassal relations.

The Cultural Revolution did, however, have an important impact. Its "cruel reality" revealed to many citizens the ugly truth about the Lin Biao system, the feudalistic nature of the Chinese state. As a result, China now had a large number of people newly dedicated to demolishing that feudalism and democratizing the Chinese state.

150

Wang Xizhe and his colleagues said that simple humanity and "the blood of the martyrs" cried out for democratization and legal rights. The survivors of the Cultural Revolution's violence were morally compelled to speak for the victims. The alternative was to institutionalize fascism, which, in the Cultural Revolution, produced, according to the series of pages posted in Canton, "massacres," "scum hole detention pens," "bloody butcheries," opponents "mercilessly dealt with," "suppression, apprehension, beating-up and execution," "framed cases," "those who were imprisoned are still in prison," "lawlessness and recklessness, gangsterism and killing, kidnapping males and abducting females and the total rejection of the rule of law," "arrests everywhere, suppressions everywhere, miscarriages of justice everywhere," "shackles, iron-bar windows, leather whips and bullets," and "savage corporal punishment." "The number of people put to death . . . was not limited to a few hundred or thousands." What was needed was full socialist democracy and a legal system that began by punishing "the 'ministers' who have committed the heinous crimes of transgressing the law, knowingly violating the law while enforcing it, creating fabricated cases, using the public to avenge personal grudges, establishing special cases without authorization, instituting prisons without authorization, using unlimited corporal punishment and practicing wanton murder."

We may not know exactly how many hundreds of thousands were killed, how many millions were tortured, maimed, or driven mad, but the claims of the group refer to known events. Having exposed the political fascism of mass vigilantism, with violence replacing legal processes, the Wang group sought the causes of China's continuing feudalism.

Wang Xizhe and those who saw as he did that the path up the mountain toward communism was grown over with feudal vines considered themselves Marxist materialists. They believed that China had to forge material tools strong enough to dig out or cut down the deep-rooted, weighty obstructions. Their adversaries claimed the major problem to climbing the mountain was capitalist-roaders, people whose consciousness, attitudes, and ideas left them without the will to make the long, hard trek. Opponents of capitalist-roaders have often been labeled "voluntarists" by foreign analysts because of their belief that if one had the will — not so much the material means — one would find the way. I will describe them as "Marxist idealists." In contrast to the Marxist materialists, who stressed material progress to defeat feudal remnants, Marxist idealists focused on changing ideas so that people would act to defeat adversaries who supposedly insisted on taking a capitalist path.

Both Marxist materialists and Marxist idealists agreed that a privileged stratum held power in China and would preclude progress through a socialist transition in which state power holders should be servants of the people, not masters standing over and above the citizenry. The two groups differed in their analysis of the source of the problem. For Marxist materialists the painful problem, so

151

cruelly manifested in the Cultural Revolution, was an institutionalized feudal state system.

Wang Xizhe depicted the dynamic principles on which this feudal state operated and replicated itself. As with all feudal systems, its dominant value was loyalty. Its holy writ was "worship of Mao Zedong thought as a kind of religion." Its feudal rulers rewarded those who incanted the magic words, who said them as morning prayers or evening penitences, who could prove themselves "the most . . . the most . . . and the most. . . ." The Wang group's description was accurate. Indeed, observant travelers to China noted such ritualism even before Wang's group posted its essays.[5] In a Chinese village where I subsequently lived, during the Cultural Revolution the family of the old village leader and other loyalists delayed the start of a meal to recite a verse from the sayings of Mao Zedong as collected and published by Lin Biao.

In the state system of Chinese feudalism, meeting halls for such rituals effectively were "gambling houses that offered 10,000 times profit for one unit of capital." The case of Zhang Tiesheng exemplified how the system worked. As a student, Zhang handed in a blank examination and got the Marxist idealists for testing him in course content instead of in revolutionary attitude, which should always come first. The powerless, vulnerable teacher giving the exam was vilified as a capitalist-roader. The incident was called to the attention of one of the lords in the Marxist idealist camp. Zhang's loyalty was rewarded. He rose swiftly. He was put forth as an exemplar of socialist loyalty (a feature that led some of the Marxist materialists to describe their opponents as social feudalists or feudal socialists) so that others would try to invent ways to prove themselves yet more loyal. People competed for favors from on high.

The result was tendencies toward redividing China into fiefs in which powerful lords in control of levers of state power extracted wealth from modern serfs tied to the land or assigned to labor for life in one guild or another and then redistributed that wealth among noble lords and their loyal followers. The emerging system was defined by personalistic relations of patron and client, lord and vassal. The individual had little or no independent mobility. This form of feudalism infected the army, the party, civil government bureaucracies, and all work units from farm and factory to school and stage.

A real feudal system was obscured by a rhetoric of proletarian dictatorship. The lords on high enjoyed "shockingly high-class luxuries." Their family and friends, vassals and courtiers, those loyally and personally connected, would inherit the state, which replicated itself on feudal criteria.

Merit was not a decisive criterion for job, reward, or promotion. Ordinary workers in farm and factory, the Wang group pointed out, were not rewarded for their productivity. Wages were not increased in line with output, and in factories bonuses were abolished. Farmers were told to prove their loyalty to the state by turning over more grain (at preestablished, low prices) and by abandoning sideline production that gave cash profits to their own local unit. Yet even if patriotic, hardworking Chinese citizens produced more, the slogan of working for socialism masked the feudal reality. The working people did not have more with which to satisfy their needs and wants. Rather, the feudal rulers had more for a luxurious life and for distribution to their loyal followers and their pet projects. The Wang group called for thoroughgoing democratization by means of reward for merit and productivity and the end of personalistic favoritism, creation of democracy and legal protection to replace nepotism with punitivism, and institutions bringing supervision of the state by the people so that corrupt and arbitrary power could not be hidden. The structured bureaucratic corruption disgusted the many good people who saw through the hypocritical rhetoric that thinly masked the fact that in the Cultural Revolution one set of overlords had replaced another. The feudal state system delighted those who learned to play and win the feudal game, which the Wang group described as a combination of grotesque rituals of religiosity and political speculation.

The reality of feudalism was exposed by the fraud of the Cultural Revolution's promise of broad and genuine democracy, as in the Paris Commune in 1871. At the outset of the Cultural Revolution, young people were invited, even prodded, to post attacks written with big characters as part of organizing to pull down capitalist-roaders. These vigilante eruptions led to thousands of sadistic atrocities. But once veteran revolutionaries, Marxist materialists, were ousted, the momentary vigilante democracy was smashed and the idealistic young rebels were disbanded, sent into internal exile, jailed, or sometimes even executed.[6] The Wang Xizhe group would suffer years of cruel incarceration.

Acts that had been encouraged and permitted were denied. Criticism was punished. Big-character posters were ripped down. The democratic forms were exposed as tactics used by feudal power holders to destroy their opponents. That power goal accomplished, the rebels were smashed.

The Wang Xizhe group addressed two new questions. How could democracy be institutionalized and legal rights guaranteed? What social group had an interest, as well as sufficient strength, to achieve democratic, antifeudal purposes?

An analogy with ancient Chinese history suggested an answer. Chen Sheng and Wu Guang, peasant revolutionaries from the third century B.C., had allied with supporters of overthrown kingdoms to dethrone the cruel rulers of the new central empire established by Qin Shi Huang Di. In like manner, the veteran revolutionaries overthrown by China's feudal fascists would be willing now to replace that feudal empire with democratized socialism. The Wang Xizhe group believed the victims of the Cultural Revolution would be willing to democratize China. The horrors of the Cultural Revolution had forced the victims to think over matters previously taken for granted. They would see that carrying out socialist democratization required a critical reconsideration of the texts of their socialist tradition. The democratizers would have to see that those who polemicized against state capitalism actually defended feudal fascism.

Even the great creator, unifier, and despot, Qin Shi Huang, that is, Mao

153

himself, would have to be examined critically and not from an attitude of reverential respect. Only then could Chinese think and move toward a democratization in which feudal power was ended, reward followed merit instead of patronage, and the living standards and opportunities of all — not just feudal lords — were raised.[7]

The task would not be easy. Millennia of Chinese history, millennia of feudal social relations had made presuppositional those feudal notions of holy writ, obedience and respect for superiors. Such reactionary ideas and habits were deeply imbued, not least of all, in the minds of the Chinese rulers. What was needed, therefore, Wang argued, was a continuation of the original, though still incomplete, democratic antifeudal struggle. Socialism could not be built on a feudal basis. Those who, in contrast, spoke not against feudalism but against capitalist restoration were actually the feudal fascists trying to entrench themselves and their own kind by preventing the extensive democracy required to complete China's antifeudal revolution. To continue toward socialism meant democratizing the state and dismantling a system of reward to friends and family; it meant ending the institutions and processes of a feudal state.

State Capitalism as the Enemy of a Socialist State

To the Marxist idealists, who saw state capitalism as the major obstacle to China's progress, the materialist attack on feudal fascism confirmed their worst fears, for it proved there were capitalist-roaders trying to reverse China's socialist gains.

Democracy, as all Marxist-Leninists supposedly knew, was a capitalist slogan. It served capitalist class purposes. Working people needed a ruling party to represent them, which would command and wield the levers of state power in their interest. To demand the democratization of a workers' party state in the name of merit and material reward meant removing power from true communists and turning power over to a system free to exploit working people.

The Marxist idealists did not claim that a privileged ruling stratum did not exist. They even acknowledged that the Lin Biao clique operated as the Wang group described, "wining and dining, making presents and promising official posts and other favors as a means of luring people into their clique."[8] But the Marxist idealists found the source of such antisocialist practices in the remnants, not of a feudal state, but of a state capitalist system.

According to an article in the party's Central Committee paper published a year and a half after the arrest of Marxist idealist leaders, the sharpest and most systematic presentation of their critique of state capitalism had been published under the name Ma Yanwen (the ideographs meaning "Essays from Marxist Research"),[9] a group that had produced four essays early in 1976 in an effort to legitimize its struggle for state power.[10]

154

The Ma group placed the contemporary struggle against state capitalism in China in the historical context of struggle against the enemies of socialism. So far, the group argued, capitalism had developed through three stages: free capitalism, monopoly capitalism, and now state capitalism. Marx had analyzed the laws of free capitalism. Lenin had revealed the imperialist logic of monopoly capitalism. Mao had pinpointed the processes of state capitalism. The Ma group focused on what revolutionary socialists had to struggle against in each stage to assure further progress toward communism.

Marx had shown that behind free capitalism's slogans of liberty, equality, and fraternity lay laws of capital, which in fact brought dependence, inequality, and dehumanizing exploitation. The laws of capital had to be exploded. Lenin had shown how misled socialists in the stage of monopoly capitalism took worker organizations into trade unionism and parliamentary socialists into reformism which, even in combination, could never force a breakthrough out of capitalism and into freedom. A Leninist party vanguard was needed. Socialist revisionists, according to Lenin, weakened the will of socialist revolutionaries with promises of peaceful evolution, public ownership, and a managed economy.

The successful struggles of Stalin after the seizure of state power pioneered the new path. Even after Lenin's Bolshevik party won power, socialist progress was not guaranteed. Bukharin was the anti-Stalin theorist of revisionism who, had he succeeded, could have reversed the conquests of socialist struggles. Bukharin insisted that with state power in the hands of a party dedicated to a transition through socialism, a capitalist class could not reemerge. Rapid, forced collectivization was therefore not necessary because rich peasants could gradually enter the general system of socialism. Stalin, fortunately in this view, forced through collectivization against the threat of capitalism in the countryside.

But even what Stalin did was not enough. Socialism lost out first in Tito's Yugoslavia and then in Khrushchev's USSR so that people had come to power in those countries who, the Ma group wrote, were far worse than Hitler's Nazis. Stalin, not seeing the danger clearly (and making errors in his policies toward party and state officials, toward intellectuals and scientists, and toward education), left an unstable situation in which Khrushchev *et al.*, using the slogan "to all according to their work," could establish a bureaucratic, monopoly capitalist ownership system.

Mao had systematically investigated the dangers of what Lenin had called "a capitalist state without capitalists." That analysis proved that China's materialist democrats could not, and would not, carry the revolution through to the end. Like Bukharin, they would stop at the democratic capitalist stage. They were mirror images of the peasants who would have stopped the revolution after land was distributed to the tillers. They were not true communists. They served only their own narrow interests, "the interests of the big bureaucrats" (*da guan de liyi*), wrote the Ma group.

Collectivization and nationalization operated by laws, Mao showed, which benefited the democratic capitalists. After liberation China still was shaped by the norms, assumptions, and notions inherited from capitalism. These included historic inequalities between city and countryside and between those who labored with their minds and those who engaged in manual labor. It included an unequal wage system for producers and a hierarchically graded payment system for officials. It included the distribution of commodities in accord with unequal monetary disbursements. This system provided a seemingly legitimate basis, which, in fact, skewed wealth and power to the benefit of mental workers, especially the highest level urban officials. The result would be that big bureaucrats became entrenched; bureaucratic state capitalism would become institutionalized. The dynamic of a capitalist state without capitalists would evolve into a capitalist state dominated by state capitalists.

Mao's great contribution was his analyses of this revisionist possibility within the third stage of capitalism created by socialist revolutionaries. Mao had exposed the hidden laws of state capitalism. To reverse those laws, the Marxist idealists had to launch a long-term struggle against bourgeois rights; that is, people had to learn to change their world-view, their values and expectations. Only if that ideational struggle were central to China's politics could capitalist restoration be prevented. At the same time, a political struggle had to be launched against those who promoted and benefited from the hidden laws of state capitalism. Either those laws and groups would be overthrown, or capitalism would be restored in China and every other state claiming to be socialist.

Khrushchev's revisionists (including China's Khrushchev, Liu Shaoqi and the capitalist-roaders) were thereby defined as the world's most dangerous enemies because they could reverse the highest achievements so far attained in socialist struggles. Khrushchev had called off class struggle and described the state he ruled as a state of all the people. For Mao, the Ma group wrote, such ideas provided the camouflage behind which capitalist-roaders could recreate capitalism. These Khrushchevian-revisionist notions blinded working people in potentially socialist states from seeing the bureaucratic capitalists in power as the class enemies of proletarian power. In short, as Marx had scientifically shown how the extraction of surplus value was the secret to capitalism's first stage, so Mao had shown how the end of class struggle was the secret to capitalism's third stage.

Mao's answer to the question, What kind of a state is it that is being built in this period? was: It is not a feudal state but a capitalist state. Consequently, everything now rested on exposing and defeating the antifeudal, materialist democratizers who reinforced the capitalist tendencies of China's state capitalism.

Capitalist inequalities had to be reversed by moving to ever larger units of distribution, ultimately to the destruction of collective ownership and local distribution and the implementation instead of state ownership guaranteeing equal distribution for all. Everything therefore turned on the attitude that informed the action of state power holders, who could and should keep pressing ahead toward communist ownership and equal distribution.

Capitalist-roaders in power were to be distinguished by their economic policies from communists who would continue the revolution. The Ma group argued that since "the new historical stage" was a struggle against the capitalist dynamics of bourgeois rights, power holders (who, on the contrary, promoted material incentives, pay according to work, economic accounting, meeting consumption needs, and the like) were objectively strengthening the hierarchical inequalities that provided a system into which their own privileged state positions fit. Ordinary workers would therefore be further exploited while bureaucrats were safely privileged.

The issue was not economic growth. The Marxist materialists may have argued that to ignore accepted notions of economic fairness would decrease work enthusiasm and lead to declining productivity, thereby actually increasing the exploitation of working people, who would get less in return for more work. But that argument obscured the more fundamental issue. In fact, the Marxist materialist insistence that increasing production — so that China could create enough new wealth to raise the poorest while meeting the legitimate wants of all working people — meant a politics divorced from continuing the transition toward communism.

The Ma group contended that the first issue to be addressed was "continuous revolution," building on the communist elements in the socialist stage so that "socialism will tend to evolve into communism." Material incentives, bourgeois rights, and so on therefore could not be considered mainly as tactical matters of economic development. They were rather "a life and death struggle determining the future and fate of socialism."

Stressing class struggle would also win economic miracles. After all, the Ma group argued, Mao had put the matter of class struggle on China's national agenda in 1962, and the next three years had seen great economic gains.[11] If stressing class struggle could win economic miracles in the worst of times, following the three difficult years 1960–1962, then, the Ma group suggested, surely nothing would be lost now, when "to prevent capitalist restoration, it was necessary to put 90 percent of one's time to carrying out a struggle with the capitalists."

A political debate was going on between, on the one hand, the Marxist idealists urging that overwhelming priority be given to transforming "the rights and ideology of the bourgeoisie" and, on the other hand, their materialist opponents who focused on overcoming backward productive forces, ending backward-

157

ness in science and related useful fields of knowledge, and confronting the problems of differences between upper and lower levels and between military and civilians. Making the Marxist materialist program one of China's national priorities, the Ma group wrote, meant abandoning the struggle, that is, the revolutionary transition to communism.

How to assure that state power would not take the capitalist road was the "important question," "especially how to prevent the class of bureaucrats from usurping Party and state power." The problem was so difficult, the Ma group found, because the state constantly created "bureaucrats, bureaucratism and a bureaucratic system." These all now had to be "thoroughly destroyed."

Mao Zedong, in addition to having comprehended the problem of state capitalism in theory, was said to have solved the problem in practice. The Cultural Revolution was the answer to preventing the usurpation of socialist power by a "class of bureaucrats." "The Great Proletarian Cultural Revolution was a major class struggle between the proletariat and . . . the class of bureaucrats, that is, the faction taking the capitalist road."

Because Lin Biao's Cultural Revolution military group had tried to seize power in a coup, the way was opened for Deng Xiaoping and other capitalist-roaders who had been removed from power during the Cultural Revolution to retake state power. A decisive politico-ideological battle was occurring in 1975. The Marxist idealists now had to legitimate recruiting and promoting new officials who would support them, while preventing the rehabilitation and return of the veteran revolutionaries who aligned themselves with the Marxist materialists.

The Ma group also had to address the related policy question of how a socialist state could prevent its officials from creating a system that would make natural and replicable their special privileges. How did people remain socialist officials without becoming members of a bureaucratic capitalist class? The Ma group argued that the issue boiled down to which people should staff the state machine. The veteran democrats poisoned by the old bureaucratic heritage of presocialist China too easily succumbed to bureaucratic corruption. Not so the new young officials schooled under socialism. Hence "how" was translated into "who."

To assure that the new power holders would not be corrupted by the continuing capitalist dynamics of bourgeois rights, the idealists developed techniques to assure correct ideas. The three related techniques were (1) the promotion of young militants whose (2) ideas were kept proletarian by engaging in manual labor and (3) by studying the analyses of Marxism-Leninism-Mao Zedong thought. Everything rested on changing the ideas, attitudes, and world-view of people in authority.

The Extraparty Program for Democratizing Socialism

In October 1976, a month after the death of Mao Zedong, leaders of the Marxist idealist camp were arrested for allegedly plotting a coup and for various other capital crimes — arson, torture, kidnapping, and murder. Soon after, Wang Xizhe and his friends were released from prison after four cruel years. Very quickly Wang entered the new debate on why China had suffered such inhumanities in the previous period. He pressed his analysis of China's feudal system to a critique of monopoly power by a Leninist-Stalinist Communist party.

The Ma group had argued that such an anti-Leninist critique had to be the hidden antisocialist essence of the Marxist materialists. It was not the old feudal system but the new proletarian power that the socialist democratizers actually assaulted. "The class enemies," the Ma group wrote, referring to the Marxist materialists, "absurdly claim that bureaucrats and bureaucratism are products of the proletarian state system itself. This is slander of red political power, reckless, reactionary logic. . . . [Bureaucracy's] poisonous roots are [actually in the old, capitalist soil of an earlier] exploitative system."

The Marxist idealists had urged Chinese to purge their state system of the capitalist democrats. The purified state machine could then continue the socialist transition to communism. How could the Marxist democrats instead win Chinese Leninists to democratizing what these Leninists had built in China? It would not be easy.

Wang was immediately in trouble again. His ideas[12] were denounced by the Communist party first secretary of Guangdong Province, where Wang lived, as "inciting" and "reactionary." The party secretary apparently was appalled that Wang blamed Mao's policies for too closely following Soviet Stalinist texts and bringing economic disaster to China, that Wang found Tito a better Marxist than Mao, and that Wang condemned the Chinese state as a "bureaucratic system" with a permanent official caste because it had abandoned Marx's Paris Commune notion that officials should be citizens rotating out of office and not a permanent caste. Wang was seen accordingly as anti-Chinese, anti-Mao and antisocialist.

In fact, Wang deepened the analysis he offered after Lin Biao fell in 1971. Wang tried to see how the system worked. In 1979 he rejected the idea of some party veterans that China's problems were the fault of the Marxist idealists. To learn how to change the system, Wang wanted to explore the social dynamics that had permitted the Marxist idealist group to practice its destructive policies.

In prison, Wang, as so many others, dedicated himself to studying Marxist texts and Chinese polemics. He emerged from prison certain that slogans like "only socialism can save China" obscured the real problems. The world had many different varieties of socialism. One had to learn why some brought such

159

inhumanity as China had suffered and what system would come to grips with China's particular difficulties. Wang concluded that it had to be a socialism premised on a "new democracy," one promising an end to the state forms that facilitated murder, torture, prison, and banishment of millions. How was this to be done?

First, one had to understand the choices and consequences when socialists won power in a state that was poor and backward, that lacked the economic abundance and democratic forms which Marx had scientifically shown were the preconditions of socialism. China was not a part of a dominant world force whose productive achievements could already meet the distribution needs of all people with a minimal involvement of necessary labor time. China's power holders were socialist-minded patriots in a poor, backward country on a planet dominated by a capitalist world market.

The Marxist idealists chose isolation from that world market. The result, according to Wang, was "regression to a feudal style 'socialist' state." Such a state — backward, vulnerable, stagnant, polarizing, premised on being shut off from and ignorant about the world, opposed to popular needs — could not freely hold people's allegiance. Its socialism would crumble.

China had no choice, therefore, but to reenter the world market with its capitalist laws, division of labor, and specialization. But to do so inevitably pushed China in the direction of "a capitalist state without capitalists." True socialist freedom was impossible. The global whole delimited the national part. Marx in *Capital*, Wang wrote, had analyzed this situation in a national society when he inquired into the consequences of workers cooperating to run one factory in a capitalist state. Inevitably, Marx concluded — and Wang concurred — the workers became their own exploiters. In like manner, in a capitalist world system, a progressive economically growing China could only be state capitalist. It had to exploit itself.

Wang thus seemed to concede a major point to the Marxist idealists. But Wang did not find the source of this capitalist danger inside China. The cause was not internal bourgeois rights, lack of manual labor by Chinese officials, or insufficient study of socialist values. The cause, Wang found, was that to increase productivity and begin to liberate workers from animal-like necessary labor time, China was compelled to enter the capitalist world market. But the impact of those capitalist relations on the Chinese Communist party, which commanded state power, must be guarded against.

Wang feared, and found to be true, that that party, especially its "leading bloc," would become a power above society in opposition to the interests of working people. Mao Zedong, Wang pointed out, warned of this danger of a "bureaucratic class" becoming "a new aristocratic stratum." But Mao, Wang continued, offered a solution that only intensified the problem. Mao abandoned Lenin's theoretical insights on how to check bureaucracy. Mao (and the Marxist

160

idealists) rested everything on the attitudes and actions of leading cliques. Lenin, Wang concluded, was a better Marxist because he saw that a solution had to lie with the citizenry, the working people, democracy.

Maoism, Wang suggested, in abandoning the popular, democratic project of Leninism, turned leaders into gods, compelling people to approach rulers in awe and worship. The feudal religion of the Lin Biao system, with its worship of leaders of special genius, was therefore a natural consequence of Mao's prescriptions. Given China's backwardness, the viciousness of the capitalist world market, and the misleading prescriptions of Mao, it was clear why the Lin Biao system with its fascistic feudal potential continued even without Lin Biao.

Where, then, if not in Mao, would one find clues to the solution of the enigma of the capitalistic bureaucratization of a socialist party? In Tito's Yugoslavia, Wang replied.

We are not privy to what Wang knows about Tito's writings or about Yugoslav theory and practice.[13] Wang merely cites a statement from the Yugoslav theorist Eduard Kardelj in 1953 (an early high point among Yugoslav leaders in thinking about how to democratize a Stalinist state) and a recent report by an important Chinese visitor, one Li Yimin, a Foreign Ministry specialist on socialist countries. Wang's purpose was to offer Yugoslavia as an instance of an attempt to build a genuine workers' state.

We do know what positive connotations Yugoslavia carried in China for Marxist materialist reformers in the debate over the socialist transition period. The model of Yugoslavia was the first alternative socialists who had achieved state power could look to if they sought an outcome that would avoid the evils of the Stalinist Soviet Union. The evil to be checked was unaccountable, centralized power in the hands of a bureaucracy of officials headed by leaders locked in a murderous internecine power struggle. The good ends to be attained were meant to prevent overcentralization, to preclude terror and mass murder, to prevent the growth of a separate stratum of officials, and to build institutions whose foundations were the cornerstones of a socialist economy that could keep as much power as possible in the hands of nonofficials, keep power at the site of work. Titoism was understood as the first practical attempt to grapple with these evils of the Stalinist-Leninist legacy.

Wang's purpose was to achieve a broad and direct democracy, which would end party administration of the economy. Progress had to be attained on the basis of "new economic relations and a new economic base." All working people would run their work units building on the lessons of Yugoslavia's experiments with worker management of the economy. Political organization then would be built on this democratized economy. Genuine power would be with people whose real interest was opposed to superexploitation by the state.

Marxist materialism teaches us, Wang argued, that relying primarily on study, campaigns, and manual labor to correct bureaucratic capitalist behavior by officials had to be of decidedly secondary importance no matter how sincerely such policies were carried out. If the material conditions of administration created a permanent division between those who administered and those who were administered, the party could not but become bureaucratized. Its leading officials could not but be a separate and special group above the reach of ordinary citizens. For Wang, the heart of the problem was that the state was distant from and not controlled by popular will. His ultimate proof of this proposition was the ease with which the ruling bloc disbanded and crushed the million people in April 1976 in Beijing's Tiananmen Square who protested the rise toward absolute power of the Marxist idealist groups subsequently vilified as the Gang of Four, or the Jiang Qing Clique.

To be sure, a scant six months later Marxist materialists at the state center were welcomed by the people when they finally arrested the leaders and plotters among the Marxist idealists. But what mattered, Wang argued, was that an unaccountable stratum of officials existed who could act one way in April and another in October.

Wang acknowledged that many people were grateful for being saved by "Uncle Deng" (Xiaoping) and therefore had no higher hope than to wish him many more healthy years full of more good deeds. But depending on a leader, no matter how great, was for Wang a feudal patriarchal project. It was not a democratized socialist state in which working people controlled their own destiny. Without fundamental change, once again officials would struggle to control a piece of the economy and pass on their patrimony to their children. Under the new signboard of the four modernizations, the old feudalism with its fascist potential would remain unchanged. This system, not the Gang of Four, was the real enemy of progress and liberation in China.

Wang asked people to think carefully about the political consequences of the social existence of party officials in administrative positions. Why, Wang wondered, did such officials sit silent while first Lin Biao and then the Gang of Four ran rampant? They were, he suggested, hoping by silence to hold onto power, as they were now doing in presenting themselves as the heirs of China's true revolutionary heritage.

Wang concluded that these people's social existence was defined by their monopoly of power. Maintaining that monopoly was their primary political motivation. The fate of democratization could not safely be turned over to people defined by such a social existence. People from below had to have the power to act.

Wang did not for a moment suggest that there were no party democrats. He praised the party members who identified with Marx's promise of the Paris Commune and Lenin's democratic prospect of rule by all working people. He even cited the shrewd analyses of people who criticized the Stalinization of the party. But social reality, not good ideas, was decisive. A party — in China or in the USSR — becomes bureaucratized, Wang found, when a relation is established between party and people such that the party gives orders and the people take orders.

Lenin argued that leadership by a party vanguard was necessary at a certain stage. Wang believed that period had passed in China. The popular action in April 1976 in Tiananmen Square proved that now the people could rule themselves. Party officials sat silent and bent with the prevailing political winds. But young workers opposed and fought against the fascist feudalists.

The meaning of that event was manifest. Marx wrote, Wang reminded his readers, that we humans set ourselves tasks only when the material conditions exist to fulfill those tasks. The task for China was to defeat fascist feudalism and democratize the state system. The people who showed the capacity to solve that problem, who understood the real enemies of socialism and were willing to struggle against those feudalists, were young workers. If workers merely obeyed party orders, the revolution would have been endangered. Top party people might never have had the courage to arrest the leading fascist feudalists in October if working people had not in April already fought against those hated forces. The proletariat had matured. The party no longer had a progressive role to play as its parent.

Wang had moved further in the democratic direction from the original position he staked out after the fall of Lin Biao. The legal rights of individuals could not be guaranteed against fascist abuses from above unless political institutions were also developed to check the monopoly of bureaucratic power. Inspired by the theory of the Paris Commune and the experiments of Titoist Yugoslavia, Wang called for a devolution of power from a separate stratum of officials to working people organized around their units of work. Only if the management of the economy were not monopolized could the superstructure of political power rest on a genuine democratic base. A separate stratum of officials above the general citizenry, exposed to and inevitably forced to compromise with world capitalism, even for the benefit of China's people, would be vulnerable to a new social existence of fascist capitalism, reinforcing the old bureaucratic culture of feudal fascism.

The only answer was democratization. A progressive socialist transition demanded that the party monopoly of state power give way to power exercised by working people. Given the long transition period imposed by China's economic backwardness and the resulting need to deal with China's economic backwardness by entering a capitalist world market, there was no guarantee of a successful transition. But democratization would facilitate the development of people accustomed to commanding their own destiny. Democratic relations would erode feudal social relations and would end a regime of blind loyalty, orders, and obedience. Officials no longer would be able to pass on their patrimony to their blood relatives and loyal retinue. The basis of self-interested bureaucrati-

163

zation would be gone and with it social relations that had permitted and replicated the legitimization and worship of any separate stratum of state power holders, whether the Gang of Four or any other.

Wang Xizhe's programmatic analysis did not appeal to many party power holders after the fall of the Gang of Four. It sounded like pure democracy, well-meaning but impractical. Such party people believed Wang's policies would produce social anarchy, economic setbacks, and military vulnerability. Many party people believed that first a socialist economic system must be built to win back people's genuine commitment and participation, to meet popular needs, to enhance the quality of life, and to defend the gains of socialist construction against potential foreign military aggressors. Wang's notion of democratizing the economy could not have priority over socialist construction.

In 1973–1974 Wang's group had argued that socialist democratization in China rested on the policy direction taken by the party people who had been cruelly victimized by the feudal fascists. Key power groups among China's party Leninists now did believe in protecting individuals against the abuses of state power, did push for legal rights, did work vigorously for ever more democratization. But the party democrats saw the problem of democratizing feudal elements in China very differently from such extraparty democrats as Wang Xizhe.[14]

The Party Democrats' Antifeudal Programs and Their Opponents

By the beginning of the 1980s, the leading communist theorist of democratization was Yu Guangyuan. Even Wang respected Yu and applauded his efforts, while wishing that Yu would move closer to his own position. Yu was considered too democratic by many in China's Communist party.

Yu was a physics major in the mid-1930s at China's Qinghua University, where he wrote a dissertation on the theory of relativity. When Japan invaded China, Yu fled Beijing and threw his life into the armed cause of Chinese revolutionary socialism. By the 1950s, Yu had emerged as one of China's foremost Marxist theorists, writing regularly in the party's leading theoretical journal. Yu addressed himself to issues as abstract as Engels and Einstein on science and socialism and to matters as immediate as voluntary, gradual collectivization and Stalinism.

At age sixty-five Yu was appointed the head of China's powerful and prestigious Marx-Engels-Lenin-Mao Zedong Thought Institute shortly after the October 1976 arrest of the plotters and leaders of the Marxist idealist group. On May Day 1979 he published an essay in *Baike Zhishi* that caught the eye and won the admiration of China's democrats, both in and out of the party. It closely analyzed Lenin's thoughts on the role of the Communist party after the revolutionary seizure of power and compared them with Stalin's writings on Lenin and the party. Yu found that Stalin had "absolutized" Lenin's views on the party. Whereas Lenin saw the leading role of the party as a necessary first stage for continuing revolutionary power, Stalin had argued that party dictatorship (a phrase Lenin almost never used) was required in all matters for the entire period of the proletarian dictatorship.

Yu stressed the democratic commitment and tactical component underlying Lenin's notion of a vanguard party. Lenin believed in the need to move on, as soon as conditions permitted, so that workers would participate in and manage the state. Practice now had proved that there was no other way than Lenin's to prevent the party from turning into a bureaucratic stratum that ruled over the mass of people.

Hence, Yu argued, it was the responsibility of the party in the first stage of the proletarian dictatorship, of party rule, to prepare the way for the second stage, rule by the organized workers, including unions. (The third stage, Yu wrote, the withering away of the state, was still in the future.) The second stage involved practicing democracy, decreasing labor time, raising political consciousness, heightening the cultural level and the standard of living, and developing the forces of production. This process in an economically backward peasant country might take longer than in an advanced capitalist country. It had been abandoned by Stalin, who stressed the role of the party under "any conditions" to the exclusion of the temporary "historical conditions," which necessitated its role for Lenin, until the workers could in a second stage of proletarian dictatorship "expand proletarian democracy," "participate in state management," and truly be their own masters, the masters of socialism. Some "clues," Yu said, could be found in "socialist Yugoslavia."

By the end of the 1970s the invocation of Yugoslavia had a special meaning to party democrats. It did not mean a complete adoption of Yugoslavia's economic system, which was found wanting because it produced high unemployment, high inflation, and dangerous international financial vulnerability. It did mean, however, that a poor, backward state committed to socialist modernization could succeed[15] (and avoid Stalinism) by importing foreign technology. Looking to "clues" in Yugoslavia meant mainly that the democratic task of involving working people in their own self-government as a necessary means of resisting the evils of entrenched, centralized party power and privilege should be on the immediate agenda.

The invocation of Yugoslavia as a model also helped make clear just how far China had yet to go in the democratic direction. Instances of Yugoslav maltreatment of democrats such as Milovan Djilas, which led Western progressives to protest to the Yugoslav government, were cited in China as examples far superior to anything China had. It seemed wondrous to Chinese party democrats that antiparty democrats could reside in Yugoslavia and write, publish, receive foreign funds, and even, miracle of miracles, keep their pensions.[16]

165

The goal of the party democrats was to make democracy serve popular needs, to make democracy at one with the interests of the mass of the citizenry. Elections began at the local level, at rural communes (for manager and accountant), in enterprises, at county levels. Nonparty candidacies were invited. Then electoral democracy could be expanded and moved to the national level, where it would include even a national legislature, perhaps at first indirectly elected by conventions of the locally elected delegates. At the same time, the role of the national legislature would be expanded, legal due process expanded and the judiciary made independent, and the civilian government would gain control over the military.

Stalinism, in the sense of abandonment of the democratic thrust of Leninism, was also used to categorize the loss of democracy within the party. China's leading economic planner at the end of the 1970s, Chen Yun, explained: "After the victory of the October Revolution in the Soviet Union, with Lenin there was normal life in the Party of that period, a very full democratic atmosphere. Afterwards, party life [under Stalin] became abnormal. This provided the likes of Khrushchev and Brezhnev, conditions in which they usurped the Party and seized power."[17]

Chen carefully avoided Stalin's name and mistakenly presented Khrushchev as pure evil. Perhaps Chen was afraid of alienating or confusing citizens and party power holders who had been raised on Mao's notion that Stalin was essentially correct and that Mao was his heir, whereas Khrushchev was antisocialist and an ideological heir of the diabolical anti-Stalinist Tito. Perhaps it was too important for their modernization cause to be able to cite Stalin on behalf of objective economic laws. Unless the party democrats could directly attack Stalin, the antidemocrats in the party could still present themselves as the legitimate inheritors of Stalinist party orthodoxy — the only leaders capable of continuing the revolution.

The party antidemocrats struck back. They claimed that broad democracy in backward China had produced the anarchy that caused the fascist violence of the earlier period. They won on their demand that democracy be taken out of the streets, that nonofficial journals be closed, that at least some of their nonparty opponents be punished as examples. The party antidemocrats feared the attempts to check abuses of party power from the outside. The party democrats had begun to inaugurate not only a system of elections, which invited nonparty candidates, but also investigative reporting (the journalists of Watergate were heroes) to ferret out corrupt and illegal or coercive party activities and then to have an independent judiciary punish such misdeeds. The party antidemocrats wanted to contain and beat back this broadened democracy. In American organizational terms, the antidemocrats opposed a civilian review process using outsiders and insisted on internal policing. To win their case, they used fear tactics, claiming that broad democracy was foreign and capitalist-inspired and led to a breakdown of order and of Chinese values, to the worst evils of the capitalist West such as street crime, sexual permissiveness, and the weakening of the family.[18]

The antidemocrats presented themselves as true Chinese socialists, heirs to the genuine Stalin-Mao synthesis. Their position became obvious on December 21, 1979, the hundredth anniversary of Stalin's birth. Whereas the party democrats pointed to a new edition of the selected works of the supposedly democratic Lenin, the antidemocrats welcomed a new edition of *Stalin's Selected Works*. The party democrats on the national party newspaper, *Renmin Ribao*, downplayed the event. They represented Stalin as someone who, in summarizing Leninism, correctly advocated scientific knowledge and winning material abundance and cultural richness.[19]

Stalin was presented very differently by *Beijing Daily*. The editorial staff of that newspaper apparently was linked to Wu De, the top capital city official still associated with the Marxist idealists. *Beijing Daily* presented Stalin as a creative genius, a giant in the ascent of Marxism, who had enriched Marxism by correctly addressing it to new conditions.[20] For Stalin, *Beijing Daily* stated, "Marxism-Leninism is a science. And science is a matter of following the development of practice by continuously advancing [theoretical] development, continuously using experience which enriches us in order to perfect old formulas and make them ever more accurate." Stalinist Leninism was promoted by the antidemocrats in China's Communist party to absolutize as an eternal principle the notion of all power to the Leninist party, especially its "correct and great leadership." "For example, Engels and Marx stated that the Paris Commune was the dictatorship of the proletariat. Everyone knows that the Paris Commune was led by two political parties and that neither one of them was Marxist. Nonetheless, afterward Lenin, basing himself . . . on new experience, said that the development of the dictatorship of the proletariat could only be carried through under the leadership of one political party, a Marxist political party."[21]

Renmin Ribao, on the other hand, associated itself with the position that Stalin's views and experiences were not universal.[22] Stalin, after all, slighted rural people to stress heavy industry, especially steel. China, on the other hand, would give ever greater weight to agriculture and light industry. Mao is presented as the one who abandoned the alleged universals of the Russian path to respond to the "concrete circumstances" of China. Mao happily dropped the thesis that revolution must originate in cities for a concept of stressing the actual conditions of China, where revolution was a matter of "the countryside surrounding the city." Building Chinese-style socialism meant innovating in response to new and real circumstances and not citing words from earlier periods which applied to different problems.

167

China's circumstances were first and foremost a multicentury of feudalism, which deeply rooted feudal values in the minds of China's people. Modernization premised on feudalism threatens to turn into fascism. Vice-Prime Minister Deng Xiaoping in a September 9, 1979, speech argued that all modern states grow out of their feudal pasts.[23] Consequently, even capitalist England and France were threatened for many generations by the prospect of a fascist outcome. Feudal remnants in Germany and Japan helped impose fascist states there. The same general danger threatened Chinese socialism; therefore, a renewed antifeudal effort had to be sustained. If the democratic forces did not grow stronger, the fascist ones would.

This antifascist position was given a most pointed form on February 13, 1979, by one of the editors of *Renmin Ribao*, Wang Roshui.[24] Wang argued that the fascist damage done by the Marxist idealists would have been impossible if Mao Zedong had not opened the way for them. Therefore the feudal culture and Stalinist party practices that permitted a Stalinist cult of the individual must be replaced by a democratic culture and a democratic party.

Stalinism was defined, in Mao's words, as expanding the targets of class struggle. Mao was found guilty of Stalinism starting in 1957, when he attacked as rightist hundreds of thousands of intellectuals, students, and others who had criticized party corruption and party privilege. Mao then became the arbiter of friends and enemies. Anyone or any group whom Mao disagreed with, or worried about, could be defined, as Stalin had defined his adversaries, as class enemies, and these included high school teachers, factory managers, party people with other ideas on modernization, or higher intellectuals. Class struggle was, in practice, a doctrine of the cult of one man, giving all power to one man, and had nothing to do with classes. Instead, people at the top such as Lin Biao and Mao Yuanxin courted Mao. Such obeisance was an aspect of feudalism, not of class struggle. Party democracy was forgotten. What mattered was the cult and the court. As Prime Minister Zhou Enlai lay dying in January 1976, Mao imperially feted Julie Nixon and David Eisenhower.

The real danger to China was a "feudal restoration." China never was capitalist. The entire program of the Marxist idealists for China was misconceived because there was no capitalism to restore. But patriarchal thought was popular in the countryside. Mao made it dominant in the party. It was a world-view that lacked faith in itself and sought refuge in an all-powerful savior. Whereas the "Internationale" of the proletariat declared that there were no saviors, China's anthem, "The East Is Red," insisted that Mao was the savior. The Stalinist cult of the individual, which Mao used, mixed with China's feudal patriarchy and opened the way for the feudal fascism of China's Marxist idealists. The only way to end the danger of fascism and feudal restoration was to break free of Stalinism, free of feudal culture, free of ultraleft dogmatism to build instead a democratic party in a democratic culture which could begin to compensate for "the democratic tradition which we lack."

Is it sufficient to locate the causes of the inhumanities that had shaken China's people and her ruling party in China's ancient cultural inheritance and in the new, foreign, imported dogmas of Stalinism? The analogy to feudalism may be helpful, but what is at issue is the causal explanation of feudal fascism.

Rene Dumont, in his devastating essay *Is Cuba Socialist?*,[25] describes the Castro regime in feudal categories. Dumont concludes that the kindest label one can give Castro's Cuba is enlightened despotism. With all its seigneurial corruptions, antieconomic calculations, aristocratic privilege, and courtier behavior, the best one can hope for in Cuba is a transition from absolute despotism to constitutional monarchy.[26]

In like manner, Milovan Djilas in *The Unperfect Society: Beyond the New Class*, reveals the anatomy of the Yugoslav political economy with the analogy to feudalism. The

> top leaders of the oligarchy distribute state functions, and sometimes economic functions, among party officials, just like the fiefs which the kings and barons used to grant to their faithful and deserving vassals. . . . In the same way that the royal prerogative, the privileges of the feudal lords, and the feudal estates, became a stumbling block to free trade and industry, which were developing under feudalism, so the despotism of the oligarchy, and the party bureaucracy's privilege in the government and the economy, together with the static, absolutized property patterns provided a basis for all this, have put the brakes on modern transport, modern management, and modern technology, and even on the socially owned property that has developed under Communism.[27]

If similar feudal patterns, which facilitate power holders to combine special privileges with technical incompetence, develop in descending levels in cultures as historically different as Yugoslavia, Cuba, and China, should one seek the cause of the feudalism in diverse cultures or in imported Stalinism? But Yugoslavia had fought Stalinism for thirty years, and Cuba was fully capitalist, not feudal, on the eve of Castro's revolutionary victory. Shouldn't the cause of what is labeled feudalism then be sought in some decisive feature which they all actually share?

Wang Xizhe had already suggested an answer to that question in his articles. The cause lies in the need to fit into a lower-ranking position in a capitalist world market and in an international military-political statist combat. The global whole delimits the statist part and, as a result, shapes for these states very constricted options.

Power holders at the national center live at an international level with special access to concentrated resources necessary for national planning and develop-

169

ment as well as national security and dignity. Given the unlimited nature of international combat, it seems functional for national leaders to be able to act secretively, swiftly, and with all necessary resources.

Other levels in the government structure become lesser parts of the same logic. Given the fact that in all three cases revolutionary power was seized by an armed force, the need for a privileged, secretive state seems presuppositional. Military logic predominates. How else deal with mortal enemies of the national revolution? There does not seem to be much room for democratization.

Worse yet, in China that army, identifying with Mao's revolutionary strategies, is not easily turned against Mao. Given its peasant base, it shares the protofascist elements of Mao's view which suspects the urban, the intellectual, and the international. To be sure, the socialist party democratizers, the Marxist materialists in China, have set out to woo village and military. But neither peasant nor soldier was the main victim of China's vigilante violence. If Wang Xizhe is right — that fascist brutality made many victims into strong socialist democrats — we must remember that comparatively few such victims exist in village and army. Besides, as Wang later noted, many revolutionary veterans, returning to power, prefer quiet over a vibrant quest for democracy. Marxist-Leninist ideology, which legitimates superior knowledge for party leaders and obedience for all others, nicely rationalized the antidemocratic feudal whole. The party democrats are aware of this and have challenged that privileged theory of knowledge which leads in the direction of feudalism. Never before in the history of the People's Republic have privileged ideas (Lenin on truth) and institutions (the military) come under assault. Party democrats are critically committed to reforming even antidemocratic forms of "socialism."

The socialist democratizers may be wise, decent, and determined. But consider their burden. No natural, strong initiative in their direction comes from army or village, or from large sections of the party and government. And scientists and writers are often too scarred to act vigorously on behalf of democracy. The party secret police is still very much on the scene and not very democratic. Besides, given the need to take on antidemocratic elements in Lenin's ideology, Stalin's party, and Mao's practice, one cannot conclude that the dominant forces in China favor the socialist democratizers. So much seems to stand against them.

When I have recited these antidemocratic odds to a couple of China's party democratizers, they have grown furious with me and lectured at me. One snapped back: "Don't tell me the obstacles to social democratization. I know them better than you do, much better. I never said our path was easy. I never said there wouldn't be reverses. I never said the struggle wouldn't be long and hard. But I also know some things you don't know. I know who the enemy is. I know how much China has suffered. I know how many of us there are who have sworn to ourselves to fight for this cause to our deaths. You may doubt it but I know *We will win*."

Chinese socialism and a democratized party and state — it is worth understanding the tradition and the vision that inspire the dedication.

PART THREE

State and Economy

7

The Dilemma of State Power:
The Solution Becomes the Problem

BENEDICT STAVIS

In the past thirty years, and indeed for the past century, China has had two broad goals. The first has been economic and technical development to modernize the economy and thereby improve the people's standard of living and strengthen the nation's military power. The second goal has been to create a new set of social and cultural values which were also harmonious with the Chinese traditions. Over the past century this goal has been expressed in both Confucian and socialist vocabulary. In the past decades, these values have been expressed in the words "red" (emphasizing social values) and "expert" (stressing economic development). Both outside observers and Chinese themselves have noted tensions in emphasis between political and economic values. There are red factions and expert factions in the Chinese leadership, and a major element of politics is considered to be struggle between these factions. Considerable analysis has focused on China's swing from one perspective to the other and on the issue of whether these two viewpoints are inevitably antagonistic or whether they might in some way be complementary.

This essay will attempt to highlight the role of the state in promoting these goals and the consequences of using state power for their attainment. To achieve these goals, it has been necessary to rely on the economic and social power of the state bureaucracy. Consequently, however, the social, economic, and political constraints on state power have all been weakened. Little has

Support for this research is derived from a broader project entitled Alternative Strategies for Rural Development, funded by the U.S. Agency for International Development, Development Support Bureau, Office of Rural Development, and Development Administration. Part of this research was done while I was a Visiting Professor of the Institute of Asian Research of the University of British Columbia. I am most thankful to the institute, its director, and associates, as well as the Department of Agricultural Economics, Michigan State University, for making this visit possible, pleasant, and productive.

prevented the state and its bureaucrats from becoming self-seeking and arbitrary. Eventually, the bureaucracy, which was given power to implement socialism and to oversee economic development, has shown signs of functioning in ways that undermine the goal of modernization and the realization of socialist values.

The problems of controlling a government, of guarding against the guardians, of course, have always been a central issue in political philosophy and are not unique to China. But they are intense in China, both because of the extensive power that has been entrusted to the state bureaucracy and because of the long and deep tradition of bureaucratic rule.

The Role of the State in Economic Development: Investment and Growth

For rapid economic growth the Chinese recognize the critical importance of investment in industry, agriculture, energy sources, technology, and infrastructure. They have enforced high rates of savings to provide funds for investment, thus in a sense redistributing income from present to future generations. In China's socialist economy, most of the activities that increase savings and mobilize investments are in the public sector.

High rates of investment require constraints on consumption; therefore, urban wages and rural incomes have been controlled by state wage and price policies. The state also controls or influences production, trade, and distribution of consumer goods. Until recently, extensive propaganda campaigns have been conducted to dampen consumer demand and to convince the people to be happy with their modest, slow-growing levels of consumption.

Both urban and rural consumption levels have grown slowly since the mid-1950s. Table 7.1, line 7, shows that total consumption has gone up at about 5.9 percent annually, which is about 3.9 percent per capita (not corrected for inflation). The level of consumption, however, is not greatly above minimal daily needs for most people. Grain predominates in the diet; clothing is functional; housing is cramped; and heating is limited. Outdoor plumbing is common. Crowded public transportation is supplemented by bicycles. Living conditions have been improved through control of drought and floods, stockpiling of grains, and distribution of food to areas stricken by natural disasters. Public health has been improved by increased access to basic health services and by mobilizing people to improve sanitary conditions. These programs permit greater overall security at low levels of income.

In contrast to the modest growth of consumption, savings and investment have been growing at roughly 9.1 percent annually (line 5). Before the 1979

Table 7.1.   National Income and National Accumulation (billion current *yuan*)

	1952	1957	1979	Annual Compound Growth Rate 1952−1979 (percent)
1. National income (material sectors)[a]	58.9	90.8	335.0	6.6
2. Personal services (13 percent of 1)[b]	7.7	11.8	43.6	
3. Total national income (1 + 2)	66.6	102.6	378.6	6.6
4. Accumulation rate (percent of material income)	18.2[c]	24.9[c]	33.6[d]	
5. Amount of accumulation: (4 x 1 ÷ 100)	10.7	22.6	112.6	9.1
6. Corrected accumulation rate (percent) (5 ÷ 3 x 100)	16.1	22.0	29.7	
7. Consumption (3 − 5)	55.9	80.0	266.0	5.9
8. National income index (constant price)[e]	100	153.0	484.9	6.0

Sources:
a. *China Economic Almanac, 1981* (Beijing: Economic Management), p. iv 4.
b. *Beijing Review*, no. 43 (October 27, 1980), p. 18.
c. Nei-Ruenn Chen, *Chinese Economic Statistics* (Chicago: Aldine, 1967), p. 144.
d. *Beijing Review*, no. 38 (September 22, 1980), p. 31.
e. *China Economic Almanac, 1981*, p. iv 5.

economic readjustment, a very large portion of this investment went into heavy industry and producer goods. In the early phases of the First Five Year Plan (1953−1955), the guideline was that heavy industry would get eight times as much investment as light industry. In 1956−1957, heavy industry's share dropped to seven times, and Mao recommended dropping it to six times.[1] During the 1960s and 1970s the ratio (and relative importance of heavy industry) went up from ten to fourteen to one.[2] The overwhelming bulk of these investments are mobilized by the state and come from taxes, including the land tax, taxes built into the prices of many industrial commodities, and profits of public sector enterprises. Private investment has been marginal because private ownership of the means of production is strictly controlled.

The strategy of limiting consumption and of emphasizing investment in heavy industry led to substantial economic transformation and growth. By the mid-1970s China had become one of the substantial industrial systems in the world economy. Its crude steel production ranked with those of France, Italy, and the United Kingdom. It was the world's fourth largest producer of primary energy, the third largest producer of synthetic ammonia (for fertilizer), the second largest producer of cotton textiles, and the fourth largest producer of cement.[3] From 1952 to 1978, the net value of industrial production (corrected for price changes) grew at a compound annual rate of about 11.3 percent, from only 8.7 billion *yuan* to 140.6 billion *yuan* (constant 1978 *yuan*).[4]

In agriculture, the long-term growth rates are, of course, not as high as for industry, but they do show growth. Table 7.2 shows that gross output, corrected for inflation, grew at about 3.3 percent annually. Because costs of production increased substantially, the net value of agricultural output, corrected for inflation, experienced a long-term annual growth rate of about 2.3 percent (line 3), a bit more than growth in population and farm labor force. Net product per worker is low and has shown no significant improvement. Within the statistical category of "agricultural output," the dynamic component has been subsidiary activities, which includes handicrafts, processing, and off-farm income. Crop

Table 7.2.   Agricultural Development

	1952	1978	Annual Compound Growth Rate 1952–1978 (percent)
1. Gross value of agricultural output (billion 1970 *yuan*)	63.4[a]	145.9[b]	3.3
2. Cost of production (percent)	25[c]	32.5[d]	
3. Net agricultural income (billion 1978 *yuan*)	59.9[e]	107.2[f]	2.3
4. Farm population (million)	503[g]	803[h]	1.8
5. Net product per farm population (*yuan* per capita) (3 ÷ 4)	119	133	.4
6. Farm work force (million)	170[i]	294[j]	2.1
7. Net product per worker (per capita) (3 ÷ 6)	352	365	0.1

Sources:
a. 1978 = 2.3 x 1952. Yang Jianbai and Li Xuezeng, "The Relations between Agriculture, Light Industry, and Heavy Industry in China," *Social Sciences in China*, no. 2 (1980), p. 183.
b. State Statistical Bureau of the People's Republic of China, "Statistical Work in New China," *Statistical Reporter*, March 1980, p. 139.
c. Nai-Ruenn Chen, *Chinese Economic Statistics* (Chicago: Aldine, 1967), p. 139.
d. Li Chengrui and Zuo Yuan, "For a Determined and Down to Earth Adjustment of the National Economy," *Jingji Yanjiu* (Economic Research), 1979, no. 12, p. 9.
e. 1978 = 1.79 x 1952. Yang and Li, "Relations," p. 183.
f. Ibid.
g. Chen, *Chinese Economic Statistics*, pp. 124–127.
h. *China Agricultural Yearbook, 1980* (Beijing: Agricultural Publishing House, 1980), p. 5.
i. Zhan Wu, "Proper Decision on Development of Agriculture, *Nongye Jingji Wenti*, (Problems of Agricultural Economy), 1980, no. 6, translated in *Joint Publications Research Service*, no. 78, 137, *Translations on China's Agriculture*, No. 140, May 21, 1981, p. 9.
j. Yang and Li, "Relations," p. 208.

production has been growing slower than the average rate. Despite virtually stagnant labor productivity, farm incomes have improved somewhat because of increases in farm prices, expansion of off-farm earnings, and small reductions in portion of farm population.

Growth in agricultural production has come from tremendous investments in labor, which have been used to change the face of the earth and to build irrigation, drainage, and terracing works. In addition, chemical fertilizer, mechanical irrigation, improved seeds, and other modern agricultural technologies have been used extensively in regions that have the water supplies and infrastructure which are necessary complements.

The long-term growth rate of the national income from 1952 to 1979 (uncorrected for price changes) has been roughly 6.6 percent annually (Table 7.1, line 1), or about 4.6 percent on a per capita basis. Making corrections for price changes is complicated because agricultural prices have inflated while industrial prices have deflated, and it is not clear how to weight these divergent trends. The Chinese estimates suggest a growth rate from 1952 to 1979 in constant prices of 6.0 percent (about 4.0 percent per capita) (see Table 7.1, line 8). The World Bank is privately estimating a real net per capita growth rate of 3.0 to 3.5 percent for the 1957 – 1979 period, depending on assumptions about prices. Compared to other large, populous countries, this growth rate is substantial but by no means spectacular. It is above those of India, Pakistan, and many other countries. But China's growth has required high levels of investment and therefore has been costly. Many economies at the same investment rate as China have grown more rapidly (Figure 7.1).

There are several important reasons why growth has not been commensurate with investment rates. China's investments have emphasized comprehensive, self-reliant development, including investment in sectors and projects with very high capital-output ratios such as heavy industry, large dams, mountain railroads and defense industries. These projects have been far more expensive than to have invested in a narrow group of industries with a high output-to-investment ratio, which could produce labor-intensive goods for export, such as textiles or assembly of electronic devices. Moreover, China may not have managed these expensive enterprises efficiently. Indeed, the Chinese admit many poorly planned and wasteful investments, such as factories without adequate electricity, neighboring factories duplicating service facilities, and overcapacity of some installations. Incentives for labor and management may have been weak.

Finally, China may have used up its "easy" forms of economic growth, so that returns are diminishing relative to investment. This hypothesis applies most easily to agriculture; virtually all of the good land is already under cultivation, and indeed some is being converted to nonagricultural uses. Other economies with limited farmland (such as Japan, Taiwan, Holland, and Denmark)

179

Figure 7.1. Investment Rates and Gross National Product Growth Rates

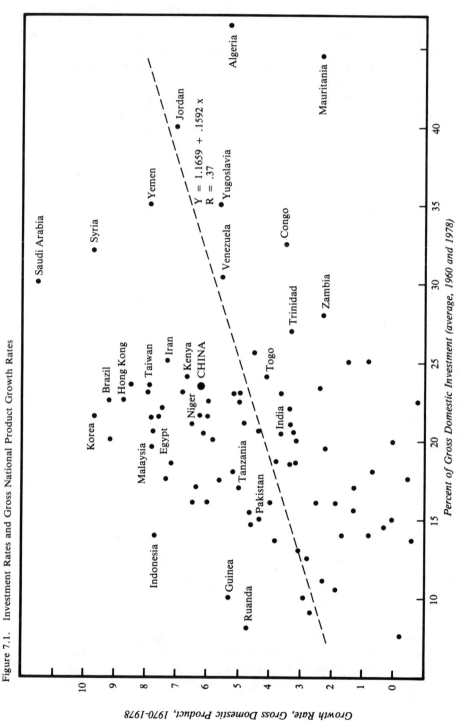

Percent of Gross Domestic Investment (average, 1960 and 1978)

Growth Rate, Gross Domestic Product, 1970-1978

$$\bar{Y} = 1.1659 + .1592\ x$$
$$R = .37$$

Sources: All economies except China: Gross domestic investment figures from World Bank, *World Tables, 1976* (Baltimore: John Hopkins University Press, 1976), p. 396. For figures for China, see text. The figures for China represent average in-

have emphasized exports of products that employ labor and technology and have imported products that require extensive land inputs. Although there are many limits on China's ability to trade on the world market, China's foreign trade has been growing rapidly since the late 1970s.

Political polemicists will debate perpetually whether China's socialist institutions should be credited for leading this economic growth and transformation or condemned for blocking more rapid growth. Such a question implies there might have been alternatives. Could a private or foreign ownership system have generated capital for heavy industrial growth in a more socially responsible way? In the rural sector, what would have been the consequences of concentration of ownership of private land, coupled with proletarianization of less efficient or less lucky farmers? What alternative institutional approaches could have mobilized labor for rural reconstruction? These issues and questions have a political fascination, but scientifically they are meaningless. History cannot be repeated in a series of controlled experiments. Regardless of a tentative answer to these questions, the past cannot be changed. China's economic strategy has been predicated on a very strong state role in mobilizing investments, allocating equipment and supplies, managing markets, and controlling consumption. Such an economic strategy automatically gave tremendous power to the state bureaucrats. In the 1980s, however, China's economy is changed tremendously. It is much larger and more complex. Transportation infrastructure permits much greater regional and firm specialization and interaction. Efficient use of new technologies is increasingly important in industry and agriculture. Regardless of whether the previous institutions are evaluated as good or bad, institutional evolution is required to meet new needs. Otherwise, economic stagnation leading eventually to serious political problems would result. And a new role for the state is required, inasmuch as the state has been at the center of economic policy.

State Power and Socialist Redistribution

A second essential role of state power has been in redistributing assets and income in conformity to socialist principles. State power has been used to distribute assets and income not only between generations by enforcing high investment rates but also within and between sectors. The general policy has been to reduce the income differentials between the top and bottom strata of wage earners and to direct the funds saved in this way from luxury consumption to long-term investment. Such a wage-control policy obviously has been contrary to many powerful interests, and state power has been necessary to implement and maintain it.

Initial redistribution and continued efforts to limit inequality have been

181

important in the rural, industrial, scientific, and cultural sectors. In the rural sector, the land reform campaign around 1949–1950 redistributed and substantially equalized assets at the local level. In following years, collective ownership of farmland assured farmers in each locality of similar wages because wages were determined primarily by labor and not by individual asset ownership. (To the extent that the quality and productivity of farmland varied because of natural conditions and long-term investments, the wages of farmers in different places could vary significantly.) Similarly, in the industrial sector, wages and salaries of workers and managers were substantially (but not completely) equalized when factories were nationalized in the early 1950s. Workers usually received 40 to 60 *yuan*, and very few managers received over 100 to 150 *yuan*.

State power played a crucial role in mobilizing masses to carry out these initial redistributions, and persistent application of state power has been needed to prevent renewed concentrations of wealth. In the rural sector, the formation of cooperatives prevented better (and luckier) farmers from buying up land or from expanding handicraft industries and engaging in petty trade. Such controls over the private sector of the rural economy have been important to assure primacy of the collective system. In the urban sector, controls over investment capital and trade prevented wealthier people from (legally) investing in business.

State power also has regulated urban-rural relations. The state has a monopoly over the marketing of crucial crops (grain, fibers, sugar, oil, seeds) and crucial inputs (fertilizer, machinery, fuel) and thereby controls prices and terms of trade of agricultural and industrial commodities. The incomes of industrial workers and administrators are roughly double to triple those of farmers (including farmers' private incomes). This inequity naturally leads to pressure to migrate from rural to urban areas. Therefore, state power is used to limit sharply this migration. Firm administrative and police controls, rationing, and extensive propaganda campaigns have been used to prevent migration to urban areas in search of industrial jobs. Perhaps one reason urban residents tolerate strict political controls is that these controls are part of the system that protects their standard of living from competition from potential rural migrants. Children of urban residents retain opportunities of going to the better urban schools, of being accepted in higher education, and of being assigned to urban locations in their work. Children born to commune members, however, have little hope of getting urban jobs or even migrating to another rural area. Even marriage to an urban resident does not assure permission to live in the city. The rural people have little alternative but to remain at home and perhaps improve their home village.

Of course these policies run contrary to the preferences of many rural people. Villagers near Dazhai, formerly the national model for labor-intensive agricultural development, disagreed with the approach taken there of huge labor inputs to improve farmland. In common with people in other countries in poor, mountainous areas, they wanted to emphasize handicrafts (mainly quilt making in this particular locality), seasonal migration (using their carts to go into the transportation business), and tourism (setting up baths and tea shops).[5] In the early 1960s roughly one-fourth of the labor force of the county in which Dazhai is situated migrated to urban areas.[6]

China has been reasonably successful in achieving equitable development. Urban-rural gaps are still substantial but probably have not increased much and are probably less than in most other Third World areas. Within the villages, extreme differences of income have been eliminated. In principle, everyone is assured food, even if it must be borrowed from the production team.[7] In practice, however, in very poor rural regions, particularly in times of climatic stress, food shortages can exist. In the urban sector, there are no extreme differences in wealth between those who own assets and those who labor because virtually no one owns productive assets (at least legally).

This does not mean that everyone is equal. Some economic differences are related to differences in family structure. Families with a large number of mature adults having good-paying jobs and few dependents do well. Families with many dependents (retired people, children) or single young adults who have low salaries are less well off.

State Power and the Enforcement of Socialist Values

The Communist leadership has always considered socialism to involve more than economic equality. Socialism has included questions of values, including selfless sharing and humility. To a certain degree, these values have been imposed by state power.

In the rural sector the issue of sharing revolves around the size of the accounting unit (the unit within which farming profits are shared). Generally, accounting has been done at the production team level, consisting of roughly twenty to forty families. In 1958 and to some extent between 1975 and 1978, some officials advocated and forced teams to adopt accounting at the brigade level, which might involve two hundred to three hundred families. This change was claimed to be ideologically advanced and a step toward even greater sharing.

Another socialist value — the integration of mental and manual labor — has had profound implications for education and science. Intellectuals have been encouraged (required? forced?) to spend substantial portions of time at manual labor in farms or factories. Of course, they then have less time for theoretical and technical training programs in both agriculture and industry.

Socialist values also influence economic incentives. To a substantial extent, industrial wages were fixed and not related to productivity. Once employed, a person could not be fired. He had an "iron rice bowl," that is, a secure, unbreakable source of income. In the rural sector, incentive systems have varied

183

greatly, but generally the range in collective wages (within a locality) has been limited. In some cases, food was assured, regardless of how much work people did. Chinese economists now argue that these patterns of wage payments reduced incentives for hard work, and new systems with greater differentials and less security are being implemented.

State Power Becomes a Problem

The above examples illustrate the omnipresence of the state in the Chinese economy. It has the power to enforce savings of over one-third of the national income; to enforce redistribution within and between the rural and urban sectors; to monopolize markets; and to determine what is produced and what is consumed. With so much power, the state also can undermine economic development, socialist values, and individual freedoms, as will be reviewed next.

Excess Accumulation, Growth, and Employment

The high investment rate combined with the overwhelming emphasis on capital-intensive heavy industry had an unanticipated consequence. Despite rapid growth in industrial output, industrial employment went up more slowly than the natural increase of the urban population. Urban youth could not find jobs. Necessity was converted to virtue, and urban high school youth were assigned to rural areas. These assignments were not always successful. Rural people saw little value in having additional residents, who were not prepared physically or emotionally for lives as farmers. Frustrated by the poor rural housing, hard work, distance from relatives, and lack of appropriate marriage opportunities, some youths came back to cities. They had no jobs, and if they came back to the city without permission, they lacked access to rationed grain. They are the group who have been involved in street crime, gang wars, prostitution, and other socially unacceptable activities. Another consequence of the job shortage has been redundant staffing, that is, two or three people essentially sharing one job. This practice is costly and inefficient, but, of course, it reduces unemployment. These problems stem from the underlying investment decisions to stress heavy industry and not to maximize employment. The government is now allowing some privately and collectively owned service units partially to provide employment.

Political Factionalism

Political factionalism flourishes in contexts that do not allow separation of economic from political power. People who wish to exercise economic or social

184

power (whether for personal or ideological reasons) can obtain power only by participating in the political arena.

Given the absence of personal economic assets in China, a person's income and security comes from his job. The modest income differentials are somewhat misleading because some jobs carry important side benefits. A good job may also include a good cafeteria, good child care facilities, access to automobiles, tickets for entertainment, consumer commodities, and other perquisites. It may include some discretionary power to allocate desirable commodities (such as movie tickets), which can be parlayed into components of complex systems of reciprocal obligations. It may provide a way of getting information and enhance opportunities to help friends get jobs, medical care, and so forth. Jobs (and to some extent housing that comes with the job) are assigned officially by various labor bureaus; unofficially a director of a factory, institute, or school may be able to open a "back door" and offer a job to a friend. In either case, job assignments are made by the bureaucracy, and personal connections have been very important in obtaining and keeping a job. Those without connections to a winning faction might fear assignment to rural areas or May 7 labor schools and might encounter difficulty obtaining assignments back to cities.

Chen Yun, vice-chairman of the CCP Central Committee, explained with remarkable frankness the importance of factions: "No one alone will be able to secure power. Only by forming factions can people secure their power and positions. As a result, there naturally are parties outside the Party, and factions within the Party. No faction dares to be careless in dealing with other factions, and they would rather suspect others than believe in them. This is the way they treat other factions, and don't they do the same to comrades of their own faction? Everyone feels insecure and is on guard all the time."[7]

An environment in which the victory of one faction might mean gain or loss of access to jobs for others is the scene of intense factional struggles, and these have interfered with routine work. Managers sometimes have been too quick to impose their superiors' views and reluctant to take any action that involves risks.

Science and Technology

One consequence of the policy of enforced egalitarianism has been partially to sacrifice scientific and technical capacity. During the years of the Cultural Revolution, intellectuals were treated as a politically unreliable group and were tightly regulated by the state (except for scientists working on military technology). Scientists were sent to farms or factories, and local political leaders were given power to make recommendations for admissions to higher educational institutions. These practices interfered with the quality of education and

185

strengthened the bureaucracy at the expense of improving China's scientific, technical, and educational resources.

In moderation, controlling elitism can help the development of education, science, and technology. The Cultural Revolution, however, was not a time of moderation. Some researchers were killed, placed under house arrest, or assigned to do manual labor. Some agricultural universities and research institutes were moved to the countryside and sometimes moved again to a second location. Research facilities were not available, libraries remained in crates, and continuity of field testing was interrupted. Sometimes living conditions were intolerable, and personnel simply dissipated. In some cases, factional struggle was severe, equipment was destroyed, and people's time was absorbed unproductively. People incompetent at science were sometimes appointed to managerial or research positions. Institutional support for serious research work evaporated. Some scientists did modest individual projects at home, while others tended flower gardens or did sewing. It was only by accident that the hybrid rice-breeding program was not destroyed. Many institutes and people flocked to tissue culture work, apparently politically safe and economically useful but hardly a comprehensive agricultural research program.

Agricultural extension also suffered. The salaries and living conditions of agricultural technicians were set relative to those of farmers, not other intellectuals, and were therefore very low. Moreover, they were distrusted as a result of the general climate of anti-intellectualism generated at various times by the leadership, especially the Maoist element. Many technicians simply left their posts.

As China's economy develops, new policies will be required to integrate science and technology with the economy. But optimal policies will be hard to find; political pendulums rarely stop at precisely the right point. The emotional dimension of political conflict during and after the Cultural Revolution makes it inevitable that new policies will swing somewhat toward the other extreme. Moreover, it will be very difficult to permit elitism in only a few fields of science without having the notion spread. Hence, for both emotional and political reasons, carefully balanced policies will be vulnerable to pressures for either extreme scientific autonomy and elitism or extreme government control in the name of enforcing socialist values.

Economic Management

In rural management, one goal of the state has been to reduce its obligation to supply rural areas with grain. Just supplying the cities has been challenge enough. Thus the state, which has a monopoly of grain trading, has enforced a policy of regional self-reliance, particularly for food. Through the Ministry of Agriculture, it has enforced land-use plans so that most of the crop areas is used to produce cereals, and only small portions of land can be devoted to cash crops and animal husbandry. In northwestern China, along the upper reaches of the Yellow River, to provide enough cereal, forests and grass have been cut, and grain has been planted in areas with marginal rainfall. Erosion has increased and grain production has faltered in some localities. The total annual silt in the Yellow River has increased from 1.3 billion tons in the early 1950s to 1.6 billion tons in the mid-1970s.[9] Deforestation of this area has resulted in a reduction of the already low rainfall, a spread of the desert, and greater irregularity in climate, including changes in the frost-free period. Misuse of the environment can, of course, occur under other social and economic systems, but it is a problem the socialist system in China has not avoided.

Because of the effects of mismanagement, this region remains very poor. A survey was made around 1978 of 123 counties of Shaanxi, Gansu, Ningxia, Inner Mongolia, Qinghai, and Shanxi, covering two hundred thousand square kilometers with a population of twenty-four million.[10] Grain yield averaged only 1.3 tons per hectare, and some regions produced only .2 to .4 tons per hectare. In 45 of 121 of these counties, the grain ration (not to be confused with per capita production) was under 150 kilograms per capita per year, and in 69 of these counties, the per capita (collective distribution was under ¥50, scarcely enough to buy food for a year. Ecological problems were not limited to the northwestern region. The mountainous southwestern region experienced similar difficulties because the policy of food self-sufficiency presumably required expanded cultivation of hillsides.

In many localities bureaucrats have compelled farmers to adopt inappropriate cropping techniques. In Sichuan and southern Jiangsu, there was an unwarranted expansion of multiple cropped rice in the summer along with a third winter crop. The expansion was considered a political issue and was thus pushed vigorously, though from an agricultural standpoint it would have been better to take one good summer rice crop, followed with a winter crop such as wheat or rape.[11] Cropping patterns have been altered in other ways, too. In Shandong, for example, cadres required the interplanting of wheat and rape as a winter crop, but not enough labor or soil moisture was available for the crop to succeed.[12]

The private sector also suffered from government constraints. In an effort to control potential rural elites, private subsidiary production of pigs, poultry, fruit trees, fishing, and vegetables was severely restricted at various times and places. Individuals who successfully expanded private production were criticized and punished. Without a vigorous program to expand collective production of these products, this policy undoubtedly hurt both nutrition and income. Exactly how widespread these problems were remains unclear. In many regions of China, the private sector was overlooked and not harmed by political zealots.

Another pattern of managerial abuse has been for commune and other offi-

187

cials to commandeer a team's labor, funds, and materials without compensation. Sometimes these funds were used for the private benefit of officials such as feasting, gift buying, and speculation.[13] Naturally, such abuses would undermine the peasants' support for collective activities. Again, the extent of such practices cannot be gauged.

In industry, analogous inefficiency, stupidity, and corruption are reported. Because government departments allocate critical inputs and market the products, factories are tempted to engage in politics to assure supplies of inputs. Cut off from market signals of consumer desires, they may make undesired products. Again, of course, the existence of such problems is well known, but the precise extent cannot be specified.

Personal Freedom

Just as state intervention in the economy has become more problematical because the economy has expanded in size and complexity, so, too, the issue of personal freedom is becoming more salient. In the first decade of Communist rule, when people remembered the poverty, war, and insecurity of the past, restrictions may have seemed reasonable. The class enemy was easily identifiable. By 1978, however, about 60 percent of China's population had been born after 1949, and nearly 40 percent after the lean years of 1959–1961. Only a minority of people in China now have personally experienced the killer famines of the past; most cannot imagine the personal and social trauma that their parents and grandparents lived through. They may be less inclined to accept low levels of consumption and high levels of social constraint on personal freedom. They are not satisfied with a simple but secure subsistence standard of living. Nor could the class enemy be identified with the categories that were relevant in the 1940s and 1950s.

At the same time, the character of the bureaucracy may have changed. When the Communist party of China was an opposition, revolutionary movement, it attracted a combination of ideologues, patriots, and poor people. After it had assumed power, however, it naturally attracted a higher proportion of people who sought political and economic power and who enjoyed the exercise of bureaucratic power. The bureaucracy was the only outlet for such desires. Over the years, these people have become the new political and economic power elite.

These long-term trends interacted with the complexities of the factional succession crisis and the proclivities of the ultraleftists to result in serious violations of personal freedom during the Cultural Revolution. Large numbers of people were killed, harassed, imprisoned, and sent away from home in enforced labor assignments for little, no, or fabricated reasons. Protesters were silenced brutally. The late 1970s have seen reactions to this suppression. People

188

are insisting on protection against arbitrary, illegal, and unjustified attacks and controls on their persons, homes, and property. This does not mean that China is necessarily moving in the direction of instituting political freedoms (of speech, assembly, organization) as in the West. Yet people are seeking some institutional reforms to prevent arbitrary, vindictive violations to persons in the future.

Limiting State Power in the Post-Mao Period

Mao Zedong was acutely sensitive to the risks inherent in using state power for economic development and social transformation. His strategy of controlling bureaucrats had several components. Government bureaucrats were controlled by the Communist party, and party members were controlled first by careful recruitment procedures and thereafter by constant ideological training. Periodic rectifications cleansed the party of opportunists. Sending them down to lower levels for long- or short-term assignments was supposed to make officials more sensitive to local realities. Investigations, meetings, wall posters, and open-door rectification meetings were supposed to assure mass participation. Criticism and self-criticism were institutionalized to separate as much as possible self-interest and ego from policy making.

China's leaders are not criticizing these approaches and are indeed reinforcing them. At the same time, however, they are in effect saying these methods of controlling the application of state power are not adequate and sometimes were misused in the context of factional struggle. New methods are being developed, and these methods are remarkably similar to those used in the West.

First, the rule of law is being developed. For both criminal and civil matters, laws are being codified, and judges and lawyers are being trained. The procurator's office is being rebuilt. The legal system will attempt to function as a constraint on the arbitrary application of state power. It will also increase the rationality, uniformity, and predictability of bureaucratic decision making to facilitate economic rationality. Law is not new in Chinese culture. The Legalists started to codify law over two thousand years ago, but the Confucian emphasis on personal relations usually overshadowed the rule of law. Both officials and commoners traditionally have been very reluctant to get involved in court cases. The acceptance and implementation of the rule of law will, at best, be a gradual process.

Second, competitive elections on an experimental basis have been carried out for selecting leaders of basic economic units (factory, workshop, commune, brigade, and team) and local government up to the county level. Thus some direct popular participation occurs in selection of leadership, and those who desire public office are forced to compete for popular support. Until now, local

189

leaders have been appointed by higher levels of government, subject to the approval of local representative bodies. Of course, electoral procedures take time to become viable political institutions. Behind-the-scene party control can be important, and voters may not take elections seriously.

In the economic realm, the responsibilities of the central state ministries are being reduced. Interenterprise coordination increasingly will be conducted by the enterprises negotiating with each other for specific contracts. Resolution of contract disputes will be through judicial processes, not through administrative channels. Enterprises will have substantial freedom to determine their own investments, suppliers, and markets. Competition between state companies may be encouraged. In general, supply and demand in the marketplace will influence many more economic decisions than previously was the case.

Interenterprise contracts seem particularly necessary because China's economic planners are now encouraging specialization, both on regional and enterprise levels. Semiarid and mountainous regions will be able to specialize more in animal husbandry and forestry products and will be able to purchase food. Specialized service companies may be set up in rural areas to provide technical services. All these forms of specialization imply much more interaction between enterprises. If government planning departments were to continue to have the responsibility for coordinating these interactions, they would grow immensely, the opportunities for inefficiency and corruption would magnify, and the attention of the government would be diverted from broad political issues to the details of economic exchange.

In rural areas, the power of the bureaucracy is being limited in important ways. A major restructuring appears to be under way in the communes. From 1958 until the early 1980s, the commune integrated government and economic functions, essentially bringing the economy directly under government supervision. In the early 1980s, separate local government offices are being reestablished to carry out government tasks and the commune is becoming solely an economic agency that is hoped to be more insulated from bureaucratic complexities of state power. It remains to be seen exactly what functions will reside in this new version of the commune; it may eventually look like a supply, marketing, and credit cooperative (similar to Taiwan's farmers' associations?).

Within the commune there have been striking changes also. In 1979 – 1980 the production team was given more autonomy to make its own economic plans and decisions. After 1981, more responsibility was given directly to individual households and small groups. These policies strengthen the property rights of both individual commune members and collective groups vis-à-vis the state, a situation somewhat analogous to that in the West, where one of the critical constraints on state power is the existence of private property rights. In China, the situation is different; rural property rights are still ill defined and incomplete (land cannot be bought and sold), and there are very few property rights in the

190

industrial sector. However, this is one of many transitional policies. Usufruct rights for farmland frequently are transformed into property rights in other countries, particularly where investment in soil fertility is needed. In the handicraft and service sectors, private investment is being encouraged both in collective and individual enterprises, leading to acknowledgment of some degree of private property rights. Foreign investment in industry is now being encouraged, and the rights of foreign investors are being put into (still imprecise) law.

As enterprises assume more responsibility for their economic management and interaction, they are being encouraged to use market criteria and incentives. Costs of production, overall profitability, and labor productivity are to be given greater emphasis. Wage systems are being developed which given material rewards and punishment for higher or lower productivity. The state is relying more on price and tax policies, which influence the economic environment in which enterprises operate. The state is reducing its direct regulation of each enterprise.

The state is also relaxing its policies of assigning urban youth to the countryside. Class labels based on pre-1949 status have been discarded. Religious expression is now given much more scope. Migration controls remain intact, however, even though peasants in chronically poor regions may desire seasonal or long-term migration to cities or richer rural regions, which may be experiencing labor shortages because of increases in cropping intensity.

Post-Mao policies to limit state power will face constraints, preeminently the issue of the political strength of the reformers. The limits must be implemented by state employees, who may not have an interest in reducing state power. Currently, a coalition of forces favors limits on state power, primarily to improve economic growth and secondarily to increase personal freedom, or at least to reduce vindictive, arbitrary attacks on individuals. The bureaucracy allows these limitations because it realizes that the government needs broader legitimacy and can ill afford further blame for economic mismanagement. But it remains to be seen whether the bureaucracy will allow its political powers to be regulated and its economic powers to be dissipated.

The reforms to date are partial and contradictory, reflecting the underlying ambiguity of their political legitimacy. Is government's task to change society or to represent it? How can lower levels be elected to represent society, while upper levels claim a revolutionary mandate to change society? Unless the basic structure of the highest levels of government is institutionalized and controlled by law, the partial autonomy at the lower levels will be very fragile. So far, there is no indication that institutionalization will happen. It would be a most radical break in China's three thousand years of political tradition to have the top leadership legitimating its power in laws and popularly elected institutions.

Within each sector, the implementation of reforms is a complex struggle.

191

When state controls over individuals and firms were relaxed, they often moved in unanticipated and undesired directions. In agriculture some farmers reduced grain production and put more emphasis on cash crops and livestock. The government feared difficulty procuring grain for the cities and was not able to purchase and store all the perishable meat and cash crops. Likewise, in industry, factories emphasized products that were profitable and ignored products that were less so. The political system has been tempted to reinstitute administrative controls to rectify these problems.

Inasmuch as state power had been expanded to speed up economic development and to assure socialist, egalitarian values, will constraints on the power of the state affect attainment of these values? With respect to economic growth, the great pressure for savings, investment, and low consumption are being relaxed. More consumer goods are available, and incentives are being improved. The economy should benefit from the new policies, although miracles must not be expected. China is still very poor, and even if the economy grows more rapidly, a major qualitative change in living conditions cannot occur soon. Modest improvements in consumption, however, can have a substantial subjective impact.

The socialist values of egalitarianism will inevitably suffer. In the industrial sector, the new powers and obligations of factory managers to emphasize profits will reduce the opportunities of workers to participate. In the rural sector, economic differences in living standards between local communities will increase. In both urban and rural areas the renewed, expanding role of individual enterprises will undermine many collectivist values. So far, there is no indication that the state will relax its basic control over urban-rural relations. Controls over grain marketing, agricultural inputs, and migration remain. If these controls were dropped, there probably would be considerable migration to cities.

One casualty of the new policies is the emphasis on ideology, socialist consciousness, and the notion of a new socialist man. It had been hoped that with enough ideological training, people would eventually adopt socialist values and would individually and collectively, spontaneously adopt socialist habits. In the long run, this evolution was assumed to obviate the need for government action, and the state could "wither away." Now these expectations are reduced; and, ironically, if anyone is to perform a welfare role (help poor regions, families, or individuals), it must be the state. In some localities there are experiments with a formal pension system for retired farmers; previously they were supported by their families. Thus even when the power of the state bureaucracy is being reduced, new tasks are being created for it.

The extent to which state power can be reduced will also be limited by broader considerations. The problems of national security will intensify in the future as China's complex interdependent economy becomes more vulnerable to military attack. Strong central power will be justified to counterbalance strong regional tendencies. The task of harnessing and controlling China's rivers will always require strong central coordination. The state is also taking on new powers by its rigid birth control campaign. By also promising long-term rewards for one-child families and penalties for multi-child families, it is positing a powerful role of the state in influencing families in their most intimate behavior. It is creating both long-term problems (children with different rights and claims against the state) and long-term obligations (promises of rewards decades in the future). The long-term impact of these promises would seem to strengthen the role of the state in the future.

These various factors suggest limits on the reduction of state power. Although some relaxation and rationalization is likely, it seems unlikely that the present policy to limit state power can be very extensive or permanent. More likely, China will continue to face the same dilemma of how to use and yet limit state power that confounds other societies. In China (as elsewhere) constant changes are likely as old solutions become new problems.

8

Marxism and the Market in Socialist China: The Reforms of 1979–1980 in Context

Dorothy J. Solinger

Up through the midpoint of 1980, the Chinese press continued, nearly daily, on the course set over a year before: presenting its readers with new designs of departure from the planned organization of the economy. To judge from its pages, model industrial enterprises (at the party's behest) were consulting market demand in determining what to produce, while retail shops were procuring where supplies were plentiful, and not from their regional wholesaler, as set down in previous plans.

Close reading shows, however, that the reforms were along the fringes and experimental, more often than not to be pursued only after administratively dictated quotas were fulfilled. Thus despite the flurry of market rhetoric that followed the December 1978 Third Plenum of the Eleventh Central Committee's injunction to "combine market adjustment with adjustment by the plan," it is safe to say that the chief sinews and the general shape of the Chinese economic system were not dismantled.

In an effort to put these experiments into a longer-range context, this essay will analyze the effects that the views of Marx have had over the thirty years from 1949 to 1979 upon the treatment toward, structure, practice, and politics of trade in the People's Republic. This analysis is meant not only as a review of the past; it intends also to point to the ways in which Marxism has struck deep roots in this sector, both in the state and in Chinese society. The result — a "socialist commerce" that eschews the market — poses barriers to "reform," promising though the new proposals appeared at first blush. Special note will be taken of these barriers.

The argument will begin by summarizing Marx's views on commerce and his vague prescriptions about its demise as capitalism passes from being. It will then show the influence on attitudes toward trade in China that these views have had when added to traditional Chinese disdain for the trader; the way they have

194

worked to determine the administrative organization of exchange as well as the semilegal divergences from the ideal model; and the manner in which Marxist ideas about the transition from capitalism to communism have set the terms of elite-level debate over how to handle the circulation of commodities in a socialist society. Finally, the political decision in 1978 to shift from full reliance on the plan to an introduction of market principles will be sketched briefly to indicate the nature of the opposition to the market initiatives.

Marx on Commerce

Three broad aspects of Marx's thoughts on commerce are relevant to the discussion that follows: first, his perceptions of it were largely negative; second, he saw it as closely linked to capitalist society and so presumed it would vanish when capitalism did; and third, he believed that when the market was gone, it would be replaced by a planned organization of the economy, although he was vague as to just when and under what conditions this transition would happen. The overall impact of these three facets of Marxism has been to limit the operation of the market in societies that honor Marx's views.

Marx's views on the role of commerce as he observed it in capitalist society, though not entirely negative, were on the whole critical. He recognized that merchant capital expands the market, promotes the productivity and adds to the accumulation of industrial capital. Furthermore, this form of capital shortens the time of circulation of productive capital and reduces industry's expenditure of energy, thereby freeing time for more production.[1] Marx's general assessment, however, was that no value is produced in the process of circulation, that is, no new wealth is created for society, so that the surplus value (profit) that it appropriates is actually merely a portion of the surplus value already yielded by productive (industrial) capital.[2] Buying and selling, then, partook of a parasitism for Marx.[3]

At one point terming at least part of commerce "unproductive exploitation," Marx did draw a distinction between "supplemental" costs in commerce (including packaging, storing, and transport), which grow from activities that continue the productive process and so add to the value of the product, and "pure" costs, which arise only because of the process of purchase and sale. It is these latter costs — for accounting, marketing, bookkeeping, correspondence, and advertising — deriving from what he saw as a worthless transfer of title of ownership (among wholesalers, speculative buyers, and other commission agents) that Marx felt to be especially unworthy.[4]

To understand the second theme above, Marx's expectation that commerce belonged to capitalism and would disappear with it, his notions of "use-value" and "exchange-value" (or, simply, "value") must be introduced.[5] The former relates to the utility of a product, its ability to fulfill a particular human need, and depends upon the totality of its physical qualities. The latter concerns the product's relation to other goods on the market and is established, according to Marx, by the amount of labor time "socially necessary" to produce it. The term "socially necessary" refers to the fact that at a given level of development of technology, an average number of hours is necessary to make an object in a particular society at a given time. The concept of exchange-value, which formed the core of Marx's labor theory of value, applies especially to market societies, in which exchange through buying and selling occurs, for Marx believed value generally set the price of a commodity.

Although neither Marx nor Engels specified explicitly the shape of postcapitalist exchange, their writings did suggest that value as price, that is, as money equivalent, would not be present in the absence of markets. Instead, one analyst concludes, Marx "seems to emphasize labor-unit bookkeeping" in socialist society, after the proletarian revolution has brought capitalism to an end.[6] On this point Engels is explicit, in a much-cited passage: "From the moment society enters into the possession of the means of production and uses them in direct association for production, the labor of each individual becomes social labor . . . the quantities of labor put into products would then be expressed in their natural, absolute measure, time . . . at that point, society will not assign values to products."[7]

Ernest Mandel, in interpreting Marx, has decided that Marx meant to say that "in socialist society the products of human labor have a directly social character, and thus have no [exchange] value . . . they are not commodities [that is, products created for the purpose of being sold], but use-values, produced for the satisfaction of human needs." Mandel holds that Marx expected that "economic categories" — commodities, value, price, wages, profit, and thus by implication the market — would cease to exist in a true socialist society. For, he maintains, the fully developed socialist economy was seen by Marx as being capable of producing an abundance of use-values. Under those conditions distribution would no longer need to be based on monetary exchange since the economy would be capable of ensuring each member of society the satisfaction of his/her basic needs.[8]

Going on, then, to the third point noted above, Marx, viewing commerce as exploitative and largely unproductive in capitalist society, expected that it would be replaced, at some point after the proletariat had seized the means of production, by a planned distribution of products. Such a distribution would be governed by the community according to the needs of individuals and not directed by the differential financial power that various consumers might command.[9] Just how far into the postcapitalist period markets were to continue to exist is not clear from Marx's writings.

196

A typical comment on this theme from the writings of Marx and Engels reads thus:

> How does it happen that trade, which after all is nothing more than the exchange of products of various individuals and countries, rules the whole world through the relation of supply and demand . . . [which] with invisible hand allots fortune and misfortune to men . . . — while with the abolition of the basis of private property, with the communistic regulation of production, . . . the power of the relation of supply and demand is dissolved, and men get exchange, production, the mode of their mutual relation, under their own control again?[10]

In this passage, Marx and Engels refer to the final, communist stage as the time when production would cease to be ruled by the market, and they discussed the market mechanism only in relation to capitalism.[11] But in at least one place they also suggest that a plan would begin to regulate production in the immediate, transitional, postcapitalist period.[12] This lack of clarity has laid the basis for much unease in socialist societies over the continued existence of marketing and has fueled frequent debates over whether and how much market exchange may exist after the revolution.

Each of these themes — negativism, disappearance and replacement by a plan, and ambiguity about timing — has an analog in Chinese stance toward the market. First, commerce has been considered lowly in the People's Republic and treated accordingly. Next, insofar as possible, planned allocation and procurement have been substituted for monetary exchange; and, third, the obscurity in Marx has fostered conflict among the leadership as to how to treat the sphere of trade. Each of these factors affects the recent efforts at reform, and each will be discussed below.

Attitudes toward and Treatment of Trade in Post-1949 China

Marx's views on trade have been laid atop a traditional disdain for the money-making dealer in goods. The Confucian morality of Chinese tradition expressed its disapproval for the merchant by ranking him fourth in a list of the four social groupings that made up society. That this culturally rooted contempt for commerce lives on in China is apparent in the following quotation from a press article of 1964, which was attempting to combat such ideas: "Who doesn't know how to do this: receiving cash with one hand and passing on the goods with the other? It's really like putting one in an inferior capacity to let us middle school graduates do this!" The author here labeled this belittling of commerce a product of history, left over by the exploiting classes.[13]

Further evidence for social prejudice against trade was provided by a former

197

commercial accountant from Beijing, who related that, when she was a commercial student in the early 1960s, her class had been taken to a special section of a Beijing department store, there to regale in the glories of viewing commodities meant for high officialdom. The visit's purpose was to try to show the skeptical students that work in the trade sector had its bright side after all.[14] Most students at her school, she explained, had been assigned there despite its low priority on their own list of preferred educational institutions.

Besides looking down upon commerce, Chinese, like Soviet Russians, entertain a socialist suspicion of trade, which has resulted in a distrust of commercial workers, who are often seen as dishonest and speculative.[15] Doubts about those involved in the commercial sphere appeared first in Mao's early postliberation policies, when he mandated "leniency for industry, severity for commerce" during *wufan*, the campaign against the "five evils" in capitalist industry and commerce. Mao also issued a call during these early years to "develop private industry within limits set by the state and reduce private commerce step by step."[16]

More recent mistrust is attested to in lines such as: "When you stand on the riverbank all the time, how can your shoes not get wet?" and "To have economic problems is an 'occupational disease' for those on the finance and trade front."[17] And, less allegorically: "The overwhelming majority of finance and trade workers and staff are directly in charge of money and commodities . . . they may easily be corrupted by bourgeois thought."[18]

The political sensitivity of the commercial sector is compounded because many of its workers "come from various strata . . . and have brought with them various non-proletarian ideas and working styles."[19] The background of commercial workers is suspect in that many of those skilled in trade before 1949 — the smaller private merchants and the former employees of capitalist commercial enterprises — were drawn into the state network, especially after the socialist transformation of commerce in 1956.[20]

Former commercial workers from the People's Republic confirmed that this suspicion operates on a daily basis in China: "Even if you lose or destroy a page in an account book by accident," said one former commercial accountant, "you'll be accused of doing it intentionally, and asked to explain your purpose." The catchword for commercial work, *cha zhang*, check up on the accounts, is a serious business.

Trade has met with another, more concrete form of discrimination in China (as it does in the Soviet Union as well), especially as against its great rival, the industrial sector. In both societies, production has taken priority and commerce has suffered as a consequence — not only in status and esteem but in state investment as well. Thus salary, career prospects, equipment, financing, work premises, and storage space all are unsatisfactory.[21] A recent article by a section of the Ministry of Commerce about that sector's new needs during the era of the four modernizations reveals the poor treatment the commercial sector has received. The article first refers to a claim by Mao from the late 1950s: "In the past several years there's been a problem in construction . . . we've paid attention only to the 'bones' and not to the 'meat'; factory building and machinery have both been done well, but urban administration and measures of a service nature have not been done correspondingly well." The problem of accommodating urban populations, though, rather than being attended to in the 1950s, grew over the years, according to the authors, as attested to by crowded shops, an insufficient number of vegetable markets, and long queues. Storage installations and transport facilities remain flawed; and sanitation, displays, and working hours continue to be problem areas. Finally, the article pleads, "commercial work is hard. Many units' personnel have long working hours and lack benefits. We should worry about their livelihood."[22]

Thus Marxism has meshed with a long-term Chinese bias against commerce to perpetuate distrust of its staff and to downgrade its material foundation. Behind these attitudes and treatment has been a desire to keep commercial activity to a minimum. As a result, its unattractiveness has hampered recruitment and its low level of funding has maintained the number of shops well below demand.[23] Whether these dispositions — in ideology and investment — can easily be turned around will be a key issue for reformers.

Commerce and the Planned Economy

The urge to restrict commerce in socialist Chinese society, then, stems in large part from Marx's teachings. Following the Soviet example, this desire has entailed acting upon Marx's dictum that a planned organization of the economy would succeed the proletarian revolution. The effect has been to try to limit market behavior — buying and selling — even as exchange persists. An important by-product is a set of officials with vested interests in running the plan, along with habits of implementing it among managers, workers, and rural cadres.

The mechanisms used over the years in ordering the Chinese economy have included plan targets written in large part in units of physical output; direct allocation of supplies in the industrial sector; total purchase of the products of industry by commercial departments and their mandatory procurement by retail shops from fixed wholesale suppliers; a heavy reliance on the state-run People's Bank for financial transactions; exchange of grain, a principal commodity, forbidden through marketing channels but carried out instead through taxation and compulsory purchase by the state; rural taxation exacted and part of rural remuneration for labor made in kind; a rationing system for scarce and vital consumer items; and state-set prices, along with price controls to keep inflation in check. Although many of these features of the economic system came under discussion and even attack beginning in 1978 and 1979,[24] none of the proposals for change has yet dislodged this basic apparatus.

Planning, which has held sway in industry[25] to a greater or lesser extent from 1949 to 1979, deals in input (raw materials, equipment) quotas, and output targets.[26] Rather than being based upon prices, the plan is drawn up according to a system of "material balances," whereby inputs are assigned in light of what is available and an attempt is made to account for all resources.[27] The allocation amounts to a transferral of goods between producing and consuming ministries, without the use of money.

Further, through the "free supply" of producer goods, which has been part and parcel of the planning system, all goods and materials are distributed to factories in amounts geared to enable them to fulfill their production plans.[28] A recent critique claims that, "because the enterprises are not required to pay for the supplies, they have frantically stockpiled goods, whether or not the goods are of any use to them. Some factories have stocks that could last more than ten years."[29]

This accounting and exchanging in physical units, along with pressures on factory managers to expand their production, has often led in both the Soviet Union and China to managers concentrating most of their attention on physical quantity of output.[30] In agriculture, too, though the peasantry may be responsive to price and income incentives, lower-level cadres have preferred instead to direct their energies to crash programs to increase production of key crops and have commanded the peasants to perform accordingly.[31] In both industry and agriculture, then, physical targets — goods and produce — have mattered more than price and have habituated cadres to orient their work around plan fulfillment.

The commercial system was formed in the earliest stages of socialist transformation, when state-owned wholesale corporations, each dealing in one (or several similar) commodities, were set up to monopolize trade in that line of product. They placed orders for processing and manufacturing with industrial departments and then either purchased their entire output or underwrote their sales. The purpose of this method in the early and mid-1950s was to control the source of goods, thereby edging out capitalist wholesalers. Purchase and allocation plans approved by the state dictated the planned distribution of goods from a given wholesale corporation to a set retail enterprise within its geographical jurisdiction.[32]

This system, though criticized on occasion and despite periodic efforts to make it more responsive to the market (in 1956, in the early 1960s, and again beginning in late 1978), has remained largely unchanged. This arrangement tends to lead to conflict, not cooperation, between industry and its marketers,

200

as factories try to overfulfill their production plans while commercial units are forced to buy products that are often defective and unrelated to market demand. In such cases, of course, the commercial units find it difficult to meet their own sales targets.[33]

Another mechanism that has obviated a genuine market approach to trade is mediation of exchange through the People's Bank. Chinese radicals explain this system as having been instituted expressly to avoid allowing cash to pass through people's hands: "To close loopholes in the flow of currency, we have adopted a series of restrictive measures. Transactions between enterprises of more than thirty *yuan* should all be settled through bank transfers. This prevents people from using money to make illegal deals."[34]

Besides the enterprise-to-enterprise exchanges within the industrial sector, the initial state directive on the establishment of the commercial system in China forbade use of currency in state-run marketing: "Currency may not be used for payment in the allocation of materials among state trade organs, for those between the state trade organs and the state enterprises, and for transportation between the state trade organs and the national transportation organs. Payment shall be made in drafts, to be cleared through the bank."[35] The bank's rigid control over capital is reinforced because it is the sole authority that can extend short-term credit, as between wholesale and retail trade organs. And for transactions outside a circumscribed locality, payments must be approved through the bank office where the buyer's credit is deposited, and all credit must be used only for the purpose specified. These regulations are designed to ensure that buyers carry and make use of only a minimal amount of cash, thus limiting opportunities for commercial exchange.[36]

In the agricultural sector, for grain, the principal crop, free marketing ceased to exist in 1953.[37] Here again, China has borrowed from the Soviet Union by abolishing the market for major crops (grain in 1953; cotton in 1954; oil-bearing crops thereafter) and substituting a system of compulsory procurement and rationed distribution through quotas. Many other products are also sold to the state on a contractual basis and can be marketed only after quotas for sales to the state have been met.[38]

Audrey Donnithorne has made the point that it is difficult to draw a dividing line between trade and taxation in the rural sector because a portion of the grain harvest (fixed at about 5 percent of gross production-team income for many years) is requisitioned as a tax in kind, for which the peasants receive no recompense; and, atop that, a further amount is purchased through the compulsory quota system by the state at fixed prices and so is not pure tax or trade.[39] Taxes were first taken in kind, in traditional fashion, by the new government in 1949, when the state needed grain and when both prices and currency systems were in a chaotic state; no change was made thereafter.[40]

201

Thus both the procurement and taxation systems force the peasantry to do less marketing than they would in the absence of these state controls.[41] This effect is reinforced by the peasants' receipt of a sizable share of the commune's payment for their labor in kind. Moreover, payment in the countryside, both in kind and in cash, is made only after the harvest, so that, according to a former rural marketing cadre, when a peasant's cash runs out, s/he falls back upon the customary practice of barter.[42] In all these ways, the socialist state in China has managed to limit the flow of cash between rural hands and to breed an unease among many cadres and peasants over becoming too involved in market activity.[43]

Rationing of scarce and vital items is yet another device that limits exchange through money in China. Formal rationing began with the institution of purchase quotas, to which it is linked: simply put, goods compulsorily requisitioned from the rural areas are distributed, through coupons, in the cities. This form of allocation avoids using inflation to cut back on demand, enables the regime to enforce population control, and serves state goals of equity.[44] In 1959 a left-wing justification of this system explained that, though high prices would limit the amount of sales of scarce consumer goods, the effect would be that those with higher incomes would enjoy relatively unlimited access to such goods, while those with lower incomes might be unable even to satisfy their most basic livelihood needs.[45] Rationing, it is hoped, will also prevent speculation and stockpiling; in fact, however, as will be discussed below, a lively trade in ration tickets somewhat undermines the system.

All the features of the Chinese economic system enumerated above — a plan often focused on the output of physical units, direct allocation of inputs, the bank as intermediary in transactions, peasantry-state grain dealings in kind, and rationing — are forms of exchange on which Marx's economic categories are not brought to bear. Despite this emphasis, prices do have a definite role in China, but they have been so designed and operated as to accentuate the same tendency toward downplaying the role of the market as do the other features. This is so because price policy has often been an important tool of state control. In the words of the director of the Ministry of Commerce's Bureau of Price Control in early 1958: "In our socialist society, the fluctuation in any commodity's market price directly or indirectly influences the state and the people's economic interest, and is related to reallocation of the nation's economic capital . . . and any price change will influence the speed of the state's capital accumulation and construction and the speed of improvement of the people's livelihood. [Thus we must] think about relationships, proportions, and economic laws in price-setting."[46]

The effect of this political concern with price has been twofold: most prices (except for those on free peasant markets in the countryside, which generally may move largely with supply and demand) have been set by the state (at various administrative levels); and long-term price stability has been a major cornerstone of policy. Over the years in China, prices fixed in light of state purposes have diminished the impact of the market on society since prices have generally neither reflected nor controlled the supply-demand relationship.

Prices of consumer goods in command economies tend to be set in accord with the rate at which planners hope to dispose of the goods, so that supply has little to do with market pressures. In the face of the shortages and resulting repressed inflation, consumers must submit to queues and informal rationing and may have money for which there is no outlet.[47] A Western journalist reported that, as of mid-1977, the feeling in much of the Chinese countryside was that "there isn't much point in working to save money if there is nothing to spend the money on."[48]

The combination of prices set by state planners who take the supply-demand relationship as only one factor among many in their calculations and long-term freezes in these prices has meant that the market has had an ambiguous role in socialist commerce in China. When demand does not regulate production, so that desired goods are not available, marketing is a very different experience for producer, distributor, and consumer from that in a capitalist society.

Marx predicted that a regulated, planned economy would one day replace money and the commodities money purchases. He did not foresee, however, that socialist states, enticed by his teachings, would rush to install the trappings of a nonmarket, nonmonetized economy — through a plan laid out largely in physical units, direct allocation of production materials, and rationed consumer goods — before his prerequisite of plenty could truly render trade obsolete. Thus exchange has continued to exist in China, but its mode has mostly not been through the market.

The "Second Economy"

Official, planned exchange, however, is only one side of the picture. When the plan fails — through inefficiency in timing, delivery of goods that fail to suit demand, and insufficiencies in coordination among units that lead to excesses and sellouts of the same stocks in different regions — habits of adaptation have helped to remedy the flaws. This "second economy," based on barter and interpersonal relations, contributes to enforce China's Marxian-inspired eschewal of the marketplace. "There was nothing wrong; no money changed hands," informants in Beijing are reported to have recently told an American journalist, in discussing their *houmen* ("back-door") activities.[49]

Besides the influence of Marxism (and the effects of scarcity) in encouraging

203

barter and a fallback on friends and connections, Chinese culture predisposes the population in these directions. In this society, 80 percent of the population still lives on the land, and produce has traditionally served as currency. The age-old custom of barter at rural fairs obviated the need for cash; in a modern-day variant, peasants trade one rationed good for another (for example a certain quantity of oil for some amount of grain).[50] An article from the 1950s refers to rural peddlers who "make purchases and sales by barter in the countryside, in line with the people's customs."[51]

When asked how widespread exchange-by-gift really was in his area of the Chinese countryside, a former rural supply and marketing cooperative worker explained that presents were necessary only to obtain items in especially short stock such as pesticides when supply was inadequate in the busy farm season. This man came from a poor, desolate area some ten hours by car from Canton, which had little finery to offer; his supplier had to be content with a small amount of tobacco or wine.[52]

A rural commercial cadre working much nearer Canton explained that when the plan failed, one had to go directly to a store or factory in the big city to find the necessary spare part or extra accessory. "But they won't sell you the thing or produce it for you specially without a gift," he explained. His commune offered peanuts and chickens in exchange for especially popular goods.[53] These gifts accompany payment at state-set prices and are made in lieu of offering to buy at a higher price.

Some consumer goods and key services that are particularly valued and hard to come by have been coined "the three treasures," referring to the three sectors whose workers — doctors, drivers, and food shop assistants — have access to highly valued and scarce goods and services.[54] Rooms in crowded urban hospitals and Western medicines are difficult to obtain without making presents to a well-placed doctor; private transport of materials is impossible without a driver in one's debt, in this society where no one owns a motor vehicle; and those who deal in foodstuffs can sometimes slyly slip out extras. Thus in a context of ideological abhorrence of the market, shortage in China is often remedied by passing around products under one's control, thereby bypassing price and market exchange.

Along with barter, *guanxi* (relationship, connections) is another functional substitute for money in the Chinese system of trade. The use of personal ties to facilitate exchange has always tempered and tampered with the cash nexus for Chinese people. The Russian concept of *blat* — influence, connections, pulling strings — plays an analogous role in the Soviet economy.[55]

Perhaps the ways and workings of this mechanism can best be appreciated through reading a set of tales about how *guanxi* develops and how it works in the Chinese commercial sector.[56] Some of these informal relationships grow up in an unexpected, even ironic manner. One informant told of a special hotel in Loyang that shelters procurement personnel from across the country who come to purchase that city's famous tractor parts. Because these personnel are likely to be carrying some cash, they are placed together in this sequestered inn to keep them safe from thieves. This hotel, meant as a haven from illegal doings, has become a hotbed for fostering personal ties and for swapping and gathering information as to what products can best be obtained where in the country and from whom. In a similar vein, political meetings for finance and trade cadres at the commune level in the countryside, planned to inspire purity, are also the breeding grounds for relationships that eventually hatch much under-the-counter barter. In these two examples, *guanxi* acts as an informal, noneconomic means of collecting market intelligence and of furthering non-planned, but still not full market, exchange.

One youth sent to the countryside to labor with peasants and learn the morality of simple agricultural toil was co-opted by the supply and marketing cooperative (SMC) when his significant city connections surfaced. In particular (to illustrate the complexity of the ties that may be drawn upon), this young man's schoolmate's older brother was a procurement agent for a Canton factory. Soon after his arrival in the countryside he was often asked to go into Canton to buy hard-to-get items for his unit; within another several years he was formally made a cooperative worker.[57]

Several informants explained how *guanxi* makes the difference in market work. Most obviously, it helps a purchaser to get the scarce, specific, or popular item unavailable otherwise from a wholesale department or factory. In a slightly more intricate mode of exchange, the SMC of one commune, in need of a special good that it is unable to obtain from its superior wholesale department, might barter with another commune's SMC if the two find each has something the other wants. In such deals each party pays the state-set price. But, in the absence of *guanxi*, exchange is far less likely to take place if one side lacks nothing the other can offer.

One final vignette concerns the free markets. In these local markets, where most sellers offer similar wares, one's placement in the marketplace is crucial to beating out competitors. Position depends, however, not just on time of arrival at the fair but on presenting gifts and having friends among the control personnel as well. "But you can't offer money," an interviewee explained. "This could cause problems, if someone where to report you. In such a case, you would certainly be sent to a very unfavorable location indeed."

Connections crop up in the course of socialist commercial work, then, just as they do for capitalist businessmen. The difference is that in China they are generally formed wholly without the aid of money, and they function as its replacement.

At the level of unit and enterprise, as well as among the populace, barter and *guanxi* take the place of purchase. One example, offered by an informant in

205

Hong Kong, is a system known as *"cengceng songli"* (present a gift at every level). Scarce, popular, or specialized goods often cannot be obtained without a host of middlemen/women; and each intermediary wants at least a token in thanks for having expedited the procurement.[58] Needless to say, the gift-bearer must engage in a bit of "indirect theft" from his/her own unit to win the desired supplies.[59]

Along with food shop attendants, retail store personnel have many opportunities for the nonmarket exchange of goods.[60] "Store leaders can get anything they want by trading goods with other store leaders," a former shop worker revealed.[61] Once the excess goods are in their hands, retail workers keep them, give them to friends and relatives, or sometimes use them for illegal exchange.[62]

Besides salespeople in shops skimming off stocks, those in other units in charge of goods also use their positions to trade outside the plan. Thus supply and marketing co-ops have been accused of bartering, a "queer way of trading" that "fosters shortages."[63] In the instance reported, two hundred piculs of melon seeds were exchanged for four hundred piculs of preserved lichee.[64] Also, factories have had to be warned against trading their products for foodstuffs and manufactured consumer goods from stores.[65]

Since free purchases at fluctuating prices have been forbidden in the planned economy, the populace and economic enterprises have drawn on custom to find functional equivalents for the market. Thus barter and connections have acted in China as semilicit ways of lubricating the fixities of administrative allocation and of helping to circumvent the disadvantages of scarcity. It seems unlikely that the regime will be able to root out these practices of informal exchange and replace them with market-based trade while shortages persist and while an overarching plan still structures the main outlines of the economy.

To recapitulate, Marx's views on commerce have added their weight to the already negative attitude toward trade in China. These views have also been responsible for the institution of a planned, hierarchically ordered, and command-managed arrangement for circulating goods that has structured the organization of production and created its own set of vested interests. In such a climate, work units and the populace at large, wary of dealing in cash, have attempted to compensate for the plan's shortcomings without resorting to buying and selling.

Marxism and Political Stances toward the Market: Three Tendencies

In the face of the seemingly widespread prominence being accorded economic reform and the pervasiveness of market jargon in the press after late 1978, it is important to recall that much leadership conflict has attended commercial policy making over the years in China. This conflict has its origins in differential understandings of Marx's design for the postcapitalist society; analytically, it revolves around three "tendencies of articulation."[66] These three can be neatly summed up in ideal-typical fashion as stances focusing respectively on class, state control, and maximum productivity, and they will be referred to here as the radical, bureaucratic, and marketeer models.[67]

Each of these three tendencies can be related to one part of the discussion above: first, it is radicals who take the most negative attitude toward trade. Thus it was the radicals who referred on one occasion to "the tinsel world of commodities and exchange by means of money," which they counterposed to what they viewed as the vastly superior "socialist relations of cooperation."[68] Then it is bureaucrats who most favor the planned approach to commercial work. And marketeers, impatient with inflexibilities in the plan but anxious to find state-sponsored ways to smooth exchange and hopeful of rectifying scarcity by stimulating productivity, are the ones who present new models of reform to do away with a need for the "second economy."

Because all the proponents are socialists, tensions and conflict among the three tendencies can best be understood as an internal dynamic within socialism. For each stresses most heavily one strain among the various prescriptions Marx set out for the transitional period, after the revolutionary victory, as the means of production came into the hands of the proletariat. Thus Marx and Engels decreed that in this period the proletariat would use the public power it had won to oppress the past ruling class, the bourgeoisie, through the class struggle emphasized by the radicals.[69]

The two philosophers also indicated, as noted above, that production and exchange could be regulated by men's own control, and not through supply and demand, once private property had been abolished,[70] and it is this aspect, planned state management, upon which bureaucrats focus. Finally, marketeers concentrate on the Marxian dictum that the proletariat as ruling class must "increase the total of productive forces as rapidly as possible."[71] Each of the three, then, draws on the one Marxian value it most prizes in designing its approach to commercial work.

Although all three groups do have some appreciation for the key values the other two hold, it sometimes seems as if each tendency is somewhat fixated upon the pursuit of its principal concern. Thus radicals, in trying to ensure that poor peasants and workers are protected, "served," or otherwise benefited by commercial policy, have at times worried that policies that aimed only at increasing economic growth or at more planning control would lose sight of a "proletarian" purpose.

Bureaucrats, intent on arranging purchases and supplies in a planned way, through vertically arranged state organs, have seemed on occasion to value controls for their own sake and may forget that these controls were instituted in the first place to serve goals of economic development and social redistribution.

And marketeers, focused on stimulating growth through a relatively free exchange with occasional fluctuating prices, do not ignore class issues and plans altogether but, in thinking of class, have shown more solicitude for those in the middling tiers of the spectrum and have advocated a plan that is moderated by the law of value.[72]

Perhaps this quality of near monomania over one value is the ultimate weakness of each position: the values that each group treats as secondary and thus tends to neglect have always come back to haunt it as its opponents call for policy changes in the name of the overlooked goals. An analysis of the stances of the three groups follows, along with a brief examination of the three central issues, taken from Marx, around which all controversy in the Chinese commercial sector has centered.

Class

Besides having a general distaste for market society as one that exploits its laboring class, Marx also made special reference to the distorting effect of class society on "social demand." This factor, he noted, "which regulates the principle of demand, is subject to the mutual relationship of different classes and their respective economic positions . . . nothing can be explained by the relation of supply to demand before ascertaining the basis on which this relation rests."[73] More simply, markets are more likely to serve and to give clout to those economically better endowed.[74] It has been suggested that in pre-1949 China, peasants at the upper end of the scale would have been more inclined to rely on the market.[75]

An essay on rural corruption written by radicals in 1965 illustrates this tendency's concern for class: "Commercial speculation and usurious activities form a bridge that leads the peasant individual economy to capitalism. A peasant must become a merchant and amass a small amount of wealth before he can be a rich peasant and capitalist. On the other hand, the activities of business speculation and usury are bound to cause some of the peasants to become impoverished and bankrupt."[76]

To guard against these eventualities, radicals in power set up standards for commercial staff and workers to determine whether their work was good: "(1) is their feeling for the workers, peasants and soldiers deep; (2) are the varieties and items they handle welcomed by the workers, peasants, and soldiers; (3) is their form of service convenient for the workers, peasants and soldiers; and (4) does their service quality and attitude satisfy the workers, peasants and soldiers?"[77]

Inspired by a morality of class struggle that gives power to the poorer, the radical assessment of commerce is that it is basically evil because, dealing in money and profits, it is both based upon and leads to further inequitable distribution. Not only should it be run by and for the least advantaged, radicals hold, but it should be kept to a minimum, with commercial workers engaging in productive as well as exchange activities: "Cloth dealers should learn to weave cloth, vegetable-mongers should learn to grow vegetables," in the words of one radically inspired editorial.[78]

State Control

A key issue for bureaucrats in market management is how to deal with the frequently surfacing problem in China of supply not meeting demand. There have been an array of bureaucratic answers to this question, all of which circumvent the straightforward approach of the marketeer, who merely relies on prices that move with supply and demand as an incentive to stimulate economic growth.

Bureaucrats believe in increasing production as a way to meet demand, but they prefer not to do so by allowing prices to rise on their own.[79] Instead, they speak of "expanding production in proportion as planned" and "using the plan to adjust [individual] prices," while keeping the overall price structure intact.[80] Another alternative they favor is to regulate distribution and guide consumption on the basis of constant supply, rather than to induce more output.[81] This approach includes rationing schemes and "planned supply."[82]

Besides shifting planning targets in production and reorganizing allocation, bureaucrats also strive to ensure that the state procures as large a proportion of productive output as possible through its own purchasing organs: "The major means [of increasing agricultural produce] is to start from the strengthening of collection and purchasing work for the expansion of the sources of supply. . . . We must stengthen measures for the purchase of those agricultural products included under the scheme of unified purchases, and strictly prohibit them from entering the free market."[83]

And, finally, a last and related option has been the institution, at times, of state-directed goods exchange meets, a form of marketing that, it is hoped, will spur production but direct its issue into the net of the state.[84]

The bureaucrats' assessment of commercial work draws on the view Marx advanced that accepts this activity as a necessary link in the chain of expanded reproduction: "Production determines the market, as well as the market determining production."[85] In addition, "Production, distribution, exchange and consumption are all members of one entity, different sides of one unit. Production predominates over all the other elements. . . . Production is also influenced by the other elements, e.g., with the expansion of the market, i.e., of the sphere of exchange, production grows in volume."[86]

Necessary though commerce may be, however, bureaucrats seek to use state organs, fixed prices, hierarchical allocation and supervision, and centrally set plans to channel it and limit its spontaneity. Their assessment that production is the basis for all economic activity gives them grounds for some sympathy with marketeers. But the ideal-typical representative of each of these two groups stresses differentially the significance that commercial work can have in spurring growth.

Productivity

Marketeers in socialist China have never gone so far as to advocate a total abandonment of all plans and rations. Rather, the thrust of their initiatives has been to try to devise arguments that justify and to design methods that permit some combination of market freedoms with a nationally guided "balance," believing this to be the best way to enhance productivity. Most obviously, because they evaluate commerce as an essentially positive force in stimulating increased growth, they have favored letting some prices fluctuate with the forces of supply and demand and have on various occasions recommended indirect planning, enterprise autonomy, and profit retention, industrial responsiveness to consumer desires, a reduction in commercial bureaucracy, and, as a consequence, direct exchanges between buyer and seller.

The periods when marketeer influence was strong and explicit have to date been relatively brief in China, normally nipped in the bud in the past by radicals (the 1956–1957 episode ended as the Great Leap got under way; the policies of the early 1960s fell victim to the gathering storms of the Cultural Revolution). Still, at several junctures over the thirty-year period under review the Chinese, like economic leaders in other Soviet-style systems, have seriously debated the question of how much market exchange can in fact exist within a planned, command economy.[87]

Debates on this theme are abstruse and arcane to the uninitiated and unfailingly are fashioned in the purest Marxist jargon at the same time that they challenge the most basic presumptions of Marx himself. At issue is the central problem of the extent to which purely economic factors, rather than social need and political decision, may govern economic activity in the period after private ownership has been largely eliminated and capitalism pronounced dead.[88]

Each tendency indeed adheres to a different central value, and that value in each case colors the manner in which each makes its normative appraisal of commercial activity. Still, in comparing the recommendations that the advocates of each make for commercial work, it becomes clear that there are certain overlaps in their views. These overlaps have made possible temporary, if uneasy, alliances on some issues between various pairs among the three in the

210

course of policy making for the commercial sector over the years.[89] The discussion below summarizes and contrasts the recommendations each has made on the following themes: the role for state organs in commercial work; the organizing principle for exchange and distribution; the method to be used in coordinating exchange and the role for the plan; the manner in which inflation ought to be handled; the degree to which state monopolies should be used; and the proper forms for market control.[90]

First, each takes a position on the role for state organs and state-set prices in commercial work. Bureaucrats and radicals tend to agree that both should be used — bureaucrats in the interests of maintaining price stability and manipulating the balance between social purchasing power and the supply of goods; radicals to ensure that state-run units crowd "class enemies" out of the marketplace and that a reduction in price differentials (regional, seasonal, wholesale-retail) will close up the loopholes that permit merchants and rich peasants to engage in speculation and profiteering. Marketeers, however, believe that the existence of many organizational links in the chain of exchange unduly prolongs and so stifles the liveliness of the trade, as well as wasting resources and adding to the depletion of the goods. Therefore, both bureaucrat and radical prefer state-managed rural fairs to freely conducted ones, a view countered by the marketeers. A radical would be most satisfied if all fairs were abolished.

Deeply distrustful of money and its tendency to promote a class polarization benefiting the economically better off, the radical hopes that local self-sufficiency can obviate a need for most marketing. Bureaucrats, however, take centralized distribution as their preferred organizing principle for exchange and distribution. The marketeer, on the other hand, believes in a mode of distribution that partakes a bit of both views and thus has sympathized at times with each of the other two: decentralized exchange is good, says the marketeer, but only insofar as it revolves around investigating the genuine local conditions of supply and attempting to satisfy demand in each separate geographic area. The purpose of attention to the locality for the marketeer is to learn its strengths and needs, so as to draw up a nationally coordinated flow of commodities, a "balance," dictated not by a fully specified hierarchical plan but by the law of comparative advantage. Marketeers also promote enterprise autonomy, a form of decentralization, for its incentive effects.

The bureaucrat synchronizes exchange among parties through the plan, with its detailed targets, vertically drawn lines of command, and administrative orders; and this plan begins in Beijing, working downward. Radical and marketeer challenge this system, both beginning their plans from the base. But the marketeer will adjust these plans through the law of value (which rules that a product's value is set by economic criteria and thus that its price should be, too), supply and demand, and economic accounting — in short, through the market;

211

while the radical favors mass participation in planning by local-level work units in an ad hoc fashion, with synthesis done purely by "socialist cooperation."

When inflation threatens, the bureaucrat controls prices and rations supply; the radical urges everyone to engage in production, practice thrift, and use scraps and waste products, all in fine guerrilla style; while the marketeer, unafraid of the movement of prices, advises that once the higher prices have incited more production, prices will fall once again.

Radicals and marketeers agree in seeing state monopoly as undesirable, but for different reasons. Radicals view monopolies, such as the state trading companies, as adding to the stifling domination of society by bureaucrats, a group they disparage for thwarting mass activism and for enjoying excessive privilege. Marketeers' distaste here centers on the negative effect of monopoly upon competition, which they value for its ability to weed out inefficient enterprises as it promotes the successful ones. It is only the archetypical bureaucrat who has no harsh words for the system of total control by the state organs, atop which he himself sits.

A last recommendation concerns forms of market control and clearly distinguishes the three positions. For each group relies on a style of market inspection that matches its interests when it goes about checking up on the implementation of state commercial policy. In periods of marketeer power, insofar as supervision is used at all, it draws in part upon former businessmen to help oversee the market.[91] Radicals have taken another extreme, relying during and after the Cultural Revolution upon the poor and lower middle peasants and in the early and mid-1970s on fearsome worker militia teams, who confiscated goods that were not permitted to be exchanged freely and who thereby enforced price controls.[92]

Bureaucrats, in their way, have designed "market control committees," composed of representatives of bureaucratic organs.[93] Bureaucrats also rely upon the bureaus for administrative management of industry and commerce at each administrative level, which were instituted to superintend price control and pass sentence on speculators, as well as to manage store and factory registration and to investigate the quality of industrial output.[94]

Thus, despite the distinctiveness of each tendency in its approach to commercial policy, there are certain grounds for limited alliances between them, as well as points of clash. The fact that no socialist would totally reject goals of social equity, state control, or increased productivity has made it possible on occasion for some two of the three to join for short-term purposes. As noted above, both bureaucrats and radicals favor the use of state organs and fixed prices, which has united members of each group against marketeers on several occasions, as in 1958. Marketeers and radicals agree on the value of decentralization and some local autonomy (if for very different reasons), both begin planning at the

212

bottom, and both have criticized the monopoly of state organs in trading. Thus some agreement was possible, for example, from the time of the Eighth Party Congress in September 1956 through the decentralization decisions that succeeded it in late 1957. And probably both bureaucrats and marketeers place more value upon economic growth than do radicals, which ultimately led radicals to attack both of these two groups during the Cultural Revolution. But the different motives and the varying goals that cause each group to opt for the tactics listed here account for the ephemeral nature of political alliances and the frequent periodic shifts in line that have marked commercial as other work in the PRC.

In the final section of the chapter, I will draw on this model to describe the lineup of political forces as official policy changed in 1978. First, though, a bit of informed speculation will suggest constituencies within the population which might attach themselves to — or themselves inspire — politicians advocating one or the other of the three tendencies. Obviously, social forces favoring the market constitute only one segment of society.

Sectoral, generational, regional, and occupational divisions within the population are likely to be the most relevant factors accounting for the position an individual or group takes in this conflict.[95] People associated with heavy industry, the sector in which state controls are both more possible and necessary and profits are less readily produced, defend adherence to the plan. Those responsible for designing and enforcing the plan would side with them.[96] On the other hand, cadres in light industrial plants find it easier in their work to respond to the incentives of the market;[97] and successful, profitable enterprises in any sector are more likely to advocate market organization. Commercial organs, attempting to fulfill a sales quota, have fought with industrial units in the past over being saddled with products to sell that do not meet consumer demand, and so they must welcome a use of market principles.

Middle-aged bureaucrats trained and educated in the 1950s, when the Soviet planning model dominated Chinese economic organization, probably remain a principal power base for plan advocacy.[98] Some older cadres, recalling the pre-1949 days of revolutionary mobilization and guerrilla warfare, must harbor nostalgia for radical approaches. And, again in generational terms, marketeers include among their numbers those educated in the West before 1949 as well as some of the youth of the late 1970s, exposed for the first time to the positive side of capitalism by the press and entranced a bit by it.[99] Sichuan Province, a major grain base, has been the pioneer in the market experiment. Its leaders in past times resented having to respond to central procurement quotas, preferring instead to use the province's wealth to enrich its home population.[100] Poorer areas, beneficiaries of nationwide redistribution of key resources,[101] must feel more comfortable as part of a plan.

213

Among occupational groups, three in particular whose work is expressly economic relish the heyday of the market: peasants who have a surplus to sell; theoretical economists who as a group champion the observance of economic laws over radically inspired political movements and rigid plans; and managers in factories whose output is thriving. Groups, whether rural or industrial, at the lower end of the economic scale, feel insecure without their safe niche within the plan[102] and have also welcomed the upheaving redistributive bursts that are part of the radical approach.

These generalities, while meant to be heuristic rather than definitive, suggest broad cuts among the masses in the conflict over how best to organize the economy. They thus shore up the view that market approaches may well meet with obstacles that could obstruct their implementation.[103]

The final section below will use the triple tendency model — three groups in partial conflict and only occasional compromise — to illuminate the period when a crucial turning point occurred in the politics of economic decision making. In mid-1978 the official political position shifted from near total reliance on planning to an admission of some market principles into economic management. As a result of this shift, official attitudes toward marketing in China became far more favorable than formerly; planned ways of doing business began to come under open attack by early 1979; and open critiques of the "second economy" were presented in the press to bolster the case for reform.[104] As the analysis above would have predicted, however, the great burst of enthusiasm for market-prone solutions that attended this shift was tempered within only about two years by criticisms and new regulations advanced by partisans of the other two tendencies.

From Plan to Market: The National Conference of Departments of Finance and Trade on Learning from Daqing and Dazhai, 1978

In the immediate aftermath of Mao's passing and the Gang's arrest, the remaining Chinese leadership roundly proclaimed the economy to be in a state of near collapse. Initially the remedy chosen was to strengthen the planning system and to enforce discipline through administrative rules and regulations. This decision was no doubt reached (or reinforced) at the Eleventh Party Congress in late summer 1977, which coincided with the reemergence of Deng Xiaoping after his disgrace at the hands of the radicals in April 1976. An authoritative article praising planning appeared in the *Renmin Ribao* shortly thereafter.[105]

The first few years after Mao was gone were complex ones in which bureaucrat and surviving radical groups sometimes cooperated and sometimes competed for the mantle of the dead leader and the legitimacy that close association with his ideas seemed then to lend. An overambitious ten-year plan produced in this period was delivered by Party Chairman and Premier Hua Guofeng in February 1978 at the Fifth National People's Congress (NPC), in which Deng, then managing the economy, could not have failed to have had a hand.[106] Its evocation of "the socialist initiative of the peasant masses" and its call to "serve the people" — both radical slogans — was coupled with good bureaucratic commands to "bring all economic undertakings into the orbit of planned, proportionate development," to "strengthen the leadership of the central authorities," and to "tighten price and market controls."

For commercial work, the June−July 1978 National Conference of Departments of Finance and Trade on Learning from Daqing and Dazhai in Finance and Trade was a significant turning point in the larger evolution from plan to market that went on between the Fifth NPC in February and the Third Plenum of the Eleventh Central Committee in December 1978. Trickles of the coming stress on market management of the economy had appeared in Hua's NPC address — he mentioned that agricultural purchase prices should be raised to promote production, which the Third Plenum realized as policy ten months later; and he called for the full use of finance, banking, and credit to supervise economic undertakings. But, on balance, this was a speech fashioned by bureaucrats and delivered by a radical sympathizer.

The summer finance-trade conference was the scene of a battle — a last-ditch effort by both radicals and bureaucrats to advance their views on the proper business of commercial work and how it ought to be run. Here, too, though, the two sets of losers — radicals in the person of Hua Guofeng and bureaucrats represented by Li Xiannian and Yu Qiuli (head of the State Planning Commission) — soon sensed the shift of the wind and properly peppered their convention addresses to accommodate it.[107] A comparison of press releases before and near the end of the meeting bears out this interpretation.

On the eve of the conference, three telltale documents went to print: a *Renmin Ribao* editorial heralding the convocation of the meeting; a *Hongqi* article in its honor by the theoretical group of the Ministry of Commerce; and a collection of essays praising model units in the commercial sector in the then year-old nationwide campaign for finance and trade to study Daqing, the exemplar oil field, and Dazhai, the famous rural production brigade.[108] The themes of the first two pieces are nearly identical. Since these themes echo as well throughout the talks of Li and Yu, they no doubt contain the mainly bureaucratic message that the conference was prepared to deliver.

The tone of these articles also recalls the spirit of Hua's February National People's Congress speech in their exhortation to let socialist commerce serve as a promoter of a great leap forward in the national economy. They also emphasize Hua's inscription for the summer meeting, which drew on a 1942 quotation of Mao's to "develop the economy and ensure supplies." In referring to the market, they evoke the "unified socialist market"; and, thinking as bureaucrats always have in socialist China, they mandate that finance and trade should work to achieve a balance between commodity supply and social purchasing power. Political and ideological work get a plug, as do party leadership and commercial workers' participation in production, all of which are radical themes. Li Xiannian's opening speech, defending the planned socialist economy, systems, and discipline, followed this line closely.[109] Either Li knew what was coming and still stuck by his guns; or, speaking first, he was unaware of the changes in store for the agenda.

The pamphlet of tales of models veered off in another vein. It is nearly completely filled with pure radical approach to commercial activity, with stories from every province attesting to the need to attack capitalism while consolidating and expanding socialism, to manage rural commerce through poor and lower-middle peasant management committees, to put politics in command, to carry out a continuous revolution under the dictatorship of the proletariat, and to wage class struggle in the market. This line creeps at times into the speech of Hua Guofeng but not into those of Li and Yu.[110]

In closing the meeting, Hua injected much marketeer jargon into his words: he spoke of "economic levers" (prices, taxes, loans), objective economic laws, problems of management, social economic accounting, and strict financial supervision. But coupled with these phrases, Hua also managed, perhaps for the last time, to take his stand for radical values in economic work. For he often quoted Mao here, asked that his listeners keep to the socialist orientation in their work, put proletarian politics in command of all work, follow the mass line, and accept mass supervision. And, holding back from full surrender to the marketeers, he reminds the audience that Mao advised reading Stalin on the law of value. Many in attendance must have known that Stalin's position on this issue was that of a bureaucrat.[111]

Yu Qiuli's speech, delivered five days before Hua's but twelve after Li's, takes from the premeeting *Renmin Ribao* editorial as does Li's and, like Hua's, bows toward the ascendant marketeers.[112] Whereas Hua's talk stands out for its frequent references to Mao, however, Yu's conceptions constantly touch on the ways that planning can influence marketeer methods: special factories and areas are to be set up according to plan for export goods; advanced technology is to be introduced in a planned way; foreign trade should be carried out in accordance with unified state policy and plan; funds are to be allocated in accord with overall planning. The head of state planning was not in a hurry to see the plan superseded!

But at the end of the conference, the *Renmin Ribao* carried a report on applying the law of value. The reporter claimed that this article was based upon notes from the conference, much to the surprise of any outside reader who had been following the proceedings as published in the press.[113] Comparing this article with the one published by the same paper on the eve of the meeting makes it clear that the agenda had shifted, that a completely new line of discussion had entered the debate after the meeting had begun. For, according to this piece, talk of the law of value had dominated the forum — its role in promoting commodity production, its ability to help formulate and enhance fulfillment of state plans, and its function as the basis for setting prices. These last two points represent marketeer positions on the law, in that they accord it, and by implication not the plan, a regulatory role in both production and exchange.

Although each of the three principal speakers had mentioned this law, none did so in the manner of a marketeer: for Yu it was to be "consciously utilized under the direction of the state's unified plans"; for Li it was to "serve planned production"; and for Hua it was to "promote the development of socialist production under the conditions of the socialist planned economy." None of these men bothered to mention this highly charged term more than once, and each showed his commitment to subordinating its role to a value he took to be a larger concern — plans and socialist production. The dominant figure at the meeting, who gave no published address there, must have been Hu Qiaomu, named in March 1978 as president of the Chinese Academy of Social Sciences.[114] His remarks on economic laws at a July State Council meeting, not printed until October, carried the selfsame message as the second *Renmin Ribao* article.[115]

The official (if temporary) victory of the marketeer line was not sealed in 1978 for some months, however. One piece of evidence is the appearance of the Thirty-Point Decision on Industry, published in the midst of the meeting on July 3, which put far more emphasis on strengthening unified state planning than it did on market principles and economic levers. Oddly enough, in light of later associations of the reform program with Deng Xiaoping, one analyst surmised that this document, like the Twenty Points of 1975 on which it is built, was drafted under Deng's instruction.[116] Another sign of resistance to the pro-market line that emerged from the meeting was a complaint aired on Beijing Radio just following the session that one batch of comrades "aims mechanically to copy, reproduce and transmit the conference documents, but their implementation comes to naught."[117]

Perhaps the most illuminating, if somewhat whimsical, shred of evidence that market considerations had finally overcome ones connected with planning, at least for that moment and at the level of rhetoric, comes from comparing two similar diatribes — one in July 1978, one in January 1979 — against "backdoor" dealings featured in the press. The interdicted behavior is nearly the same in both — in one, a mill sold high-quality cloth cheaply to its workers and other units for "trial use"; in the second, some enterprises were giving away commodities to their staff and workers "under all sorts of names — year-end bonuses, labor safety devices."[118]

But an entirely different moral was drawn in each case. In July the journalist queried: "If all enterprises operate like that, how can there be any unified policy and planning?" By January, however, concerns had shifted, as the commentator revealed: "Not everyone should receive goods in kind . . . it increases pressure on the market and creates an imbalance in the supply of certain commodities." It was the Third Plenum in December and the triumph of the pro-market reformers that changed for a time the official perspective on (if not necessarily the actual practice relating to) the proper channels for the distribution of goods.[119]

In the several years that followed the Third Plenum, conflict eventually cropped up among the leadership, with some preferring to stress "reform" or "restructuring" of the economic system through decentralization or market principles; others supporting "readjustment," which entailed tighter central planning and more government intervention through administrative means; and yet others, attacked as "leftists," championing the interests of heavy industry and speedy growth, or criticizing the speculation and inflation that had accompanied the experiments with marketing.[120] Thus the issue is a long way from being definitively settled at the time of this writing.

But the admission of far more material incentives than ever before into economic life in China has raised questions among observers as to the future of the socialist ideas and institutions that have dominated Chinese economic organization for thirty-odd years. Recent developments call into doubt for some the durability of the framework outlined in the first part of this chapter: the disparaging attitudes toward trade, coupled with disadvantageous treatment of traders; a plan whose thrust is to eliminate monetary transactions as much as possible; and a set of semilegal practices, which mesh well with Chinese culture, that aim to compensate for the rigidities in this system.

I have tried to show, however, that the question should best be turned around: is it not equally likely that Marxism and its plan will continue to exert an influence in some form in China — bolstered as they have been by the blend in this sector of Marxism with traditional Chinese values; the support lent by habits from three decades of planning (and habits of evading planning that fit Chinese custom); the resonance of the plan with the needs of certain social groups within the Chinese population who have come to depend upon its security; and, perhaps most important, a half century of commitment to Marxist ideology among the top leadership, of which at least one strong opinion group continued to fight for the plan, well after market ideas had appeared on the scene.

Thus despite the glamorous billing that the Western press gave to the trial of market forces in China beginning in the late 1970s, these various influences still work to limit the speed and check the extent to which market can even compete on a par, much less override plan altogether in the People's Republic for some time to come.[121]

PART FOUR

Center and Locality

9

Between Center and Locality:
State, Militia, and Village

VICTOR NEE

The major organizational achievement of the first decade of the People's Republic of China was the creation of a subcounty government capable of sustained mobilization of rural resources. This new government claimed a broad base of participation and rested on three pillars of support —the party, the people's commune system, and the militia — all of which extended down to the village. In the villages the party branch functioned as an elite organization responsive to national policy and regulations yet composed of indigenous political leaders with deep roots within the community. By the early 1960s the people's commune was a three-tiered system that incorporated peasant households into collective agricultural production. The militia was a paramilitary organization that sought to harness young peasants for the purposes of state control and mobilization. The capability of the party-state to reach down to the villages through this newly established network was unparalled in Chinese history.

Philip Kuhn's analysis of local government in the late Qing and Republican periods pointed to a tension between state control and local autonomy. He argued that because the lowest level of the Qing government extended only to the county, the ability of the state to maintain control in the villages depended upon enlisting the services of local people. "Thereby was established the characteristic interaction between state control and local autonomy that marked the government of Ch'ing [Qing] China."[1] Kuhn argued that state control and local

I would like to express appreciation for the criticism I received on an earlier draft of this essay from Mark Selden, Brett de Bary, Sherman Cochran, Ko Yiuchung, Alan Liu, David Mozingo, Ezra Vogel, and Zhang Xinxiang. The research for the essay was conducted with the support of the Social Science Research Council, International Postdoctoral Grant, 1979–1980. The Center for International Studies and the Rural Development Committee at Cornell University provided a stimulating and supportive environment for research and writing.

autonomy were not mutually exclusive but were, rather, complementary and mutually interdependent characteristics of local government. Though in contemporary China subcounty government has been greatly developed and rationalized, there are important areas of continuity with the past. The rule of avoidance has been upheld in that the highest county official continues to be an outsider. As was the case with county magistrates in the past, the county party secretary has depended upon local support to govern effectively. Likewise, bureaucratic units at the subcounty level have been based upon natural social units, which Kuhn maintained was characteristic of late Qing and Republican local government. In light of these continuities, the question can be asked, in what way are state control and local autonomy mutually dependent aspects of state and society interactions in contemporary China? This essay seeks to analyze the militia system in China in order to explore the intersection of control and autonomy as a structural feature of local government. By control I mean the ability of the state to manage society, the allocation of resources, and the flow of events. Autonomy is defined as the power of communities to govern themselves and to influence the outcome of policy implementation pushed by the party-state.

The people's militia embraces nearly the entire youth and young adult population in rural China. As a coercive organization, based upon the capability for organized violence, the militia is the principal instrument for state control in the countryside. As a mobilization organization, the militia can effectively harness the energies of youthful villagers. Yet although the militia was developed to serve these functions of state control, there were also important counterbalances. First, the militia men and women were local people undetached from production and villages, as opposed to full-time professionals in the standing army. Their primary commitments were to their households and community. Second, militia commanders at the subcounty level were also local people with deep roots in the locality. Though the local military district supervised the training of the militia, the local peasant militia commanders maintained direct organizational control at the village level. Thus state control was filtered through local commanders and members, whose primary loyalties and ties were to the locality and community and who viewed the concerns of the party-state through a lens colored by localist preoccupations.

Marx maintained that in primitive societies with no organized monopoly of coercive forces, it was impossible for a minority to coerce the majority.[2] In Marx's view, state power rested upon the capability to coerce through the organized violence of the standing army and police. Thus the more the capability for violence is diffused in society and the weaker the state's monopoly on armed forces is, the less power holders at the center can resort to coercive means to achieve state objectives. In societies without state monopoly of the capability for organized violence, such as Lebanon in 1982, where coercive power was

224

fragmented into warring militias, the Palestine Liberation Organization, and foreign armies, state power is likely to be weak. The existence of large militias breaks the state's monopoly over the means of coercion. As Eric Nordlinger has argued, "A relatively large militia force serves as a powerful counterweight to the regular army."[3] In late Qing China, according to Kuhn, the rapid growth of local militias in response to the Taiping Rebellion resulted in a diffusion of power into provinces and localities and a fundamental weakening of centralized state power which was to persist well into the twentieth century.[4]

The Chinese Communists took careful measures to safeguard the militia from falling captive to localist interests and control. The army and the party were assigned dual control over the militia; only politically reliable villagers were allowed to enter the elite armed militia; and weapons and ammunition were carefully registered and controlled by the local military district. There is little evidence that the militia was similar to its nineteenth-century counterpart, providing a quasi-independent power base for subcounty elites. The weight of evidence clearly reinforces the view that the militia was very much integrated into a local system of state control and mobilization.[5]

Yet to view the militia simply as an instrument of state control would be to make the mistake of viewing it only from the top down, based on its formal functions and chains of command. The militia must also be viewed from the bottom up, considering the ways peasants make claims on state resources and exert leverage to further local interests. Viewed from the bottom up, the militia appears more multifaceted; it assumes more fully the characteristics of a local government institution staffed by local cadres and composed of youthful villagers. It is from this perspective that we must examine state-society interaction within the institutional framework of the militia and the maintenance of a balance between control and autonomy.

What happens when those at the center of state power in Beijing impose policies that fly in the face of sentiment in areas of critical interest to the locality? The Great Leap Forward was one such occasion, as is evident in the fact that it gave rise to three bitter years of severe deprivation and famine conditions in many rural areas. In the Great Leap Forward the militia was rapidly developed into an instrument for mass mobilization, absorbing peasants into construction projects outside their villages, which contributed to the collapse of agricultural production in 1960.[6] In the Four Cleans Campaign, the militia was frequently used by party work teams as an organizational weapon to conduct rectification of the village party branch.[7] These instances appear to confirm the view that the mobilization and control functions of the militia are dominant. What they share in common is that they took place during mass campaigns, when the party-state sought to exploit its organizational resources in the subcounty arena to mobilize society behind its goals.

Yet during periods less characterized by mobilizational politics, localist as-

225

pects are likely to be manifest, and state supervision of the local militia slackens. Moreover, even in the most intense mass campaigns, limits to state control imposed through organizations such as the militia can be detected. Accordingly, in the final section of this essay, I will discuss the role of the militia in the Cultural Revolution, suggesting the limits of state control in a period when mobilizational pressures were intense.

Historical Background of the People's Militia

A survey of the historical evolution of the people's militia sheds light on its role in contemporary society. The first Communist militia organizations were closely tied to the rise of peasant associations (1925–1927) during the period of the first united front between the Guomindang and Chinese Communist party when Communists mobilized peasants along the anticipated path of the Northern Expedition.[8] Following the Guomindang purge of Communists in 1927 and the subsequent repression of the peasant movement, Mao Zedong and Zhu De led the survivors of the Nanchang and Autumn Harvest uprisings to the mountainous regions of Jiangxi, where they established soviet base areas, expanded the Red Army by drawing recruits from marginal groups in society, and sought to arm and give rudimentary military training to poor peasants.[9] The peasant militia that emerged in this period was unstable, because the Communists never succeeded in establishing a firm footing in the villages of Jiangxi and Fujian. Nonetheless, when the Red Army was nearby or able to secure villages, the militia was active in carrying out radical land reform and class struggle against local landlords and providing defense for villagers against landlord militias when the Red Army departed. It was during the Jiangxi soviet period, however, that Mao and Zhu developed a military system whereby a village-based militia was integrated into more mobile guerrilla forces that operated in the locality.[10] The village-based militia was also used as a source of recruitment for the Red Army.

After the defeat of the Jiangxi and other southern and central base areas by the Nationalist Army and landlord militias, the Communists embarked on the Long March, which took them to the remote areas of Shaanxi province in North China. During the anti-Japanese war (1937–1945) and the civil war (1945–1949) periods, a second major building of peasant militia took place throughout North China. The Japanese invasion provided the Communists with the opportunity for rapid expansion of their base areas in regions where the Guomindang army and administrative apparatus retreated under the onslaught of the Japanese advance in North and Central China.[11] Communist organizational penetration of villages in many areas was initiated by army work teams that traveled from village to village to help peasants to establish militias, sometimes incorporating existing militias.[12]

226

From the years of war mobilization in the Communist base areas a new state system emerged, characterized by close integration between the basic components of the state: the bureaucracy, army, party, and village-based mass organizations.[13] The militia system was a basic component of the state, providing the primary organizational means for Communists to mobilize the villages for war, economic recovery, and social transformation. It formed the base of a three-tiered defense system made up of the militia, local guerrilla forces, and the main force army. It came to be closely identified with new forms of economic organization in the villages of North China, as vividly described by Franz Schurmann:

> Work and battle teams composed of young peasants were organized in the villages. When danger threatened, the teams marched forth to engage in battle. . . . One of the most interesting things about these new forms of village organization was that everything relating to production and struggle was regarded as work. War, like work, was integrated into the pattern of daily life. Time spent in battle was reckoned as the equivalent of so many days of work in the village. . . . The whole population was mobilized, freeing men for military service. Women were made to do work normally done by men. When no fighting was necessary, the fighters returned to the fields to do their own work or help other peasants. The linkage between war and production based on the natural village was one of the great organizational achievements of the Chinese Communists.[14]

After the Chinese Communists seized state power in 1949, the militia appeared to fall into a period of abeyance, probably because no definite functional role could be found for it other than short-term and tactical tasks.[15] In the early 1950s the militia was linked to a conscription plan for the People's Liberation Army (PLA), but this apparently was not widely implemented. In 1950–1951, the militia was mobilized to support the land reform campaign in the villages and to round up bandits and remnant Guomindang forces.[16] It continued to be closely tied to the army, which was responsible for its supervision and training. But the army was undergoing transformation and modernization along Soviet lines, and it seems to have viewed the militia as a burden. John Gittings reported that from 1954 to 1957 there was virtually no mention of the militia in the Chinese press or official documents.[17]

Militia-building appeared to correspond to periods of mass mobilization when the central government sought a means to reach down into village society to mobilize the peasantry. Not until the Great Leap Forward (1958–1960) did the militia once again assume a central organizational role in the society and economy. During this period its national membership increased dramatically from approximately twenty-five million to two hundred million. Even more than in the period of revolutionary war, during the Great Leap the militia assumed the status of an organizational model for society and was closely associated with the people's commune system.[18] The massive militia buildup was integral to the militarized conception of the people's commune.

Mao emerged as the leading exponent of the people's commune – militia system, which became the cornerstone of his agrarian policy. The commune-militia system was a conduit through which the party-state could reach directly down to the villages. At the same time, these two organizations provided the basis for a strong local government, staffed by cadres from the locality. This center-local linkage was seen as providing the organizational capability for state power holders to mobilize and unleash the energies and creativity of the masses, which for Mao was the key to successful long-term rural development.[19]

The all-out mobilization that characterized the Great Leap Forward proved short-lived. It is not necessary to provide an account of the failures associated with the Great Leap Forward and the severe economic crisis that it precipitated. After the Great Leap, the large-scale, all-out mobilization of the village population for massive basic construction projects was sharply curtailed. Reports appeared in the press criticizing militia work as disruptive of agricultural production when training was not circumscribed to limited slack season periods. As the economic situation in the countryside worsened in 1960 and 1961, militia work was virtually halted. The PLA *Work Bulletin* reported that in many areas the militia system was in disarray, its organization greatly overextended, existing frequently only on paper; moreover, control and maintenance of weapons were lax, and in some localities, the militia had fallen into the hands of "bad elements" who abused it to further selfish interests.[20] There were also reports that local militia commanders in many areas had resorted to "commandism" and coercion in mobilizing peasants for construction projects during the Great Leap Forward.[21] The PLA was assigned to resume supervision of the militia, which during the Great Leap Forward was controlled instead by the commune administration. Reassignment of militia control to the local military district contributed to the weakening of the power of the commune administration in the post – Great Leap period. It may also have reflected Mao's growing disillusionment over the political reliability of the party and his sense that the army more fully supported his policies.[22]

The Army and Militia

According to Franz Schurmann, by 1966 Lin Biao as minister of defense "stood undisputed at the head of that chain of command" that extended from the Ministry of Defense down through the army and basic militia.[23] This view of a monolithic army-militia system, however, is flawed in that it failed to take into account the strong regional and provincial loyalties and ties of the PLA ground forces. In a sense, the PLA was divided into two armies, the elite main forces and the regional-provincial army units in charge of regional and local defense. The main forces, which were mobile and could be rapidly deployed anywhere they were needed, were directly under the command of Lin Biao. The army ground forces, however, were assigned to geographical areas broken up into eleven military regions and twenty-three provincial military districts and were further dispersed within the provinces into military subdistricts. The stationary nature of their deployment integrated the ground forces into the regional and provincial party-government establishment. Typically, the party secretary of the provincial party committee also held the position of the political commissar of the military district. The commander of the military district was concurrently a member of the standing committee of the provincial party committee. The settled character of the military district forces tended to promote, over time, horizontal integration into the provincial power structure and modulate vertical integration into the national military system.[24]

Charged with the defense of the area assigned to it, a military district's major responsibility was to supervise and train the militia.[25] The actual training was assumed by the military subdistrict, an administrative subunit of the military district. Both the district and subdistrict were linked horizontally to civilian administrative centers below the province, at the prefectural and county levels. At the county level, the military subdistrict maintained an office in the county government to administer militia work, the people's arms department. Its commanding officer and staff continued to wear military uniforms while assigned to the county militia office. Like the military district, the military subdistrict was a settled and geographically contained unit of the PLA ground forces. It enjoyed considerable autonomy from Beijing in militia work, compared to its command over the army forces. Local military commanders were required to get Beijing's permission to deploy army units, a regulation designed to prevent the reemergence of warlordism, which plagued China in modern times.[26] Little is known about the horizontal linkages of the military subdistrict with the prefectural administration, but it is likely that the settled character of the subdistrict forces gave rise to a local garrison mentality and to close ties with the civilian bureaucracy. Thus the vertical structure of command from Beijing down to the ground forces was modulated by horizontal integration at the provincial and local levels. The strength of the provincial ties of the ground forces became manifest in the Cultural Revolution and helped to determine its outcome.

Militia Organization

The people's arms department is generally considered among the more important bureaus of the commune administration. Not only is it responsible for

229

militia work, but it also cooperates with the county public security office to solve criminal cases in the commune's jurisdiction. The militia commander, especially after the Cultural Revolution, has been regarded as an influential cadre in the commune and is usually a vice-chairman of the commune party committee or at least a member of the party standing committee. Like other subcounty cadres, the militia commander is from the county, though typically from outside the commune in which he serves. With few exceptions, a military background, either as a guerrilla leader or a PLA veteran, is required of militia commanders.

The village militia organization is entirely indigenous in both leadership and membership. Its commander is a production brigade cadre whose salary, like that of other brigade cadres, is paid in work points, making him dependent upon the village collective economy. He is appointed by the commune militia commander. Male villagers usually between the ages sixteen and forty-five and female villagers between sixteen and thirty-five belong to the ordinary militia, except the children of former landlords and rich peasants.[27] The ordinary militia is largely a paper organization with little activity or training under normal circumstances. The basic militia, on the other hand, is among the most active organizations in the village.[28] Its membership is recruited from among the village "activist" youth population of men between sixteen and thirty and women between sixteen and twenty-five years of age. Generally members of the basic militia are the politically reliable and active youths: members of the Young Communist League, team cadres, ambitious village youths who aspire to be socially and politically mobile. At least in the past, it was considered an honor to be asked to join the basic militia. Demobilized soldiers and veterans returning to the village are recruited into and form the mainstay of the elite armed basic militia; for them the age limit is raised to forty.

The concern for maintaining state control over the local militia is evident in critical areas of organizational life. Admissions into the elite armed militia must be approved by the commune party committee after a recommended investigation conducted by the village party branch. Weapons and ammunition are carefully registered by the commune militia office, and militia members are prohibited from transferring weapons without the approval of the county people's arms department. Both are issued to the village militia in very limited quantities. Most villages probably have only a few rifles. Party leadership is maintained; the party secretary of the brigade is also the militia's political commissar.

What role does the militia play in the village? The consensus of opinion among Western experts is that the military preparedness of the militia is not high.[29] This conclusion is not surprising. China has not mobilized the militia for war since the civil war (1945 – 1949). Moreover, for the basic militia the training period, lasting from two to three weeks during the agricultural slack season, consists primarily of political indoctrination accompanied by brief, largely perfunctory military exercises.[30] Some communes, however, appear to provide rigorous military training for the armed militia.[31] The emphasis on political indoctrination is an accurate reflection of the actual role of the militia in village life. As Richard Madsen's essay in this volume shows, the militia plays an important role in the political socialization of village youth. During periods when the party-state seeks to mobilize the peasantry, the militia is geared up to spearhead the campaign or project. Thus it is frequently called up to participate in rural construction projects. In normal times, it is expected to set an example as a highly motivated work force in collective agricultural production. In the border areas and coastal villages, the armed basic militia often patrols strategic roads and waterways. At times the militia guards the village's fishponds, orchards, or crops before harvest. If a crime is committed in the village, the militia cadre is expected to help in the investigation together with the commune militia chief and the county public security office. Finally, the militia has overall responsibility for maintaining the social order, until recently a duty largely understood to mean keeping an eye on the activities of former landlords and rich peasants. We shall see that in the Cultural Revolution, however, maintaining the social order took on a different dimension.

The Militia and Local Society

The view of the militia from Beijing is likely to emphasize its formal organization as a hierarchical local system, controlled by the provincial army and the county government. Viewed from the village level, however, the militia takes on a more "human cast" as an organization made up of local individuals. The militia appears to be an informal network of human relations that tie militia cadres to friends, kinsmen, fellow villagers, and other local cadres in the county. Villagers may not be entirely clear about the chain of organizational command, reaching down from the military district through the county people's arms department to the commune militia commander, nor about the carefully conceived system of control that renders their militia battalion a dependent organization. But they are likely to know in detail the life histories of the militia cadres in the village, as well as of the local cadres from the village who serve in the subcounty or county government. Whether the militia should or should not be controlled by the state is a moot issue; its existence is largely taken for granted. Villagers instead are likely to think of ways the militia or relations with its cadres can be useful in pursuing individual or village interests. Whereas Beijing views the militia as an organizational resource for the control and mobilization of the peasantry, villagers are likely to be attentive to the ways in which ties to local militia cadres might enhance preferential access to state resources.

231

Much of the following discussion of the village view of the militia is preliminary and tentative. It is largely based upon field work I conducted in a Fujian county, in March and April 1980, and on informant interviews in Xiamen and the United States.[32]

To understand the "human" ways in which villagers view subcounty organizations such as the militia, it is useful first to show the degree to which the administrative center of the militia is enmeshed in the local social structure. To villagers, the county government appears as a distant entity. Only infrequently might the ordinary villager travel to the county seat to visit a spouse who works there, to use the health facilities, or to purchase agricultural implements not available in the commune stores. The militia command, however, is located in the commune administration, which, as G. William Skinner has pointed out, is also often the location of the standard marketing town.[33] Once a week members of each household come to the commune to make their purchases and socialize with friends and relatives from other villages. The local militia system bears a certain structural resemblance to the multiplex militia in the late Qing, described by Kuhn,[34] both being based upon villages in a marketing community and coordinated by an administrative center usually located in the marketing town. Thus when the commune militia commander calls together the village militia cadres to plan the annual training session, these cadres belong to a lower-level elite, bound by the common sentiment and ties that characterize the marketing community.[35]

The commune militia commander, however, is an outsider to the marketing community, though he may come from a neighboring commune within the county. But the top county officials may consider him an insider by virtue of his local origin.[36] Though he may not have the same density of particularistic ties as a subcounty cadre serving in his own commune, the militia commander understands the local customs and, more important, is part of the same subcounty local elite. The degree to which the subcounty elite is integrated through networks of personal ties is difficult to determine, because data on this aspect of local leadership are extremely fragmentary. Neither Michel Oksenberg's study of local leadership nor A. Doak Barnett and Ezra Vogel's study of county government provides data on this aspect of local leadership.[37] Ethnographic accounts of local leadership in Taiwan, however, have pointed to the importance of patron-client relations and "connections" (*guanxi*) in subcounty politics and social life.[38] Similarly, recent accounts of the bureaucratic process in China stress the pervasive importance of personal ties and connections.[39] My evidence is based upon my study of Yangbei Village in Wuping County. The limited data I collected on the local elite suggested the existence of an "old boy" network of subcounty cadres developed over years of tenure in local government.

In the militia system, for example, the commune militia commanders in Wuping were army veterans, some of whom had joined the army together or served in the same unit. One of the two commune militia commanders from Yangbei Village, Lian Fuling, was militia chief of Shangdang commune near the county seat. Because of the strategic location of Shangdang commune, close to the county seat, this militia chief was considered to be among the most influential subcounty cadres from Yangbei. He was friends of many county cadres, including the PLA officer who headed the Wuping people's arms department, who had been his superior officer in the army. He was also known to be a close friend of the militia commander of Xiangdong, the commune in which Yangbei Village is located. This friendship also went back to army days. According to villagers, Fuling helped his boyhood friend, Lian Chenqi, also a veteran, to land a prized job as head of the new commune hydroelectric plant, through his friendship with Xiangdong's militia commander, who in the Cultural Revolution rose to the position of the commune's party secretary. Though this example does not provide a chart of the network of personal ties that made Lian Fuling so influential, it does illustrate the principles according to which particularistic ties develop and function within the subcounty political elite. It also reveals how personal ties crisscrossing the subcounty government may be efficacious in providing access to state jobs and resources. It is through these informal networks that local leaders devise ways to render local government more responsive to local interests, whether of the individual or group. "Going through the back door" *(zouhoumen)*, a practice whereby personal ties are exploited to gain preferential access to public resources, is the popular expression of this aspect of local government.

A discussion of the way state-sponsored formal organizations have been adapted to basic social and political processes in village life illustrates the intersection of the functions of control and autonomy at the village level. There is a very close correspondence between the militia leadership and the village's political elite. In Liu Ling Village, Shaanxi Province, virtually all of the militia cadres were either party members or members of the Young Communist League, and they were concurrently important cadres in the production brigade.[40] The same situation prevailed in Yangbei Village. The militia is not the basis of political power, but it plays an important role in village organizational life. In Yangbei, membership in the basic militia was a certification of good political standing as an activist with promise for a bright future. It was the badge of admission into the "in" group in the village. In the four production teams among whom I conducted household surveys, all of the young team cadres were members of the basic militia. The next generation of brigade leaders were likely to emerge from this group. Perhaps more important, the basic militia is an important base for upward mobility to opportunities and jobs outside the village.

A favored source for cadre recruitment in rural China is the army. In the army, a young peasant could participate in a large organization whose ethos of disciplined service to country was expected to broaden his outlook and range of experience, making him less susceptible to localist values. Moreover, the army provided a context for sustained political study and opportunities to join the party. In Shandong Province veterans and demobilized soldiers were reported to constitute approximately 30 percent of the local cadre force, and in old base areas, as many as 60 percent of local cadres had had military experience.[41] The militia in particular had a high percentage of demobilized soldiers in leadership positions. According to Oksenberg, "It is known that many PLA veterans, who usually were party members as well as the recipients of some advanced technical training, played important leadership roles in rural China."[42]

Though in theory it was possible for a young peasant to gain admission into a technical middle school or university, extremely few Yangbei youths ever progressed to higher educational institutions that promised a state sector job upon graduation. The army not only gave Yangbei male youths a means to gain experience outside the village; it made them prime candidates for cadre jobs in local government, state-run factories in the county or prefecture, or at least village and subvillage organizations. In interviews with village youths, I learned that the greatest aspiration for a young peasant was to work for the state, to become a salaried worker, and "eat state rice," as opposed to being a peasant. Households whose members worked for salaries in the state sector were among the most prosperous in the village. Only the basic militia members were chosen to join the PLA. Because the village militia chief selected the young men for the PLA to evaluate, youth anxious to join the army were attentive to developing good connections with him. According to my informants, this role was an important basis of the militia chief's power in the village. The desire of the most activist village youths to make favorable impressions and to please the militia leadership only strengthens the social control functions of the militia. At the same time, the militia cadres' power of discretion in selecting youths for the army, who later have the best chances of getting ahead, is evidence of considerable local autonomy.

In the course of my field work, I was struck by the degree to which what villagers said about subcounty and county cadres from Yangbei reflected the role these cadres played in village life. Lian Fuling, for example, was held in higher esteem among villagers than were the other two commune militia commanders from Yangbei. It appeared that the perception that Fuling was an influential cadre in Wuping impressed villagers, whereas the other commune commanders were assigned to peripheral communes far from the county seat. My informants' description likewise reflected the emphasis on influence and status in the evaluation of the cadres. Neither villagers nor informants seemed to have detailed knowledge about what these cadres actually did in their government posts, but they did have a great deal to say about influence, connections, and attitude toward fellow villagers, enemies, friends, and kinsmen. Among county cadres I interviewed, there seemed to be a strong awareness of the village origin of local cadres in Wuping. One cadre from another commune was proud to tell me that his home village had more cadres in Wuping than did Yangbei, implying in this comparison that his home village was of greater consequence. Villagers were proud to have cadres from Yangbei working in Wuping and in the subcounty government and regarded them as an asset to the village. As we shall see, it is very much to the interest of a village to have as many of its own people as possible serving as cadres in local government in well-placed and influential positions. As one county cadre said to me, "We try to help our own village if we can, within the bounds of the law. It's natural to want to see your village do well."

Perhaps the clearest way to explain why the village view is focused on its native sons is through an account told to me in Yangbei. Several years before my field work in Yangbei, the brigade cadres decided to purchase a large tractor mainly for transport purposes. The brigade director was sent to Wuping to order a used tractor. Upon his arrival he visited several of the Yangbei cadres, including Fuling, the Shangdang militia commander. A dinner was organized to which all Yangbei cadres came, and the plan to purchase the tractor was discussed, while news of family and village was passed on to the county cadres by the brigade director. The brigade director was advised to go to the agricultural machinery department to order the tractor. The order was placed, but there was a waiting list. After nearly half a year, the brigade sent its director back to Wuping. The Yangbei cadres in Wuping met again. This time the public security cadre agreed to take the matter to friends in the agricultural machinery department. Shortly afterward Yangbei learned that a tractor was available. I learned that the downpayment was loaned to the brigade from money pooled by all of Yangbei's subcounty and county cadres.

During their sojourn in Wuping, the brigade and team cadres are attentive to the needs of the cadres' wives and children. Some villagers complain that the subcounty and county cadres' children are given special consideration in getting into the PLA and in recruitment for the few state sector jobs that opened up for villagers. According to my informants, villagers generally try to build up good ties with these cadres, as a form of investment in the future. When a subcounty or county cadre returns to Yangbei to visit his family, villagers and friends flock to his home to visit, especially young men and village cadres eager to learn about local politics and bureaucratic affairs or to pick up pointers on how to launch their own careers as local cadres. In a sense, the favorable consideration extended from the brigade to the dependents of the subcounty and county cadres can also be interpreted as an exchange for past and future help in gaining preferential access to resources controlled by the state.

The great achievement of the Communist local government system was the ability to extend state power down to the villages. Whereas in the Qing, state control over the subcounty was weak, the Communists built strength through a complex skein of state-sponsored local organizations centered on the party, the people's commune system, and the militia. My analysis has focused on the local militia, yet this has led us back to the relationship between local cadres and their villages. The militia system and its cadres, after all, are a part of local government and society and must be treated in this light. The balance between control and autonomy which was analyzed in the militia can be generalized to local government as a whole. Just as with the militia, it would be misleading to assume that the formal organization of local government, and the unprecedented degree of state control structured into it, provides the definitive view of state and society relations. Future research must be more focused on the underpinnings of the formal organizations, the social linkages between state and society, whether based upon patron-client, social class, locality, or factional lines of affiliation. It is in the interplay between the formal organizational processes of local government and the informal, particularistic networks that bind the subcounty and county elite to state and village that the new balance between state control and local autonomy has crystallized.

What is new about state and society relations in contemporary China is that the local elite has become fully incorporated into local government while maintaining its ties to village and locality. Previous Chinese states strictly followed the rule of avoidance and sought to prevent the local elite from gaining control of local government, allowing instead the lowly *yamen* runners and *bao* chiefs to serve as the agents of control for the county magistrate. Only in periods of decline and crisis did the local elite encroach on the bureaucratic barriers that set them apart from formal positions in local government, as in the late Qing, when central state power was weakening and leading to the eventual collapse of the dynasty. Yet the exclusion of the local elite severely limited the capability of the state in building up local government. Instead, in traditional China, the county *yamen* was the lowest effective level of state power, leaving the subcounty arena the weak link in state and society relations. By incorporating the new village-based elite that rose to power following the revolutionary land reform into the expanded local government, informal networks of social power could be fused with the formal organizations of state power. The organizational result was that the processes of control and autonomy became inextricably intertwined. On the one hand, for the first time in history, a Chinese state succeeded in creating strong local government capable of mobilizing society. On the other hand, the local elite gained access to and control over jobs and resources that stemmed from the development and extension of local government.

If state control over society has been strengthened through its deep penetration into local society, does this imply that there is no effective limit or check on state power, as suggested in the writings of totalitarian theorists? The final section of the essay will analyze the role of the militia in the Cultural Revolution, when pressures from Beijing were intense for mobilization and control along lines defined by one group of power holders, the Cultural Revolution Left. As Franz Schurmann wrote: "During the Cultural Revolution, the villages of China, so far as could be gathered, remained quiet. Whether that was due to the successful implementation of the militia system is hard to say. Nevertheless, with the disarray of the party as a result of the Cultural Revolution, the militia under the direction of the army must be accounted one of the major stabilizing forces in the land."[43]

The Militia in the Cultural Revolution

Since the death of Mao and the arrest of the remnants of the Cultural Revolution Left, the so-called Gang of Four, both Chinese and many Western accounts have tended to speak of the decade of turmoil between 1966 and 1976 as a reign of terror. These accounts, for the most part, have dwelled on the fate of urban people during the Cultural Revolution.[44] The suffering of peasants is seldom mentioned. The strife and violence of the Cultural Revolution lapped at the shores of China's villages but usually without disrupting the flow of life, although some villages near urban centers were swept into the maelstrom.[45] But why were villages on the whole quiet, while the cities were turbulent? It could be argued that the original guidelines of the Cultural Revolution, the Sixteen Points document, stipulated that agricultural production was not to be disrupted by the political movement.[46] The Sixteen Points also stipulated that factories were to continue production and could not be drawn into the struggle. Yet within the first year of the Cultural Revolution, China's factories were swept into the storm of political strife as were other urban social units that were originally declared off-limits to Red Guard agitation.

Martin Whyte has argued that, in effect, China is divided into two social systems, rural and urban, with different social structures.[47] According to Whyte, urban society is much more bureaucratic, because voluntary and neighborhood associations were eliminated. Urbanites, as a result, are more dependent on the state bureaucracy to satisfy their basic needs and have no social buffer to reduce their exposure to state power. On the other hand, peasants continue to live and work in their traditional setting, in the same subvillage groupings where kinship and neighborhood solidarities continue unbroken. In rural society, the apex of the system, the people's commune, is bureaucratic, but the base, the brigade and team, is nonbureaucratic. The village cadres, who are indigenous and not state cadres, "constitute a buffer between the peasants and the bureaucracy above, and their total loyalties make it difficult for higher authorities to crack down."[48] An additional dimension is the close relationship

237

between subcounty and county cadres and their native villages in providing yet another buffer between center and locality. I hypothesized the existence of an elite, entrenched in local government and integrated through networks of personal ties in such a manner that loyalties to locality counterbalance bureaucratic accountability. This essay has also pointed out the interlocking of administrative nodes and natural social units, so that power frequently flows along preexisting social channels. These features of rural society provide an explanation for why the villages were spared the worst effects of the Cultural Revolution.

Data on the Cultural Revolution in the subcounty arena are much more limited and sketchy than the now voluminous material available on the cities during the Cultural Revolution. My analysis of the role of the militia in the Cultural Revolution is based upon three sources, the *Foreign Broadcast Information Service* daily press and radio reports from 1966 to 1976, probably the best source on provincial and local news available to researchers outside of China, my field work in Yangbei Village, and a review of the secondary literature on the Cultural Revolution, particularly concerning the army and local military forces. From the *FBIS* sources, I collected reports on local militia for each province for the Cultural Revolution years. The following account, though based upon these composite sources, holds specific references to the FBIS and secondary literature to a minimum.

In analyzing the role of the local militia in the Cultural Revolution, I have identified three stages.

Stage 1: During the first year of the Cultural Revolution, there was very little mention of the militia in the Chinese press. But according to Harvey Nelson, an expert on the Chinese military, the militia played an important part in the suppression of indigenous Red Guard organizations that sought to bring the urban movement to the villages.[49] A village youth who was attending college in Fuzhou returned to Yangbei in 1966 and helped form an indigenous Red Guard organization, made up largely of his friends and acquaintances. This organization then began to call the brigade party secretary a "capitalist-roader" and demanded that he step down. The party secretary stepped aside and was preparing a self-criticism when the basic militia set itself up as a rival Red Guard organization and came to the defense of the village party leadership. I do not know what role, if any, the party secretary played in setting the basic militia against the Red Guard group. But in the initial confrontation, the basic militia rounded up the Red Guards, beat them severely, and bound and gagged them. According to my informants, the leaders were being taken up to the mountains to be executed when Lian Fuling, the Shangdang commune militia commander, rushed in from Wuping to stop the execution. After this event, there were no further attempts to organize a village Red Guard organization. Richard Madsen in this volume describes a similar confrontation in Chen Village, where discontented urban youths, assigned to live and work in the village, organized a Red Guard band and mounted an attack on the party leadership. As in Yangbei, members of the basic militia organized a loyalist Red Guard group to defend the party leaders and, under the guise of "law and order," restored order. These accounts apparently reflect a widespread pattern among the village-level elite, displaying a defensive reaction to threats by Red Guards, whether they were indigenous units or units traveling to the village from the cities. The village party leadership's response to Red Guard groups was much like that of their urban counterparts, who used party work teams to put down rebels. But in the villages Red Guard groups were more easily isolated, and the basic militia was more powerful than were the party work teams in the urban setting. In the cities, the Cultural Revolution leadership could intervene to disband and discredit party work teams that suppressed urban Red Guard groups, but in the subcounty arena, their power failed to filter down to the villages, a reflection of the local autonomy held by the subcounty elite.

We have no concrete evidence as to whether this early suppression of Red Guards took place on a village-to-village basis or was coordinated at the subcounty level in the commune militia command. Lian Fuling's appearance at the crucial moment to stop the execution of the Yangbei Red Guard leaders suggests that Wuping's people's arms department was kept abreast of developments in Yangbei. Xie Fuzhi, the minister of public security, estimated that nationwide 80 percent of the county and subcounty people's arms departments supported the party establishment, which is strong evidence that there was little opposition from the county and subcounty militia commands to the village-based suppression of Red Guards, even if there was no active encouragement.[50] The *Liberation Army Daily*, the PLA official newspaper, in an editorial on August 6, 1967, pointed to the widespread use of the local militia to suppress Red Guards; not only in villages but apparently in many suburban communes, peasant militiamen were sent to the cities to attack urban Red Guard groups as well. The editorial intimated that the instigation to send militiamen to the cities came from elites above the village level. Informants in Fuzhou, the provincial capital of Fujian, described pitched battles in the city between peasant militiamen sent in from suburban communes and Red Guard factions.[51] This level of militia mobilization could only have been coordinated at the county level, if not higher.

Stage 2: If villages were, in effect, closed off to Red Guard rebellion early in the Cultural Revolution, who participated in the county and subcounty "seizures of power" attempts following the nationwide January 1967 leftist upsurge? In county towns, where the urban population is sizable, Red Guard groups existed among youth, workers, and office staff, following the basic pattern prevalent in the larger cities in the provinces. But in the subcounty arena, the commune population is often no larger than a village. It is not surprising, therefore, that the commune-level power seizures did not occasion the same chaos experienced by urban centers in the January power seizures of 1967. Instead, under the supervision of the military subdistrict, "three-in-one" revolutionary committees were established in communes, as a bureaucratic matter, with the militia commander given the dominant position. According to Harvey Nelson, the militia administrative organ simply replaced the party committee as the leadership organ in the new revolutionary committees at both county and commune levels.[52] Since the commune people's arms department was under the direct supervison of the military subdistrict, it was a way to extend army control down to the subcounty government at a time when the national party organization was in disarray.

By this time, in the wake of the January seizures of power, the provincial and local armies had sided emphatically with forces that sought to defend the established party-government-army elite from youthful radical Red Guard challengers and from the Cultural Revolution Left in Beijing. The provincial army's intervention on the side of order reflected the strength of its provincial and local loyalties. Indeed, the social and political ties that linked the provincial army to the civilian party establishment were longstanding and extensive, as the following commentary suggests: "There were many connections and intimate relationships; many dependents worked in the local organizations; and sons and daughters studied in local schools. If work was to proceed according to familiar ways and habits, if work relationship, feelings, face, family and intimate friendships were to be considered, it would be easy to take the side of the municipal party committee and oppress the revolutionaries."[53]

The conservative nature of the army-militia control of the county and subcounty government is suggested in an account of mop-up operations in Guangxi Province, where the Cultural Revolution factional strife was among the most violent in the nation, taking on civil war proportions involving positional warfare. The Guangxi military district coordinated the suppression of the rebel faction, relying on the county and commune people's arms department in rural counties where the rebel factions had established strong enclaves, and proceeded to root them out from county to county until the last rebel stronghold surrendered in the spring of 1968.[54]

Stage 3: From late 1968 to 1973 militia-building in rural areas became a major campaign, closely associated with the consolidation of revolutionary committees and the rehabilitation of the rural party organization. The training of the local militia and rectification of militia cadres became the primary task of the military subdistricts. In the Xuzhang Military Subdistrict of Henan Province, the subdistrict administrative structure underwent a major reorganization so that it could devote more of its staff to militia work. The subdistrict party committee assigned three of its five members to devote full time to militia work and formed a special team made up of ten cadres from different departments to supervise that work. It then sent army cadres to the county and commune militia offices in small teams to strengthen the militia administrative organs.[55] In the course of the militia rectification campaign, the provincial newspapers filed numerous reports of army work teams traveling from commune to commune to supervise the training and lead the rectification of the local militia to tighten up organizational discipline.

Although the provincial newspapers published a steady stream of reports on militia-building and rectification from 1968 to 1973, the underlying politics of the campaign cannot be easily deciphered from these accounts. A murky picture emerges of competition for control of the county government between the army and the newly reorganized party. It appeared that the army gained the upper hand. Indeed, in county after county reports were written attempting to justify the predominance of militia cadres in the county and subcounty party committees. In Minho County, Qinghai Province, the people's arms department published an article maintaining that even though the leading cadres of the militia office were appointed the first secretary and deputy secretary of the county party committee, civilian party members should not think "that problems of the armed forces' accepting the leadership of the party could no longer be solved."[56] The PLA commander of the Wuping County militia office assumed the position of party secretary, as did many militia commanders at the commune level. In my provincial files, a pattern whereby county and subcounty militia cadres were appointed to top party positions appears in articles and reports on the militia and problems of party reorganization in virtually every province. The composite picture that emerges of army-militia control of county and subcounty party organization is consistent with David Mozingo's essay in this volume, which analyzes the political power of the provincial and local armies.

The peasant origins of the PLA officers and soldiers has helped to keep the army close to the pulsebeat of China's villages. Army men during their years of service keep their dependents in their home villages, where the production team is supposed to provide them with special consideration and benefits. Regular home visits keep the men informed of and sensitive to conditions in their village. Upon retirement or demobilization they return to their village and family. And, as I have pointed out, as members of the elite armed militia, they become the backbone of the village basic militia organization. Moreover, they form the primary source of commune militia cadres, as well as an important source of cadre recruitment in the subcounty and county government.

It may be that the real significance of the provincial army's ascendancy to power was to give greater voice to peasant interests in provincial government. The Cultural Revolution was an urban movement, led by the Cultural Revolution Group, a coterie of urban ideologues, whose primary bases of power were the great cities of China, Shanghai and Beijing. This urban movement was defeated to a large extent by the refusal of the provincial army to support the

241

urban-oriented politics of the Cultural Revolution Left. In the county and sub-county arena, the ascendancy of the militia organization and its commanders to top positions of power enhanced the local power of the ground forces, especially since militia commanders were almost entirely from army back-grounds. The quiet of the villages by contrast to the cities can be understood as an outcome of the three stages of militia and army response to the Cultural Revolution.

If a new pattern of state and society interactions has emerged in contemporary China, it must be reflected in the relationship between center and locality. As Theda Skocpol has argued, the Chinese revolution, like its earlier counterparts, the French and Russian revolutions, was a state-building event, giving rise to a highly centralized, bureaucratic state, with far greater organizational resources for mobilization and control than previous Chinese states.[57] This new system, I have argued, was possible because of the success of the Chinese Communists in building strong local government, capable of sustained mobilization of the villages and effective control over the allocation of rural resources in propelling the villages along a trajectory of state-sponsored rural development. The party-state was the principal actor. It defined the strategies and parameters of rural development along essentially collectivist, noncapitalist lines; it sought to transform rural social relationships and peasant culture on the basis of a vision of uninterrupted revolution; and it sought to control rural-urban relationships to curb rural-urban migration, to set the terms of trade between city and countryside, and to levy the villages' share in the cost of socialist construction. Though the central organs of the party-state gained considerable autonomy from society, at the base of the state was a network of local organizations, rooted in natural social units, that facilitated the participation of the local elite and the masses. Not only did this network enhance the power of the party-state, but it also laid the basis for a new relationship between center and locality.

This essay has focused on the militia as a key organizational link between state and local society. Through an analysis of the militia, I have pointed to the mutual dependence of state control and local autonomy. The leaders of the village militia usually are among the village elite. The commune militia commander, though typically selected from outside the commune he serves, is nonetheless part of a cohesive subcounty elite. Thus though the militia is an important instrument of control and mobilization, the local character of its leaders and members builds a considerable counterbalance to state control. The militia is multifaceted and is deeply rooted in the organizational life of the village as an instrument of social control, as an avenue for upward mobility, as a youth organization, and as a force for production and basic construction. All of these functions are directly administered by rural cadres and thereby reflect the militia's role in promoting local autonomy. Although in post-Mao China the militia has been cut back, the local elite can be expected to continue to play its role in linking the state with local society.

Underpinning subcounty government are the informal networks of social power, consisting of the personal ties or connections that help in gaining access to opportunities, jobs, and resources in the state sector. This network system results in an emphasis on the "human cast" in local government, because villagers are interested in knowing who knows who in what position. The role of local cadres as gatekeepers to opportunities and resources, and the importance of cultivating personal ties or connections with them, suggest yet another dimension of local autonomy.

In the Cultural Revolution, the localist orientation of the subcounty elite, witnessed in the political behavior of the village militia, helped to seal the villages from the worst disruptions of this decade of strife. Emerging as the dominant forces for defending the social order, the provincial army and militia assumed the center stage in provincial and local politics. The response of the militia and the local elite to the Cultural Revolution upheaval reflects the ability, under certain conditions, of the localities to resist the policies and politics of a small group of power holders at the center of state power. The most notable of these conditions appears to be the existence of intraelite divisions at the national and provincial levels.

In the first half of the twentieth century, Chinese governments attempted to penetrate more deeply into the subcounty arena, and incorporate local elites into formal organs of state power.[58] But it was not until the social revolution unleashed by land reform, which swept away the old landowning elite, that it became possible to expand fully local government in the subcounty arena and incorporate the new village-based elite into the local state system. This new elite is in a position both to act as an agent of state control and to provide a buffer between center and locality; to assist the state in channeling agricultural resources from the locality and to act as patrons who provide access to jobs and resources controlled by the state sector; and to push down to the village campaigns and programs of the party-state and also to blunt and even sabotage unpopular policies.

10

Harnessing the Political
Potential of Peasant Youth

RICHARD P. MADSEN

The contribution of young people — those in the "green years" (*qing nian*) between the age of fifteen and marriage — to the history of the Chinese revolution has been of major importance. Most scholars who have studied the role of youth in social change in China have focused on urban youth: students in urban schools, urban Red Guards during the Cultural Revolution, city youth who were sent to the countryside.[1] Little systematic attention has been given to peasant youth. One reason for this neglect is that the role of peasant youth has not been as spectacular as that of urban youth. In the Cultural Revolution, peasant youth did not revolt against the political establishment to the extent that urban youth did. And after the Cultural Revolution, peasant youth have not generally posed serious threats to social order such as were created by discontented "sent-down youth," unemployed and underemployed young workers, and disillusioned young intellectuals. Nevertheless, over the past thirty years peasant youth have played distinctive, important roles in rural Chinese politics. In this essay I will describe some of those roles and show how they have been shaped by interactions between state political organizations and social processes at the village level.

I will base my argument mainly on ethnographic data concerning two generations of village youth in Chen Village, a single-surname-lineage community of about thirteen hundred residents in South China.[2] The first generation entered the political process in the late 1960s, and it played an important part in the creation of new levels of socialist organization and consciousness during that time. The second generation entered the political process in the mid-1970s and was involved in the retreat from the socialist experiments of the 1960s. The focus on a particular village will enable me to highlight the concrete ways in which social and political processes interact within a community framework,

244

and the comparison between different generations will enable me to analyze changes within the configuration of social and political processes over time.[3]

The main difference between the political roles of urban and peasant youth comes from differences in their mobility prospects. Compared with urban youth, peasant youth have a narrow range of opportunities for mobility, either upward or downward. Because government regulations severely restrict migration from the countryside to the city, most peasant youth can expect to become farmers like their parents. Peasant boys, indeed, can expect to remain in the same village as their parents, while peasant girls will be married into a community only a short distance from their homes. Until very recently, I will argue, the lack of mobility opportunities has caused the attitudes and values of peasant youth to be much closer to those of their parents than is the case with urban youth. Although urban youth have had many more opportunities for upward mobility than peasant youth, they have also been much more vulnerable to downward mobility. Because industrialization has not kept pace with urban population growth, the threat of unemployment and underemployment is much more real to many urban youth than the hope of ascending the ladder of occupational success. As a result, urban youth commonly share acute anxieties and grievances that alienate them from urban adults with stable jobs. On the other hand, since most peasant youth can expect to grow into a certain niche in their village community, they tend to remain committed to the outlooks of their families and take the same sides as their parents in village conflicts, differing from their parents not in the substance of their interests but in the vehemence with which they are willing to pursue them.

The characteristic vehemence of peasant youth has until recently been an extremely important resource for the Communist party in pursuing social and political change at the village level. In the 1950s and 1960s, the Communist strategy for "making revolution" within Chinese villages involved fanning up "class conflict" — not only conflicts between richer and poorer villagers but between rival kinship groups, traditional factions, and the like.[4] Once the appropriate conflicts were identified, it was necessary to turn them into organized confrontations. But adult peasants were often reluctant to fight against fellow villagers, even hated oppressors or rivals. To turn latent conflicts into confrontations, the party needed to rely on the brashness of village youth. In the 1960s and early 1970s, at least, the main instrument for harnessing this resource was the village militia. The militia, however, could be used for such purposes only under particular social and historical conditions. I will argue that those conditions, which were present in the 1950s and 1960s, began to disappear in the 1970s, with a resultant loss in the party's ability to use " class struggle" as a strategy for social change in the countryside.

Richard P. Madsen

Social Status and Behavioral Style of Young Peasants

At about the age of fifteen, a boy[5] in Chen Village is ready to leave school and take up full-time farm work. Nowadays, he will probably have just finished lower middle school. About 60 percent of the parents in Chen Village send their children to the local lower middle school, which was established about 1970; the others give their children only the five years that constitutes a full primary school education. If a boy's parents have reckoned that a junior middle school education would be wasted on their son, they will probably have interrupted his schooling for a year or two after the first or second grade, so that when he finishes primary school and begins full-time farm work, he is about fifteen years old, the same age as those boys who completed junior middle. Only a few young villagers have ever gone on to the senior middle school, which is located at the commune seat. And no one has ever gone on to college. So by and large it is a cohort of fifteen-year-olds that enters the village's full-time labor force every year.

"Full-time labor" in Chen Village usually means farm labor, carried out in the collective fields (mostly rice but some sugarcane, peanuts, and assorted collectively grown vegetables as well), which belong to the five production teams into which the village is divided. During the planting and harvest seasons, the work day is about fourteen hours long; but during the agricultural slack season, work on collectivized land lasts for only about seven hours. A fifteen-year-old would be expected to do the same kind of work as anyone else in his production team, but he would not be expected to work as fast or as skillfully as his elders. Adult peasants give him advice about how to improve his agricultural skills. By the time he is about eighteen, his strength and skill will have developed sufficiently that he is as good at normal field work as any adult villagers, though not as skilled as older, more experienced men in determining exactly when, where, and with what techniques to plant crops so as to assure maximum yields.

As a full-time farm laborer, the fifteen-year-old is eligible to participate on a formally equal footing with village adults in major political activities. He can and indeed must attend meetings of his production team at which problems related to agricultural cultivation and such issues as how labor within the team is to be allocated, how work points are to be distributed, and who should be elected to positions of leadership within the team are discussed. He also attends general meetings of his local production brigade, that political organization, in this case coextensive with the boundaries of the village, which comprises the basic unit of the political apparatus of the Chinese state in the countryside. In all these meetings, the fifteen-year-old has as much formal right to speak his mind as any other full-time laborer in the village and, when relevant, the right to vote. But his participation is limited by social expectations. He would not normally dare to speak out, because he could not presume to have anything significant to say. If he spoke up, his parents would probably berate him after the meeting for speaking nonsense and not knowing his place. When he is about seventeen or eighteen, he will have earned the right to speak at political meetings by proving his ability to do farm work with full adult strength and normal adult competence.

Thus a fifteen-year-old peasant who has just taken up full-time farm work has the same formal economic and political roles within the village as his elders. He differs from them mainly in his ability to perform those roles. He is embarking on a process of apprenticeship which will enable him to be a fully competent participant in the same small social world within which his parents live. He is not involved in a process of education which would give him the opportunity to move outside of the world of his parents. Moreover, at least until he is married and has children of his own, the peasant youth remains deeply dependent on his family, both economically and morally. He will have no income of his own to spend. The income he earns from his labor on the collective fields is not even given to him to give to his family; it goes directly to the head of his household. Any money he makes in private "sideline enterprises" is supposed to be handed over to his parents. He is supposed to be a filial son and to contribute to the prosperity and solidarity of his family. Any young man who flagrantly defies these moral obligations will be held in contempt by his fellow villagers.

Yet the ties that bind a son to his family begin to be loosened somewhat when he reaches fifteen and begins a full routine of farm work. Indeed, truly to honor his parents and effectively to support his family, he must now begin to shoulder responsibility and take independent initiative. If he does not do so in the course of his farm work, his economic contribution to his family will be deficient. And if he does not begin to stand on his own in social and political interaction, the honor he can bring to his family will be lacking. It is to his family's benefit that he become a distinguished representative of his generation. If he does so, he may someday be given positions of power and responsibility in the political structure of the village, the glory from which will reflect back on his parents. And when it is time for him to marry, if he is judged by fellow villagers to be an outstanding member of his generation, it will be relatively easy for his family to arrange his marriage to a good wife, a sturdy, hardworking, and obedient woman connected to a well-thought-of family who will help her husband build a prosperous, stable, and respected household of his own and therefore be of great help to her husband's parents in their old age. Thus a truly filial son will want to stand out among his peers.

So, in part, precisely because he wants to honor and provide for his family, a young man who has just begun farm work will be attentive to the standards set by his peers and will want to excel with respect to those standards. But the approach toward life celebrated by his peers will not be quite the same as that

247

deemed appropriate for members of his parents' generation. The Confucians believed that a young person's moral training should begin with poetry and then as he reached toward adulthood be complemented by ritual. The purpose of poetry was to bring into order the exuberant emotions of the young; the purpose of ritual was to order his relationships with society.[6] I am not suggesting that young peasants are today in any explicit way followers of Confucius. But the old Confucian idea of a progress from poetry to ritual points to an important difference between the mode of life of Chen Village's youth and their parents. Young villagers tend to be physically exuberant and emotionally impulsive; and villagers generally seem to think that it is natural and right that they be this way, so long as they are learning to direct their strength and impulses toward socially useful purposes. Married people are much more concerned about the rituals of social propriety which enable them to live in harmony with their fellow villagers, and it seems to be commonly felt that a mature person ought to have these concerns.

During the harvest season, the young men of the village like to go to the place where the grain is being weighed and show off their strength by seeing who can lift to their shoulders the heaviest sacks of grain. They like to engage in contests to see who can work the longest and hardest before becoming exhausted. Older people are proud of their strength, too. An adult has to be strong and full of stamina to gain the respect of his fellow villagers. (It is, for example, almost impossible for a weakling to become a village cadre; no one would look up to such a person enough to follow his leadership.) But older people, for all the value they place on physical prowess, have to husband their energy if they are to be able to give constant adequate attention to their responsibilities. They cannot waste their energy in extravagant bursts of physical power. Young people can; and the fifteen-year-old who has just begun full-time farm work will exercise his body in hard work toward the day when he can match any of the nineteen- or twenty-year-olds in exuberant displays of raw power and stamina.

Young men also value brashness and reckless courage, the ability to enter and win tough verbal brawls in defense of their interests. Like physical strength, these are traits appreciated by almost all villagers, young and old alike. The people of Chen Village have a special reputation, which at least some of them seem to glory in, for being stubborn, crudely direct, and fiercely determined. But adults with families have to temper these traits with a modicum of prudence. They have, after all, probably assured a stable position for their families within the village by slowly cultivating a network of cordial alliances with neighbors, relatives, and friends. They must be careful not to destroy these valuable alliances through ill-advised displays of hotheadedness. The young men of the village do not share this need for caution to the same degree as their elders. They know that when they are ready to marry, raise a family of their own, and settle into a stable niche in the village's social and political structures,

248

they will not be able to rely simply on the alliances their fathers have set up. They will have to make alliances of their own, and their ability to do so will depend to no small degree on the prestige they have developed through their interaction with their peers when they were young. That prestige will depend in part on how well they have demonstrated the toughness of their personality among their youthful peers. Villagers seem to accept the fact that young people are likely to be more recklessly brash than older people, and if, for instance, a family's unmarried son says something during a political meeting that upsets some adult family friends, the son's action will not necessarily destroy that friendship. At the same time, the brashness a son exhibits during his late adolescence may eventually help his family, if through displaying this brashness he proves that he is someone not to be pushed around and thus is eventually able to settle into a prestigious position within the village.

The young peasant just beginning farm work will not exhibit the same brashness as those who are four or five years his senior, just as he cannot hope to match their physical strength. But he will look up to the eighteen-, nineteen-, or twenty-year-olds and gradually try to emulate them. His behavior, oriented toward his slightly older peers, will thus take on a style distinct from that of his parents, even though the difference is often more a matter of emphasis than substance.

The distinctive character of youthful behavior will be reinforced by the young adolescent spending much of his nonworking time in informal interaction with other adolescents of the same sex. In Chen Village there may be even more of such informal youthful interaction than in many other rural villages because of a particular village custom which, though not uncommon in southern Guangdong, is not generally practiced throughout China. This is the custom of having young men and women sleep away from their homes in dormitories called "girls' houses" (*meijian*) and "boys' houses" (*zhaijian*).[7] Young men start to sleep in the boys' houses around the age of fifteen. There are about fifteen boys' houses in the village, most of them sleeping about three or four young men apiece. But the main dormitory for young men is the loft of the building that serves as the brigade militia headquarters, where about twenty-five young men sleep. They sleep in the boys' houses until they are married. While spending their nights in these dormitories, they still remain part of their household's economy, symbolized by eating their meals with their household. But sleeping in the boys' dormitories gives them plenty of time to associate with unmarried young men from around the village and through such association to develop a young person's point of view and a commitment to young people's behavioral standards.

The style of behavior which gives a young villager prestige among his peers — the zest for explosive displays of physical prowess and the enthusiasm for blunt brashness — can be very useful to the pursuit of certain Communist pro-

249

grams in the village, if it is properly tapped and harnessed — if, in a manner of speaking, the "poetry" the young people learn is orthodox *political* poetry.

Political Potential of Young Peasants

"Political potential" is defined in terms of the particular political challenges posed by a given period and the ability of particular groups to respond to those challenges. In the 1960s, the Chinese government was facing the challenge of building up its system of collective agriculture and of deepening its population's commitment to socialist moral ideals. Young peasants could make important contributions to these processes.

The government's commitments to build up the system of collective agriculture were based on ideological convictions — that an egalitarian socialist economic system is good in itself — and on practical considerations — the awareness that well-organized collective agriculture can be more productive than individualized agriculture. For many peasants, however, the government's ideology seemed abstract and irrelevant to practical concerns. Villagers tended to be committed to collective agriculture to the extent that it increased their standard of living. They were potentially interested in such a system but would not become actually interested unless it could be demonstrated to work to their advantage, which it could not do unless they were motivated to work hard on it. Therefore, a vicious circle developed. Collectivized agriculture would not be seen by peasants to be clearly in their interests unless they worked very hard at it; but they would not work hard at it unless they were sure that it would be in their interests.

This vicious circle was made even more vicious by the fact that in the Great Leap Forward the Chinese government had attempted to impose a radical collectivization that disastrously failed. By the early 1960s, peasants had every reason to be suspicious of further attempts to introduce new forms of collectivization. In the early 1960s, the government had allowed collectivized agriculture to become only minimally collective. Agricultural land was owned collectively by small production teams consisting of about twenty-five neighboring households. But agricultural work was not done by production team members working as a single team. Individual families (or in some cases groups of several neighboring families) were given plots of collective land to work on their own and could manage the land as they wished and keep what they produced minus a quota of grain which they had to give over to the production team. Though collective in name, this system was close to private agriculture. But by the mid-1960s, the Chinese government was trying to make agriculture more collective again. Members of production teams were pushed to work together on their team's collectively owned fields. The greater degree of cooperation had

250

the potential for making agriculture more productive and peasant standards of living higher — if peasants could be motivated to work enthusiastically. But how could villagers who were suspicious of such collective enterprise be motivated to put an all-out effort into it?

One resource that could be called upon to create this motivation was the village youth. Young peasants, as I have shown, found great prestige in manifesting their physical strength and stamina. If that desire for prestige could be so directed that the youth manifested their strength and stamina in collective production, then the government might further its interests in maximizing the productivity of collective agriculture. And if collective agriculture were successful, peasants in general might become more committed to it. Thus, especially during the critical weeks of the transplanting and harvest season, the government would call on village young people to be pacesetters in production.

Young people were not necessarily any more interested than their elders in adopting new degrees of collective agricultural cooperation within the village. But because of their interest in sometimes pouring a great amount of physical energy into whatever they did, they could be led to help make new levels of collectivization work and thus create a general interest in it among residents of the village.

Besides maximizing the efficiency of collective agriculture, the Chinese Communist party, under Mao, was committed at least in principle to continuing a social revolution that would produce a relatively egalitarian society bound together by selfless commitment to the common good. To this end, the party in the 1960s continued to carry out political rectification campaigns in the rural areas against people who had corruptly acquired privileges or who had in other ways manifested ways of thinking and acting that contradicted the austere egalitarian ideals of Maoist thought. For instance, in the Four Cleans campaign of the mid-1960s, the party directed villagers to attack cadres who had been lazy and arrogant and had misused public funds.

The Maoists within the Chinese government seemed to believe that political campaigns that directed villagers to attack selected examples of common peasant failings could educate villagers to raise the standards of political conduct and make them more willing to sacrifice narrow self-interests for the collective good of a socialist society. They seemed to believe that once peasants got caught up in the frenzied enthusiasm of political campaigns they would begin to see that their truest interests lay in a wholehearted devotion to the public good.

The ritual center of political rectification campaigns was the "struggle session" or "denunciation session" in which campaign "targets" were dragged onto a stage and verbally humiliated and sometimes physically attacked by the enraged peasant "masses." Such campaigns were painful, exhausting affairs for attackers as well as victims; and the campaigns could have many unintended consequences. People who took the lead in doing the attacking, for instance,

251

could often find themselves subject to serious reprisals by friends of the victims or by the victims themselves if (as not infrequently happened) the victims made political comebacks. Here, young people, proud of their brash boldness, could make an important contribution to the government's political purposes, if their brashness could be properly tapped and channeled. During political campaigns, the activists — those who actually did the criticizing, cursing, and pummelling — were almost all young people.

But only if their emotional enthusiasm and physical exuberance were properly channeled could young people play an important role in the development of new commitments among villagers to collective production and socialist revolution.

Political Organizations for Harnessing Youth's Potential

In Chen Village, there are several organizations for tapping energy and enthusiasm generated by villagers passing through the youthful phase of their life cycle and channeling that energy and enthusiasm into the political projects of the Chinese state. These are the Young Communist League, the Propaganda Team, the Mao Zedong Thought Counselors,[8] and the village's basic militia company.[9] But the most important of these seems to be the militia company.

Under the right management and in the right historical circumstances, the militia's ideology can enfold the natural enthusiasms of young people in such a way that political ideals of working for the glory of the state can be made to resonate with youthful enthusiasm to achieve glory within one's village; and formal organization to carry out public political projects can mesh with the informal organization of the village's youth. Then the enthusiasms of the village's small core of youthful political activists can be used to pull along the imagination and aspiration of the middle-of-the-road youth and so provide a powerful striking force to be used for official political purposes.

When a young man or woman reaches fifteen years of age, he or she is eligible to join the basic militia company. Applications are scrutinized by the militia chief. Young people of upper-middle peasant background may be admitted only if they show above average political enthusiasm. People with rich peasant or landlord backgrounds need not apply.[10] Almost all young people of poor and lower-middle peasant class background apply to join the militia, and almost all are accepted. There is no law requiring young poor and lower-middle peasants to apply, but if such persons did not apply, they would feel left out of the work of good people of their generation. As an interviewee put it: "They won't let you join only if you are a bad person; if you refuse to join, aren't you then being like a bad person?" The official age limit for militia members is thirty; but almost all women drop out after getting married and almost all men

252

after their wives have their first child. They drop out because militia work is unpaid and done in one's free time; and the responsibilities of marriage and children curtail the amount of free time one can use on unpaid activities. Thus from the point of view of poor and lower-middle peasant youth, the basic militia comprises all "good" young people in the village between the age of fifteen and marriage.

Official political status within the militia is granted as a reward for performing well the militia's official tasks. To see how the political status structure of the militia might be made congruent with the "natural" status structure of peasant youth and thus might enable the militia to tap the energy and enthusiasm of village youth for political purposes, let us describe briefly the main tasks the militia is supposed to perform.

The avowed primary purpose of the militia is to organize an effective guerrilla fighting force to be used in case of war and to carry out paramilitary activities like sentry duty within the village during peacetime. Thus militia members are given a basic training in guerrilla war tactics and in the use of weapons. (Weapons training is carried out with dummy rifles; the basic militia does not handle real weapons.) Organized into platoons and squads, the militia members take turns in doing sentry duty in the village at night — an especially important activity around harvest season, when dishonest persons might be tempted to steal some of the newly harvested grain lying out in the open. But the paramilitary tasks are not the main work of the militia. The militia is also supposed to take a general role in "grasping revolution and promoting production," and it is in this capacity that the militia makes its major contribution to political life in the village. In times of political calm when the attention of the village is turned to farm work, the most important function of the militia is in production. The militia promotes production by encouraging the tendencies of young people to display their physical energy and by focusing that energy on collective farm work. The militia's contribution comes across vividly in the following quote from an interview describing the way the militia platoon in the village's poorest production team dramatically raised the team's productivity: "The labor power of the team was very poor, especially that of the adults. But the militia in that team used to call out to them and urge them and push them to work like hell, to work like fools. They worked in what seemed to be an especially joyful way, different squads having contests with one another. So the work went very quickly. This was the militia's work, since old people weren't able to push forward like that."

The militia can be most effective in promoting production during the agricultural busy season when the tasks of harvesting and planting require a tremendous amount of fast, intensive labor — just the work young people are good at and proud of. A well-organized militia unit aids production not only through the productive labor which its members directly perform but also through the im-

253

pact their hard work has on the older workers in a production team. Hardworking militia members act as "rate busters" in a production team, setting a standard for work that pulls along the older members of the team.

During political rectification campaigns the militia's youthful members can perform a political rate-busting function. They raise the pitch of struggle and criticism against political offenders higher than many adults would want it to go. As an informant put it: "During big struggle meetings, you have to rely on the militia to push things forward. Old people, middle-aged people, don't like to struggle. They are afraid to hurt the feelings of people. But young people aren't afraid. They don't know anything at all about personal relationships, and during the struggle meetings will struggle and struggle with all their might. When they come home, their parents are liable to yell at them: 'Bastard! What the hell do you think you are trying to do? Minding so much of other people's business!' " In Chen Village, at least half the people taking active roles in political "struggle sessions" during rectification campaigns were militia people.

The young person who, proud of his physical strength, shows off that strength by heeding the calls of his militia commanders to drive himself like a fanatic in bringing in the collective harvest, and who, proud of his brash boldness, lashes out as directed against political offenders during rectification campaigns will rise to the top of the political status hierarchy formed by the militia. His militia work will win him entrance to the Young Communist League; and though his duties as a League member will go beyond his formal militia duties, a crucial part of his work will be to set standards for activist behavior within the militia. If he is in outstanding physical condition and from an impeccable class background, he may be chosen to be a member of the armed militia — an elite corps of (in Chen Village at least) about twenty militiamen entrusted with the responsibility of bearing weapons.[11] He may also be given awards such as that of "militia pacesetter," which will make him an official model for other militia members. He will have achieved such distinctions by doing within a political context an activity that might have won him the respect and admiration of his young peers, even if there had been no village militia. Thus political honor, achieved in the militia, can become fused with social honor, acquired by excelling in the standards of one's peer group.

Political status and social status can thereby reinforce one another. The role of politically active militia person gains luster in the eyes of a generation of young militia men and women because the peers whom they would naturally most admire are militia activists. Conversely, the status of physically tough, strong-willed young persons is given extra luster because such people are accorded a high level of political honor. When this happens, an intense militia esprit de corps can develop. Most militia members will want to follow the lead of their pacesetters even if they cannot keep up with them. The militia can capture the allegiance of the majority of a youthful generation and can systematically turn that generation's energy and daring to political purposes.

In Chen Village, from the mid-1960s to the early 1970s, about two-thirds of the village militia members routinely received the award of "Five Good Militiaperson." This award did not distinguish a small elite from the body of the militia, but rather delimited the basically dependable militia members from those not so dependable. There were about 150 people in the militia. If 100 young people were basically dependable and could be mobilized by the militia around a given cause, the militia might be an important force indeed in the village's life.

Young People, the Militia, and Chen Village History

In describing the way organizations like the militia might channel and focus the energies of village youth, I have written mostly in the subjunctive mood. Thus "political status and social status *can* reinforce one another," and "the militia *might* be an important force in village life." These were potentialities which were realized in the village under certain concrete configurations of historical circumstances. Now I wish to switch to the declarative mood, to talk about the flow of historical action engaged in by specific persons in specific settings.[12]

In early 1965 the militia sprang into action as the Four Cleans campaign engulfed Chen Village. Launched by Mao in late 1962, this campaign was inspired by Mao's fears that a new class of privileged officials was arising in the countryside. (As it developed, the course of this campaign often shifted back and forth toward more or less radical directions because of infighting among factions led by Mao and Liu Shaoqi; and the high-level controversies over the correct course of this campaign were a prelude to the Cultural Revolution.) A work team composed of outside cadres entered the village to organize a movement to clean up cadre corruption in the community.

The work team members were a mysterious group of thirteen people who refused even to tell the peasants their surnames. They were skillful organizers. Their first three months in the village were spent in "sinking roots and linking up" — making contacts with and gaining the cooperation of peasants who had grievances against the village cadres. There were plenty of grievances: economic grievances common to villagers whose income had slipped below average for the village because, through physical weakness, lack of planning abilities, bad luck, or lack of good personal connections with local families, they had been unable to take advantage of the resources given to them in land reform and collectivization; and personal grievances resulting from real or imagined slights received at the hands of the local cadres. But in spite of these various grievances, the first reaction of the peasants was to remain silent. As an informant put it: "Most of the masses were afraid. The cadres were like emperors. . . . If you complained about them, they might want to take revenge, something very frightful because a peasant has no way of leaving a village." To overcome this endemic fear, the work team needed to rely on brash young peasants.

The work team's first step in mobilizing young people was to tighten up the leadership of the militia. At that time the village militia chief was a late-middle-aged man (a poor peasant) who had been forcibly conscripted by the Guomindang in the late 1940s and later "liberated" by the Communists and made a member of the People's Liberation Army. He had apparently been chosen for his militia post in the early 1960s because he was one of the few villagers who knew anything about military affairs. But he was a rather bumbling person with little local prestige. Young people could not readily look to him as a role model, and he was a generally ineffective militia leader. The Four Cleans work team suspended this man and temporarily took over the militia. Through the militia, they then whipped up some of the strongest, brashest of the poor and lower-middle peasant young people into a strong activist fervor.

The best young activists were eighteen- or nineteen-year-olds who knew that if they performed well they would probably be able to enter the Communist party and eventually move into important positions within the village. But the work team, backed up by an intense propaganda campaign that enveloped the entire country, helped to create a powerful esprit de corps among the militia, so that even relatively moderate young people were inspired by the zeal of their activist pacesetters. Even young people who had no hope that their activism would result in Communist party membership got caught up in the enthusiasm to play dynamic parts in the campaign. When mass struggle sessions were organized to condemn the local cadres, it was the village militia, sitting as a group in front of the audience, which provided the loud chorus of angry voices to curse or denounce "bad" cadres dragged out before the masses by the work team.

Almost all of the village cadres were denounced for such faults as using their posts to obtain personal privileges for themselves, for playing favorites, and for ruling in an overbearing, "undemocratic" way. The village's young people did not give focus and direction to the struggles against the cadres. The work team gave the overall direction; and adult villagers, resentful about receiving what they felt to have been unfair treatment from the cadres, provided the specific evidence against hapless village officials — young people could not be presumed to know enough to do that. But it was the young people organized in the militia who provided the explosion of outrage which gave the struggles against the old local political leadership their devastating force. The result was that villagers now had an interest in setting and enforcing higher standards for their cadres — and themselves — than ever before. One might well question the moral correctness of trying to create an interest in new moral standards by such means, and one might also question the long-range effectiveness of such an enterprise. But in the short run at least, a new public spirit was created in the village. Villagers had gained new interests in public virtue — interests approximating those which the state wanted to cultivate — and the youth, their natural enthusiasm carefully focused through the militia, had played an important role in this transformation.

When the "struggle phase" of the Four Cleans wound down, the work team directed the task of rebuilding the village leadership. In accordance with policy established at higher levels (apparently after considerable debate), most of the village's criticized cadres were rehabilitated and reinstated. There was to be no fundamental reshaping of the old political order as had happened during land reform, when the party had used class struggles spearheaded by young people to break the power of the leaders of the old political order and replaced those leaders by new Communist cadres drawn largely from the ranks of activist young peasants. Now in the mid-1960s, the Communist party's policy was only to teach local cadres and masses some lessons about correct morality in a socialist society. Thus most of the old political elites returned, although a few of the most corrupt and least competent cadres were weeded out. In Chen Village, one of the main persons thus weeded out was the village militia chief, not because he was especially corrupt but because, it seems, the work team wanted a more competent militia head. So a new militia chief was picked, a young adult who had no military experience but who gave some promise of being an effective leader of village youth.

By now it was late 1965, and an intense campaign to study Mao Zedong's works was sweeping the country. A contingent of fifty sent-down city youth had settled in the village, some of whom were thoroughly caught up with idealistic hopes of transforming the country in accordance with Mao Thought. The most zealous of these city youth were made Mao Thought Counselors for the village. It was their job to criticize "feudal customs" and selfish behavior in the village in accordance with the moral ideals of Mao's teaching. These city youth showed much more gusto than the village youth in fearlessly criticizing peasant customs and interests. The radical nature of the urban youths' response to village affairs threw the essentially moderate nature of peasant youth activism into sharp relief. But the extremism of the sent-down city youth had an effect on the peasant youth. It solidified the moral mood that had been established in the Four Cleans. It helped make it more plausible than before to the peasant youth that exuberant brashness in the service of the revolution was a glorious thing — not just a way up within the social status system of the community but a mark of morally redemptive service to the country.

The prevalence of this moral mood, coupled with the skillful management of

257

the new militia chief, helped to maintain the esprit de corps that had been established among the militia during the Four Cleans. Even basically moderate youth could be led to vigorous support of state-sponsored projects to advance the village toward the socialist ideals then being propounded by the party.

The "moral revolution" advanced by the Four Cleans campaign and the Mao Study movement was then used to support a new experiment in collective production. A system of "Dazhai work points" was introduced, which made collective agriculture more a cooperative enterprise than ever before. Around 1964, the government had turned away from the system of collective agriculture management in which individual peasant households took responsibility for tilling their own portion of the collective land and had instituted a system in which peasants tilled the collective fields in organized teams. But according to this system, workers were remunerated for their labor by piece rates. Thus individual rewards were directly correlated with individual work. This system led villagers to compete against one another rather than cooperate together for maximum collective efficiency, and it allowed the strong to reap considerably more rewards than the weak. But under the Dazhai system, remuneration was by a time rate, and the value of a day's labor for different workers was determined by a worker's peers, who decided what overall contribution he had made to his production team. Thus the emphasis was on maximum cooperation. Moreover, according to the Dazhai system, the differentials between the highest paid and the lowest paid workers were much smaller than under the piece-rate system. So the Dazhai system was more in accord with Maoist socialist ideals, maximizing the importance of cooperation and minimizing the difference in material reward.

With its greater emphasis on cooperation, the Dazhai system held out the promise of increasing the general productivity of the village and thus might eventually turn out to be in the interests of all villagers. But it could fulfill this promise only if workers were properly motivated, and it was more difficult to motivate workers if their pay was not directly related to the actual amount of labor but only to general production team's standards for a good day's work. If the standard slipped down, the general level of work intensity might also slip. The youth of the village, organized through the militia, played an important role in solving the motivation problem. Especially during the crucial harvest and planting seasons, the young people, whipped up in the militia, set a high standard for hard work. If older people wanted to be considered top-flight laborers and thus get the maximum remuneration possible for a day's work, they had to meet or exceed the standard set by leaders among the militia people. By being "rate busters" the youth helped keep the intensity of collective labor at a high level.

During chaotic phases of the Cultural Revolution (1967), the village's peasant youth, organized through the militia, made a crucial contribution to the village's stability. By this time, many of the sent-down city youth, discouraged at the prospect of spending the rest of their lives living like ordinary peasants in a remote country village, were becoming restless. They formed a Red Guard organization to overthrow the local cadres in the name of the ideals of the Cultural Revolution, and then many of them fled back to the city. The village was left in political chaos; but key elements of the local militia, banding together into a Red Guard organization of their own, helped to hold the village together, by backing the village's cadres, vigorously preaching the need for law and order, and energetically urging people on to carry out production. After the Cultural Revolution, there was a Purify the Class Ranks campaign (1968-1969), in which the militia, under the direction of local (adult) village cadres, provided the driving force for massive attacks against scapegoats for the disruption of local law and order during the Cultural Revolution.

But after 1970, the role of the militia — and with it the role of young peasants — in the village began to change. There were fewer political campaigns, and the campaigns that did occur were less intense than those of the 1960s. Trying to recover from the chaos of the Cultural Revolution, shaken by the attempted coup of Lin Biao, and torn by factions trying to position themselves to win the succession struggle after Mao's passing, the Communist party was in no condition to make vigorous, sustained attempts to change the moral ideals of villagers and intensify their collective cooperation. Accordingly, there was not much need to mobilize the enthusiasm of young people to provide the emotional force behind political campaigns.

Moreover, even when central party officials tried in the early 1970s to carry out political campaigns in the countryside, Guangdong officials seem to have managed to block those campaigns. Thus, the One Hit, Three Anti campaign of 1970, the Criticize Confucius campaign of 1973, and the Study the Dictatorship of the Proletariat campaign of 1975 all failed to have a deep impact on Chen Village.

In the early 1970s, an attempt was still being made to use the militia to whip up a rate-busting enthusiasm for production, with some continued success. But government policy toward agricultural collectivization began to change. In 1975 in accordance with a new official policy, the Dazhai system was scrapped in Chen Village, to be replaced by a piece-rate system. By 1979, under the policies of the Deng Xiaoping regime, agriculture was, in effect, decollectivized. Now, individual households took responsibility for the cultivation of their own pieces of collective land. The Chinese government had retreated from its earlier attempts actively to change village moral standards and village production systems to correspond to socialist ideals. The enthusiasm and exuberance of village youth was thus no longer needed for political purposes.

One sign of the new times was a change in the mood of Chen Village's youth. They were still headstrong and still proud of their physical prowess, but these

259

qualities were now disoriented. Youth were now more mischievous than purposively involved in political affairs.

The change seems to have begun with news of the fall of Lin Biao, received in Chen Village in 1972. According to several former Chen Village youth interviewed in Hong Kong — persons who in the late 1960s and early 1970s were young militiamen — the fall of Lin Biao was a shattering blow to the moral vision of many young people. It was disorienting to see the person who had been hailed as the main paragon of revolutionary virtue next to Mao himself now being branded a traitor. As one peasant informant put it, after the fall of Lin Biao, "who the hell wanted to work anymore." There was still a core of active young people in the village — people striving to get into the party and to achieve cadre positions — but such people were now increasingly looked upon by middle-of-the-road youth as simple careerists, rather than as models to be imitated or leaders to be followed. As one of our peasant interviewees (who by his own account had been politically middle-of-the-road, not an activist) put it: "During the Cultural Revolution, because of these campaigns, a lot of youths became activists in criticizing people and in labor. But after the Cultural Revolution, these same youths became lazy, very lazy. . . . Yes, the youths believed Mao Thought. In their hearts they really felt this Mao Zedong was something. Thought every quote had true meaning. I felt so too. . . . Then everyone was more progressive, public spirited. Now, after Mao's Cultural Revolution, people are more backward, even do bad things. It was really counterproductive."

Such growing cynicism made it next to impossible in the 1970s to mobilize youth through the militia to be a striking force for revolution and production. By 1975 the Chen Village militia was not even bothering to have evaluations for "Five Good" militia members, apparently because the general level of activism among the militia was so low that giving such awards to a significant number of people would have all too obviously been a charade.

By 1979, the morale of young people in Chen Village had sunk so low that they jumped at the chance to desert the community. Although Chen Village was no more than a two-day journey by foot from the border with Hong Kong, very few natives of the village had up until then attempted to cross the border illegally. But in the spring of 1979, inspired by (false) rumors that the police were no longer preventing people from crossing the border, an extraordinary exodus of the village's youth occurred. Between May and October more than two hundred young people — practically the entire younger generation — made the dangerous crossing to Hong Kong. (Because the young people have gone, village households now have to hire laborers to help with their agriculture.) These youth were not rebelling against their parents or against the village's political leaders. Many of them left with at least the tacit approval and sometimes the active encouragement of parents and local cadres. They continue to send large sums of money and quantities of consumer goods back to their families in the village (by 1982 about half of the village households had TV sets sent by their children from Hong Kong); and the youth in Hong Kong have formed a village association that recently raised U.S.$10,000 to buy a truck and a boat for the village to use in transporting its products.

This extraordinary turn of events was possible only because of circumstances that make Chen Village atypical: the village's proximity to Hong Kong and the fact that in the spring of 1980 the village was made part of a "special economic zone" around the border with Hong Kong and thus became an integral part of the Hong Kong market. But the swiftness with which village youth jumped at the chance to leave the village in 1979 may indicate basic changes in peasant attitudes which may be widely shared in China. Border controls were relatively lax in 1962, but there was no such massive exodus of youth from Chen Village then, even though the village was enduring economic hard times caused by the failure of the Great Leap Forward. Then, village youth were willing to live out their commitments to family and community by working within government organizations to fight for social changes proposed by the Communist party. Then even middle-of-the-road youth could in ways described above be induced to follow the lead of their activist peers. Now village youth manifest their commitments to family and community by scrambling to take maximum advantage of economic forces. Middle-of-the-road youth follow not the few remaining young political activists — whom they despise as rank opportunists — but persons seeking economic betterment by making an illegal trek to Hong Kong. It would not be surprising if analogous shifts in attitudes were taking place among peasant youth throughout China, even though these shifts cannot be expressed in the dramatic ways open to Chen villagers because of their community's peculiar circumstances. Peasant youth are still characterized by exuberant energy, but there are now lacking the moral and organizational resources to teach the youth political "poetry" — that is, to discipline their impulses and turn them toward public service.

I have tried to assess the political potential of peasants passing through the youthful phases of their life cycle and to specify the institutional framework that was established in Chen Village to harness that potential. In the 1960s at least, the political potential of peasant youth seemed to differ significantly from the potential of urban youth. It seemed out of character for young peasant activists to fly in the face of local sensibilities or radically oppose local interests, as some of the "radical" sent-down youth did for a time in Chen Village in the mid-1960s. The reason was that peasant youth in a fundamental way shared the sensibilities and interests of their elders, a sharing bolstered by the knowledge that they would probably live out their lives in their home village and their social and political success would depend on achieving the long-term support and respect of their fellow villagers. We have seen how certain tendencies in

261

youthful conduct could be evoked and harnessed by village political institutions (with the militia playing a key role) to drive villagers to exert themselves in collective labor during the agricultural busy seasons and to criticize political offenders during rectification campaigns. But we have also seen how very concrete concatenations of historical circumstances determined exactly how and with what consequences this "youth connection" was actualized. Thus the general ideological mood of the country helped determine the degree to which village young people could be led to link their quest for local glory to a larger quest for national glory. Thus the structure of the village's (adult-dominated) political leadership helped determine whether the young people would be mobilized for revolutionary ends. And thus the particular managerial skills of particular adult militia chiefs helped determine the amount of political morale the village young would have. What this analysis points to is the need to link sociological analysis of the institutional links between state and society to a careful account of the flow of Chinese history.

My own research has focused mainly on situations in rural China from the mid-1960s to the early 1970s. But I have tried to suggest how earlier and later historical contexts both gave shape to and were shaped by different patterns of participation of youthful peasants in politics.

In his chapter on villages in *Ideology and Organization in Communist China*, Franz Schurmann stressed the importance of Communist organization of young peasants for the revolutionary transformation of rural society in the late 1940s and early 1950s.[13] Traditional village leadership positions, he said, were dominated by older men, who exercised their leadership through the civil arts of persuasion and the political manipulation of personal loyalties. Young people had no power, but they had strength, the potential ability to lead people through the military arts of disciplined violence. The Communist party recruited and organized young peasants and encouraged them to struggle militarily against the old chiefs. The Communists offered strong young people of poor peasant background a special hope — the hope that they could become the leaders of the new social order that was being established. Then the Communists armed and organized the young peasants and encouraged them in the struggle. The destruction of the power of the old chiefs and their replacement by a young elite oriented to military activities made it possible for the Communists to drive their organization deep into the fabric of the villages. When combined with the political organization of poor peasants, the military organization of young people made it possible for the Communists to carry out the revolutionary projects of land reform and eventually of collectivization. The "youth connection" could be used by representatives of the state to bypass the leaders of the old rural society for the sake of political and economic revolution.

The process Schurmann describes seems indeed to have taken place in Chen Village in the 1950s. That is when the present leadership of the village rose to power. They were tough, young, poor peasants then, and they led the struggles for land reform and collectivization, thus creating new patterns of village life and linking the village's history to national political movements. But by the mid-1960s, this generation of 1950s young revolutionaries had become adult family men in their early thirties. Many of them had begun to temper their youthful exuberance, to worry about the welfare of their newly formed families, and to practice the adaptive social rituals of compromise and accommodation.

Political leaders in Beijing became worried about such phenomena and eventually launched the Four Cleans campaign to chastise this new generation of village chiefs. But the government was not willing totally to replace this 1950s generation by a new 1960s generation. It could not mobilize young peasants simply by promising them the positions of power which belonged to their elders. But it skillfully used their desires to be strong and bold to provide the physical and moral power behind carefully orchestrated efforts to develop a new economic and moral order for the village.

By the mid-1970s, however, the evidence suggests that the "youth connection" had begun to disappear. If our informants are correct, the youthful phase of the peasant life cycle — in Chen Village at least — now seemed increasingly to be producing a rebelliousness, not an active, disciplined rebelliousness but a passive, dispirited kind, the result of frustrated rising expectations and a breakdown in the credibility of government ideology. Perhaps new forms of ideology and organization will be needed now to harness anew the constructive political potential of China's village youth.

Notes

Chapter 1. The Postrevolutionary Chinese State

1. For a discussion of political changes and continuities, see Ho Ping-ti, "Salient Aspects of China's Heritage," in Ho Ping-ti and Tang Tsou, eds., *China in Crisis* (Chicago: University of Chicago Press, 1968), vol. 1, pp. 1–41. Ho does not mince his words: "While the Maoist ideology and the unprecedented power of organization are distinctly new wine, this new wine is contained in a 2000-year-old bottle of authoritarianism" (p. 25). In the Marxist tradition, these continuities are often couched in terms of the persistence of "Oriental despotism" or the "Asiatic model of production": see, for example, Rudolf Bahro, "The Alternative in Eastern Europe," *New Left Review* 106 (November–December 1977): 3–38; Umberto Melotti, *Marx and the Third World* (London: Macmillan, 1977); Karl A. Wittfogel, *Oriental Despotism: A Comparative Study of Total Power* (New Haven: Yale University Press, 1957).

2. T. H. Rigby, ed., *Stalin* (Englewood Cliffs, N.J.: Prentice-Hall, 1966), p. 24. For Stalin's own definition of the role of the state, see J. V. Stalin, *Problems of Leninism* (Peking: Foreign Languages Press, 1976), esp. pp. 38–52, 168–267, 734–765, 927–936.

3. The *locus classicus* is Mark Selden's *The Yenan Way in Revolutionary China* (Cambridge, Mass.: Harvard University Press, 1971). Compare Carl E. Dorris, "Peasant Mobilization in North China and the Origins of Yenan Communism," *China Quarterly*, no. 68 (December 1976), pp. 697–719; I. J. Kim, "Mass Mobilization Policies and Techniques Developed in the Period of the Chinese Soviet Republic," in A. Doak Barnett, ed., *Chinese Communist Politics in Action* (Seattle: University of Washington Press, 1969), pp. 78–98.

4. Edward Friedman and Mark Selden, eds., *America's Asia: Dissenting Essays on Asian-American Relations* (New York: Vintage, 1971), pp. 360–365.

5. This argument is developed more fully by John W. Lewis in "Leader, Commissar, and Bureaucrat: The Chinese Political System in the Last Days of the Revolution," in Ho Ping-ti and Tang Tsou, eds., *China in Crisis*, pp. 449–481.

6. Mao Tse-tung, "Speech at the Hankow Conference" (April 6, 1955), in *Miscellany of Mao Tse-tung Thought* (Arlington, Va.: Joint Publications Research Service, 1974) (hereafter *Miscellany*), vol. 1, pp. 86–87.

7. Zhang Chunqiao refers to criticisms of the "rural style" or "guerrilla habit" in his important article, "Renouncing the Bourgeois Concept of Legal Rights," *Renmin Ribao* (People's Daily), October 13, 1958, translated in *Union Research Service* (Hong Kong: Union Research Institute), vol. 13, pp. 150–157. This article is also steeped in nostal-

gia for the egalitarian days of Yanan, an emotion also visible in Mao's work of the late 1950s and early 1960s; for example, see his comments on the "egalitarian life" in Yanan in "Reading Notes on the Soviet Union's 'Political Economics' " (1961–1962), in *Miscellany*, vol. 2, p. 182.

8. Ying-mao Kau, "Patterns of Recruitment and Mobility of Urban Cadres," in John W. Lewis, ed., *The City in Communist China* (Stanford: Stanford University Press, 1971), p. 113.

9. The relationship between the party and the unions illustrates this disciplinary process; see Paul Harper, "The Party and the Unions in Communist China," *China Quarterly*, no. 37 (January–March 1969), pp. 84–119.

10. To date, there have been three state constitutions. The first, adopted on September 30, 1954, by the First National People's Congress, defined the PRC as "a people's democratic state led by the working class and based on the alliance of workers and peasants." Both the second (January 17, 1975) and the third (March 5, 1978) changed the phrase "people's democratic state" to a "socialist state of the dictatorship of the proletariat." Each constitution was accompanied by an authoritative report explaining and defending its content. These were presented by Liu Shaoqi, Zhang Chunqiao, and Ye Jianying respectively.

11. These congresses have not constituted a significant locus of power (with the possible fleeting exception of the mid-1950s) so I shall largely ignore them. Though certain "democratic" reforms in the representative system were introduced in 1979– 1980 (notably the extension of direct elections for "people's representatives" up to the county level), it is as yet too early to assess whether changes are anything more than cosmetic.

12. For the 1975 constitution, see *The Constitution of the PRC* (Peking: Foreign Languages Press, 1975); for the 1978 constitution, see *Peking Review*, no. 11 (March 17, 1978), pp. 5–14.

13. See Pierre M. Perrolle, ed., *Fundamentals of the Chinese Communist Party* (White Plains, N.Y.: International Arts and Sciences Press, 1976), p. 71.

14. Ibid., p. 78.

15. For a critique from the late 1970s, see Wang Xizhe, "For a Return to Genuine Marxism in China," translated in *New Left Review* 121 (May–June 1980): 33–48. Wang argues (p. 47) that "administrative leadership by the party is not the only form the party's leading role can take."

16. *Peking Review* 36 (September 2, 1977): 16–22.

17. Mao Tse-tung, "Talk at an Enlarged Central Work Conference," (January 30, 1962), in S. R. Schram, ed., *Mao Tse-tung Unrehearsed: Talks and Letters, 1956–71* Harmondsworth: Penguin, 1974), p. 164.

18. Perrolle, ed., *Fundamentals of the Chinese Communist Party*, p. 89.

19. For the most recent effort, see "Ensuring Full Democracy Inside the Party," *Renmin Ribao*, January 11, 1979.

20. In the 1978 state constitution, the dominance is mentioned retrospectively in the preamble (p. 5): "Chairman Mao Tse-tung was the founder of the PRC. All our victories in revolution and construction have been won under the guidance of Marxism-Leninism-Mao Tse-tung Thought." For a detailed analysis of Mao's policy role, see Michel C. Oksenberg, "Policy Making under Mao, 1949–68: An Overview," in J. M. Lindbeck, ed., *China: Management of a Revolutionary Society* (Seattle: University of Washington Press, 1971), pp. 79–115.

21. For example, see "On the Role of the Individual in History," *Beijing Review* 32 (August 11, 1980): 17–21.

22. For a discussion of the central work conference, see Parris H. Chang, "Research Notes on the Changing Loci of Decision in the Chinese Communist Party," *China Quarterly*, no. 44 (October–December 1970), pp. 169–194.

23. Both of the quotations are in John W. Lewis, *Leadership in Communist China* (Ithaca, N.Y.: Cornell University Press, 1963), pp. 140–143.

24. The complex "class enemies" category can be simplified into two main groups: people designated with a class status (*chengren*) of "landlord" or "rich peasant" in the early 1950s and those on whom the party has pinned various invidious political "labels" ("hats," *maozi*) notably "rightist," "counterrevolutionary," or "bad element."

25. A label like "present-day counterrevolutionary" (*xianxing fangeming*), which includes spies and saboteurs, has been far more serious than the label of "rightist," which usually denoted a political *lapsus linquae* or *calami*.

26. See the table in Lewis, *Leadership*, p. 108.

27. James R. Townsend, *Politics in China* (Boston: Little, Brown, 1974), p. 251.

28. The respondent noted that all technicians count as "cadres," but they are distinct from their political and administrative counterparts in that they "manage professional matters" (*guanli yewu*) while the latter "manage people" (*guanli ren*).

29. "Constitution of the CPC" (August 18, 1977), in *The Eleventh National Congress of the CPC (Documents)* (Peking: Foreign Languages Press, 1977), pp. 127–145.

30. *Peking Review* 11 (March 17, 1978): 8.

31. Benjamin I. Schwartz, "A Personal View of Some Thoughts of Mao Tse-tung," in Chalmers Johnson, ed., *Ideology and Politics in Contemporary China* (Seattle: University of Washington Press, 1973), p. 367.

32. "Decision of the Central Committee of the CCP concerning the Great Proletarian Cultural Revolution," August 8, 1966, translated in K. H. Fan, ed., *The Chinese Cultural Revolution: Selected Documents* (New York: Monthly Review Press, 1968), pp. 162–173.

33. For the best account of events in Shanghai during this period, see A. B. Walder, *Ch'ang Ch'un-ch'iao and Shanghai's January Revolution*, Michigan Papers in Chinese Studies, No. 32 (Ann Arbor: 1977).

34. Ibid, p. 62.

35. Mao admitted to party colleagues in late 1966 that "I myself had not foreseen that the whole country would be thrown into turmoil" and that the Reds Guards "in one rush swept you [party officials] off your feet" (ibid., p. 25).

36. Sheng Wu Lian, *Whither China?* (January 6, 1968), *Guangyin Hongqi* (Canton Printing Red Flag), no. 5 (March 1968), translated in *Survey of China Mainland Press* (Hong Kong: U.S. Consulate General), no. 4190 (June 4, 1968), p. 3.

37. Ibid., pp. 8–12.

38. This commitment continued into the 1970s. For example, the 1975 state constitution contained several radical-inspired formulations, one of which emphasized the direct representation of the masses in organs of administration. The italicized portion of the following quotation from Article 3 is missing from both the 1954 and 1978 constitutions: "The organs through which the people exercise power are the people's congresses at all levels, *with deputies of workers, peasants and soldiers as their main body*." Article 13 of the 1975 constitution also guaranteed the right to exercise the basic forms of "extensive democracy" practiced during the Cultural Revolution, describing them as "new forms of carrying on socialist revolution created by the masses of the people."

39. Li Yizhe, "Concerning Socialist Democracy and Legal System" (November 7, 1974, translated in *Issues and Studies* (Taibei) 12 (January 12, 1976): 110–148.

Chapter 2. Back from the Brink of Revolutionary-"Feudal" Totalitarianism

1. "Communiqué of the Third Plenary Session of the Eleventh Central Committee of the Communist Party of China" (adopted on December 22, 1978), *Peking Review*, December 29, 1978, pp. 8, 15.

Later, the phrase to shift the "focus of work" was used in the English translation in place of to shift the "emphasis." For example, see *Beijing Review*, January 7, 1980, p. 14.

For an analysis of the events and ideological debates surrounding the struggle for succession to Mao in the years just before and after his death, as well as a forecast on the likelihood of a revival of the call for integration of universal principles with concrete practice, see Tang Tsou, "Mao Tse-tung Thought, the Last Struggle for Succession, and the Post-Mao Era," *China Quarterly*, no. 71 (September 1977), pp. 498−529.

2. *Peking Review*, December 29, 1978, p. 11. As published in the revised version of his famous speech, "On the Correct Handling of the Contradictions among the People," Mao's statement reads, "The large scale, turbulent class struggle of the masses characteristic of the times of revolution have in the main come to an end, but the class struggle is by no means entirely over." *Selected Works of Mao Tse-tung*, 5 vols. (Peking: Foreign Languages Press, 1977), vol. 5, p. 395. It has a different emphasis from the way in which it is used in the Communiqué.

3. Richard Lowenthal, "Development vs. Utopia in Communist Policy," in *Change in Communist Systems*, ed. Chalmers Johnson (Stanford: Stanford University Press, 1970), p. 54.

4. Samuel Huntington, "Social and Institutional Dynamics of One-Party System," in Samuel Huntington and Clement H. Moore, eds., *Authoritarian Politics in Modern Society* (New York: Basic Books, 1970), pp. 3−47.

5. Lowenthal, "Development vs. Utopia," p. 108.

6. Ibid., p. 115; italics in the original.

7. Juan Linz, "Totalitarianism and Authoritarianism," in Fred Greenstein and Nelson Polsby, eds., *Handbook of Political Science* (Reading, Mass.: Addison-Wesley, 1975), Vol. 3, pp. 175−411.

8. N. S. Timasheff, "Totalitarianism, Despotism, and Dictatorship," in Carl J. Friedrich, ed., *Totalitarianism* (Cambridge, Mass.: Harvard University Press, 1954), p. 39.

9. For a more extended theoretical discussion of the concept of totalitarianism and the definition of politics, see my paper with the same title as this chapter (pp. 3−12), which was presented on May 30, 1980, at the Luce Seminar, University of Chicago.

For a suggestion to use a new phrase "political totalism" in the place of "totalitarianism," see my paper "Political Totalism, Authoritarianism, and Hegemony: A Proposed Theoretical Scheme for the Study of the Transformation of the Traditional Sociopolitical Order into a Communist System in China," presented at the Northern Illinois University, October 27, 1982.

For a sequel to the present essay, and a more detailed and concrete discussion of events since 1980, see "The Middle Course in Changing the State-Society Relations and in Reforming the Political Structure," a revised and updated version of a paper presented at a conference on China held at the University of Chicago in November 1981.

10. *Dagong Bao* (Impartial Daily), November 28, 1979, p. 8.

11. Ding Ling, "Some Remarks from the Heart," *Hongqi* (Red Flag), 1980, no. 12, p. 51.

12. It is now widely recognized that there were "leftist" errors in the policies toward literature and the arts before the Cultural Revolution. These "leftist" policies helped the ultraleftists to seize control after 1966. See the article by Zheng Wen in *Renmin Ribao* (People's Daily), August 10, 1979, p. 4; editorial, November 17, 1979, p. 1.

13. Ding Ling, "Some Remarks from the Heart," p. 52.

14. See Ba Jin, "Random Thoughts," a series of short essays and reminiscences published since December 17, 1978, in *Dagong Bao* and *Huaqiao Ribao* (China Daily News). See particularly numbers 7, 11, 14, 15, 27, 29, 34, and 36. One of the most moving pieces is number 36, in which he describes the fate of two dogs and his feelings toward his own dog. The force of these short pieces derives from Ba Jin's honesty and frankness in analyzing his thoughts, feelings, and role in these traumatic years as well as from his ability to express an understanding of the reality of that period.

15. Liu Binyan, "The Call of the Times," *Wenyi Bao* (Literary Gazette), 1979, nos. 11-12, pp. 36-46. The article consists of his remarks made at the Fourth Congress of Writers and Artists.

16. Some of the lower-level cadres were executed for "counterrevolutionary crimes."

17. According to the editor-in-chief of the *Renmin Ribao*, Hu Zhiwei, the tragic and painful lessons of the ten years during the Cultural Revolution enabled "us" to realize profoundly and personally that unless "democracy" inside and outside the party was fully developed the party's system of centralism could become "feudal autocracy" and a "feudal, fascist, dictatorial system" (Hu, "How to Develop Criticism and Self-Criticism in Newspapers," *Xinwen Zhanxian* (The News Battlefront), 1979, no. 6, p. 5).

18. Brantly Womack, "Politics and Epistemology," *China Quarterly*, no. 81 (December 1979), pp. 768-792.

19. "The Tree of Practice Is Forever Green," *Renmin Ribao*, March 21, 1979, p. 3. This report gives an account of the genesis of Hu's article "Practice Is the Sole Criterion for Testing Truth." The possibility or even likelihood that Hu's article was the product of prompting by leaders at a higher level or of an unannounced meeting of a group of like-minded party leaders and cadres at different levels cannot be excluded.

20. *Peking Review*, June 23, 1978, pp. 14-21, 29.

21. *Hongqi*, 1977, no. 3, p. 18.

22. *Beijing Review*, July 6, 1981, p. 23.

23. For the theoretical problems raised in this article, see "China: New Theories for Old" by the editors, *Monthly Review*, May 1979, pp. 1-19. For a debate over the post-Mao developments, see Charles Bettelheim, "The Great Leap Backward," ibid., July-August 1978, pp. 37-130, and Reader's Comment on *China since Mao*, ibid., May 1979, pp. 21-55.

24. Hu Qiaomu, "Observe Economic Laws, Speed up the Four Modernizations," *Peking Review*, November 10, 1978, pp. 8, 9. For more details, see the new or republished works of Xue Muqiao, Sun Yefang, Yü Guangyuan, and Xu Dixin.

25. As a Marxist, Mao recognized that there are laws governing all things. In particular, he urged his comrades to study the "laws of war" and to plan their actions "in accordance with these laws in order to overcome the enemy facing us" (*Selected Readings from the Works of Mao Tse-tung* [Peking: Foreign Languages Press, 1967], pp. 51-52). But Mao also emphasized that war is a continuation of politics and that military strategy must be subordinated to political objectives. This is as it should be. How much Mao's thinking on political-military relations influenced his ideas on the relationship between politics and other spheres is an interesting but unresolved problem.

26. Hua Song, "Repel the Interference of Anarchism," *Hongqi*, 1980, no. 2, p. 23; italics added.

27. For example, to establish virtue was considered to be the highest personal achievement, to be followed by the performance of meritorious deeds and formulation of ideas and views, in that order.

28. The term "latent dysfunction" is derived from Anthony Giddens, "Functionalism après la lutte," *Social Research*, Summer 1967, pp. 325–366.

29. For a more detailed discussion of this idea of Mao, see Tang Tsou, "Mao Tsetung Thought."

30. Article by Lin Zili, in *Hongqi*, December 1979, p. 2. For a reaffirmation of Mao's formulation coupled with a repudiation of its interpretation and use by the ultraleftists, see Jin Shougeng's article in *Zhexue Yanjiu* (Philosophical Research), 1980, no. 1, pp. 16–23.

31. The New Years editorial of the *Guangming Ribao* (The Light Daily), a newspaper specializing in education, culture, and science, hailed this reversal as "a change of historical significance" (January 1, 1980, p. 1).

The term "intellectual" embraces "professors, scientists, senior engineers and writers who are commonly known as highly qualified intellectuals as well as ordinary technicians in factories, primary school teachers and other mental workers with professional knowledge." In 1949, there were about three million intellectuals. Now, there are twenty-five million intellectuals, including six million scientific and technical workers. Ninety percent of the total trained after 1949 came from "working people's families" (*Beijing Review*, June 23, 1979, p. 14).

32. This term came into vogue after the publication of Yao Wenyuan's article, "The Working Class Must Take Over the Leadership in Everything," *Hongqi*, 1968, no. 2, pp. 3–7.

33. Deng's speech at the All-Army Political Work Conference, June 2, 1978, *Peking Review*, June 23, 1978, pp. 14–21, 29.

34. Quoted in *Dagong Bao*, December 29, 1979. Peng Chong was elevated to be a member of the Secretariat in February 1980.

35. *Beijing Review*, February 2, 1979, pp. 10–15.

36. *Renmin Ribao*, July 14, 1979, p. 1. Before the Cultural Revolution, this department had slightly more than 2,000 researchers and cadres. Before 1976, 1,042 persons were investigated at one time or another. It is not known how many of these persons were disgraced. In July 1979, it was announced that more than 800 of those disgraced had been rehabilitated after 1977, that is, the adverse decisions against them were reversed, the labels removed, and their reputations reaffirmed. (The eminent economist Sun Yefang was denounced as a "counterrevolutionary revisionist.")

37. For the public response to this exposure of a case of corruption, see Liu Binyan, "The Call of the Times."

38. *Dagong Bao*, December 14, 1979, p.1.

39. From January 23 to February 23, 1980, the Chinese Associations of Playwrights, Writers, and Movie Makers held several joint discussions on the new situation and new problems that had emerged during the past two years. The discussion was focused on three plays (*The Impostor, The Female Thief*, and *In the Dossier of the Society*). Although the majority of the participants pointed out the "serious defects" of these plays and scripts, the view of the other side was also put on record. More important, no label was put on the writers.

40. Article by Wang Roxui, *Renmin Ribao*, April 28, 1982, p. 5. For a brief report on Hu Qiaomu's talk, see *Dagong Bao*, June 28, 1982, p. 1. For the criticism of Bai Hua's

Bitter Love, see my paper "Paradoxes in Political Reform in China," presented at a conference in November 1981 held at the University of Chicago.

41. Deng's speech at the National Conference on Science, March 18, 1978, *Hongqi*, 1978, no. 4, p. 17.

42. Article by Zheng Yan, *Hongqi*, 1980, no. 3, p. 35.

43. *Renmin Ribao*, March 25, 1980, p. 2.

44. This remark was made by the poet Ke Yan (*Dagong Bao*, December 28, 1979, p. 7).

45. *Dagong Bao*, December 14, 1979, p. 7; December 28, 1979, p. 7; *Ming Bao* (The Bright Daily), November 23, 1979, p. 3.

46. For a discussion of the functions of these mass organizations in the scientific and technological fields by a leading theoretician in China, Yu Guangyuan, see *Renmin Ribao*, March 14, 1980, p. 5. Under the All-China Association for Science and Technology there are more than one hundred societies on special subjects.

47. *Huaqiao Ribao*, January 12, 1980. Xia's leg was broken by the mob during the Cultural Revolution and he was permanently crippled. He was also imprisoned for a period of time. Only in 1978 did he become active again (*Dagong Bao*, December 28, 1979, p. 7).

48. *Dagong Bao* (Hong Kong), March 24, 1980, p. 1.

49. *Beijing Review*, June 16, 1979, p. 9.

50. *Beijing Review*, February 16, 1979, p. 8. In 1978, there had been more than five million landlords and rich peasants. By 1979, only fifty thousand retained these labels (*Beijing Review*, January 21, 1980, p. 14). To what extent this change actually occurred in the countryside cannot be ascertained.

In 1950, the State Council adopted a regulation under which the labels of landlord and rich peasant could be removed if the landlord had worked in the field for five years and the rich peasant had worked three years without violating laws and regulations and without doing evil things ("On Certain Problems concerning Classes and Class Struggle," *Xinhua Yuebao [Wenzhai Ban]* [New China Monthly (Selected Articles)], 1980, no. 10, p. 1). But this regulation was never enforced.

51. *Beijing Review*, June 21, 1980, p. 10.

52. The discriminatory treatment of the descendants of landlords and rich peasants has contributed to the magnification of class struggle in the countryside simply as a result of population growth. For example, there remained in one province about 50,000 persons who had originally been classified as landlords or rich peasants. But their second generation numbered more than 250,000 persons and the third generation, 500,000 (*Hongqi*, 1980, no. 2, p. 29).

53. *Beijing Review*, November 16, 1979, p. 16; italics added. The implications of this view are far-reaching. Would struggle between classes as a whole be replaced by conflicts among institutional interest groups and corporate professional and occupational groups? What role would the party play in the resolution of these conflicts?

54. *Beijing Review*, October 5, 1979, p. 21.

55. *Beijing Review*, November 23, 1979, p. 16. The Chinese now admit their error in their criticism of Stalin's view expressed in 1936 that exploitative classes had disappeared in the Soviet Union. At the same time, they reaffirmed their criticism of Stalin's judgment expressed in 1937 that class struggle had sharpened. See "On Certain Problems concerning Classes and Class Struggle," pp. 4–5.

56. "A Study in the Planned Management of the Socialist Economy," *Beijing Review*, October 26, 1979, pp. 14–21.

57. By 1980, these experiments were being undertaken in more than three thousand

factories, or 7 percent of the industrial enterprises owned by the state. This 7 percent produced more than 30 percent of the total industrial output or around 40 percent of the total profits derived from industry (speech by Liu Guoguang, *Wenhui Bao* [Literary Catchment Daily] [Hong Kong], March 8, 1980, p. 7). On a report on the experiment in one hundred factories in Sichuan in the first half of 1979, see the article by Ren Tao of the Institute of Planned Economy of the State Planning Commission in *Jingji Yanjiu* (Economic Research), December 1979, pp. 6−9, 33. Six of these factories were studied more intensively than others. Many of the one hundred factories formerly held the title of "enterprises of the Daqing type." For a report of a survey of these experiments in Sichuan, Anhui, and Zhejiang, see the article by Lin Zili, *Renmin Ribao*, April 4, 1980, p. 5. See also ibid., April 4, 1980, p. 1.

58. By early 1980, there were thirty-six thousand rural markets, close to the total number existing in 1965. The monetary transactions at these markets in 1979 increased by 36 percent over 1978 (*Renmin Ribao*, March 10, 1980, p. 2). According to G. William Skinner there were forty-five thousand market towns in China in the mid-nineteenth century. There are now approximately fifty thousand communes. The number of rural markets given refers most likely to the large local market and does not include many small ones.

59. According to a later report, the preliminary calculation shows that the peasants' average per capita income from the collective units in 1979 was 84 *yuan*, an average increase of 10 *yuan*, 2 *yuan* more than the projected figure (Report of the Vice-Chairman of the Planning Commission, Li Renjun, by the New China Agency, *Dagong Bao*, April 11, 1980, p. 1).

60. *Renmin Ribao*, July 5, 1978, p. 1.

61. Ibid., August 3, 1978, p. 1.

62. For a detailed discussion, see Tang Tsou, Marc Blecher, and Mitchell Meisner, "The Responsibility System in Agriculture," *Modern China* 8 (January 1982): 41−103.

63. *Wenzhai Bao* (Journal of Selected Reports), December 15, 1981, p. 1.

64. *Liaowang* (The Lookout), 1982, no. 4, p. 8.

65. *Renmin Ribao*, April 28, 1982, p. 4.

66. *Dagong Bao*, June 17, 1982, p. 1.

67. Xu Dixin, Dong Fureng, and Liu Guoguang, in their capacities then as respectively the director and vice-directors of the Institute of Economic Research of the Chinese Academy of the Social Sciences, made three informative speeches in Hong Kong on the new policies. The full texts are printed in *Wenhui Bao* (Hong Kong), March 8, 1980, pp. 6−7. These speeches are among the best summaries of the policies at that time. See also Xue Muqiao's three-part article in *Beijing Review*, February 4, 1980, pp. 16−21; March 24, 1980, pp. 21−25; and April 7, 1980, pp. 20−25.

68. For example, "Never Forget the Relationship between Fishes and Water," by "our special commentator," *Renmin Ribao*, August 19, 1978, p. 2.

69. The translation used is taken from *Peking Review*, October 13, 1978, p. 7.

70. Ye accused the ultraleftists of suppressing "every social stratum" (*Beijing Review*, October 5, 1979, p. 18).

71. Ibid., p.19.

72. The term "science" now refers specifically to systematic scientific theory and research, as well as generally to the scientific attitude that was stressed during the May Fourth period as a weapon to attack traditional superstition, attitudes, and values. The term "democracy" can be best understood in the broad sense as a system of freedoms or rights which preceded the establishment in the West of a system of democratic govern-

ment in the strict sense of the term and made it possible for science to develop even under a monarchical or autocratic government. It refers primarily to "limited government" and only secondarily to "democracy" in the narrower sense.

73. "Academic Freedom and Political Democracy: A Discussion in Academic Research Sponsored by the Beijing Guangming Daily," *Eastern Horizon*, November 1979, p. 6.

74. *Beijing Review*, October 5, 1979, p. 23.

75. For a concise report on the changes in the system of election and nomination, see *Dagong Bao*, February 12, 1980, p. 1.

76. For the notion of "binding oneself" and "precommitment" in a theory of rational choice, see Jon Elster, *Ulysses and the Sirens* (Cambridge: Cambridge University Press, 1979).

77. *Hongqi*, 1980, no. 6, pp. 3−4.

78. *Renmin Ribao*, March 23, 1980, p. 1.

79. Tito may have provided a precedent or example for this new step.

80. "Constitution of the Communist Party of China," *Beijing Review*, September 20, 1982, p. 19. This practice of "being a lifelong cadre" corresponds to the practice of giving an "iron rice bowl" to the workers. In some factories the son or daughter can take over his or her parent's job, if the latter retires.

81. For an early diagnosis of this problem, see the insightful article by Mike Oksenberg, "The Exit Pattern from Chinese Politics and Its Implications," *China Quarterly*, no. 67, September 1976, pp. 501−518.

82. Li Honglin, "What Kind of Leadership by the Party We Uphold," *Xinhua Yuebao (Wenzhai Ban)*, 1979, no. 11, p. 3. For a report on separating the party committee from the administrative leadership at Nankai University, see *Renmin Ribao*, March 29, 1980, p. 3.

83. Lin Zili, *Hongqi*, December 1979, p. 3. In its March 29, 1980, issue, *Ming Bao* carried what purports to be excerpts from a speech made by Vice Chairman Chen Yün at a meeting of the Politburo in July 1979. Chen remarked that the constant guide used by the cadres is not "Marxism-Leninism," but the "will of their senior officials" and the "hints given with the eyes of the upper-level officials." After the Beijing regime publicized a directive to reaffirm the necessity of keeping party and government secrets and noted that much important information about China came back to China from outside, *Ming Bao* carried an editorial saying that this speech was given to it by travelers from China and that it could not verify its authenticity. Several days later, the New China News Agency challenged the authenticity of several documents published by *Ming Bao*. But the thrust of the remarks cited here is consistent with all the published articles and official statements, although the existence of many expressions and phrases not generally used in China suggests that the document as a whole is not authentic.

84. We do not yet have sufficient evidence to show whether Deng set these limits because he was under pressure from the standpatters and his position was momentarily weakened. My guess is that he did so out of conviction.

85. *Beijing Review*, October 5, 1979, p. 16.

86. See "Communiqué of the Third Plenary Session of the Eleventh Central Committee of the Communist Party of China" (adopted on December 22, 1978), *Peking Review*, December 29, 1978, p. 15. See also Tsou, "Mao Tse-tung Thought," p. 524 for a forecast of this formulation.

87. *Renmin Ribao*, January 2, 1980, p. 1.

88. This phrase is borrowed from Linz, "Totalitarianism and Authoritarianism," p. 191.

89. The future thus contains a wider range of possibilities for good or evil than we can envisage at this time. Yu Guangyuan, a leading theoretician, a vice-president of the Academy of the Social Sciences at that time, and the head of Institute of Marxism-Leninism and Mao Zedong Thought, makes a distinction between realization of the dictatorship of the proletariat *"through the party"* and its realization *"through an organization embodying the entire proletariat."* He attributes to Lenin the ideas that the Communists must create the conditions so that the dictatorship of the proletariat through its vanguard could be advanced to the dictatorship of the proletariat through an organization embodying the entire proletariat. The implication of Yu's idea is that the leadership of the party may one day be downgraded. The downgrading of the principle of party leadership coupled with the emphasis on "an organization embodying the entire proletariat" may in the future provide the ideological foundation of a greater degree of political and economic pluralism (*Xinhua Yuebao* [Wenzhai Bao], 1979, no. 6, pp. 22−31; italics added). One must also point out, however, that this article was published at the high point of the trend toward liberalization. Since 1981, this trend has been checked and even reversed in some specific areas in various degrees.

90. The real issue is the use of "big-character" posters; the other three phrases are mainly rhetorical flourishes.

91. Qi Xin, "Let's Look at How the Chinese Communist Party Strengthens Its Organization," *Qishi Niandai* (The Seventies), 1980, no. 4, p. 58.

92. Aside from the problem of political succession, the problem of a generation gap has been raised and discussed in China. For example, see *Zhongguo Qingnian* (Chinese Youth), 1980, no. 1, pp. 14−18.

93. See Guillermo O'Donnell, "Tension in the Bureaucratic-Authoritarian State," in David Collier, ed., *The New Authoritarianism in Latin America* (Princeton: Princeton University Press), 1979, pp. 314−318.

94. As R. M. MacIver once paraphrased Aristotle, "We can learn the nature of anything only when it has reached — and passed — its maturation. Events and process, theories and actions, appear in a new perspective" (Foreword to Karl Polanyi, *The Great Transformation* [Boston: Beacon Press, 1957], p. ix).

95. The concept of totalitarianism as formulated by most Western social scientists from Friedrich to Linz applies to the regime, not to a revolutionary movement. An implicit assumption underlying my reformulation of this concept is that it can be extended to discuss the tendency inherent in some revolutionary movements. This extension of the applicability of the concept is also made necessary by the fact that the CCP established its own army, government, and base areas during the revolutionary period and was in fact a state within a state.

96. These phrases are borrowed from Yu-sheng Lin, who uses them to develop a different theme in *The Crisis of Chinese Consciousness* (Madison: University of Wisconsin Press, 1979), pp. 29, 41.

97. Among other things, Mao asserted that "literature and art are subordinate to politics" (*Selected Readings from the Works of Mao Tse-tung*, p. 221). In the version of Vice-Premier Deng's speech on January 16, 1980, as published in *Ming Bao*, Deng declared that "we . . . would no longer raise the slogan that 'literature and art are subordinate to politics' because this slogan can easily become the actual justification for arbitrary interference with literature and art" (*Ming Bao*, March 3, 1980, p. 2). For a comment on how Mao's ideas were being pushed step by step to the extreme, see Luo Xun, "Literature and Arts, Life, and Politics." *Wenxue Pinglun* (Literary Criticism), 1980, no. 1, p. 2. See also note 40, above.

98. In 1924 there were in the border area of Shenxi-Gansu-Ningxia, only sixty pub-

licly owned enterprises employing four thousand workers and staff members (*Jingji Guanli* [Economic Management], October 1979, p. 46).

99. Frederick C. Teiwes, *Politics and Purges in China, 1950–1965* (White Plains, N.Y.: M. E. Sharp, 1979). See also Tang Tsou, "Revolution, Reintegration, and Crisis in Communist China: A Framework for Analysis," in *China in Crisis*, ed. Ho Ping-ti and Tang Tsou, vol. 1, Book 1 (Chicago: University of Chicago Press, 1968), p. 318.

100. Xu Bing, "On Human Rights and Rights of Citizens," *Xinhua Yuebao* (*Wenzhai Ban*), 1979, no. 7, p. 4.

101. These slogans may or may not have been used by Lin Biao and the ultraleftists. They do accurately describe their mentality.

102. For the documentation of these charges, see Tsou, "Mao Tse-tung Thought." There is no way to confirm their accuracy. But they are consistent with the published writings of Zhang and Yao and the articles in *Xuexi yu Pipan* (Study and Criticism), a journal under the exclusive control of the ultraleftists.

103. This statement by Lin Biao was contained in his speech of May 18, 1966 (*Zhonggong wenhua da geming zhongyao wenjian huibian* [Collection of Important Documents of the CCP Great Cultural Revolution] [Taibei: Zhonggong yanjiu zazhi she, 1973], p. 341).

104. In a political system such as that in China, the politics and behavior pattern at the top are immediately copied by those at the lower level and infect the entire system. "A person sent from Chairman Mao's headquarters" was supposed to be obeyed and followed closely. For a vivid account, see Liu Binyan, "Between a Human Being and a Monster," *Renmin Wenxue* (People's Literature), 1979, no. 9, p. 85.

Chapter 3. The Chinese Army and the Communist State

1. This power dispersion first became apparent from the biographic sketches of communist leaders collected by Edgar Snow in the late 1930s. See *Red Star over China* (New York: Grove Press, 1968), pp. 490–564.

2. General summaries of the PRC's political history which stress this theme include Jurgen Dömes, *The Internal Politics of China, 1949–1972* (London: C. Hurst, 1973); A. Doak Barnett, *Communist China: The Early Years, 1949–55* (New York: Praeger, 1964); and Franz Schurmann, *Ideology and Organization in Communist China* (Berkeley and Los Angeles: University of California Press, 1964).

3. The crucial importance of loyalty patterns within the PLA officer corps which began in the original five great field armies, and existed for the most part independent of the civilian Communist party machine, is developed in William W. Whitson (with Chen-hsia Huang), *The Chinese High Command: A History of Communist Military Politics* (New York: Praeger, 1973).

4. For an analysis of the limited information available on the purge of Gao Gang and Rao Shushi, see Frederick Teiwes, "Rectification Campaigns and Purges in Communist China, 1950–61" (Ph.D dissertation, Columbia University, 1971), esp. pp. 247–249.

5. The best documentary collection is Union Research Institute, *The Case of Peng Teh-huai, 1959–1968 (Hong Kong: Union Press Limited, 1968).

6. Studies of the early phases of the Cultural Revolution which deal with this question include Edward E. Rice, *Mao's Way* (Berkeley and Los Angeles: University of California Press, 1972); Stanley Karnow, *Mao and China: From Revolution to Revolution* (New York: Viking Press, 1972); and David and Nancy Milton, *The Wind Will Not Subside: Years in Revolutionary China* (New York: Pantheon, 1976).

7. On the conflict regarding China's response to the Vietnam War crisis of 1965–1966, see Donald Zagoria, "The Strategic Debate in Peking," and Uri Ra'an, "Peking's Foreign Policy 'Debate' 1965–66," in Tang Tsou, ed., *China in Crisis* (Chicago: University of Chicago Press, 1968), vol. 2, pp. 237–268 and 23–71, respectively.

8. This conclusion emerges from the charges brought against the Lin Biao group by the special procuratorate in the trials of the Gang of Four. See *A Great Trial in Chinese History* (Beijing: New World Press, 1981), p. 188.

9. During extensive travels in China the past three years, I have talked at length with scores of senior managers, specialists, and technicians at state and provincial level organizations and in economic enterprises. For more than half the cadres I have spoken to, a typical pattern emerged: military service in the late 1940s and early 1950s, followed by transfer to posts in the civilian administration.

10. The significance of this conception of rural revolution in the formative period of the late 1930s and early 1940s is closely examined in Mark Selden, *The Yenan Way in Revolutionary China* (Cambridge, Mass.: Harvard University Press, 1971).

11. For example, Alice Langley Hsieh, *Communist China's Strategy in the Nuclear Era* (Englewood Cliffs, N.J.: Prentice-Hall, 1962), and Raymond Garthoff, ed., *Sino-Soviet Military Relations* (New York: Praeger, 1966).

12. The perception of the issue as fundamentally a conflict between modernizing and guerrilla-war traditions within the PLA (between "professional" and "political" soldiers) was common to most Western analyses in the 1960s. Examples are Ralph Powell, *Politico-Military Relationships in Communist China* (Washington, D.C.: Georgetown University Press, 1963), and Ellis Joffe, *Party and Army: Professionalism and Political Control in the Chinese Officer Corps, 1949–1964* (Cambridge, Mass.: Harvard University Press, 1967).

Chapter 4. The Concept of the Dictatorship of the Proletariat in Chinese Marxist Thought

1. For example, Benjamin Schwartz, *Communism and China: Ideology in Flux* (Cambridge, Mass.: Harvard University Press, 1968), p. 14.

2. "Critical Marginal Notes on the Article 'The King of Prussia and Social Reform. By A Prussian,'" in Karl Marx and Friedrich Engels, *Collected Works* (New York: International Publishers, 1975), vol. 3, p. 199.

3. Ibid., p. 198.

4. Ibid.

5. Karl Marx, "Critique of the Gotha Program," in Karl Marx and Friedrich Engels, *Selected Works* (Moscow, 1949), vol. 2, p. 29.

6. Friedrich Engels, *The Origin of the Family, Private Property and the State*, in Marx and Engels, *Selected Works*, vol. 2, p. 290. The classic formulation is of course expressed in the *Manifesto* in Marx's well-known and oft-quoted characterization of the modern capitalist state as "but a committee for managing the common affairs of the whole bourgeoisie" (Marx and Engels, *Selected Works*, vol. 1, p. 35).

7. Karl Marx and Friedrich Engels, *The German Ideology* (New York: International Publishers, 1960), p. 59.

8. Ibid.

9. Engels, *The Origin of the Family, Private Property and the State*, p. 290. An enlightening debate that bears on the controversial question of the relationship between state power and social classes in early modern Europe is to be found in Paul Sweezy,

Maurice Dobb, et al., *The Transition from Feudalism to Capitalism* (New York: Science and Society, 1954), as we shall observe shortly.

10. Karl Marx, *The Eighteenth Brumaire of Louis Bonaparte*, in Marx and Engels, *Selected Works*, vol. 1, p. 302.

11. Ibid., p. 303.

12. Marx, "Critique of the Gotha Program," p. 29.

13. Engels, *The Origin of the Family, Private Property and the State*, p. 289.

14. Ibid., p. 290.

15. Marx, *The Eighteenth Brumaire of Louis Bonaparte*, p. 301; italics added.

16. Marx, "On the Jewish Question," in Marx and Engels, *Collected Works*, vol., 3, p. 152.

17. Bertell Ollman, "Marx's Vision of Communism: A Reconstruction," in Seweryn Bialer, ed., *Radical Visions of the Future* (Boulder: Westview Press, 1977), pp. 35−83.

18. Marx and Engels, "Manifesto of the Communist Party," in *Selected Works*, vol. 1, pp. 50−51.

19. H. Meyer, "Marx on Bakunin," *Etudes de Marxologie* 91 (October 1956): 108−109, as quoted in Ollman, "Marx's Vision of Communism," p. 47.

20. Marx, "Critique of the Gotha Program," p. 23

21. Karl Marx, *The Civil War in France*, from the 1902 translation reprinted in *The Paris Commune* (New York: Labor News Co., 1965), p. 78.

22. Ibid., p. 70.

23. *The Paris Commune*, pp. 17−18. In the 1891 introduction Engels makes his famous reaffirmation that the Paris Commune is the Marxist historical model of the dictatorship of the proletariat: "The German philistine has lately been thrown once again into wholesale paroxisms by the expression 'dictatorship of the proletariat.' Well, gentle sirs, would you like to know how this dictatorship looks? Then look at the Paris Commune. That was the dictatorship of the proletariat" (ibid., p. 20).

24. Marx, *The Civil War in France*, pp. 74−75.

25. Ibid., p. 76.

26. Ibid., p. 77.

27. Marx, "On the Jewish Question," p. 168.

28. For example, the celebration of the historically progressive nature of the czarist state of Peter the Great and Ivan the Terrible in Stalinist historiography and the Qin state in effecting the transition from "slavery" to "feudalism" in Maoist historiography.

29. Z. Mosina, "The Discussion of the Problem of Absolutism," *Istorik Marksist*, no. 6 (1940), p. 69, as quoted by Christopher Hill in Sweezy, Dobb, et al., *The Transition from Feudalism to Capitalism*, p. 73.

30. Paul M. Sweezy, "A Critique," in Sweezy, Dobb, et al., *The Transition from Feudalism to Capitalism*, pp. 1−20.

31. Maurice Dobb, "A Reply," ibid., p. 26.

32. Christopher Hill, "Comment," ibid., p. 75.

33. "State and Revolution in Tudor and Stuart England," *Communist Review*, July 1948, p. 212, quoted by Hill, ibid., pp. 73−74.

34. "Report to the Second Plenary Session of the Seventh Central Committee of the Communist Party of China" (March 5, 1949), in *Selected Works of Mao Tse-tung* (Peking: Foreign Languages Press, 1969), vol. 4, p. 372.

35. Mao Tse-tung, "On People's Democratic Dictatorship," ibid., vol. 4, pp. 411−412, 418−419.

36. As announced in the lengthy *Renmin Ribao* (People's Daily) editorial of April 5,

1956, "On the Historical Experience of the Dictatorship of the Proletariat," and elaborated upon in *Renmin Ribao* in December 1956 under the title "More on the Historical Experience of the Dictatorship of the Proletariat."

37. Schwartz, *Communism and China*, p. 19.

38. Mao Tse-tung, *On the Correct Handling of Contradictions among the People* (Peking: Foreign Languages Press, 1957), p. 50; italics added.

39. Ibid., p. 49.

40. "Comment on Comrade Ch'en Cheng-jen's Stay in a Primary Unit" (January 29, 1965), *Joint Publications Research Service*, no. 49826, February 12, 1970, p. 23.

41. For a discussion of this aspect of Maoism, see Maurice Meisner, "Leninism and Maoism: Some Populist Perspectives on Marxism-Leninism in China," *China Quarterly*, January – March, 1971, pp. 2 – 36.

42. This, of course, is one of the main themes of Mao's 1957 treatise "On the Correct Handling of Contradictions among the People."

43. For example, Guan Feng, "A Brief Discussion of the Great Historical Significance of the People's Communes," *Zhexue Yanjiu* (Philosophical Research), 1958, no. 5.

44. The enemy was identified as early as January 1965 in the directive known as the "Twenty-three Articles." For a translation of the text, entitled "Some Problems Currently Arising in the Course of the Rural Socialist Education Movement," see Richard Baum and Frederick C. Teiwes, *Ssu-Ch'ing: The Socialist Education Movement of 1962 – 1966* (Berkeley and Los Angeles: University of California Press, 1968), Appendix F, pp. 118 – 126.

45. The most theoretically sophisticated version of this thesis has been presented by the French Maoist Charles Bettelheim. See Paul M. Sweezy and Charles Bettelheim, *On the Transition to Socialism* (New York: Monthly Review Press, 1971).

46. Chen Chih-ssu, "Great Revelations of the Paris Commune," *Hongqi* (Red Flag), no. 4 (March 24, 1966), *Joint Publications Research Service*, no. 35137, pp. 14 – 17.

47. Mao Tse-tung, "Talks at Three Meetings with Comrades Chang Ch'un-ch'iao and Yao Wen-yüan," in Stuart Schram, ed., *Mao Tse-tung Unrehearsed: Talks and Letters, 1956 – 1971* (Harmondsworth: Penguin, 1974), pp. 277 – 278.

48. See, for example, Chang Ch'un-ch'iao, "On Exercising All-Round Dictatorship over the Bourgeoisie," *Peking Review*, April 4, 1975, p. 10.

49. Ibid., pp. 5 – 7.

50. Ibid., p. 10.

51. Ma Yanwen, "The Bureaucratic Class and the Dictatorship of the Proletariat," *Beijing Daxue Xuebao* (Peking University Journal), 1976, no. 4, p. 6.

52. Ibid., pp. 3 – 12.

53. "On Exercising All-Round Dictatorship over the Bourgeoisie," p. 8.

54. Yu Tung, "Programme for Consolidation of Dictatorship of the Proletariat," *Hongqi*, 1973, no. 12, translated in *Peking Review*, January 18, 1974, p. 6.

55. Ibid., p. 5.

56. "On Exercising All-Round Dictatorship over the Bourgeoisie," p. 7.

57. Guo Moruo, "Zhongguo gudaishi di fengyi" (Selections from ancient Chinese history), *Hongqi*, 1972, no. 7, pp. 56 – 62.

58. "Dead Soul of Confucius, Fond Dream of New Tsars," *Peking Review*, February 8, 1974, p. 14 (translation of an article by the Beijing University and Tsinghua University Group for Mass Criticism, originally published in *People's Daily*).

Chapter 5. The Chinese State and Its Bureaucrats

1. The evidence for increased state power has been reviewed recently by Theda Skocpol, *States and Social Revolutions* (London: Cambridge University Press, 1979), esp. chap. 7, pp. 236–281.

2. Seymour Melman, *The Permanent War Economy* (New York: Simon and Schuster, 1974).

3. Nicos Poulantzas, *Political Power and Social Classes* (London: New Left Books, 1973); James O'Connor, *The Fiscal Crisis of the State* (New York: St. Martin's Press, 1973).

4. C. Wright Mills, *The Power Elite* (New York: Oxford University Press, 1956); Ralph Miliband, *The State in Capitalist Society* (New York: Basic Books, 1969); G. W. Domhoff, *The Higher Circles: The Governing Class in America* (New York: Vintage, 1970).

5. Charles Bettelheim, *Cultural Revolution and Industrial Organization in China* (New York: Monthly Review Press, 1974); *The Transition to Socialist Economy* (Atlantic Highlands, N.J.: Humanities Press, 1975).

6. *Selected Works of Mao Tse-tung,* 5 vols. (Foreign Languages Press, 1977), vol. 5, p. 345.

7. Charles Tilly, "Reflections on the History of European State-Making," in *The Formation of National States in Western Europe,* ed. Charles Tilly (Princeton: Princeton University Press, 1975), pp. 39–40.

8. A. Doak Barnett, *Cadres, Bureaucracy, and Political Power in Communist China* (New York: Columbia University Press, 1967).

9. Ye Jianying, *Speech at the Meeting in Celebration of the 30th Anniversary of the Founding of the People's Republic of China* (Beijing: Foreign Languages Press, 1979), p. 25.

10. "The Ghostwriter of Marshal Ye's Speech," *Cheng Bao* (Hong Kong), November 6, 1979.

11. Suzanne Pepper, "Chinese Education after Mao: Two Steps Forward, Two Steps Back and Begin Again?" *China Quarterly,* no. 81 (1980), pp. 1–65.

12. Richard Kraus, William E. Maxwell, and Reeve D. Vanneman, "The Interests of Bureaucrats: Implications of the Asian Experience for Recent Theories of Development," *American Journal of Sociology* 85 (1979): 135–155.

13. Quoted in Roy Medvedev, *Let History Judge* (New York: Vintage, 1973), p. 425.

14. Milovan Djilas, *The New Class* (New York: Praeger, 1975).

15. Fred Block, "The Ruling Class Does Not Rule," *Socialist Revolution* 33 (1977): 6–28.

16. Louis Althusser, *Essays in Self-Criticism* (London: New Left Books, 1976).

17. Immanuel Wallerstein, "The Rise and Future Demise of the Capitalist World System: Concepts for Comparative Analysis," *Comparative Studies in Society and History* 16 (1974): 387–415.

18. Martin Shaw, "The Theory of the State and Politics: A Central Paradox of Marxism," *Economy and Society* 3 (1974): 429–450.

19. Leon Trotsky, *The Revolution Betrayed* (New York: Pathfinder Press, 1972).

20. Livio Maitan, *Party, Army and Masses in China* (London: New Left Books, 1976).

21. Wlodzimierz Brus, *Socialist Ownership and Political Systems* (London: Routledge & Kegan Paul, 1975).

22. Karl Marx and Friedrich Engels, *Selected Works* (New York: International Publishers, 1968), pp. 171–172.

23. Pepper, "Chinese Education after Mao."

24. Martin King Whyte, *Small Groups and Political Rituals in China* (Berkeley and Los Angeles: University of California Press, 1974).

25. Richard Curt Kraus, *Class Conflict in Chinese Socialism* (New York: Columbia University Press, 1981).

26. Joseph R. Levenson, *Confucian China and Its Modern Fate,* 3 vols. (Berkeley and Los Angeles: University of California Press, 1972), vol. 3, p. 113.

27. Max Weber, *The Religion of China* (New York: Free Press, 1951); *Economy and Society* (New York: Bedminster Press, 1968).

28. Reinhard Bendix, *Max Weber: An Intellectual Portrait* (Garden City: Anchor Books, 1962), p. 100.

29. The relationship between Levenson's and Weber's writings on patrimonialism is discussed in Frederic Wakeman, Jr., "A Note on the Development of the Theme of Bureaucratic-Monarchic Tension in Joseph R. Levenson's Work," in *The Mozartian Historian: Essays on the Works of Joseph Levenson,* ed. Maurice Meisner and Rhodes Murphey (Berkeley and Los Angeles: University of California Press, 1976), pp. 123–133.

30. Weber, *Economy and Society,* pp. 1028–1031.

31. Ibid., pp. 1030–1031.

32. John R. Watt, *The District Magistrate in Late Imperial China* (New York: Columbia University Press, 1972).

33. Michael T. Dalby, "Court Politics in Late T'ang Times," in *The Cambridge History of China,* ed. Denis Twitchett (London: Cambridge University Press, 1979), vol. 3, pt. 1, pp. 561–681.

34. Middle-class efforts to weaken patrimonialism through a stronger legal system in Indonesia are discussed by Daniel S. Lev, "Judicial Authority and the Struggle for an Indonesian Rechstaat," *Law and Society Review* 13 (1978): 37–71. His analysis is highly suggestive of parallels in the Chinese political struggles for legal reform after Mao's death.

35. Etienne Balazs, *Chinese Civilization and Bureaucracy* (New Haven: Yale University Press, 1964); Guenther Roth, "Personal Rulership, Patrimonialism and Empire-Building in the New States," *World Politics* 20 (1968): 194–206; Norman Jacobs, "Max Weber, the Theory of Asian Society, and the Study of Thailand," *Sociological Quarterly* 12 (1971): 525–530; S. N. Eisenstadt, *Traditional Patrimonialism and Modern Neopatrimonialism* (Beverly Hills: Sage, 1973); Randall Collins, *Conflict Sociology* (New York: Academic Press, 1975); Simon Schwartzman, "Back to Weber: Corporatism and Patrimonialism in the Seventies," in *Authoritarianism and Corporatism in Latin America,* ed. James M. Malloy (Pittsburgh: University of Pittsburgh Press, 1977), pp. 89–106; Lloyd I. Rudolph and Susanne Hoeber Rudolph, "Authority and Power in Bureaucratic and Patrimonial Administration: A Revisionist Interpretation of Weber on Bureaucracy," *World Politics* 31 (1979): 195–227.

36. For a recent autopsy, see Perry Anderson, *Lineages of the Absolutist State* (London: New Left Books, 1974).

37. Karl A. Wittfogel, *Oriental Despotism* (New Haven: Yale University Press, 1957).

38. James Scott, *The Moral Economy of the Peasant* (New Haven: Yale University Press, 1976).

39. Recent examples include Lucien W. Pye, *The Dynamics of Factions and Consensus in Chinese Politics: A Model and Some Propositions* (Santa Monica: Rand, 1980); and Michel Oksenberg, "Economic Policy-Making in China: Summer 1981," *China Quarterly,* no. 90 (1982), pp. 165 – 194.

Chapter 6. The Societal Obstacle to China's Socialist Transition: State Capitalism or Feudal Fascism

1. See my "Maoism, Titoism, Stalinism," in Mark Selden and Victor Lippit, eds., *The Transition to Socialism in China* (Armonk, N.Y.: M. E. Sharpe, 1982), pp. 159 – 214. I find that none of the strategies will attain the socialist goal.
2. K. E. Brodsaard, "The Democracy Movement in China, 1978 – 1979," *Asian Survey* 21 (July 1981): 752ff.
3. Li Yizhe, "Concerning Socialist Democracy and the Legal System," in *The Revolution Is Dead, Long Live the Revolution* (Hong Kong: The Seventies, 1976), pp. 249 – 283; in Chinese, *Li Yizhe da zibao,* ed. Ting Wang (Hong Kong: Ming Bao Publishers, 1976). The Li of Li Yizhe, one Li Zhengtian, in 1979 claimed that the inspiration for their work came from a senior party member who suffered greatly during the Cultural Revolution. The following quotations are from this source.
4. *Qishi Niandai* (The Seventies), no. 2 (February 1982), pp. 88 – 90.
5. See Albert Moravia, *The Red Book and the Great Wall* (New York: Farrar, Straus, Giroux, 1968).
6. One notorious case is that of Yu Luoke, whose life and death are discussed in the Hong Kong journal *Zhengming* (Contention), 1979, no. 24. His diary appears in 1980, no. 29. His class origin theory is discussed by Gordon White, *The Politics of Class and Class Origin* (Canberra: Contemporary China Centre, The Australian National University, 1976).
7. Perhaps Wang Xizhe did not know that the Lin Biao group had come to the same conclusion. It also described Mao as a "contemporary Qin Shi Huang" taking the revolution backward. It described the Marxist idealists as using "false revolutionary rhetoric" to "deceive and mislead" the people and permit "disguised exploitation." People's "blind faith" in the leader made this situation difficult to change. In sum, for Mao and the Marxist idealists, "their socialism is, in essence, social fascism. They have turned China's state machine into a kind of meat grinder for mutual slaughter and strife, and they have made the Party and whole country's political life into a patriarchal life of the feudal, dictatorial and autocratic type" (*The Lin Piao Affair,* ed. Michael M. Y. Kao [White Plains: International Arts and Sciences Press, 1975], pp. 83 – 85).
8. Yao Wenyuan, *On the Social Basis of the Lin Piao Anti-Party Clique* (Peking: Foreign Languages Press, 1975), p. 23. The materials circulated in China to serve as a basis for criticizing the Lin Biao group found them guilty of attempting "to lure Communist Party members to become philistines and politicians by such nasty means as making promotions and promises, giving parties and feasts, and handing out gifts" (*The Lin Piao Affair,* p. 235).
9. *Renmin Ribao* (People's Daily), April 8, 1978.
10. *Beijing Daxue Xuebao* (Beijing Universal Journal), 1976, no. 2, pp. 22 – 29; no. 3, pp. 15 – 29; no. 4, pp. 3 – 12. The following quotations are from this source. I am indebted to the Orientalia Section of the Library of Congress for finding these essays for me.

11. China's great economic recovery from 1962 to 1966 is indisputable. But economic policy in that period was premised on the prescriptions of China's Marxist materialists, not on the class struggle line of the Marxist idealists.

12. Reprinted in Hong Kong's *Guangchajia* (Observer), 1979, no. 9, and *Qishi Niandai* 1979, no. 9, from Canton's *Voice of the People,* "Strive to Achieve the Dictatorship of the Proletariat." This essay does not consider Wang's post-1979 writings, "The Direction of Democracy," "An Open Letter to the Delegates to the Fifth National People's Congress about the Liu Qing Affair," "Mao Zedong and the Cultural Revolution," and others.

13. In an October 1979 interview reprinted in *Wuyue tongxin* (May Letter), no. 8, Wang expressed a need to collect more materials on Yugoslavia and other East European experiences. Wang supported the democratic movement in all those countries, including the 1956 Hungarian Revolution, which Mao, in contrast, had urged Khrushchev to crush.

14. In April 1981 Wang and other spokespeople of the nonparty young democrats were arrested. He was tried in secret — apparently for revealing state secrets — and sentenced to fourteen years in prison. See "Before and After the Arrest of Wang Xizhe," *Zhengming,* no. 44 (June 1, 1981), pp. 22–24, and AFP, Hong Kong in *Foreign Broadcast Information Service,* June 11, 1982, p. k2.

15. Yu Guangyuan and Su Xiaozhi in *Guangming Ribao* (Enlightenment Daily), May 8, 1980, p. 3.

16. Wang Pingnan in *Renmin Ribao,* May 8, 1980, p. 7.

17. *Renmin Ribao,* January 25, 1979.

18. See my "Exploding the China Myth," *Book World,* June 13, 1982, p. 9.

19. *Renmin Ribao,* December 21, 1979, p. 4.

20. In contrast, Marxist materialists claimed that Marxist idealists such as Trotsky ignored new realities and dogmatically applied old formulas ("The Origins and Manifested Forms of Revisionism," *Hongqi* [Red Flag], 1980, no. 1, pp. 42–45). Thus even Stalinists had to present themselves as reform-minded materialists.

21. *Beijing Daily,* December 21, 1979, p. 3.

22. *Renmin Ribao,* July 17, 1979, p. 1.

23. Reproduced in Chinese November 16, 1979, in the Hong Kong magazine *Wide Angle.* Deng's theory resonates with Barrington Moore, Jr.'s, *Social Origins of Dictatorship and Democracy* (Boston: Beacon Press, 1966).

24. Reproduced in Chinese in February 1980 in the Hong Kong magazine *Ming Bao,* no. 170, pp. 2–15.

25. Rene Dumont, *Is Cuba Socialist?* (New York: Viking Press, 1974), esp. pp. 109, 110, 118, 124, 127, 139, and 141.

26. In answer to a July 9, 1981 question as to how he responded to pointed criticism from his closest colleagues, Fidel Castro said he did not receive or need such criticism because he was his own severest critic.

27. Milovan Djilas, *The Unperfect Society: Beyond the New Class* (New York: Harcourt, Brace and World, 1969), pp. 191–192.

Chapter 7. The Dilemma of State Power: The Solution Becomes the Problem

1. Tadao Miyashita, *The Currency and Financial System of Mainland China* (Seattle: University of Washington Press, 1966), p. 108.

2. Special Commentator, "The Aim of Socialist Production Must Be Really Understood," *Beijing Review,* no. 51 (December 21, 1979), p. 11.

stood," *Beijing Review*, no. 51 (December 21, 1979), p. 11.

3. Central Intelligence Agency, *Handbook of Economic Statistics* (Washington, D.C.: Central Intelligence Agency, 1978).

4. State Statistical Bureau of the People's Republic of China, "Statistical Work in New China," *Statistical Review*, March 1980, p. 139.

5. H. V. Henle, Personal communication, 1975.

6. Tang Tsou, Mark Blecher, and Mitchell Meisner, "Organization, Growth, and Equality in Xiyang County," *Modern China* 5 (April 1979): 139−185.

7. William L. Parish and Martin King Whyte, *Village and Family in Contemporary China* (Chicago: University of Chicago Press, 1978), pp. 47−52.

8. Chen Yun, "Speech at the CCP Central Committee Work Conference," April 1979, translated in *Issues and Studies* 16 (April 1980): 83.

9. "Silt Control," *Beijing Review*, no. 19 (May 11, 1979), p. 30.

10. Tung Dalin, "The Questions of the Direction of Construction of the Northwest Yellow Soil Plateau," *Renmin Ribao*, November 26, 1978.

11. Chou Chin, "Szechwan Today," *Beijing Review*, no. 48 (December 1, 1978), p. 22.

12. *Foreign Broadcast Information Service*, April 19, 1979, p. 0−2.

13. "Lighten the Peasants' Burden," *Peking Review*, no. 30 (July 28, 1978), pp. 20−21.

Chapter 8. Marxism and the Market in Socialist China: The Reforms of 1979−1980 in Context

1. Karl Marx, *Capital*, 3 vols. (Moscow: Foreign Languages Publishing House, 1962), vol. 3, bk. 3, pp. 275, 298; bk. 2, p. 131.

2. Ibid., bk. 3, pp. 274, 277. See Ernest Mandel, *Marxist Economic Theory*, trans. Brian Pearce, 2 vols. (New York: Monthly Review Press, 1968), vol. 1, p. 84.

3. Jere L. Felker, *Soviet Economic Controversies: The Emerging Marketing Concept and Changes in Planning, 1960−1965* (Cambridge, Mass.: M.I.T. Press, 1966), p. 17.

4. Marshall I. Goldman, *Soviet Marketing: Distribution in a Controlled Economy* (New York: Free Press of Glencoe, 1963), p. 3; and Felker, *Soviet Economic Controversies*, pp. 16−17; Marx, *Capital*, vol. 3, bk. 3, p. 284.

5. A clear presentation of the definitions of the terms used here is found in Ernest Mandel, *An Introduction to Marxist Economic Theory*, 2d ed. (New York: Pathfinder Press, 1973), pp. 9−10; also see Mandel, *Marxist Economic Theory*, chap. 2.

6. Deborah D. Milenkovitch, *Plan and Market in Yugoslav Economic Thought* (New Haven: Yale University Press, 1971), pp. 21−24.

7. Frederick Engels, *Anti-Dühring* (Peking: Foreign Languages Press, 1976), pp. 401−402.

8. Mandel, *Marxist Economic Theory*, pp. 10, 565−567. See also Alec Nove, *The Soviet Economic System* (London: George Allen & Unwin, 1977), p. 257; Milenkovitch, *Plan and Market*, p. 14.

9. Milenkovitch, *Plan and Market*, pp. 9, 15−20. See also Dwight H. Perkins, *Market Control and Planning in Communist China* (Cambridge, Mass.: Harvard University Press, 1966), p. 210.

10. Karl Marx and Frederick Engels, "Excerpts from The German Ideology," in Lewis S. Feuer, ed., *Marx and Engels: Basic Writings on Politics and Philosophy* (Garden City, N.Y.: Doubleday Anchor Books, 1959), p. 257.

11. Milenkovitch, *Plan and Market*, p. 15.

12. For example, item seven in a list of measures for the proletariat, once having seized the means of production, to use in "entirely revolutionizing the mode of production," states: "Extension of factories and instruments of production owned by the state; the bringing into cultivation of wastelands, and the improvement of the soil, generally in accordance with a common plan." See Karl Marx and Frederick Engels, "Manifesto of the Communist Party," in Feuer, ed., *Marx and Engels*, p. 28.

13. *Survey of the Chinese Mainland Press* (hereafter, *SCMP*), no. 3295 (1964), pp. 4, 6. In August 1964, Beijing commercial departments conducted training classes to indoctrinate new young workers in the value of commerce, and the economic newspaper *Dagong Bao* (Impartial Daily) (Beijing) carried a series of articles on this theme. See also *Gongren Ribao* (Workers' Daily) (Peking), March 13 and 14, 1965.

14. Interview in Hong Kong, October 18, 1979.

15. Nove, *Soviet Economic System*, p. 256; Gur Ofer, *The Service Sector in Soviet Economic Growth: A Comparative Study* (Cambridge, Mass.: Harvard University Press, 1973), pp. 156, 161.

16. *Selected Works of Mao Tse-tung*, 5 vols. (Peking: Foreign Languages Press, 1977), vol. 5, pp. 66, 69.

17. *Selections from Chinese Mainland Magazines* (hereafter *SCMM*), no. 665 (1969), p. 25.

18. *SCMP*, no. 3249 (1964), p. 2.

19. *Current Background*, no. 760 (1965), p. 29.

20. Barry M. Richman, *Industrial Society in Communist China* (New York: Vintage Books, 1972), p. 883; Audrey Donnithorne, *China's Economic System* (London: George Allen & Unwin, 1967), p. 316.

21. Nove, *Soviet Economic System*, p. 255–256, 261–262.

22. *Hongqi* (Red Flag), 1978, no. 7, pp. 74–78. The "four modernizations" were the modernization of industry, agriculture, science and technology, and the military, the name given to the programs of speedy economic development put into effect after 1976.

23. See *Guangming Ribao* (Light Daily) (Beijing), February 9, 1980, which states that the number of urban "commercial points" (retail stores, food and drink shops, and other service centers) had been reduced by 82 percent since 1957, from one million in that year to 180,000 in 1978; and that the personnel working in such points represented 3.57 percent of urban population in 1957 but fell to an average of 2.34 percent by 1978 and was as low as 2 percent in some cities. The articles cited in notes 22 and 23, complaining about these conditions, are the products of an official shift in attitude toward commerce and the consumer that began in early 1978.

24. The first major critique of the system was Hu Qiaomu's seminal article on observing economic laws, in *Renmin Ribao* (People's Daily), October 6, 1978. Another article of import in that paper was one by Xue Muqiao on June 15, 1979. The journal *Jingji Yanjiu* (Economic Research) printed many articles calling for reforms beginning in 1979 such as changing the method of allocation of production materials to one of commodity circulation (that is, through supply-and-demand-determined prices), using floating, not fixed, prices for nonessential goods; allowing prices to influence production, and permitting prices to be flexible in reflecting market needs, as they float within a range, among other suggestions.

25. Perkins, *Market Control*, pp. 65–67, explains that planning was attempted in agriculture as early as 1951 but was largely abandoned by mid-1958.

26. See Dorothy J. Solinger, "Some Speculations on the Return of the Regions: Parallels with the Past," *China Quarterly*, no. 75 (1978), pp. 623–638, on the history of planning in China, 1949–1977; p. 633 surveys the changing use of targets.

27. Charles E. Lindblom, *Politics and Markets* (New York: Basic Books, 1977), p. 292. Unified distribution of key raw materials and major equipment began in 1950. See Perkins, *Market Control*, p. 100. Yu-min Chou, "Wholesaling in Communist China," in Robert Bartels, ed., *Comparative Marketing* (Homewood, Ill.: Richard D. Irwin, 1963), pp. 259–260, describes the operation of the direct allocation system.

28. Donnithorne, *China's Economic System*, chaps. 6 and 17; and interview with a factory accountant in Hong Kong, October 23, 1979.

29. *Zhengming* (Contention) (Hong Kong), no. 19 (May 1979), p. 9–13. An article from the mid-1950s explains the disjunction between the prices and the allocation of producer goods: "Since the production tasks of the enterprises are determined by the state, the quantity of producer goods needed by the enterprise is allocated by the state according to the plan. Therefore, the level of prices for producer goods does not regulate the quantity of producer goods required by the enterprise." This statement is taken from Ch'en Hsi-jun, "Chia-ko chi-hua" (Price planning), *Ji-hua jing-ji* (Planned Economy), 1956, no. 7, pp. 30–33, translated in Nicholas R. Lardy, *Chinese Economic Planning* (White Plains, N.Y.: M. E. Sharpe, 1978), p. 95.

30. Goldman, *Soviet Marketing*, p. 135; Perkins, *Market Control*, pp. 119–120; Nove, *Soviet Economic System*, p. 258.

31. Perkins, *Market Control*, pp. 67–68.

32. See the statement by Tseng Shan, then minister of commerce, to the Eighth Party Congress in 1956 in *Extracts from China Mainland Magazines* (hereafter *ECMM*), no. 423 (1956), p. 2. The analysis here is borrowed from Chen Yun's speeches of June 1956 to the Third Session of the First National People's Congress, in *Guangming Ribao*, July 1, 1956, and to the Eighth Party Congress, in *Eighth National Congress of the Communist Party of China, Volume II: Speeches* (Beijing: Foreign Languages Press, 1956), pp. 157–176.

33. Chen's 1956 critique of this system reappeared daily in the press during 1979–1980, as factories were told to produce according to the market — but in accord with the plan's dictates.

34. *SCMM*, no. 822 (1975), p. 22.

35. Government Administrative Council, "Decisions on the Procedures Governing the Unification of State-Operated Trade in the Nation," March 10, 1950, in Chao Kuo-chün, *Economic Planning and Organization in Mainland China: A Documentary Study (1949–1957)*, 2 vols. (Cambridge, Mass.: Harvard University Center for East Asian Studies, 1960), vol. 2, pp. 20–23.

36. Chou, "Wholesaling," pp. 267–268. More material on the bank's role in commerce can be found in Donnithorne, *China's Economic System*, p. 316.

37. According to *New China News Agency* (Beijing), November 11, 1978, grain is now allowed on the free markets in Sichuan — a most unusual situation.

38. Perkins, *Market Control*, pp. 50 ff. Beginning in 1955, the earlier system, "planned purchase, planned supply" for these three rationed crops, was supplemented by a system entitled "unified purchase" by which quotas were set for delivery to the state of a wide range of other agricultural products whose supply was not rationed.

39. Donnithorne, *China's Economic System*, p. 273; see also ibid., chap. 13. The workings of the procurement and taxation systems in the Guangdong countryside in the mid-1970s are described in William L. Parish and Martin King Whyte, *Village and Family in Contemporary China* (Chicago: University of Chicago Press, 1978), pp. 48–51.

40. Perkins, *Market Control*, pp. 43–44.

41. Since 1949 free markets, like those operating in 1980, have existed legally in the countryside in 1956–1957 and 1961–1965 but usually not for rationed goods.

42. Interview in Hong Kong, November 27, 1979. See Gordon Bennett, *Huadong: The Story of a Chinese People's Commune* (Boulder, Colo.: Westview Press, 1978), pp. 96−97, on disposal of the collective income in the countryside.

43. Starting in 1978 the press featured articles assuring the rural populace that the party endorsed fairs in the countryside (for example, *Renmin Ribao*, June 20, 1978; *Guangming Ribao*, August 18 and September 30, 1978). On March 3, 1980, *Renmin Ribao* mentioned those who are hesitant about the fairs.

44. Perkins, *Market Control*, on pp. 177 and 191, distinguishes between "formal" and "de facto" rationing. The latter occurs when supply for many items falls short of demand and desire runs particularly high (as for bicycles, radios, and, more recently, television sets), resulting in waiting lists and thus informal rationing. Both formal and de facto rationing take the place of a market distribution. See also ibid., pp. 192 and 197, on the values of rationing for the regime.

45. This analysis was offered by none other than Xue Muqiao in *Hongqi*, 1959, no. 10 (reprinted in *Xinhua Banyuekan* [New China Semimonthly], 1959, no. 10, p. 167. Years later, in an era when rightwingery was the vogue, Xue argued instead for floating prices and against rations. See note 24 above.

46. Zhang Yifei, "Guojia guiding shangpin shichang jiage de genzhu" (The basis for state-set commodity market prices), *Jingji Yanjiu*, 1958, no. 4, pp. 50−51.

47. Lindblom, *Politics and Markets*, p. 303; Philip Hanson, *Advertising and Socialism* (White Plains, N.Y.: International Arts and Sciences Press, 1974), pp. 7 and 81; Nove, *Soviet Economic System*, p. 257; Gregory Grossman, "The 'Second Economy' of the USSR," *Problems of Communism*, nos. 9−10 (1977), p. 39.

48. Ross Munro, "Why China's Peasants Don't Want to Work," *San Francisco Chronicle*, July 29, 1977.

49. Fox Butterfield, "In China, Austerity Is Less Austere if One Has Friends in Right Places," *New York Times*, December 11, 1977.

50. Interviews in Hong Kong, September 7 and November 12, 1979.

51. *Dagong Bao*, March 3, 1956.

52. Interview in Hong Kong, November 27, 1979. Very popular items also are hard to obtain without presenting the wholesale workers with gifts. Personal relationships may do the trick as well. An official source describes two production teams bartering produce for fertilizer when the planned amount fell short. See *Renmin Ribao*, August 20, 1979.

53. Interview in Hong Kong, October 19, 1979.

54. Butterfield, "In China." An informant in Hong Kong told me the same tale on October 23, 1979.

55. Charles A. Schwartz, "Corruption and Political Development in the U.S.S.R.," *Comparative Politics* 11, no. 4 (1979): 437. Also see Hedrick Smith, *The Russians* (New York: Ballantine Books, 1977), chap. 3, esp. p. 115. Grossman, "'Second Economy,'" p. 32, also refers to a Russian custom of bringing gifts to one's superior as "a general and regular way of ingratiating oneself with authority ... expected by both parties."

56. The material here is drawn from interviews in Hong Kong on October 19, November 27, November 29, and December 11, 1979.

57. Work for the cooperative is something of a plum in the countryside, according to an interview on September 7, 1979. One can work on rainy days and so continue to earn work points; one can buy necessities without ration coupons and without waiting. In the city, commercial work is considered less special.

58. Interview on October 17, 1979 in Hong Kong.

59. Schwartz, "Corruption and Political Development," p. 437, used this term to describe the way enterprise officials in the USSR use state money or goods to obtain preferential treatment in the distribution of goods in short supply or in the delivery of a better assortment of goods to retail stores.

60. In the Soviet Union workers in shops take advantage of their positions in this way, too. See Grossman, "'Second Economy,'" p. 29; and Smith, *The Russians*, pp. 117 – 118.

61. Interview in Hong Kong, November 29, 1979.

62. *SCMM*, no. 822 (1975), pp. 22 – 27.

63. *Renmin Ribao*, December 30, 1956.

64. The picul is equal to fifty kilograms.

65. *Yangcheng Wanbao* (Yangcheng Evening News) (Canton), August 22, 1962.

66. Franklyn Griffiths, "A Tendency Analysis of Soviet Policy-Making," in H. Gordon Skilling and Franklyn Griffiths, eds., *Interest Groups in Soviet Politics* (Princeton: Princeton University Press, 1971), p. 360, defines a "tendency of articulation" as "a mass of common articulations which persists over time." On p. 337, he says that "specific policies are made through tendency conflicts," which is true for China as well. Use of this concept keeps vague who the particular proponents of each tendency might be and leaves open the possibility that given individuals might shift from one tendency to another over time, or might contain in their personal approaches elements of more than one tendency at a given time.

67. These three models parallel but are not identical to Lindblom's three "politico-economic alternatives" (authority, exchange, persuasion) (*Politics and Markets*, p. 4).

68. *SCMP*, nos. 5869 (1975), pp. 13 – 14, and 5932 (1975), p. 81.

69. Marx and Engels, "Manifesto of the Communist Party," in Feuer, ed., *Marx and Engels*, p. 29.

70. "The German Ideology," in ibid., p. 257.

71. "Manifesto" in ibid., p. 28.

72. The law of value states that the value of a commodity is established by the amount of labor, across enterprises on an average, that is necessary to produce the commodity in a given society at a certain point in time. Since price is the monetary expression of value, most simply, marketeers want an object's price to be set not according to political decision but to its economically determined worth. The law also indicates that allocatory decisions ought to be based upon profit considerations, according to which enterprises and sectors are best able to use labor and capital inputs efficiently.

73. Marx, *Capital*, vol. 3, bk. 3, p. 178. His concern here is echoed in different words by Oskar Lange in Oskar Lange and Fred M. Taylor, *On the Economic Theory of Socialism*, ed. Benjamin Evan Lippincott (Minneapolis: University of Minnesota Press, 1938), p. 20.

74. Uma J. Lele, *Food Grain Marketing in India: Private Performance and Public Policy* (Ithaca: Cornell University Press, 1971), pp. 44 and 79, explains some reasons why having more capital gives one a head start in the marketplace: those with more wealth can hold stocks in anticipation of higher prices when prices are low; they have the wherewithal to take risks and to acquire more information; they may spread their investments and provide their own transportation; and they may work safely on much smaller profit margins.

75. Perkins, *Market Control*, pp. 25 – 26. Another point of view, however, is offered by the Chinese marketeers of 1980, in whose mouthpiece, *Shichang* (Market) (Beijing), (1980), no. 12, p. 6, there appeared a short tale of a poor, many-mouthed peasant family that benefited from the recent opening of free markets, enabling it to earn a bit of cash

from its surplus vegetables. Old indigent people in China gain from marketing the products of sideline enterprises in China too. See Parish and Whyte, *Village and Family*, p. 76.

76. In Gordon Bennett, *China's Finance and Trade: A Policy Reader* (White Plains, N.Y.: M. E. Sharpe, 1978), p. 99.

77. *Xuexi Yu Pipan* (Study and Criticism) (Shanghai), 1974, no. 10, p. 96.

78. *SCMP*, no. 4286 (1968), pp. 6–12.

79. See the article by Zhang Yifei on how the state sets prices, cited in note 46 above.

80. *Dagong Bao*, April 13, 1959; and *Hongqi*, 1963, nos. 7–8, p. 9.

81. *Hongqi*, 1963, nos. 7–8, p.7.

82. Bennett, *China's Finance and Trade*, p. 88; *SCMP*, no. 894 (1954), p. 8; *ECMM*, no. 31 (1956), p. 12; Yao Yilin, "Shinian lai de shangye" (Ten years of commerce), in *Jianguo Shinian, 1949–1959* (Ten years of national construction) (Hong Kong: Jiwen chubanshe, 1959), 1: 269; *Xinhua Banyuekan*, 1959, no. 10, p. 167; *Hongqi*, 1963, nos. 7–8, p. 9.

83. *ECMM*, no. 119 (1957), pp. 33–34.

84. Examples are the state grain markets of 1954 (*SCMP*, no. 822 [1954], pp. 20–21) and the goods exchange meets for third-category produce of 1959 (Yao Yilin, "Shinian lai de shangye," p. 269).

85. Marx, *Capital*, vol. 3, bk. 3, p. 187.

86. Karl Marx, *A Contribution to the Critique of Political Economy*, trans. N. I. Stone (Chicago: Charles H. Kerr and Co., 1918), p. 291.

87. For discussions of debates elsewhere in the Soviet world, see Felker, *Soviet Economic Controversies*, esp. chap. 2, "Value and Trade Theories in Evolution"; Hans-Hermann Höhmann *et al.*, *The New Economic Systems of Eastern Europe* (Berkeley and Los Angeles: University of California Press, 1975), chap. 10, on pricing, refers to law of value debates of the 1950s that were joined by experts from all countries that had adopted the Soviet economic system (p. 281); Alfred Zauberman, "The Soviet Debate on the Law of Value and Price Formation," in Gregory Grossman, ed., *Value and Plan* (Berkeley and Los Angeles: University of California Press, 1960), pp. 17–35; and Milenkovitch, *Plan and Market*, pp. 24, 33, 38 for Soviet debates and pp. 123–126 for Yugoslav debates.

88. E. L. Wheelwright and Bruce McFarlane, *The Chinese Road to Socialism* (New York: Monthly Review Press, 1970), pp. 82–86, discusses the 1959 debate on the law of value, on the basis of several articles in *Guangming Ribao* from that period. Other representative articles that deal with this issue are Gu Zhun, "Shilun shehui zhuyi zhidu xia de shangpin shengchan he jiazhi guilu" (A preliminary discussion of commodity production and the law of value in a socialist system), *Jingji Yanjiu*, 1957, no. 6; Zhang Chunyin et al., "Bochi Gu Zhun guanyu jiazhi guilu de xiuzheng zhuyi guandian" (Refuting Gu Zhun's revisionist viewpoint on the law of value), ibid., (1957) no. 6, pp. 27–38; Yuan Lian and Di Wen, "Wo guo jingji xuejie guanyu shangpin shengchan he jiazhi guilu wenti de taolun" (The discussion in my country's economic circles on problems of commodity production and the law of value), ibid., 1958, no. 12, pp. 77–80, 76 (this article reviews debates over the years 1953–1957); "Beijing bufen jingji lilun gongzuozhe zuotan guanyu shehui zhuyi zhidu xia shangpin shengchan yu jiazhi guilu de taolun qingkuang" (Discussions at the forum held by some economic theoretical workers in Beijing on commodity production and the law of value in a socialist system), ibid., 1959, no. 2, pp. 31–33; Xue Muqiao, "Shehui zhuyi zhidu xia de shangpin shengchan he jiazhi guilu" (Commodity production and the law of value in the socialist sys-

tem), *Xinhua Banyuekan*, 1959, no. 10, pp. 165 – 170 (this article refers to the 1956 debate); "What Is the Law of Value?" *Jingji Yanjiu*, 1963, no. 2, pp. 17 – 23, translated in *Translations from Ching-chi Yen-chiu, Joint Publications Research Service*, no. 18,684 (1963); *Hongqi*, 1963, nos. 7 – 8, pp. 1 – 9; and "On Commodity Exchange, Commodity Circulation, and the Uniformity and Divergence of Commerce," *Jingji Yanjiu*, 1964, no. 8, pp. 44 – 51, translated in *Translations from Ching-chi Yen-chiu, Joint Publications Research Service*, no. 26,800 (1964).

89. Griffiths, "Tendency Analysis," p. 367, notes that "the content of a given tendency consists of values, analyses and recommendations."

90. The following analysis is based principally on a reading of articles in *Xuexi Yu Pipan* (1973 – 1976) on marketing, commerce, and planning for the radical view; and on all articles in *Jingji Yanjiu* (1978 – 1979) and *Foreign Broadcast Information Service* (hereafter *FBIS*) (1976 – 1979) on commerce, the law of value, and planning for the bureaucrat and marketeer views. A few old speeches of Vice-Premier Chen Yun from the 1950s also helped in constructing the marketeer view.

91. As an example, *Guangzhou Ribao* (Guangzhou Daily) (Canton), November 2, 1979, has an article on enforcing price discipline, in which a municipal price inspection group was composed to check on stores' implementation of state price changes. The group included members of the Municipal Political Consultative Committee, whose membership is drawn from former capitalists.

92. Described in interviews in Hong Kong on September 7, October 23, November 29, and December 11, 1979.

93. Gordon Bennett, "Activists and Professionals" (Ph.D. dissertation, University of Wisconsin, 1973), p. 307, lists the members of the committee set up in 1954 in Guangdong.

94. Interview with city commercial official in Guilin, November 1979. A Hong Kong informant told me on November 12, 1979, that these organs have lost prestige in recent years and so can no longer fulfill their responsibility.

95. Griffiths, "Tendency Analysis," p. 369, suggests that the following variables may account for the propensity of diverse actors to articulate a similar approach to a given policy; organizational affiliation, occupation, role, age, career, ideological orientation, self-interest, and responsiveness to authority. In the following remarks I hazard educated guesses on the basis of scattered bits of information.

96. This section is based on an interview at Stanford University, November 1979, with officials from the Anshan Steel Works. Impressions were supplied by C. Thomas Fingar. Also, Yu Qiuli, head of the State Planning Commission, put heavy emphasis on planning in an article in *Renmin Ribao*, September 12, 1977, and in his speech at the National Conference on Learning from Daqing and Dazhai in Finance and Trade, in ibid., July 3, 1978, pp. 1, 3. Most interesting, perhaps, when Yu presented the 1979 economic plans, he barely mentioned the program of economic reform, noting that "we must carry out this work energetically and systematically, *under the unified plan* of the State Council" (emphasis added); and said that "*light industries and the textile industry* should be allowed to sell, in conformity with the price policy set by the state, products which the state does not purchase" (ibid., June 29, 1979). See *China News Analysis*, no. 1165 (1979). Experiments with the market principle beginning in 1979 focused on light industry, in which profits could be earned and measured readily. Industries carrying out this experiment mentioned in various articles included textiles, shoes, and rubbers (*Renmin Ribao*, December 18, 1979), leather goods (ibid., December 11, 1979), typewriters (November 25, 1979), and fans (November 12, 1979). Several of these articles mention light industry or a Municipal Light Industry Bureau specifically.

97. *Beijing Review*, 1980, no. 23, pp. 5–6, states that in Shanghai the new reforms, such as they are, apply in far greater force to the textile (light) than to the metallurgy (heavy) industry. Textile factories remit only 90.5 percent of their profits to the state and the entire trade (that is, the bureau, not the individual enterprise) may keep the other 9.5 percent, to be used for technical transformation of the entire trade. For enterprises producing metallurgical products, the increased part of the profit a factory has earned, using 1978 as the base year, is divided between the bureau (again, on behalf of the entire trade) and the state, in the proportion 40 (to the bureau and the enterprises it controls) to 60 (to the state).

98. Michael Yahuda, "Political Generations in China," *China Quarterly*, no. 80 (1979), pp. 800–802.

99. Problems of youthful cynicism in the wake of the Cultural Revolution are the subject for official concern and propaganda, as the regime tries at once to inspire better productivity through visions of the developed Western economies while promoting the notion of the "superiority of socialism." See *Renmin Ribao*, March 25, 1980. The new urban collective enterprises, promoted by the government beginning in 1979, are essentially a form of private enterprise and are largely staffed by the unemployed young people who have returned to the cities after their Cultural Revolutionary stint in the countryside. Experience working in these collectives may be building up cohorts for market management among the young. Youths encountered in Changsha in November 1979 were very excited by the new magazine *Shichang*.

100. A major line of attack against Li Jingquan, then first party secretary there, during the Cultural Revolution, was that he hoarded Sichuan's grain.

101. See Nicholas R. Lardy, "Centralization and Decentralization in China's Fiscal Management," *China Quarterly*, no. 61 (1975), pp. 25–60, for a description of how this system worked.

102. *Renmin Ribao*, December 18, 1979, p. 1, has an article claiming that "industries feel that if their products have a plan, they have a right to exist."

103. There is some evidence for open opposition to market approaches in the official press. For instance, *Guangzhou Ribao*, November 9, 1979, p. 2, mentions leadership cadres in a Canton plastics factory who did not see why the factory should produce products not listed in the plan, even if they drew a profit. *Renmin Ribao*, November 19, 1979, p. 2, contains an article supporting the plan, warning that chaos will result from any alteration in present arrangements.

104. One example, from Beijing Radio, August 2, 1978, decrying the tendency of units to fight for control over commodities, states: "The more controls there are, the more obstacles, detours and stockpiling will occur in the flow of commodities. This is the main reason why the commercial departments of our country have three billion *yuan* worth of commodities staying on the roads." Another broadcast from the same station ten days later reads: "'When the flow of commodities is organized according to economic zones, we can no longer control the commodities' — this is the true thinking of those who want to organize the flow of commodities according to administrative zones. Indeed, if the flow of commodities is organized according to economic zones, some localities will lose part of their controls over commodities. But the loss of these unnecessary controls . . . will help develop the economy and ensure supplies."

105. For an analysis of this period, and the effort to rectify chaos through plans that marked it, see Solinger, "Some Speculations on the Return of the Regions." The authoritative article, authored by the State Planning Commission, is in *Renmin Ribao*, September 12, 1977.

106. *Peking Review*, 1978, no. 10, pp. 7–40.

107. These three delivered the key published speeches at the meeting. Li actually never gave in at this conference, as noted below.

108. *Renmin Ribao*, June 21, 1978; *Hongqi*, 1978, no. 7, pp. 74–78; *Quanguo caimao xue daqing xue dazhai huiyi dianxing cailiao xuanbian* (Selected model materials from the National Conference to Study Daqing and Dazhai in Finance and Trade) (Beijing: Zhongguo caizheng jingji chubanshe, 1978). The campaign was launched at a May 1977 conference to study Daqing and Dazhai in industry; Hua was the keynote speaker.

109. *Renmin Ribao*, June 27, 1978, in *FBIS*, June 28, 1978, E1–E13.

110. *Renmin Ribao*, July 8, 1978, in *FBIS*, July 11, 1978, pp. E1–E12.

111. See note 72 above. Stalin's position in his authoritative treatise on the roles of the plan and market under socialism (*Economic Problems of Socialism in the U.S.S.R.* [Peking: Foreign Languages Press, 1972], p.18) is that the law of value regulates commodity circulation, but it only *influences* production, having no regulatory function in that sphere. Stalin also held that that law applied only to exchange between the state sector and the collective economy (and within the collective sector), but not to that within the state sector (between state-owned enterprises, that is). Typically, bureaucrats, hoping to shore up the plan they manage, assert that it is the plan and not profit indicators that sets production policies and decisions about where to allocate capital.

112. *Renmin Ribao*, July 3, 1978, in *FBIS*, July 6, 1978, pp. E1–E13.

113. *Renmin Ribao*, July 5, 1978.

114. *Issues & Studies* (Taipei) 14, no. 7 (1978): 75–80.

115. *Renmin Ribao*, October 6, 1978, in *FBIS*, October 11, 1978, pp. E1–E22. That Hu did attend the finance and trade meeting is confirmed in *FBIS*, July 10, 1978, p. E1.

116. See *I&S*, 15, no. 1 (1979): 48–63, and 14, no. 11 (1978): 90. Articles 9, 11, 12, 20, and 28 heavily stress the plan. The Twenty Points appear in *I&S*, 13, no. 7 (1977): 90–113. Both are derived from the Seventy Articles for Industry of 1961, in Union Research Institute, *Documents of the Chinese Communist Party Central Committee, 1956–1969*, 1 (Hong Kong: Union Research Institute, 1971), 689–693. *SCMP, Supplement*, July 8, 1968, p. 37, claims that Deng also helped prepare this document.

117. Beijing Radio, July 9, in *FBIS*, July 14, 1978, p. E2.

118. *Renmin Ribao*, July 27, 1978, in *FBIS*, August 1, 1978, pp. K1–K3 (see also *FBIS*, January 26, 1979, pp. E22–23).

119. *Renmin Ribao*, April 3, 1980, p. 5, says that the spirit of the Third Plenum called for "combining regulation by the plan with regulation by the market, using the plan as primary, but still paying full attention to the role of the market." Of course, planned distribution still remained by far the predominant mode of goods distribution after the Third Plenum. But experiments with use of the market did begin then, and a market consciousness began to pervade the official press.

120. For a detailed discussion of debates over the organization of the economy and strategies for modernization over the years 1978 through 1981, see Dorothy J. Solinger, "The Fifth National People's Congress and the Process of Policymaking: Reform, Readjustment, and the Opposition," *Asian Survey* 22 (December 1982): 1238-1275.

121. The experience of reform in other socialist states provides a clue. Höhmann et al., *New Economic Systems*, p. 297, notes that more than twenty years of efforts in Eastern Europe to increase the adaptability of prices has not yet resulted in a departure from the system of state-administered price-fixing.

Chapter 9. Between Center and Locality: State, Militia, and Village, 1927–1980

1. Philip Kuhn, "Local Self-Government under the Republic: Problems of Control, Autonomy, and Mobilization," in *Conflict and Control in Late Imperial China*, ed. Frederick Wakeman and Carolyn Grant (Berkeley and Los Angeles: University of California Press, 1975), p. 258.

2. Karl Marx, *The Critique of the Gotha Program* (New York: International Publishers, 1938); Frederick Engels, *The Origins of the Family, Private Property, and the State in Light of the Researches of Lewis H. Morgan* (New York: International Publishers, 1942); Stanley Moore, *The Critique of Capitalist Democracy* (New York: Paine Whitman, 1957), p. 17.

3. Eric Nordlinger, *Soldiers in Politics: Military Coups and Governments* (Englewood Cliffs, N.J.: Prentice-Hall, 1977), pp. 32–49, cited in Alan Liu, "The 'Gang of Four' and the Chinese People's Army," *Asian Survey* 19 (September 1979): 829.

4. Philip Kuhn, *Rebellion and Its Enemies in Late Imperial China: Militarization and Social Structure, 1796–1864* (Cambridge, Mass.: Harvard University Press, 1970).

5. Shohei Kumano, "The Militia System of Communist China," *Review* (Tokyo) 9 (June 1966): 1–17; John Gittings, "China's Militia," *China Quarterly*, no. 18 (April–June 1964), pp. 100–117; Franz Schurmann, *Ideology and Organization in Communist China* (Berkeley and Los Angeles: University of California Press, 1968), pp. 412–497; C. K. Yang, *A Chinese Village in Early Communist Transition* (Cambridge, Mass.: MIT Press, 1959), pp. 170–177; Ting Li, *Militia of Communist China* (Hong Kong: Union Research Institute, 1955).

6. Numerous reasons have been cited to explain the severe economic setbacks that followed the Great Leap Forward, including natural disasters, arbitrarily large commune units that ignored the traditional boundaries of the marketing system, and an overly egalitarian distribution system. To be sure, these factors were important, yet the disruptions caused to agriculture by large-scale deployment of the village labor force outside the village for basic construction projects may have been more immediately responsible for the dramatic drop in crop yields. In Wuping County in Southwest Fujian Province, where famine conditions were especially serious in 1960, peasants attributed the precipitous drop in grain production to the diversion of a large part of the labor force to building roads, leaving the villages with inadequate labor to farm the fields.

7. Ezra Vogel, *Canton under Communism* (Cambridge, Mass.: Harvard University Press, 1969), pp. 321–349.

8. Ho Kan-chih, *A History of the Modern Chinese Revolution* (Peking: Foreign Languages Press, 1959), p. 102, and Yang Lu-hsia, "The Chinese Communist Militia," *Issues and Studies*, no. 9 (June 1973), pp. 48–52.

9. Chen Xuxiang, *Wuping Nongmin Wuzhuang Baodong* (The armed peasant movement) in *Wuping Wenyi* (Wuping County, Fujian: Local Historical Society, 1979), pp. 93–105, and interview with Jinggangshan Local History group in April 1972.

10. Liu Yuzheng, "Zhongguo Renmin Geming Zhanzhen de Minbing," (The militia during the Chinese People's Revolutionary War,) *Renmin Ribao* (People's Daily), June 28, 1962, p. 3.

11. Chalmers Johnson, *Peasant Nationalism and Communist Power* (Stanford: Stanford University Press, 1962).

12. See David and Isabel Crook, *Revolution in a Chinese Village: Ten Mile Inn* (London: Routledge & Kegan Paul, 1959), pp. 40–42; and William Hinton, *Fanshen: A Documentary of Revolution in a Chinese Village* (New York: Monthly Review Press, 1966), pp. 82–124.

13. Victor Nee, "Community and Change in Revolutionary China" (Ph.D. dissertation, Harvard University, 1977), pp. 24–156.

14. Schurmann, *Ideology and Organization*, p. 427. For a description of how militia organizations were developed into local defense systems that linked villages in a locality in a complex underground tunnel system see Jack Belden, *China Shakes the World* (New York: Harper, 1949), p. 60.

15. John Gittings, *The Role of the Chinese Army* (New York: Oxford University Press, 1967), pp. 205–209.

16. Chang Ching-wu, "Strengthen Militia Work," *Collection of Important Chinese Communist References* (Taipei: Central Publication Service), pp. 111–112. See also G. William Skinner, "Peasant Organization in Rural China," *Annals of the American Academy of Political and Social Science* (September 1951).

17. Gittings, "China's Militia," p. 103.

18. "Yingjie Renmin Gongshe de Gaozhao" (Welcome the high tide of the people's commune), *Hongqi* (Red Flag), 1958, no. 7, pp. 14–15. According to this editorial, the organizational needs of the people's commune require militarization in order to mold the peasantry into a work force that is disciplined and efficient, comparable to factory and army organizational environments. Thus the militia was seen as an instrument to modernize the peasantry, so that peasants, like workers, could work autonomously (*ziyou diaodong*) in a large organizational setting.

19. The comparative research of Cornell's Rural Development Committee points to a strong correlation between strong local organization and successful rural development, concurring with Mao's views on this issue. See Norman Uphoff and Milton Esman, *Local Organization for Rural Development in Asia* (Ithaca: Cornell Rural Development Committee, 1974), and Benedict Stavis, "China's Rural Local Institutions," *Asia Survey* 16, no. 4 (1976): 387–396.

20. Fu Ch'iu-t'ao, "Report on Inspection into the Question of Militia work in Honan," in *Bulletin of Activities*, no. 4, 1961.

21. Gittings, *The Role of the Chinese Army*, pp. 213–219.

22. Schurmann, *Ideology and Organization*, pp. 533–574.

23. Ibid., p. 567.

24. Joseph Heinlein, "The Ground Forces," in *Military and Political Power in China*, ed. William Whitson (New York: Praeger, 1972), pp. 153–168.

25. "The main duty of the provincial military district, military sub-district, and people's arms department at all levels is to conduct militia work" (Ministry of National Defense, "Regulations on Militia Work," August 1978, translated in *Issues & Studies*, no. 2 [February 1980], p. 85).

26. Harvey Nelsen, "Military Forces in the Cultural Revolution," *China Quarterly*, no. 51, (July–September 1972), pp. 444–451.

27. Ministry of National Defense, "Regulations on Militia Work," p. 78.

28. William L. Parish and Martin King Whyte, *Village and Family in Contemporary China* (Chicago: University of Chicago Press, 1978), p. 40.

29. Ralph Powell, "Communist China's Mass Militia," *Current Survey* 7 (November 1964): 1–7; see also William Whitson, ed., *The Military and Political Power in China in the 1970s* (New York: Praeger, 1972).

30. Informant interviews on Yangbei's militia training.

31. See Chu Li and Tien Chieh-yun, *Inside a People's Commune* (Peking: Foreign Languages Press, 1974), pp. 124–139.

32. For a discussion of my field work experience see Victor Nee, "Post-Mao Changes in a South China Production Bridgade," *Bulletin of Concerned Asian Scholars* 13 (April–June 1981): 32–39.

33. G. William Skinner, "Marketing and Social Structure in Rural China," *Journal of Asian Studies* 24, pt. 3 (May 1965): 382–399.

34. Kuhn, *Rebellion and Its Enemies*, p. 225.

35. G. William Skinner, "Marketing and Social Structure in Rural China," *Journal of Asian Studies* 24, pt. 1 (November 1964): 32.

36. See Michel Oksenberg, "Local Leaders in Rural China, 1962–65: Individual Attributes, Bureaucratic Positions, and Political Recruitment," in *Chinese Communist Politics in Action*, ed. A. Doak Barnett (Seattle: University of Washington Press, 1969), pp. 176–179.

37. Ibid., and A. Doak Barnett with Ezra Vogel, *Cadres, Bureaucracy and Political Power in China* (New York: Columbia University Press, 1967).

38. See, for example, J. Bruce Jacobs, "The Cultural Bases of Factional Alignment and Division in a Rural Taiwanese Township," *Journal of Asian Studies* 36 (November 1976): 79–97.

39. See B. Michael Frolic, *Mao's People* (Cambridge, Mass.: Harvard University Press, 1980), and Fox Butterfield, *China: Alive in the Bitter Sea* (New York: Times Books, 1982), pp. 44–49, 94–99, 149–150.

40. Jan Myrdal, *Report from a Chinese Village* (New York: Pantheon, 1965).

41. "Shandong Qishiwan Fuyuan Junren he Geming Canfei Junren Zhongxin Tuanjie Qunzhong Fazhan Nongcun Jiti Jingji" (700,000 Shandong demobilized and disabled armymen sincerely unite with the masses to develop the collective agricultural economy) *Renmin Ribao*, January 17, 1963.

42. Oksenberg, "Local Leaders in Rural China," p. 165.

43. Schurmann, *Ideology and Organization*, p. 571.

44. See, for example, Chen Jo-hsi, *The Execution of Mayor Yin* (Bloomington: Indiana University Press, 1978); Ken Ling, *Revenge of Heaven: Journal of a Young Chinese* (New York: Putnam, 1972); and Butterfield, *China*.

45. William Hinton, personal communication; his forthcoming book on developments in Long Bow Village since land reform gives an account of how a suburban village was drawn into urban political struggles in the Cultural Revolution (New York: Random House).

46. "Decision of the Central Committee of the Chinese Communist Party concerning the Great Proletarian Cultural Revolution," *Renmin Ribao*, August 11, 1966, in Wen-shun Chi, ed., *Readings in the Chinese Communist Cultural Revolution* (Berkeley and Los Angeles: University of California Press, 1971), pp. 223–230.

47. Martin Whyte, "Family Change in China," *Issues & Studies* 15, no. 7 (1979): 48–62.

48. Ibid, p. 56.

49. Harvey Nelson, "Regional and Paramilitary Ground Forces," in *Military and Political Power*, ed. Whitson, p. 144.

50. Ibid., p. 144.

51. Interviews with Fuzhou residents conducted in April 1972.

52. Nelson, "Regional and Paramilitary Ground Forces," p. 145.

53. Quoted in Thomas Mathews, "The Cultural Revolution in Szechuan," *Cultural Revolution in the Provinces* (Cambridge, Mass.: East Asian Research Center, 1971), p. 129.

54. Victor C. Falkenheim, "The Cultural Revolution in Kwangsi, Yunnan and Fujian," *Asian Survey* 9 (August 1969): 581–597.

55. *Foreign Broadcast Information Service*, May 23, 1972, p. D.3.

56. Ibid., January 25, 1972, p. H.1.
57. Theda Skocpol, *States and Social Revolutions* (Cambridge: Cambridge University Press, 1978).
58. Kuhn, "Local Self-Government," pp. 257–298.

Chapter 10. Harnessing the Political Potential of Peasant Youth

1. Good recent examples of such scholarship include Stanley Rosen, *Red Guard Factionalism and the Cultural Revolution in Guangzhou* (Boulder, Colo.: Westview Press, 1982); Susan L. Shirk, *Competitive Comrades: Career Incentives and Student Strategies in China* (Berkeley and Los Angeles: University of California Press, 1982); Jonathan Unger, *Education under Mao* (New York: Columbia University Press, 1982); and Thomas P. Bernstein, *Up to the Mountains and Down to the Countryside: The Transfer of Youth from Urban to Rural China* (New Haven: Yale University Press, 1977).
2. Chen Village is a single-lineage farming village in the southern part of Guangdong Province. The village constitutes a single production brigade, currently divided into five production teams. It is one of nine brigades in its people's commune. When in this essay, I refer to "village leaders," I mean cadres on either or both of the interlocking organizations that administer the brigade: the brigade revolutionary committee and the brigade party branch committee. This essay is based on my own interpretations of data gathered with Anita Chan and Jonathan Unger from twenty-six former residents of that village — fourteen sent-down youth who came into the village from the city of Canton in 1964 and began leaving in the early 1970s and twelve former peasants who migrated to Hong Kong in the latter half of the 1970s. We have carefully cross-checked the accounts of different interviewees so as to minimize the effects of bias. For a discussion of the methodological issues involved in this research see Anita Chan, Richard Madsen, and Jonathan Unger, *Chen Village: The Recent History of a Peasant Community in Mao's China* (Berkeley and Los Angeles: University of California Press, 1983); and Richard Madsen, *Morality and Power in a Chinese Village* (Berkeley and Los Angeles: University of California Press, forthcoming).
3. I wrote the first draft of this account of the status of young peasants before the publication of William L. Parish and Martin King Whyte, *Village and Family in Contemporary China* (Chicago: University of Chicago Press, 1978). I find that my description of the status of young people generally agrees with the account given in their book. Since their book is based on interviews with persons from a wide variety of villages in Guangdong, I am encouraged to believe that my analysis may be generally true, at least of rural society in southeastern China.
4. For extensive descriptions of the economic, social, and political conflicts that gave rise to such grievances, see Chan, Madsen, and Unger, *Chen Village*, chap. 2; and for an analysis of the cultural framework shaping the grievances, see Madsen, *Morality and Power*, chaps. 2 and 3.
5. Chen Village is still a male-dominated community. No peasant women have been given any positions of authority in the village outside of that of head of the women's association. The position of women in the village is beginning to change, especially with a recent change in local marriage customs which makes it possible for young women to marry within the village. But in writing about the political potential of youth as it manifested itself over the past ten years, it makes sense to refer mainly to the potential of young men. See Parish and Whyte, *Village and Family*, pp. 235–247.

6. Tu Wei-ming, "The Confucian Perception of Adulthood," *Daedalus* 105 (Spring 1976): 115–116. The Confucians believed that having mastered "ritual," a person reaching the fulfillment of his life in old age should take special care to discipline himself by music.

7. Parish and Whyte have found similar "youth houses" in their sample (*Village and Family*, pp. 231–232).

8. Unlike longstanding youth organizations like the Young Communist League and village-level propaganda teams, the Mao Zedong Thought Counselor (*fudao yuan*) organization was relatively new. It was established in the course of the Mao Study campaign in the mid-1960s, and its purpose was to use the enthusiasm of young people to teach peasants quotations from Mao's works and to explain the meaning of those quotes.

9. The basic militia, a functioning organization, is different from the ordinary militia, which exists only on paper. All able-bodied villagers (with the exception of "class enemies") were officially registered as members of the ordinary militia, which meant only that they could be called into action in a military emergency. In this essay, when I refer to "militia," I mean basic militia unless otherwise noted.

10. During land reform in 1953 each villager was assigned an "official class status" (*cheng fen*) based mainly on his or her sources of income within the five-year period before liberation in 1949. The basic official class statuses (in order of official desirability) are poor peasant, lower-middle peasant, upper-middle peasant, rich peasant, and landlord. One's official class status is an important determinant of the degree to which one is allowed to participate in politics: only officially designated poor and lower-middle peasants were admitted into the Communist party and allowed to hold sensitive posts in the local government; rich peasants and landlords were denied civil rights until 1979, when under a new policy of the Deng Xiaoping regime, the official stigma attached to their class status was removed.

11. See Parish and Whyte, *Village and Family*, p. 40, for an account of village militia organization which dovetails with the one given here. The one difference between my account of the militia and the Parish and Whyte account has to do with the composition of the armed militia. Parish and Whyte (p. 40) say that "the armed militia, consisting mostly of retired army men, is usually organized directly under the commune's armed forces department. . . . The average villager has little regular contact with this unit." In Chen Village, the armed militia was composed not of retired army men but of the strongest and most politically reliable of the young people in the basic militia. (It provided a path for these people for mobility into the PLA.) The armed militia functioned as an elite within the basic militia so that average villagers had considerable contact with this unit. In the area around Chen Village, the armed militia seemed to have been more important than in many other parts of Guangdong — a fact that one of our interviewees suggested was attributable to its proximity to the border with Hong Kong.

12. For a detailed account of this history see Chan, Madsen, and Unger, *Chen Village*.

13. Franz Schurmann, *Ideology and Organization in Communist China* (Berkeley and Los Angeles: University of California Press, 1968), pp. 427–431.

Index

agricultural production: government constraints, 186–188; growth, 178, 179; militia's role in, 253–254; responsibility system, 71; youth's role in, 251, 258. *See also* collective agriculture.

Althusser, Louis, 137

Association of Chinese Writers and Artists, 67, 68

authoritarianism, postrevolutionary: background, 28; characteristics, 32, 54; critiques of, 44–52; kinds, 33

authority: of cadres, 69, 134; government crisis in, 72; meanings, 62

autonomy: definition, for communities, 224; for individuals in economy, 72, 186, 190, 287n; local, 234, 242, 243; meanings, 67; for rural groups, 71, 223; for social groups, 79; state, 111–114

Ba Jin, 57

Bai Hua, *Bitter Love,* 66

Beijing Daily, presentation of Stalin, 167

"bourgeois liberalization": attack on, 80; future of, 80–81

Brus, Wlodzimierz, 138

bureaucracy: expansion, 30–31, 188; historical dominance of, 87; limits on, 190; problems, 77; as structure, 140; tradition, 141

bureaucratic class: advantages for, 136, 139, 146, 234–235; during Cultural Revolution, 20, 41, 43, 123, 136, 185–186; Engels on, 136; Marx on, 136–138; theories of, 136–138

bureaucratic reform: conservative approach, 44–46; leftist democratization, 47–52; liberal democratization, 46–47; need for, 64

bureaucrats, 20; attacks on, 126–127;

divisions among, 146; in marketing, 209; patrimonial model, 142–144; power of, 33, 44, 77, 176, 181; and property, 134; revisions by, 140; as ruling class, 123–124, 141, 146; strong leadership of, 133; upward social mobility of, 136

CCP. *See* Communist party, Chinese

cadres: control of government by, 39, 42; definition, 42, 134, 267n; expansion of, 30–31; functions, 134; lack of education among, 84; military, 97, 231–235, 236, 240–241; organization, 42–43, 134–135, 273n; power of, 69; recruitment, 31, 233–234, 276n; special position of, 136, 139, 146, 234–235; in villages, 237, 243, 256–257, 273n; work style of, 44–46

capitalism: development of, 155; as enemy of socialist state, 154–158; Mao's theories, 155–156, 158; Marxist views, 195–197; state, 136–138

"capitalist-roaders," 149, 151–158

Central Committee, 37, 48; Eleventh (December 1978), 53; decisions by, 68–69; security for, 103

Chen Boda, 124, 150

Chen Village: description, 295n; study of youth in, 224–249, 252–263; youth exodus from, 260–261

Chen Yun, vice-premier, 75, 166, 185

Chiang Kai-shek, 96

class(es): military, 91; rural, 68–69; status, assignment of, 296n; theories, 86–87. *See also* bureaucratic class; class structure; class struggle; intellectuals; peasant class

class structure: "class enemies," 267n; new perception of, 65–69, 77; and politics, 145–147; as variable, 138

class struggle, 47, 126, 268n; and cadre

297

Index

Index

Red Army, 226
Red Guard, 237; local defiance of, 239, 240; urban youth in, 259
reforms, governmental: bureaucratic, 44–52, 64; economic, 70, 194, 289n–290n; electoral, 74–75, 266n; implementation, 192–193; legal, 72–74, 189; in party structure, 75–78; political, 78–81; in popular participation, 189–190
Renmin Ribao, 72, 76; antifascist position, 168; on economic planning, 214, 215, 216, 217; presentation of Stalin, 167
revisionism, 60; by bureaucrats, 140; by Khrushchev, 156; socialist, 155
revolution, Chinese, 89; activity areas during, 29, 90; character, 120–121, 242; consequences of, 132; groups during, 91; history, 226–227; militia, 227; roots in past, 144
revolutionary movement: in China, 90–91; egalitarian tradition in, 30; strength of, 29; of ultraleftists, 55
revolutions, Communist, 89; centralized party-state, 89; in Cuba, 89; in Hungary, 89; in Poland, 90; in USSR, 166; in Yugoslavia, 90

"second economy," 203–206, 207, 286n; barter and culture, 203–204; reliance on connections, 204–206, 237
"sectarianism," 57
Schurmann, Franz, 227, 228, 236, 262
Scott, James, 145
Shanghai radical group, 38, 48
Sheng Wu Lian, 49; program of, 49–50
Sino-Japanese War, 83, 226–227
Sixteen Points document, stipulations, 237
Skocpol, Theda, 242
socialism, Chinese: and the cadres, 135; Chinese aspects of, 145; as historical novelty, 133–134; liberalization in, 78, 274n; principles of, 78, 79; state commitment to, 148–149; values, 183, 192
socialist democracy: changes under, 74–75; future, 174; meaning of, 74, 273n; role of people in, 79
socialist state: democratization program (extraparty), 159–163; democratization program (within party), 163–166, 170; "feudal fascism" as obstacle, 149–154, 162–164; future of, 170–171; move for liberalization, 150–154; state capitalism as enemy, 154–158
socialist thinkers in China: Marxist democrats,

159–164; Marxist idealists, 151, 154, 158–161, 164, 167, 168, 281n, 282n; Marxist materialists, 151, 153, 157–159, 161, 162, 282n
society, Marxist: economic abundance in, 115–116; and state, 110–112, 134
Soviet models: in army, resistance to, 97–98; state-building, 28–32, 39
Soviet Union: under Khrushchev, 155–156; and Marxist ideology, 131; and the PLA, 32, 98; polemical battle with, 121–122; after revolution, 166; Stalinist, 161; state-building model, 28–32, 39; view of trade, 198
specialists: political support for, 64, 67; role in society, 62, 63, 64
Stalin: Chinese views of, 167; on economy, 291n; historiography, 119–120; state system, 28, 30, 164–165
Stalinism, 164–166; and Chinese regime, 90, 91; interpretations of, 168–170; negative view of, 166
state: autonomy, 62, 111–114; Bolshevik model, 28–29; Communist, 33; definition, 33; imperial, 22; as product of society, 110–112; role in Chinese history, 128–129, 242; role of party in, 33, 34–43, 77; role in society, 19–20, 115, 236, 237–238; studies of, 132–133; views of, 110–111. *See also* Marxism-Leninism; Marxist theory; socialist state
state, postrevolutionary: beginnings, 27–30; characteristics, 32; definition, of apparatus, 120–121; establishment, 30–32; structure, 33–43, 275n
state-building: background, 28–30; difficulty of, 89–91; goals, 175; models, 28–29, 30–32, 39; need for, 28
state institutions, and distribution of power, 33–43. *See also* Chinese Communist party; government, in China; government, local; People's Liberation Army
state power: and distribution of assets, 181–183; to implement goals, 175; institutionalized, 34, 132, 242; problems of, 184–189; relaxation of, 190, 191; in rural society, 69, 71, 182, 224, 225; socialist values, 183–184; types, 33–34
supply and demand, as problem in China, 200, 203, 209
Sweezy, Paul, 119

Tiananmen incident, 51, 80, 162, 163
Titoism: economic program of, 150, 161;

302